Detroit
in Its World Setting

Published with the assistance of the Detroit Public Library
and also the friends of the Detroit Public Library
as part of Detroit's Tricentennial Celebration in 2001

Detroit
in Its World Setting

A Three Hundred Year Chronology, 1701–2001

Edited by David Lee Poremba

Wayne State University Press Detroit

Great Lakes Books

A complete listing of the books
in this series can be found
at the back of this volume.

Philip P. Mason, Editor
Department of History, Wayne State University

Dr. Charles K. Hyde, Associate Editor
Department of History, Wayne State University

Library of Congress Cataloging-in-Publication Data

Detroit in its world setting : a three hundred year chronology,
1701-2001 / edited by David Lee Poremba.
      p. cm. — (Great Lakes books)
Includes bibliographical references and index.
   ISBN 0-8143-2870-9
1. Detroit (Mich.)—History—Chronology. I. Poremba, David Lee II.
Series.
   F574.D457 D49 2001
   977.4'34'00202—dc21

                                        00-011565

Table of Contents

Introduction

In anticipation of Detroit's 300th birthday, the Friends of the Detroit Public Library, with the encouragement of the McGregor Fund, decided to revise and reissue *Detroit in Its World Setting,* originally published in 1953 in celebration of the city's 250th anniversary. The object of the chronology is to show Detroit in its world setting, so that events in the city can be seen against events of national and international importance.

Since the scope of the chronology covers nearly three hundred years and so many subjects, each entry is of necessity brief. Great selectivity was used in choosing the events to be included. Events were chosen to show change and progress, such as the development of an idea or an object, and the goal has been to present people's daily lives and interests, so the everyday things, as well as the great, have been included.

Detroit in Its World Setting is not an all-inclusive history but an enlarged time line on which to organize memories of people and events. It not only indicates rulers, dynasties, and conflicts but also what people were reading, how they spent their leisure time, what music they sang along with, and what inventions and discoveries affected their lives. With this chronology, it is possible to illuminate particular events in any year or trace a subject through nearly three centuries.

There are many chronologies available in published form. This one differs from others in that it is local in focus specifically to Detroit and its environs. Events in Detroit and, to a lesser extent, the state of Michigan are given a separate listing at the beginning of each year and are included whether or not they had national influence.

This edition improves on the original by adding new areas of coverage and broadening those that have carried over. The coverage of women's achievements, events involving the African American community, information on immigrants and Detroit's ethnic neighborhoods, major landmarks in the city, and public education is particularly enhanced. Further, the addition of three appendices provides the reader with a chart of the political leadership of Detroit from the earliest days of French command to the reelection of Mayor Dennis Archer. Finally, the revised edition includes an index, allowing readers to access particular items of interest with ease.

The chronology, under each year, is divided into four sections. Within the Detroit and Michigan section the reader will find coverage of local events generally listed in the following order: statistics, government and politics, dated events, undated major events, daily life/settlement, religion, education, culture, sports, recreation, science and medicine, transportation and construction, business, and Michigan settlements outside Detroit. The World History heading provides an international backdrop for the reader, against which life in Detroit can be seen. Statistical information is provided first, then entries in chronological order if dates are known, or geographically, working away from Detroit (events occurring closest to Detroit are listed first, for example, Ohio River

Valley, then colonial, English, European, African, and so on). The Cultural Progress section lists entries under education, literature and other publications, music and dance, theatre, art, fashion, architecture, entertainment, and sports. The Scientific and Commercial Progress heading presents scientific and medical entries followed by business and industry. U.S. entries are generally listed first.

The items themselves were taken from books, magazines, manuscripts, and other reference sources, a complete listing of which is included at the back of the book.

The finished product could not have been completed without the expertise and dedication of Rebecca N. Ferguson. Special thanks go to Jack Schramm and to Great Lakes Books editorial board members of Wayne State University Press, in particular Philip P. Mason, Charles K. Hyde, JoEllen Vinyard, Stanley Solvick, and DeWitt S. Dykes. At Wayne State University Press I would like to recognize the efforts of Arthur Evans, Alice Nigoghosian, and Jane Hoehner.

Finally, I would like to thank the Friends of the Detroit Public Library whose generous financial support has made the publication of *Detroit in Its World Setting* possible.

David Lee Poremba, Editor

Categories and Their Scope

Detroit and Michigan

Conflicts—government and politics—business and industry—labor—culture—sports—recreation—religion—education—ethnic groups—immigration—landmark buildings—women's firsts—population statistics

World History

Exploration—U.S. government and politics—wars and conflicts—diplomacy—law—religion—labor—social welfare—crime and famous trials—disasters—public health

Cultural Progress

The arts—literature—education—sports—recreation—entertainment—publications—famous people

Scientific and Commercial Progress

Science—medicine—inventions—industry—transportation—technology—agriculture—business—finance—advertising—household items—food—famous people

Detroit in Its World Setting
1701-1800

Artist's conception of Fort Pontchartrain in 1701. Ste. Anne's Church can be seen above the bastion on the extreme right.

Antoine de la Mothe Cadillac (c. 1658–1730). The founder of Detroit envisioned a permanent colony controlling the fur trade for France.

An artist's engraving showing the proud bearing and dress of the Huron tribe as they pose with their newly elected chief.

A painting by Detroit artist John Mix Stanley showing the Ottawa Indian woman Catherine informing Major Henry Gladwin of Pontiac's conspiracy in 1763.

Artist's depiction of the Ottawa Indian village at Michilimackinac. A similar village was maintained at Detroit in 1763.

Detroit, 1794. This watercolor view of Detroit shows the British flag over the ramparts of the port as sailing vessels tie up at King's Wharf.

1701

Detroit and Michigan

Michigan is vast area of forest, home to about 15,000 American Indians; most settlements are in St. Joseph and Saginaw river valleys. Principal tribes are Chippewa (Ojibway), Ottawa, Potawatomi, Huron.

Early June. Commander Antoine de la Mothe Cadillac, second-in-command Alphonse de Tonty, Cadillac's 9-year-old son (Antoine), 2 priests (a Jesuit and a Recollet), 50 soldiers, and 50 workmen set out from Montreal in 25 canoes; they are accompanied by a contingent of Algonquins. Follow Ottawa River to Lake Nipissing and French River, then into Georgian Bay, paddle into Lake Huron and head south through St. Clair River and Lake St. Clair. Aim is to establish permanent French settlement to control trade routes through Great Lakes.

July 23. Cadillac and company spend night on Grosse Isle. They canoe upriver the next morning. Site of Detroit is selected because it is defensible: river is narrow and unobstructed by islands; land rises roughly 40 feet above the water. Small river (Savoyard) runs diagonally to southwest.

July 24. Cadillac and company begin building palisade (occupying area now bounded by Griswold and Shelby, Jefferson and Larned). Fort to be called Pontchartrain de Détroit (Pontchartrain after Cadillac's benefactor, *Détroit* meaning "the Strait"). They erect log houses by placing trees set on end in a trench, not more than 6 feet high. No beasts of burden; construction is labor intensive.

July 26. Saint Anne's Day is observed. Founding of Ste. Anne's Church dates from this service. Foundations laid for first chapel (corner of Griswold and Jefferson).

Late summer/fall. Father Vaillant, Jesuit priest in company, departs Detroit.

Sept. Mesdames Marie-Therese Cadillac and Anne Picote de Tonty, wives of the commanders, arrive, signaling to settlers it is safe for them to bring their families. Six-year-old Jacques Cadillac accompanies his mother.

Winter. Cadillac's efforts to induce area Indians to settle near Detroit for mutual protection and better trading are successful: 4 villages (Huron, Miami, Ottawa, Chippewa) are built.

World History

Population of American colonies, about 275,000.

Jan. 18. First Prussian king crowns himself; Frederick I rules for next 12 years.

July 6. Notorious pirate Capt. (William) Kidd hanged in England.

Aug. 4. French sign peace treaty with Iroquois enabling settlement of North American interior. French move quickly to settle lands in Ohio River Valley and in Great Lakes region. (Antoine Cadillac moved out in advance of official peace.)

Louisiana becomes province of France; covers area drained by Mississippi, Ohio, Missouri rivers. One of 3 French colonies on North American mainland; other 2 are Acadia and Canada. Together all three are known as New France.

War of the Spanish Succession begins (to 1714) in Europe.

Great Northern War is under way in Europe (began 1700; continues to 1721); nations, chiefly Russia and Poland, ally to break power of Swedish empire. England and Denmark, early Russian allies.

Cultural Progress

Yale University founded.

Scientific and Commercial Progress

Rice is South Carolina export staple.

Jethro Tull invents seed drill to plant seeds in rows. Also improves plow.

1702

Detroit and Michigan

Fort Pontchartrain, roughly 200 feet square, encloses a church, priest's house, Antoine Cadillac's and Alphonse de Tonty's houses, warehouse, 2 guard houses, and 13 smaller houses. Large gate opens to the river; smaller gate opens on one of the inland sides of the fort (probably to the west). On riverbank, Cadillac erects a windmill; used for grinding.

First white child born in the village is the daughter of Alphonse de Tonty and his wife. She is named Therese, in honor of Madame Cadillac. Exact date unknown.

June. Recollet priest Constantin Delhalle arrives in Detroit.

World History

England's King William II concludes campaign (begun 1689) to more centrally rule American colonies: all British warships under his control; colonial power to appoint officials revoked; governors selected and sent by king.

Triangular Trade (Europe-Africa-America route), which began five years ago, going strong.

March 8. King William II dies in horse-riding accident; Queen Anne ascends English throne (to 1714). Anne's reign marks transition to parliamentary government. Last Stuart monarch.

Queen Anne's War (known as War of Spanish Succession in the colonies) begins.

East and West Jersey are united into royal province of New Jersey.

Yellow fever epidemic kills hundreds in New York.

French make first Gulf Coast settlement, Fort Louis (later Mobile, Alabama).

Cultural Progress

March 11. First daily newspaper in London, *The Daily Courant,* is published.

Queen Anne approves horse racing.

Scientific and Commercial Progress

Many German towns lit by oil.

Serfdom abolished in Denmark.

1703

Detroit and Michigan

Village of Detroit first appears on a map, by Guillaume Delisle.

World History

April 21. Sweden defeats Russia at Battle of Pultusk.

May 1. St. Petersburg founded by Russia's Peter the Great.

Nov. Storm batters England; thousands dead.

Dec. Japanese earthquake and fires kill an estimated 200,000.

Isaac Newton elected President of Royal Society.

Work begun in London on Buckingham Palace.

1704

Detroit and Michigan

Feb. 2. Antoine and Therese Cadillac's daughter, Marie Therese, is baptized. Becomes the first recorded christening in church's books.

Cadillac reports some 2,000 American Indians live near Detroit settlement.

Fall. Cadillac travels to Quebec; Alphonse de Tonty is temporary commander (to 1706).

World History

Delaware separates from Pennsylvania; receives own legislative assembly but remains under governor of Pennsylvania (to 1776).

Feb. 29. Canadian French and Indians massacre 49 British colonists at Deerfield, Massachusetts; another 112 taken captive, including children.

Aug. In War of Spanish Succession, British take Spanish peninsula, Gibraltar; retain control (to present day).

Aug. England wins decisive victory over French and Bavarians at Battle of Blenheim.

Cultural Progress

April 24. America's first regular newspaper begins publication: the *Boston News-Letter* is published weekly (to 1722).

Johann Sebastian Bach writes his first cantata.

John Harris writes first English-language dictionary of the arts and sciences, *Lexicon Technicum.*

Scientific and Commercial Progress

Isaac Newton publishes *Optics,* defense of the emission theory of light.

First newspaper advertisements appear in *Boston News-Letter.*

1705

Detroit and Michigan

So many Ottawa and Huron Indians have moved from northern Michigan in St. Ignace to Detroit that Jesuits abandon mission. Jesuit priests stir opposition to Antoine Cadillac.

June 15. Cadillac is arrested in Quebec, where he is tried and acquitted of misdeeds in the fur trade.

World History

Oct. 14. In War of Spanish Succession, Austrian and British forces take Barcelona.

Rebellion against Peter the Great's westernization of Russia.

Cultural Progress

First performance of George Frideric Handel's *St. John's Passion.*

First copper mine worked in what would become United States, at Simsbury mine, Granby, Connecticut.

Thomas Newcomen improves steam engine (invented 1696).

Astronomer Edmund Halley predicts return in 1758 of comet seen in 1682.

Queen Anne confers knighthood on Isaac Newton.

1706

Detroit and Michigan

Jan. 29. Sieur de Bourgmont is temporary commander of Detroit (to Aug.).

June 6. Quarrel between Ottawa and Miami Indians leads to capture of Father Constantin Delhalle. He is released, but then shot by the Ottawa. Soldiers are ordered to fire and 30 Ottawa are killed.

Aug. Antoine Cadillac returns; following acquittal in Quebec, he has full control over Detroit (to 1711).

New influx of settlers.

World History

Charleston (South Carolina) successfully defended against French and Spanish.

Albuquerque (New Mexico) founded in northern part of New Spain.

Sweden's Charles XII defeats Russians and Saxons at Battle of Franstadt.

England conquers the Spanish Netherlands.

Austrians expel French from Italy.

Cultural Progress

First evening paper, *The Evening Post,* issued in London.

1707

Detroit and Michigan

March 10. Antoine Cadillac begins making land grants (to 1711)—68 small lots within fort and 75 long, narrow plots of farmland northeast of fort. The "ribbon farms" front the river; some are as narrow as 200 feet and extend as far as 3 miles inland. (Beaubien, St. Aubin, Chene, and Dequindre among early farmers.)

Lot number 59, within fort, is given to Marie Le Page—the only record of a conveyance to a woman in early Detroit.

Cadillac acts as feudal landowner, or seignior; requires farmers to pay him annual rent and a percentage of their grain (for use of his mill), as well as work on his farm a specified number of days each year. Work of craftsmen and traders strictly controlled.

Land grant to Francois Fafard de Lorme stipulates that he plant, or help plant, a Maypole in front of Cadillac's door; May Day celebration held there.

Cadillac orders that horses and cattle be sent from Montreal.

Aug. 6–10. Great council of Indian chiefs held at Fort Pontchartrain to settle matters relating to Indian attack last year. Cadillac takes charge of councils.

Deserter (named La Roze) hanged in Detroit, first recorded capital case in settlement.

Dec. 28. Marie Agatha Cadillac, daughter of Antoine and Therese, is born.

World History

British land in French settlement at Acadia (Nova Scotia), Canada.

May 1. Act of Union unites England, Wales, and Scotland as United Kingdom of Great Britain. Adoption of Union Jack as national flag.

Japan's Mount Fujiyama erupts.

Religious migration of thousands of Protestants (Calvinists, Lutherans) from Rhineland-Palatinate (Germany) to England begins.

Sweden invades Russia.

Scientific and Commercial Progress

English physician John Floyer invents watch to measure pulse; first precision instrument for medical diagnosis.

French engineer Denis Papin invents high-pressure boiler.

1708

Detroit and Michigan

Patent of land given to Joseph Parent specifies he must shoe Cadillac's horses.

Francois Clarembault, Sieur d'Aigremont, subdelegate of the Surveyor and Kings Deputy for surveying the military posts in Canada, arrives in Detroit, staying 19 days.

D'Aigremont's report on the conditions at Detroit and on Cadillac replete with petty charges against commander and recommends establishment of a post at Mackinac (Michilimackinac), which has become almost a ruin. Antoine Cadillac attempts to regulate sale of brandy to settlers and American Indians; small rations please no one.

New church built; structure is roughly 35 by 24 feet.

World History

Sweden's Charles XII invades Ukraine; attempt to take Moscow thwarted.

British capture Minorca and Sardinia.

Cultural Progress

Palace at Versailles is completed (begun 1661); symbolizes extravagance of age of King Louis XIV.

Scientific and Commercial Progress

Alchemists near Dresden discover formula for making Chinese porcelain.

Dutch physician Hermann Boerhaave publishes theory of inflammation.

Rival British companies merge to form United East India Company, strongest European power on Indian coasts.

1709

Detroit and Michigan

March 27. Francois Cadillac, son of Antoine and Therese, is born.

Cadillac's French patron, Count Pontchartrain, writes the commander, complaining he shows "too much greed" and too little moderation in his dealings with settlers at Detroit.

World History

Transatlantic slave trade accounts for an estimated 20,000 African slaves a year shipped to British possessions in Caribbean.

Portuguese begin settling Brazil's interior.

July 8. Peter the Great defeats Sweden's Charles XII at the Battle of Poltava; marks end of Swedish supremacy in northern Europe, rise of Russia as major power. Charles XII flees to Turkish territory as Great Northern War continues (to 1721).

Sept. 11. Battle of Malplaquet is bloodiest of War of Spanish Succession; some 20,000 allied lives are lost.

Frosts devastate crops and orchards as far south as Mediterranean; causes famine in Europe, food riots in France.

Black Death (the plague) ravages Prussia; hundreds of thousands dead.

Russia occupies Poland; begins sending prisoners to Siberia.

Cultural Progress

First pianoforte made by Bartolomeo Cristofori, Florentine maker of harpsichords.

The Tatler begins publication in England.

Song "For He's a Jolly Good Fellow" becomes increasingly popular among British after Battle of Malplaquet.

Scientific and Commercial Progress

Thermometer invented by Daniel Fahrenheit in Germany.

Hippocratic method of medicine (in which aim is to cure the patient) revived in Europe.

1710

Detroit and Michigan

Responding to political pressure from Cadillac's enemies in Paris and Quebec, French government relieves Cadillac of his post at Detroit and names him governor of the new French colony of Louisiana. Although it is a promotion, it leads to financial ruin—Cadillac is required to leave his property at Detroit.

May 5. First recorded marriage of whites at Detroit, Jean Baptiste Turpin and Margaret Fafard.

May 9. Church records note a doctor's name—M. Henry Belisle, possibly the first in Detroit.

World History

Great German migration to America begins.

British forces occupy Acadia (Canada).

To illustrate British power in America, 5 Iroquois chiefs are presented by military to Queen Anne.

Cultural Progress

Influential Boston clergyman Cotton Mather writes *Essays to Do Good.*

First piano built.

First copyright act introduced in Britain.

Irish philosopher George Berkeley publishes *Principles of Human Knowledge*.

Collected works of English dramatist William Congreve published.

Scientific and Commercial Progress

Second paper mill in America is set up near Philadelphia.

1711

Detroit and Michigan

Summer. Antoine Cadillac leaves Detroit to assume duties as governor of Louisiana. He does not return. Some of his followers desert village, precipitating a drop in population.

Joseph Guyon du Buisson is appointed commander of Detroit (to 1712).

More than 1,000 Fox Indians arrive from Wisconsin on the invitation of the now-departed Cadillac. Other tribes are hostile; Commander du Buisson asks Fox to leave. They refuse to do so; tension mounts.

World History

Tuscarora War: Settlers and American Indians fight in Carolina; 200 settlers dead.

Rio de Janeiro is captured by the French.

Aug. British invasion of French Canada thwarted.

War begins between Russia and Turkey; Peter the Great forced to sign Treaty of Pruth, returning land to Ottoman Turks and allowing Sweden's king safe return passage.

April 17. Holy Roman Emperor Joseph I dies of smallpox; succeeded by his brother, Charles VI (until 1740).

Black Death (the plague) ravages Europe; hundreds of thousands dead.

Cultural Progress

In London, *The Spectator* (paper of social satire and literary criticism) begins publication, replacing *The Tatler*.

Alexander Pope writes influential *Essay on Criticism*.

London Academy of Arts established.

Queen Anne establishes the Ascot Races.

1712

Detroit and Michigan

Fox Indians attack Fort Pontchartrain. Detroit is under siege for 19 days; church and other buildings catch fire. Fox retreat, only to be overtaken by Huron, Ottawa, and Potawatomi at Windmill Point. Only 100 Fox escape back to Wisconsin, where, in retaliation, they block French passage to the West (until 1734).

June. Francois Daupin, Sieur de la Forest, is commander of Detroit (to 1714).

World History

Slave revolts take place in New York.

Pennsylvania forbids further importation of slaves.

Carolina separates into two colonies, North and South Carolina.

In Scotland, Rob Roy is declared an outlaw.

Last execution for witchcraft occurs in England.

Peace Congress opens at Utrecht to settle War of Spanish Succession.

Religious warfare in Switzerland; Protestants defeat Catholics.

Peter the Great marries Catherine, his former mistress.

Cultural Progress

Jonathon Swift writes *A Proposal for Correcting the English Language*.

Scientific and Commercial Progress

Nantucket whalers capture first sperm whale. Launches new age in whaling.

In England, Thomas Newcomen invents working steam engine to pump water from mines.

1713

Detroit and Michigan

French settlements, including Detroit, enter period of relative peace (to 1744).

Farmers are hardworking but, by all reports, fun loving. Fur trade continues to dominate settlement.

World History

Feb. 25. First Prussian king, Frederick I, dies; succeeded by his son, King Frederick William I (to 1740), who creates strong, absolutist state.

April 11. Treaty of Utrecht is signed, ending War of Spanish Succession. Spain agrees to give Gibraltar and Minorca to Great Britain; France's Louis XIV agrees not to unite France and Spain, cedes Acadia (Nova Scotia) and Newfoundland to British, recognizes Protestant succession in Britain. Marks the beginning of the dissolution of the French colonial empire in the Great Lakes; paves way for English world domination.

Pragmatic Sanction issued by Holy Roman Emperor Charles VI; states female right of succession is legal in Hapsburg domains (allowing for future ascendancy of his daughter, Maria Theresa) and lands are not to be divided.

Peace of Adrianople signed by Turkey and Russia.

Swedish King Charles XII captured (and held for 15 months) by Ottomans.

Cultural Progress

Original works by George Frideric Handel commissioned by Queen Anne for celebration of Peace of Utrecht to be held in St. Paul's Cathedral.

Scientific and Commercial Progress

World's first schooner is constructed, in Massachusetts colony; distinctively American sailboat becomes widely imitated.

French establish post at Natchez (Mississippi); becomes important trade center.

Board of Longitude established in London.

Smallpox immunizations first described.

1714

Detroit and Michigan

Nov. 12. Lt. Jacques Charles Sabrevois is commander of Detroit (to 1717).

World History

Queen Anne of England dies; succeeded by King George I of the House of Hanover (to 1727); speaks no English.

March 6. Peace of Rastatt between Austria and France supplements Treaty of Utrecht.

Turkish-Venetian War begins.

Charles XII returns to Sweden but Great Northern War continues.

Battle of Storkyro establishes Russian domination over Finland.

Scientific and Commercial Progress

Virginia colony establishes ironworks; brings German ironworkers to settle.

Account of smallpox vaccination published by Royal Society of London; arouses interest in Britain and America.

July 8. Parliament passes Longitude Act: Will award £20,000 prize to anyone who can devise means of determining a ship's longitude.

French surgeon Dominique Anel invents a fine-pointed syringe for surgical purposes.

Daniel Fahrenheit develops mercury thermometer with temperature gauge.

1715

Detroit and Michigan

French build fort at Michilimackinac (Mackinac), to control upper lakes.

World History

American Indian uprising in South Carolina; Yamasee nation kills hundreds of British settlers; troops force tribe and allies into Florida (across Spanish border).

Black slaves comprise 24% of Virginia's population.

First Parliament of King George I opens.

Jacobite rebellion in Scotland attempts to restore Stuart monarchy; fails.

Sept. 1. The Sun King, Louis XIV, of France dies after longest reign in history (72 years); 5-year-old great-grandson Louis XV to reign (to 1774), at first with regent, Duke of Orleans.

Cultural Progress

Vaudevilles, popular musical comedies, appear in Paris.

English painter and architect William Kent frees the English garden from formality.

1716

Detroit and Michigan

French King Louis XV revokes all land grants given by Antoine Cadillac on grounds that they were not given in ordinary form and that too much was exacted from the occupants. However, settlers are left in possession.

World History

Virginia colonists cross Blue Ridge Mountains into Shenandoah River Valley.

Concerned by French encroachment, Spanish reoccupy Texas, establishing series of missions.

Jan. Scottish royalists disperse Jacobite troops; James III, the Old Pretender, leaves Britain for France.

Aug. Holy Roman Empire enters war against Turks.

Cultural Progress

First company of English actors appears in America at Williamsburg, Virginia.

First Italian daily newspaper, *Diario di Roma,* published.

Scientific and Commercial Progress

First lighthouse in America is erected on Little Brewster Island, Maine; Boston Light is also built this year.

Scottish economist John Law establishes *Banque Royale* in France.

1717

Detroit and Michigan

Louis de la Poste, Sieur de Louvigny, is commander of Detroit. In July he is succeeded (to 1720) by Henri de Tonty, younger brother of Alphonse.

"Card Money," ordinary playing cards cut into 4 pieces, each piece stamped with a fleur-de-lis and a crown (and signed by the governor, intendant, and clerk of the treasury), is in use in Detroit.

Fox Indians attack the fort but do little harm.

World History

German Mennonites, Moravians, Dunkers begin great migration to Pennsylvania.

Spain sets up viceroyalty of New Granada, separating territory of present-day Colombia, Panama, Venezuela, and Ecuador from viceroyalty of Peru.

Jan. 4. Triple Alliance formed by Britain, France, and Dutch Republic forces Old Pretender James III to leave France.

Dutch Lowlands begin period of commercial decline following more than a century of prosperity.

Cultural Progress

In London, Freemasons organize first Grand Lodge; origins of secret fraternal order espousing fellowship, religious tolerance, political compromise. Attracts many influential men.

School attendance is made mandatory in Prussia.

George Frideric Handel's *Water Music* is first performed on the Thames.

Scientific and Commercial Progress

John Law's Compagnie d'Occident is given a 25-year trade monopoly and government in Louisiana; in return, he must send at least 6,000 white and 3,000 black settlers to the vast territory.

Inoculation against smallpox introduced in England by Lady Mary Wortley Montagu.

1718

Detroit and Michigan

Fort Pontchartrain strengthened.

Father Antoine Delino, pastor.

World History

New Orleans is founded by French gov. of Louisiana, Sieur de Bienville.

Spanish establish mission at San Antonio, Texas.

French and Spanish fight (to 1720) for control of Texas territory; becomes Spanish possession.

Scots-Irish migration to American begins.

William Penn, Quaker founder of Pennsylvania colony, dies; leaves 21 million-acre estate.

Feb. 18. Russia's Peter the Great has son and heir, Alexis, murdered for "imagining" rebellion against his father.

July 21. Peace of Passarowitz ends war between Venice (backed by Holy Roman Empire) and Turkey.

Aug. Quadruple Alliance is formed by France, Holy Roman Empire, Britain, and the Netherlands. Determines to prevent Spain's Philip V from overturning peace settlement that followed War of Spanish Succession; Spain has threatened the agreement by taking over Sicily.

Dec. 11. Sweden's Charles XII killed during expedition against Norway. Succeeded by his sister, who hastens to bring Great Northern War to an end.

Cultural Progress

First theater in America is built at Williamsburg, Virginia.

Voltaire (Francois-Marie Arouet) is released from Bastille after 1-year imprisonment; his *Oedipe* is performed in Paris.

Scientific and Commercial Progress

The potato (originated in South America) arrives in North America; brought by Irish immigrating to Boston.

First table of chemical affinities presented by French chemist Etienne Geoffroy.

First bank notes are issued in England.

Edmund Halley discovers proper motion of fixed stars.

1719

World History

Father Pierre de Charlevoix explores America's inland waterways to try to find westward route.

Ireland is declared inseparable from England.

Nov. 20. Peace of Stockholm ends hostilities between Sweden and Britain's George I.

Jesuits are expelled from Russia.

Cultural Progress

Daniel Defoe publishes *Robinson Crusoe*.

James Figg, who popularized boxing in England, is crowned first boxing champion.

Scientific and Commercial Progress

Science of pathological anatomy is initiated by Italian physician Morgagni.

American Mercury is published in Philadelphia.

Boston Gazette is founded by William Brooker.

Oriental Company is founded in Vienna for trade in the Far East.

1720

Detroit and Michigan

Church records show 43 baptisms, 7 marriages, and 15 deaths.

Detroit's population has climbed back to about 200—its count before Antoine Cadillac left (1711).

Charles Joseph, Sieur de Noyelle, is commander of Detroit. Succeeded later that year by Alphonse de Tonty (to 1727).

World History

Jan. South Seas Bubble, English speculation craze, bursts; financial losses are widespread.

John Law is named controller-general, giving him authority over Louisiana. He succeeds in increasing shipping between New Orleans and France, but his Compagnie d'Occident fails this year, ruining many French investors.

Jan. Spain's Philip V joins Quadruple Alliance of Britain, France, Holland, and Holy Roman Empire, assuring peace in Europe.

Feb. 17. Treaty of the Hague is signed: Spain gives up Italian claims; Holy Roman Empire gives up claims to Spain.

Last major occurrence of Black Death (the plague) in western Europe claims some 50,000 lives.

Sweden's queen abdicates in favor of her husband; monarchy is stripped of former powers in favor of government by House of Nobles.

Tibet becomes a Chinese protectorate (until 1911).

Cultural Progress

Old Haymarket Theater opens in London.

George Frideric Handel is named director of the Royal Academy of Music, London.

First serialization of novels occurs in newspapers.

Wallpaper becomes fashionable in England.

First yacht club is established at Cork Harbor, Ireland.

Scientific and Commercial Progress

First English patent on a plow is granted.

1721

Detroit and Michigan

June 6–18. Father Pierre de Charlevoix, on his way through Great Lakes, visits Detroit and describes it as almost abandoned due to neglect by the French government.

Alphonse de Tonty, commander of Detroit, is summoned to Quebec to answer charges made against him by American Indians and leading citizens of Detroit.

World History

Summer. Smallpox epidemic in Boston strikes thousands; kills hundreds.

Smallpox epidemic in London.

Aug. 30. Great Northern War ends (began 1700) with signing of Treaty of Nystad; gives Peter the Great a "window" on the West—Russia gains Estonia, some Baltic islands, and other territories from Sweden; Peter is proclaimed Emperor of All the Russias. Russia emerges as great force in Europe; Sweden is diminished.

April. John Aislabie, former chancellor of the exchequer, is sent to the Tower of London for fraud (South Seas Bubble).

April. Robert Walpole becomes British prime minister (to 1742) and chancellor of the exchequer; restores public credit.

China suppresses revolt on Formosa (Taiwan).

Cultural Progress

Johann Sebastian Bach completes his *Brandenburg Concertos.*

New England Courant is first published in Boston by James Franklin.

Scientific and Commercial Progress

Regular postal service begins between London and New England.

1722

Detroit and Michigan

July 17. Church records begin to be inscribed "Parish of Ste. Anne's" (first reference to official name).

World History

Boston's population reaches 12,000.

Iroquois sign treaty with Virginia agreeing not to cross Blue Ridge Mountains or Potomac River without permission.

Tuscarora join Iroquois, which becomes League of Six Nations, tribal alliance.

New Orleans is made capital of Louisiana Territory.

Peter the Great, on Russian throne since 1689, assumes title of czar.

Ottoman sultans wage fierce battles to extend influence.

Peter the Great's attack on Ottoman Empire thwarted by sickness; horses and troops ingest deadly bacteria.

Persia is overcome by Afghan invaders.

China's Manchu emperor dies after 52-year reign of expansion; 3 new provinces added.

Easter Island (Polynesia) is discovered by Dutch explorers.

Cultural Progress

Daniel Defoe writes *Moll Flanders.*

Scientific and Commercial Progress

First technical treaty on steelmaking is published.

British Parliament forbids journalists to report debates.

1723

Detroit and Michigan

A new Ste. Anne's Church is erected on north side of present Jefferson Avenue (between Griswold and Shelby).

World History

Louis XV attains majority; begins ruling without regent.

Oct. Treaty of Charlottenburg signed by England and Prussia: grandson of George I will marry a Prussian princess; Prussia's Prince Frederick to marry daughter of the prince of Wales.

Yellow fever strikes Europe for first time.

Fifteen-day massacre by Afghans in Persia.

Scientific and Commercial Progress

American coffee industry has its beginnings with seedling planted on Caribbean island of Martinique.

British industry expands at rate of 1% per year.

Britain reduces duty on tea, which has been less popular than coffee and cocoa.

1724

World History

In South Carolina, black slaves outnumber whites 2 to 1.

New Orleans' French territorial governor passes codes to control black population, expel Jews.

Philip V of Spain abdicates; his successor, Luis I, dies and Philip is king again.

Russia and Ottoman Empire sign treaty to divide Persia between them; Persia's Afghani Shah Mahmud goes mad and orders massacre.

Peter the Great crowns his wife, Catherine, czarina.

Cultural Progress

Gin becomes popular drink in England.

Peter the Great founds Russian Academy of Sciences.

Scientific and Commercial Progress

Longman's, England's oldest publishing house still extant, founded.

1725

World History

Jan. 28. Russia's Peter the Great dies and is succeeded (to 1727) by his wife, Catherine.

Aug. 15. France's 15-year-old King Louis XV weds Maria Leszczynska of Poland, daughter of former king; marriage was arranged.

Famine and bread riots in France.

In Persia, still under siege by Ottomans, Afghani Shah Ashraf succeeds Mahmud, who has gone insane.

Cultural Progress

Antonio Vivaldi writes *The Four Seasons.*

Alexander Pope publishes his translation of Homer's *Odyssey.*

Scientific and Commercial Progress

New York Gazette is issued.

French geographer Guillaume Delisle publishes *Map of Europe.*

St. Petersburg Academy of Science is founded by Catherine I.

1726

World History

German settlers from Pennsylvania begin settling Shenandoah Valley, Virginia.

Cardinal Fleury becomes Chief Minister and virtual leader (to 1743) of France.

Voltaire is banished from France; takes refuge (to 1729) in England.

Holy Roman Empire and Russia agree on alliance against Turkey.

Cultural Progress

Jonathan Swift writes *Gulliver's Travels,* his satirical masterpiece.

Scientific and Commercial Progress

English clergyman and physiologist Stephen Hales is first to measure blood pressure.

Lloyd's List begins publishing shipping news; issued twice weekly in London.

Gen. George Wade builds 250 miles of military roads and bridges in Scotland.

1727

Detroit and Michigan

Nov. 10. Commander Alphonse de Tonty dies and is buried in churchyard at northwest corner of Griswold and Jefferson. On Dec. 19, M. le Chevalier de Lepernouche assumes temporary command.

World History

First convent in America is established in New Orleans by Ursaline nuns.

Britain's King George I dies and is succeeded by his son, George II (to 1760).

Quakers demand abolition of slavery in colonies.

First failure of Ireland's potato crop.

War erupts between Spain and England; Spain lays siege to Gibraltar.

Catherine I dies; Peter II, grandson of Peter the Great, becomes czar of Russia.

Russian-Chinese border is fixed by treaty.

Ottoman army advances on Persia.

Cultural Progress

American Philosophical Society founded in Philadelphia.

First performance of Johann Sebastian Bach's *St. John's Passion.*

Ottoman foreign minister returns to Constantinople with printing press; will be used to spread Islamic beliefs.

Scientific and Commercial Progress

Coffee first planted in Brazil.

English clergyman and physiologist Stephen Hales's essays, *Vegetable Staticks*, published; beginning of experimental plant physiology.

1728

Detroit and Michigan

Detroit has string of commanders: Jean Baptiste Deschaillons de St. Ours, followed by Charles Joseph (Sieur de Noyelle), and then M. de Boishebert (to 1734).

Jesuits of Quebec establish a Huron mission—across river from Detroit to avoid conflict of ecclesiastical jurisdiction with the Recollets. Huron bands begin to settle there; trading with woodsmen closely monitored by the priests.

World History

March. Spain ends 14-month siege of Gibraltar; Britain retains possession of peninsula.

Cultural Progress

Madrid lodge of Freemasons founded; soon suppressed by the Inquisition.

Ephraim Chambers writes *Cyclopedia, or Universal Dictionary of Arts and Sciences,* 2 volumes, inspiring others to compile encyclopedias.

English novelist and playwright Henry Fielding pens first comedy for the stage, *Love in Several Masques.*

Scientific and Commercial Progress

Danish navigator Vitus Bering, employed by Russia, traverses Bering Strait; first European to make passage of waterway between Asia and North America.

English astronomer James Bradley announces his discovery of aberration of light of fixed stars.

1729

Detroit and Michigan

Robert Navarre arrives from France to become Sub-Intendant, responsible for civil affairs.

Schools are not regularly kept; many are illiterate. Some families send children to Montreal or Quebec to be schooled by priests.

World History

City of Baltimore founded.

Nov. 28. Natchez tribesmen in Louisiana attack settlers and soldiers; 200 are killed, several hundred taken prisoner. Retaliation for colonists' demand that Natchez give up sacred burial ground.

North and South Carolina become crown colonies.

Nov. 9. Treaty of Seville is signed by Spain, England, France. Outlines Spanish succession in Italian duchies, provides for Britain's retention of Gibraltar.

Portugal returns control of African seaport city Mombasa to Arabs.

Scientific and Commercial Progress

Benjamin and James Franklin publish *The Pennsylvania Gazette.*

Diamonds discovered in Brazil; gold already mined there. Begins rush.

Isaac Newton's *Principia* translated into English.

English edition published of Charles Perrault's (1697) *Histories or Tales of Past Times with Morals,* a retelling of folktales including "Little Red Riding Hood," "Sleeping Beauty." (Origins of Mother Goose.)

1730

Detroit and Michigan

Ste. Anne's parish register records 106 baptisms, 16 marriages, and 44 deaths.

Oct. 16 or 18. Antoine Cadillac dies in France.

World History

Russian Czar Peter II dies of smallpox; cousin Anna Ivanovna and cohorts overthrow supreme privy council (Feb. 26) to gain control. Czarina to rule for 10 years.

Crown Prince Frederick of Prussia is imprisoned by his father.

The Netherlands' Frederik IV dies, ending 31-year reign during which country has ceded some of its German territories. Succeeded by son, who reigns as Kristian VI.

Ashraf, Shah of Persia, is murdered.

Sultan Ahmad XII of Turkey is deposed and succeeded by Mahmud I, who restores order following Istanbul uprising.

Cultural Progress

Henry Fielding's *Tom Thumb* performed in London; Voltaire's *Brutus* in Paris.

Scientific and Commercial Progress

Philadelphia inventor Thomas Godfrey improves mariner's quadrant.

Cabinet Minister Charles Townshend resigns from public life and introduces scientific farming to England: develops ways to keep cattle through winter, allowing year-round sale of meat; also improves cultivation and crop rotation methods.

1731

Detroit and Michigan

French government makes slight improvements in the governing of Detroit.

World History

First permanent settlement in western Virginia.

French fortify Crown Point on Lake Champlain, New York.

Louisiana again becomes French royal province following failure of John Law's scheme to develop territory.

French begin expedition into western Canada.

March 16. Treaty of Vienna is signed by Britain, Holland, Spain, Holy Roman Empire— all agree to recognize Holy Roman Emperor Charles VI's Pragmatic Sanction (*see* 1713).

Mass expulsions of Protestants from Salzburg, Austria.

Persia fights Ottoman invaders.

Cultural Progress

First circulating (subscription) library in America is organized in Philadelphia by Ben Franklin.

Public concerts are held in Boston, Massachusetts, and Charleston, South Carolina.

Scientific and Commercial Progress

First botanic garden in America is planned in Philadelphia.

English factory workers are prohibited from immigrating to America.

English mathematician John Hadley invents reflecting quadrant that sailors can use to determine latitude at noon or at night.

London residence of British prime minister is built at 10 Downing Street.

Porcelain factories multiply in Europe; demand for china brisk.

France prohibits barbers from performing surgery; founds Royal Academy of Surgery.

1732

Detroit and Michigan

Louis XV directs that all Detroit land grants are settled on pain of forfeiture.

World History

Englishman James Oglethorpe obtains charter to establish Georgia.

Conrad Beissel founds Seventh Day Baptists in Germantown, Pennsylvania.

Prussian King Frederick William I settles 12,000 Salzburg Protestants in East Prussia.

Rain and grasshoppers ruin crops in western Japan; famine affects 2.6 million; 12,400 die.

Cultural Progress

Ninepins played for first time in New York.

First performance of London professional theatrical company in British colonies, in New York.

Covent Garden Opera House, London, opens.

Scientific and Commercial Progress

Benjamin Franklin issues *Poor Richard's Almanack*; also launches first foreign-language newspaper in British colonies—*Philadelphia Zeitung*.

Franklin revolutionizes colonial postal service, greatly increasing revenues.

English scientist Stephen Gray discovers some bodies are conductors and others nonconductors (insulators) of electricity.

1733

Detroit and Michigan

Outbreak of smallpox claims many lives.

Antoine Cadillac's widow and sons ask permission to go to Detroit to settle his estate.

World History

Georgia, 13th colony, established; first settlement at Savannah.

Nov. 5. First issue of John Peter Zenger's *Weekly Journal* is released; includes scathing criticism of New York's royal governor.

Smugglers evade Britain's Molasses Act.

Spanish fleet, laden with South American silver and gold, shipwrecked off Florida Keys.

France and Holy Roman Empire begin War of Polish Succession (to 1735) for control of Poland; France supports Stanislaw I; HRE supports Augustus III as king of Poland.

Conscription introduced in Prussia.

Persian army lays siege to Baghdad.

Cultural Progress

Alexander Pope's *Essay on Man* published in England; popular 18th-century poem.

Latin abolished in British courts.

First German Freemason lodge established at Hamburg.

Scientific and Commercial Progress

New York Weekly Journal is first issued.

John Kay patents flying shuttle loom; demand for thread increases.

Parliament passes Molasses Act prohibiting American trade with non-British West Indies.

Stephen Hale publishes account on determining blood pressure.

1734

Detroit and Michigan

Dam is built across Cabacier's Creek and a grist mill erected.

Robert Navarre is appointed sub-intendant and royal notary; as only civil officer in Detroit, also acts as justice, surveyor, collector, and sub delegate.

Thirteen grants of land are made to citizens and confirmed by Louis XIV.

June 10. Hughes Jacques Péan, Sieur de Livandière, is appointed commander; soon succeeded by Lt. Jacques Charles Sabrevois (to 1738).

World History

Great Awakening is begun by charismatic evangelical preacher Jonathan Edwards: fire-and-brimstone sermons spark 15-year religious revival in colonies.

Forced out of Salzburg, 8,000 Protestants settle in Georgia.

War of Polish Succession (begun last year) spreads through Europe: Spain and Sardinia join French side; Russia allies with Holy Roman Empire.

Turk tribesman Nader Shah invades Persia.

Cultural Progress

The Boston Weekly Post-Boy first issued.

First horse race in America is held at Charleston Neck, South Carolina.

Voltaire exalts British constitution, representative government.

The Koran, Islamic holy book, is translated into English.

Scientific and Commercial Progress

William Bull, of Charleston, South Carolina, becomes first American-born doctor to receive a degree when he is graduated from University of Leyden.

English seaman cures himself of scurvy by eating grass; doctors take note.

1735

Detroit and Michigan

Father Prisque Daniel is the pastor of Ste. Anne's.

World History

Aug. John Peter Zenger, printer and publisher of New York *Weekly Journal,* is acquitted of seditious libel in landmark trial establishing freedom of the press.

Scarlet fever epidemic strikes New England.

French make settlement at Vincennes (Indiana) on Wabash River.

French fur traders found Ste. Genevieve, first permanent white settlement on Missouri River.

War of Polish Succession ends with Treaty of Vienna; dynastic reshuffling in Europe.

Russia allies with Persia against Ottoman Turks.

War between Turkey and Persia ends.

Chi'en-lung (Hung-li) becomes Emperor of China (to 1796) and fourth ruler of Ch'ing (Manchu) dynasty; expands empire to widest limit.

Cultural Progress

Feb. 18. First opera (*Flora*) is performed in America at Charleston, South Carolina.

Scientific and Commercial Progress

First American medical society founded in Boston.

First American agricultural experimental farm is established at Savannah, Georgia.

Explorer Charles Marie de La Condamine gathers samples of hardened latex (rubber) in Peru and takes them back to France (1743); French call new material caoutchouc.

Swedish naturalist Carl Linnaeus publishes his *Systema Naturae,* basis for modern system of biological classification and nomenclature.

1736

Detroit and Michigan

Census lists 200 Ottawa, 200 Huron, 100 Potawatomi and their families living near Detroit.

French government makes more land grants at Detroit.

World History

British Parliament repeals statutes against witchcraft.

Russia (to be backed by Austria) declares war (to 1739) on Ottoman Empire.

Persian dynasty that has ruled since 1502 ends when last shah in line dies; Turk leader Nader Shah, who has effectively been ruling for 5 years, assumes power (to 1747).

Cultural Progress

George Frideric Handel's *Alexander's Feast* is performed at Covent Garden, London.

Scientific and Commercial Progress

Boston physician William Douglass gives first clinical description of scarlet fever.

English surgeon Claudius Aymand performs the first successful appendix operation; described in medical literature.

English inventor John Harrison presents his first ship's chronometer to London Board of Longitude; the instrument is accurate to within 1.3 miles of longitude per day, but is cumbersome (weighing more than 60 pounds) and delicate; Harrison spends years refining instrument.

Swiss mathematician Leonhard Euler publishes first systematic textbook of mechanics.

Swedish astronomer Anders Celsius leads French expedition into Lapland to measure degree of meridian in polar regions.

1737

Detroit and Michigan

Recollet priest Father Francis la Morinie, pastor at Ste. Anne's.

World History

William Byrd founds Richmond, Virginia.

French explorer Pierre de La Vérendrye founds fur-trading posts west of Lake Superior and reaches Missouri River in search for an overland northwest passage.

Calcutta, India earthquake kills hundreds of thousands.

Cultural Progress

Germany's new Göttingen University is first to espouse belief than the function of a university is to discover as well as pass on knowledge.

Licensing Act restricts number of London theaters and requires all plays to be subjected to censorship of Lord Chamberlain before public performance.

Scientific and Commercial Progress

Philadelphia police force organized by Benjamin Franklin is first city-paid constabulary in America.

1738

Detroit and Michigan

Antoine Cadillac's son, Joseph, sells his father's holdings in Detroit for $9,750, of which only $4,875 is paid.

Charles Joseph, Sieur de Noyelle, is made commander of Detroit (to 1741).

Distinguished Recollet priest Father Louis Marie Bonaventure Carpentier succeeds to pastorate of Ste. Anne's (to 1754).

Huron Indians move from Detroit to Sandusky Bay, where they can trade with the British.

World History

British troops are sent to Georgia to settle border dispute with Spain.

John Wesley converts; Societies of Methodists begin organizing.

Food production in France declines; linked to higher death rates.

French finance director Jean H. L. Orry devises the corvee, a system of forced labor to construct roads.

Papal Bull issued against Freemasonry.

Cultural Progress

Work begins on Royal Palace, Madrid.

Scientific and Commercial Progress

French mathematician and astronomer Pierre de Maupertius returns from Lapland expedition with information confirming Isaac Newton's theory of Earth's shape.

Swiss physicist Daniel Bernoulli publishes *Hydrodynamica,* a treatise on pressure and velocity of fluids; includes early version of his kinetic theory of gases.

1739

World History

Slaves revolt in South Carolina; quashed by quickly assembled force.

Moravian Church is founded in America.

Oct. War of Jerkins' Ear: Spain and Britain fight for control of North American and Caribbean waters.

Ireland's potato crop fails; effect is devastating as crop is staple of Irish diet.

Russo-Turkish War (begun 1736) ends. In Treaty of Belgrade, Russia gains Azov but agrees not to build Black Sea fleet; compelled to sign treaty after former ally Austria abjures. Austria yields Belgrade and northern Serbia.

Persia defeats large Mughal army and takes Delhi; Afghans invade from northwest. In response, India's leaders begin establishing independent states. Infighting among them leads to chaos and opens door for European incursion into Indian subcontinent.

Cultural Progress

George Frideric Handel's oratories, *Saul* and *Israel in Egypt* are first given at the King's Theater, London.

Scientific and Commercial Progress

German-American glassmaker Caspar Wistar sets up New Jersey factory, first of note in America.

American astronomer John Winthrop IV publishes *Notes on Sunspots.*

1740

Detroit and Michigan

Detroit records 156 baptisms, 27 marriages, and 73 deaths.

First farmhouse west of Fort Pontchartrain is built about this time, by Jean Baptiste Baudry.

World History

May. Frederick William I dies and is succeeded by his son, Frederick II, "the Great" (to 1786); greatly expands Prussia, which becomes military state, major European power.

Oct. Austria's Charles VI dies and is succeeded by his daughter, Maria Theresa.

War of Austrian Succession (to 1748) is begun by Prussia's Frederick the Great against Maria Theresa; European rulers refuse to recognize her right to rule in spite of their earlier acceptance of the Pragmatic Sanction. England allies with Austria (and others) against Prussia, Spain, France (and others).

Famine in France and Russia.

Oct. Russian Czarina Anna Ivanovna dies; secures succession to her great-nephew Ivan VI, who rules with regent.

Cultural Progress

University of Pennsylvania is founded.

First American orphanage with continuous existence founded in Savannah, Bethesda Home.

English novelist Samuel Richardson's *Pamela* published; becomes American bestseller 4 years later.

Scottish philosopher David Hume writes *A Treatise of Human Nature*.

Prussia's Frederick the Great introduces freedom of the press, worship.

Scientific and Commercial Progress

Post roads connect American colonies from Massachusetts to South Carolina. Packet boats operate on regular schedule, servicing major ports.

British Admiral George Anson sets out on around-the-world voyage.

English inventor Benjamin Huntsman improves the crucible process for smelting steel.

Enclosure of English farmlands is hastened by act of Parliament.

1741

Detroit and Michigan

July 28. Pierre Poyen de Noyan is commander of Detroit (to 1742).

World History

New York bakers strike; probably first strike in America.

British Prime Minister Sir Robert Walpole uses phrase "balance of power" in House of Commons speech; becomes guiding principle for British foreign policy.

Prague is occupied by French, Bavarian, Saxon troops; Austrian defense weakened by typhoid.

Typhoid epidemic kills tens of thousands in France; also strikes Sweden.

Yellow fever hits Spain (Cadiz); thousands die.

Elizabeth Petrovna, daughter of Peter the Great, overthrows government of Anna Leopoldovna, regent of Ivan VI; becomes czarina (to 1762).

Cultural Progress

Benjamin Franklin publishes *Philadelphia Magazine*.

Moravians who have founded Bethlehem, Pennsylvania, mark Christmas with celebration, including German tradition of visit from St. Nicholas.

Scientific and Commercial Progress

Indigo cultivated in South Carolina; initiates North American dyestuffs industry.

Vitus Bering explores coast of Alaska, discovers Aleutian Islands.

1742

Detroit and Michigan

Pierre de Celeron, Sieur de Blainville, is commander of Detroit (to 1743).

Jesuit priest Armand de la Richardie establishes mission on Bois Blanc to administer to Hurons at Detroit.

World History

Battle of Bloody Marsh: British troops under James Oglethorpe repel Spanish attack on Fort Frederica, St. Simons Island, Georgia.

Feb. Robert Walpole, Britain's first prime minister, resigns after 21 years in office. Created cabinet and party systems.

Feb. Elector of Bavaria Charles Albert is crowned Holy Roman emperor; supported by Maria Theresa's opponents, France and Prussia, he rules as Charles VII (to 1745).

Prussians defeat Austrians at Chotusitz (Czech Republic).

Peace of Berlin ends First Silesian War; Maria Theresa cedes Silesia to Prussia.

Austrian Empress Maria Theresa allies with British, raises armies, and drives allied forces out of Bavaria, in ongoing War of Austrian Succession.

Cultural Progress

English cardplayer Edmond Hoyle publishes *Short Treatise on Whist,* providing rules for game that becomes bridge.

George Frideric Handel's *Messiah* is first performed, at Dublin Cathedral.

Johann Sebastian Bach composes the *Goldberg Variations.*

Karl Heinrich Graun introduces Italian opera to Berlin.

Scientific and Commercial Progress

Coal is found in western Virginia.

Benjamin Franklin invents iron fireplace for heating. Becomes known as Franklin stove.

Merchant Peter Faneuil gives red-brick meetinghouse to city of Boston.

Cotton mills open in Birmingham and Northampton, England.

Swedish astronomer Anders Celsius devises centigrade scale of temperature.

1743

Detroit and Michigan

Joseph Lemoyne, Sieur de Longueil, is commander of Detroit (to 1747).

World History

June 27. English defeat French at Battle of Dettingen, forcing Emperor Charles VII to take refuge at Frankfurt in ongoing War of Austrian Succession. Dutch ally with British on the side of Austrian Empress Maria Theresa, also joined by Saxony.

War resumes between Persia and Ottoman Empire.

Russian pogroms kill thousands of Jews.

Cultural Progress

First London performance of Handel's *Messiah*.

Scientific and Commercial Progress

American Philosophical Society formed (Philadelphia); first scientific society in America.

French explorers reach Rocky Mountains.

French naturalist Charles-Marie de La Condamine makes first scientific exploration of the Amazon.

Dutch East India Co. richer and more powerful than Britain's United East India Company.

1744

World History

King George's War (to 1748) begins as North American counterpart to War of Austrian Succession: French struggle to protect sugar shipments from British fleets in Caribbean.

France deserts Prussia and declares war on England and on Maria Theresa.

Maria Theresa begins pogroms to evict Jews from Bohemia and Moravia.

Sept. Prussian King Frederick the Great takes Prague but is driven back to Saxony by Maria Theresa's forces.

Frederick the Great issues edict requiring peasants to plant potatoes.

Mount Cotopaxi erupts in viceroyalty of Peru (present-day Ecuador).

Cultural Progress

Sotheby's art auction house has its beginnings in London.

Anthem "God Save the King" (later "God Save Our Gracious King") published in London.

Tommy Thumb's Pretty Song Book is published in London; contains earliest versions of popular nursery rhymes "London Bridge Is Falling Down," "Hickory, Dickory, Dock," others.

First golf club is Honourable Company of Edinburgh Golfers, Scotland.

Johann Sebastian Bach releases part II of *Well-Tempered Clavier*.

Scientific and Commercial Progress

Gyroscope stabilizer first used on ships.

British Admiral George Anson returns from his voyage around the world, but has lost most of his crew to scurvy.

1745

Detroit and Michigan

More private land claims are granted.

World History

British, aided by New England settlers, take French fortress at Louisburg, Canada.

Second Jacobite rebellion (to 1746) in Britain: Charles Edward "Bonny Prince Charlie" Stuart, the Young Pretender, attempts to restore Stuart monarchy but fails.

Holy Roman Emperor Charles VII dies; his son succeeds him as elector of Bavaria and signs peace treaty with Maria Theresa. He regains lands conquered by Austria but renounces any claim to Austrian throne.

Dec. 25. Treaty of Dresden. Peace agreement made by Prussia, Austria, Saxony. Prussia recognizes Pragmatic Sanction but retains Silesia. Fighting in the War of Austrian Succession, nevertheless, continues.

Britain withdraws its support of Maria Theresa; troops return home to quell Jacobite rebellion.

Cultural Progress

Scottish national song, "The Campbells Are Coming," published.

Quadrille becomes fashionable dance in France.

Scientific and Commercial Progress

Basic electrical device, Leyden jar condenser, invented by Ewald Jurgen von Kleist.

Charles Bonnet writes *Traite d'insectologie,* a treatise on insects.

1746

Detroit and Michigan

Fort is attacked by northern Indians. Pontiac and his tribe aid in defending.

World History

Feb. French victorious at Raucoux, freeing Netherlands from Austrian control.

Spain's Bourbon King Philip V dies; succeeded by his son, Ferdinand VI.

Madras (India) falls to French forces.

Cultural Progress

College of New Jersey is chartered; later becomes Princeton University.

Wearing of tartans prohibited in England.

Joshua Reynolds paints *The Eliot Family.*

Scientific and Commercial Progress

Benjamin Franklin begins experiments with electricity.

1747

Detroit and Michigan

More land claims granted to settlers.

Boats carrying 150 soldiers arrive from Montreal to strengthen post against possible American Indian attacks, which are encouraged by the English.

June. 5 French traders returning to Detroit are captured and killed by Huron warriors.

Huron warriors plot attack on Detroit, but American Indian woman, overhearing the conspiracy, betrays them and averts the massacre.

World History

Ohio River Valley Company (also called Ohio Company of Virginia) established; King George II grants London merchants and landed Virginians 200,000 acres west of Alleghenies. Company later fails due to conflicts with French.

Britain's Royal Navy dominates European and Caribbean waters.

Prussia and Sweden ally for mutual defense.

Death of Persian shah leaves country in state of anarchy.

Barkzai dynasty rises to power in Afghanistan; remains in power to 1929.

Cultural Progress

Samuel Johnson begins work on his *Plan of a Dictionary of the English Language*.

Scientific and Commercial Progress

German chemist A. S. Marggraf discovers sugar in beets and carrots.

First school of civil engineering established in Paris.

1748

World History

Russian troops march through Bohemia toward the Rhine.

Peace of Aix-la-Chapelle ends War of Austrian Succession; recognizes Pragmatic Sanction (*see* 1713) and (Francis I) as Holy Roman Emperor. Prussia now major European power.

Cultural Progress

Subscription library opens in Charleston, South Carolina.

David Hume publishes *Philosophical Essays Concerning Human Understanding*.

Scientific and Commercial Progress

English physician John Fothergill describes diphtheria.

Baron de Montesquieu writes *L'Esprit des lois* (*The Spirit of the Laws*), pioneering sociology. Best-selling book influences European and American political thought.

Excavation begins of Pompeii, buried in Mt. Vesuvius eruption, A.D.79.

1749

Detroit and Michigan

Gov. of New France (La Galissonière) offers farm animals and equipment to any Frenchman who will settle in Detroit. Only 46 men respond this year.

Fort is expanded—walls pushed northward and southward. Houses within the walls are crowded together, mostly along 4 main streets, running east and west: Rue St. Joseph, Rue St. Jacques, Rue Ste. Anne, and Rue St. Louis. Footpath runs around the village.

Detroit's population (including neighboring farms), about 900.

Lt. Jacques Charles Sabrevois is commander of Detroit.

Pierre de Céloron, Sieur de Blainville, arrives in Detroit after burying lead plates throughout the Ohio Valley, claiming land for France.

French life in Detroit reportedly pleasant; habitants are sociable, observe religious calendar, attend weekly market, enjoy dances and horse races.

Aug. 20. French engineer Joseph de Lery draws plan of Detroit.

World History

Halifax, Nova Scotia, founded by British.

First settlement is made by the Ohio Company.

Consolidation Act reorganizes the British Royal Navy.

Cultural Progress

English novelist and playwright Henry Fielding writes realistic novel *Tom Jones*.

Scientific and Commercial Progress

London cabinetmaker Thomas Chippendale opens his first furniture factory.

1750

Detroit and Michigan

Detroit records 236 baptisms, 24 marriages, and 114 deaths.

Another 57 Frenchmen settle in Detroit, responding to governor's offer of material assistance (made last year).

World History

World population, about 750 million.

European population, about 140 million.

Population of American colonies, about 1.2 million.

Iron Act passed: Parliament prohibits American colonists from making finished goods of iron.

Treaty of Madrid grants most of (present-day) Brazil to the Portuguese.

Famine in France.

Cultural Progress

First playhouse opens in New York.

Johann Sebastian Bach dies; prolific composer invented tempered scale and initiated keyboard technique that becomes standard.

Scientific and Commercial Progress

American land speculator/explorer Thomas Walker is first white man to discover Cumberland Gap, mountain pass through Appalachian Mountains. Facilitates move westward.

Bituminous coal is first mined in America on the James River, Virginia.

German mathematician/astronomer Johann Tobias Mayer publishes *Map of the Moon*, lunar tables.

French astronomer Nicolas de Lacaille leads astronomical expedition to Cape of Good Hope to determine solar and lunar parallax.

1751

Detroit and Michigan

Feb. 15. Pierre de Celeron, Sieur de Blainville, is commander of Detroit (to March 19, 1754).

Michael Yax, probably first German settler in Michigan, begins farming in Grosse Pointe.

World History

Dutch ruler William IV dies; his son, William V, succeeds him (to 1795), his widow, Anne (daughter of Britain's George II) is regent.

Sweden's Frederick I dies, ending 31-year reign.

Sept. 12. Britain's victory at Arcot checks French hegemony in India.

China invades Tibet.

Cultural Progress

English poet Thomas Gray pens "Elegy Written in a Country Churchyard."

First volume of Diderot's *Encyclopedia* appears in France (last volume published 1772).

Minuet becomes fashionable dance in Europe.

Scientific and Commercial Progress

First incorporated hospital in U.S., Pennsylvania Hospital (Philadelphia), chartered.

Sugarcane brought to Louisiana from Santo Domingo.

1752

Detroit and Michigan

Famine and smallpox threaten Fort Pontchartrain.

June. Governor of New France, Marquise Duquesne, orders war party to be organized in Detroit against the British, who have encroached on trade with American Indians. Some 250 Frenchmen and Ottawa warriors set out from Detroit, attack British fort and Miami village at Pickawillany (Piqua, Ohio). French and Ottawa win decisively. Several tribes return to trade with French.

World History

June. Treaty of Logstown: Iroquois and Delaware Indians cede lands south of Ohio River to British.

Georgia becomes crown colony.

Great Britain and its colonies adopt Gregorian calendar. Wed. Sept. 2 is followed by Thurs. Sept. 14 to make adjustment. New Year's Day to be celebrated Jan. 1.

Cultural Progress

David Hume publishes *Political Discourses*.

English poet/novelist Charlotte Lennox writes *The Female Quixote*.

Scientific and Commercial Progress

Philadelphia installs street lamps.

June 15. Benjamin Franklin conducts kite experiment; shows relationship between lightning and electricity.

Franklin helps found American colonies' first mutual fire insurance company: Philadelphia Contributionship for the Insurance of Houses from Loss by Fire.

Pennsylvania Hospital founded in Philadelphia; oldest permanent general hospital in America.

1753

World History

Canadian French troops occupy Ohio River Valley, erecting Forts Presque Isle and Le Boeuf. British send George Washington out (in Dec.) with letter demanding that they withdraw.

British Parliament passes act permitting naturalization of Jews; opposition prompts repeal (next year).

Cultural Progress

British Museum, London, is founded.

Scientific and Commercial Progress

Conestogas, broad-wheeled covered wagons, originate in Pennsylvania; used to carry heavy loads westward before advent of railroads.

Scottish naval surgeon James Lind publishes findings that citrus wards off scurvy.

Carl Linnaeus publishes *Species Planetarum*; foundation for modern system of botanical nomenclature.

1754

Detroit and Michigan

Detroit becomes staging point in French and Indian War. Over 400 French militia are sent to outpost with supplies.

Jacques d'Anon, Sieur de Muy, is commander of Detroit (to May 25, 1758).

Recollet priest Simple le Bocquet, pastor of Ste. Anne's.

French engineer Joseph de Lery makes another plan of fort.

World History

June 19. Albany Congress: With advance of French, British colonial representatives and Iroquois (Six Nations) sign treaty, plan joint defense.

July 10. Plan of Union. Albany Congress issues proposal (sponsored by Benjamin Franklin) calling for voluntary union of 13 British colonies. Later rejected by colonial legislatures, crown.

Fighting breaks out between French and British in America; French and Indian War is fought (to 1760), mostly over control of lucrative Ohio River Valley. Last major conflict before American Revolution.

Fort Duquesne built by French on site of present Pittsburgh.

Cultural Progress

First concert hall in Boston opens.

King's College, New York, founded; later becomes Columbia.

American Puritan preacher Jonathan Edwards publishes *Freedom of the Will.*

Rules of Golf published in Scotland by St. Andrews Golfers, later called Royal & Ancient Golf Club.

David Hume writes *History of Great Britain, vol. 1*; completed 1762. Popular in England and America.

Scientific and Commercial Progress

First iron-rolling mill opens in Fareham, Hampshire, England.

1755

Detroit and Michigan

Some Acadians banished from Nova Scotia seek refuge in Detroit.

Fort Pontchartrain enlarged to accommodate new settlers.

Ste. Anne's Church rebuilt; new structure includes a belfry.

Body of Father Constantine d'Halle, killed in 1706, is reinterred in new church.

World History

British expatriate French Acadians; many settle in Louisiana.

King George II dispatches Gen. Edward Braddock to North America as commander in chief.

July 9. British army under Gen. Braddock defeated by French at Fort Duquesne.

Sept. 8. Battle of Lake George ends in defeat for French.

Nov. 1. Lisbon earthquake; generates tsunami (tidal wave). At least 30,000 dead.

China begins campaign (to 1760) to eliminate Turk and Mongol threats.

Cultural Progress

Richard Skuckberg, English surgeon with Gen. Braddock, writes verses to "Yankee Doodle."

Samuel Johnson publishes *A Dictionary of the English Language.*

Scientific and Commercial Progress

Philadelphia's Independence Hall completed.

Scottish chemist-physician proves magnesium is an element.

1756

World History

Population of 13 colonies, about 1.5 million, including 250,000 slaves. Largest cities, Boston and Philadelphia.

Population of Canada (including Michigan), about 80,000.

Seven Years' War (to 1763): Prussia fights Austria for control of Germany and supremacy in Europe. Great Britain supports Prussia; France, most German states, Russia, and Sweden join Austria. Struggle encompasses French and Indian War (begun 1754).

June 20. Black Hole of Calcutta: Overnight imprisonment of 146 Europeans by an Indian Nawab in a tiny, poorly ventilated room, results in death of all but 23.

Robert Clive sets out from Calcutta against the Nawab of Bengal.

Scientific and Commercial Progress

English civil engineer John Smeaton rediscovers hydraulic cement (unknown since fall of Rome).

First chocolate factory built in Germany.

1757

Detroit and Michigan

French soldiers from Fort Duquesne arrive at Detroit.

Detroit's population (per government report), about 200.

American Indians and the French hold foot races with bets of furs.

World History

May. Prussia's Frederick the Great invades Bohemia; forced to withdraw.

June. Robert Clive defeats French at Battle of Plessey, destroying French claims and establishing British supremacy in India.

Nov. Prussia's Frederick the Great crushes French at Battle of Rossbach. One month later he is victorious over Austrians.

Famine accompanies Seven Years' War.

Cultural Progress

Tobias Smollett's *Complete History of England* published; rivals David Hume's work in popularity.

Scientific and Commercial Progress

Sextant is invented; improves navigation.

Swiss biologist Albrecht von Haller publishes first volume of *Elementa Physiologiae,* marking beginning of modern physiology.

1758

Detroit and Michigan

May 25. Capt. François Picoté, Sieur de Bellestre, assumes command; last French commander of Detroit.

World History

William Pitt becomes British prime minister; vigorously pursues battles with French in Canada, Africa, India.

In French and Indian War (to 1760), British capture Fort Duquesne; rename it Fort Pitt. British take Louisburg.

In Seven Years' War, Prussia's Frederick the Great ousts Russian invaders, also wins battle against Austria.

As astronomer Edmund Halley predicted, comet last seen in 1682 reappears; becomes known as Halley's comet.

1759

Detroit and Michigan

In French and Indian War, British destroy French posts at Presque Isle, Venago, Le Boeuf; soldiers from these posts are sent to Detroit, causing shortage of provisions.

World History

French troops are sent to reinforce Fort Niagara, but are captured when fort is surrendered. British also seize French forts at Ticonderoga and Crown Point.

Sept. 13–18. British troops under Gen. James Wolfe defeat French (led by Gen. Louis-Joseph de Montcalm) at Battle of Quebec. Both commanders are killed.

Cultural Progress

Voltaire publishes masterpiece, *Candide*; satirical tale explores nature of good and evil. (Eventually translated into more than 100 languages.)

Joseph Haydn composes Symphony No. 1; regarded as first great master of the symphony.

First American song, "My Days Have Been So Wondrous Free," composed by Francis Hopkinson.

Scientific and Commercial Progress

Colonies' first life insurance company incorporated in Philadelphia: Presbyterian Ministers' Fund.

Irishman Arthur Guinness begins brewing beer.

1760

Detroit and Michigan

Sept. 12. British Maj. Robert Rogers, Capt. Donald Campbell, and regulars from Fort Pitt are dispatched to Detroit to secure Fort Pontchartrain.

Nov. 29. Fort Pontchartrain is formally surrendered to the British, whose captains report it is among finest forts they have seen. The *fleur-de-lis* comes down and British colors are raised. Change is reportedly regarded with indifference by French settlers, who are compelled to swear oath of allegiance to King George II of England.

French notary Robert Navarre reportedly assists British officers in transition.

Fort and town have an area of 372 feet north and south and 600 feet east and west. There are about 2,000 inhabitants and 300 dwellings.

Maj. Rogers orders British parties at Detroit to secure possession of Ohio forts; he leads northern excursion to secure Michilimackinac. Lake ice forces his return overland through Detroit.

Capt. Donald Campbell is commander of Detroit (to 1762).

Winter. French merchants and farmers entertain British officers and the favor is returned.

Dress is similar to what might be worn in London and Paris, though a bit behind (as news travels slowly). Merchants wear brocaded waistcoats, lace jabots, long-tailed coats, breeches with buckles at knees; hair is powdered. Their wives and daughters wear long, full gowns, shawls; hair is usually worn up. Farmers, craftsmen wear brightly colored shirts, trousers with belt or sash, straw hats, moccasins; their wives wear short gowns (to knees) with petticoats to ankles, broad-brimmed straw hats.

Copper is obtained in northern Michigan by Alexander Henry who sinks a mine shaft but soon abandons it.

World History

Population of 13 colonies, about 1.6 million.

France surrenders Canada to British.

Oct. 9. Russians occupy and burn Berlin.

Oct. 25. Britain's King George II dies, ending 33-year reign, and is succeeded by his grandson, George III (to 1820).

Cultural Progress

First exhibition of contemporary art at Royal Society of Art, London.

London's Botanical Gardens open at Kew.

Scientific and Commercial Progress

Josiah Wedgewood opens pottery works at Staffordshire, England.

1761

Detroit and Michigan

Early summer. Capt. Donald Campbell learns of Iroquois plot to unite western bands of Indians in attack on British forts, including Detroit. Scheme fails to win support, but threat is heeded. Reinforcements and peace negotiators are sent to Detroit.

Sept. 3. Troops under command of Henry Gladwin arrive in Detroit with Sir William Johnson and George Croghan, both influential with various tribes. The reinforcements are greeted with much festivity.

Sept. 9. Grand council with American Indians opens. Meeting is a success for both sides (though there is no record that powerful Chief Pontiac attends).

Forts at Michilimackinac and St. Joseph reinforced with small garrisons.

World History

Colonial advocate-general James Otis protests Writs of Assistance (general search warrants).

France, Spain, and Italian Bourbon states sign pact against Britain.

Oct. 5. William Pitt resigns as British prime minister when Parliament, king refuse to declare war on Spain.

Cultural Progress

Collected works of Voltaire are translated by Smollett and others; published in England.

Scientific and Commercial Progress

Austrian physician Leopold Auenbrugger introduces percussion tapping as method of medical diagnosis of lungs.

German botanist Josef Kölreuter discovers the function of plant nectar and recognizes the role of insects and the wind in the pollination of flowers.

1762

Detroit and Michigan

August. Maj. Henry Gladwin arrives in Detroit to take command (to 1764).

German-born trader Abraham Chapman arrives from Montreal; first known Jewish settler in Detroit.

Tribes become increasingly dissatisfied with British traders and officers.

World History

French and Indian War officially ends with Treaty of Fontainebleau; France's power in North America is broken.

France cedes claim to lands west of Mississippi River to Spanish, vastly expanding New Spain.

Due to expense of Seven Years' War, commander of British forces in America, General Amherst, decides there will be no further gifts to American Indians during times of peace. Policy leads to dissatisfaction among various tribes whose anti-British sentiments are encouraged by some French settlers.

In Caribbean, British capture Martinique, Grenada, Havana. Also capture Manila, in Philippines.

In Seven Years' War, Spain joins Austrian alliance; Russia withdraws and makes peace with Prussia; Sweden also signs treaty with Prussia. France and Austria soon to make peace with Frederick the Great as well.

Czarina Elizabeth of Russia dies and is succeeded by Peter III, who is overthrown, put to death, and succeeded (to 1796) by his wife, Catherine II (the Great).

Cultural Progress

French philosopher Jean-Jacques Rousseau publishes *Social Contract*. Highly influential work argues it is incumbent upon people to establish their own government, that they "have a duty to obey only legitimate powers."

Child prodigy Wolfgang Amadeus Mozart composes his first violin sonatas and improvisations

Scientific and Commercial Progress

Cast iron converted for first time into malleable iron, at Carron ironworks in Scotland.

Swedish physician Nils von Rosenstein establishes science of pediatrics.

1763

Detroit and Michigan

April 27. Angered by methods of trade employed by the British, Ottawa Chief Pontiac holds council on Detroit River (at Ecorse River) to outline his plan to capture Detroit. Maj. Henry Gladwin is warned of the plot and makes preparations.

May 7. Pontiac, 10 chiefs, and 60 warriors enter fort but seeing the British garrison readied, they withdraw. Pontiac realizes command at Detroit has been warned of his plan; tries to identify the informer, but when confronted by Pontiac's emissaries, Maj. Gladwin refuses to disclose his source.

May 8. Pontiac and three chiefs enter fort, requesting that his warriors be allowed entrance the next day to smoke the peace pipe with British. Gladwin denies the request, saying only the chiefs would be admitted. Pontiac withdraws in frustration.

May 9. Pontiac and the Ottawa cross river to the fort. Met with word that only he and his chiefs may enter, he turns away. The Ottawa return to their village. Pontiac prepares to seize fort.

May 10. Pontiac lays siege to Detroit (for 153 days). But Gladwin, British soldiers, and loyal French inhabitants hold out. Pontiac's example sets off uprising throughout region west of Alleghenies. Only Detroit, Niagara, and Pitt are not captured by American Indians.

Late May/early June. Potawatomi warriors overwhelm small garrison at Fort St. Joseph; within the week, the Chippewa capture fort at Michilimackinac. In wake of uprisings, British do not reestablish permanent garrisons at Sault Ste. Marie or Fort St. Joseph.

July 29. Capt. James Dalyell, Maj. Robert Rogers, and 260 reinforcements reach Detroit to help defend the settlement.

July 31. British forces emerge from fort during night; launch attack on Ottawa. Intercepted, fighting erupts on Parent's Creek (renamed Bloody Run after event), claiming 20 British lives, including Capt. Dalyell. An uncounted number taken prisoner; 42 are wounded.

Aug. Detroit continues to receive supplies by ship.

Sept. 9. Potawatomi arrive at Detroit to seek peace. Tribal support for Pontiac's War wanes.

Oct. More tribes seek peace with Gladwin in Detroit.

Oct. 31. Pontiac sends Gladwin a message saying he is abandoning his siege and is willing to begin peace talks.

Nov. Chief Pontiac and a few followers leave Detroit, spending winter near the Maumee River.

Britain's Proclamation of 1763 draws a line from Ottawa River along the Appalachians to mark limit of their settlement; west of the line (including all of Ohio River Valley), Indian trade is to be conducted strictly through British-appointed commissioners.

World History

Feb. 20. Treaty of Paris signed, in which Great Britain acquires all of New France except for a few islands, New Orleans, and French possessions west of the Mississippi, which are ceded to Spain. Spain cedes the Floridas (East and West) to England.

France cedes Louisiana to Spain, which recognizes Mississippi River as western boundary of British holdings in America.

Charles Mason and Jeremiah Dixon begin survey of boundary between Pennsylvania and Maryland; completed 1767.

First American synagogue, Touro, is completed in Newport, Rhode Island.

Cultural Progress

Excavations at Pompeii and Herculaneum reveal Roman way of life.

Scientific and Commercial Progress

English clockmaker and inventor John Harrison develops a marine chronometer for determining longitude at sea.

1764

Detroit and Michigan

Aug. 31. Maj. Henry Gladwin is relieved of his command; Col. John Bradstreet takes over; arrives with force of 1,200 men.

Fort at St. Joseph is not reinforced; becomes trading post. Michilimackinac is reoccupied by British.

Sept. Council is held; chiefs, tired of war, agree to peace with British.

Freemasons among the British officers organize Zion Lodge.

Detroit loses numerous inhabitants to new settlement at St. Louis; population seriously reduced.

World History

St. Louis (Missouri) is founded.

April. Parliament passes Sugar Act (replaces ineffective Molasses Act of 1733) to raise taxes in American colonies and Currency Act, forbidding colonists to print paper money.

May. Boston lawyer James Otis denounces "taxation without representation."

Jesuits are expelled from France.

Stanislaw Poniatowski becomes King of Poland (to 1795); last Polish monarch.

Deposed Czar Ivan VI murdered in prison.

Cultural Progress

Oct. 29. *Connecticut Courant* begins publication (today known as *Hartford Courant,* the oldest continuously published newspaper in the nation).

Castle of Otranto by English writer Horace Walpole is first Gothic novel; sets standard.

Literary salons are founded in Paris.

Wolfgang Amadeus Mozart (age 8) writes his first symphony.

Scientific and Commercial Progress

Brown University, Providence, Rhode Island, founded.

London introduces practice of numbering houses.

1765

Detroit and Michigan

British hold council with American Indians at Detroit; 18 tribes are represented.

Lt. John Campbell succeeds Bradstreet as commander of Detroit.

World History

Population of Philadelphia reaches 25,000; 2nd largest city (after London) in British Empire.

March 22. Parliament passes Stamp Act. Colonists respond by assembling Stamp Act Congress (Oct. 7) in New York; delegates from 9 colonies draw up declaration of rights and liberties, which are sent to King and Parliament.

May 15. Parliament passes Quartering Act, requiring colonists to provide British soldiers with room and board.

Economic depression begins in Boston.

Holy Roman Emperor Francis I dies; succeeded (to 1790) by his son, Joseph II. His widow, Maria Theresa, is co-regent.

Cultural Progress

More than 20 newspapers currently published in American colonies.

Scientific and Commercial Progress

First medical college in America is established in Philadelphia.

Tobacco is biggest American colonial export—amounting to twice the exports of bread and flour. Fish, rice, indigo, and wheat are among other exported goods.

William Stiegel begins producing fine glassware in Lancaster County, Pennsylvania.

Scottish engineer James Watt invents modern condensing steam engine.

Potato becomes the most popular foodstuff in Europe.

Paris tavern-keeper named A. Boulanger becomes first restaurant proprieter.

1766

Detroit and Michigan

Aug. 26. Maj. Robert Bayard appointed commander of Detroit.

World History

March 18. Parliament repeals Stamp Act but Declaratory Act states Britain's right to tax colonies.

July. Pontiac and Sir William Johnson meet at Fort Ontario (Oswego, New York): in formal treaty, chief agrees to give allegiance to British; British promise to remove settlers from American Indian lands.

Presidio of San Francisco founded; Spain's northernmost frontier post.

British gain control of Madras (India).

Cultural Progress

Rutgers University chartered.

Christie's art auction house opens in London.

Scientific and Commercial Progress

Construction begins on Britain's Grand Trunk Canal, connects North Sea and Irish Sea.

Royal Astronomer Nevil Maskelyne issues (first annual) *Nautical Almanac*.

French naval officer Louis de Bougainville sets out on around-the-world expedition (returns to France 1769); finds Tahiti, Solomon Islands, New Guinea.

1767

Detroit and Michigan

Capt. George Turnbull becomes commander of Detroit (to 1769).

World History

Parliament passes Townshend Acts, placing duties on various items, including tea, glass, and paper; colonies organize nonimportation agreements, especially in Boston.

Crown suspends New York Assembly for refusal to support quartering of British troops.

King Charles III expels Jesuits from Spanish empire, opening door for Franciscan conquest of California.

Cultural Progress

The Prince of Parthia by Thomas Godfrey, Jr., is first drama written by a native American to be professionally produced (in Philadelphia).

First parish school in America is established in Philadelphia.

Scientific and Commercial Progress

Daniel Boone traverses Cumberland Gap, makes trips into Kentucky.

Joseph Priestley publishes *The History and Present State of Electricity.*

1768

Detroit and Michigan

Village tax levied on lots in fort—1 shilling per foot.

World History

Regulator movement begins in North and South Carolina: back country settlers oppose corrupt officials; ends in 1771 with restoration of law and order.

Anti-British riots in Boston. Colonists draft grievances.

Crown dissolves Massachusetts Assembly for refusal to assist in tax collection; Britain sends more troops to Boston.

Oct. 14. Treaty of Hard Labor confirms cession of Cherokee lands in Carolinas, Virginia to British crown.

Nov. 5. Treaty of Fort Stanwix confirms cession of Iroquois lands between Ohio and Tennessee rivers to British crown.

Russo-Turkish War begins (ends 1774).

Cultural Progress

John Dickinson's *Letters from a Farmer in Pennsylvania* widely read in American colonies; author later called the "penman of the revolution."

Royal Academy, London, founded; portrait painter Joshua Reynolds is president.

Mother Goose's Tales first issued by John Newbery publishing house in London, England.

Scientific and Commercial Progress

Capt. James Cook sets sail; circumnavigates globe (returns 1771).

Chamber of Commerce of State of New York is formed, first of its kind.

1769

Detroit and Michigan

Lt. George McDougall buys Hog Island (Belle Isle) from American Indians for 8 barrels of rum, 3 rolls of tobacco, 6 pounds of vermilion paint, and wampum belt.

World History

First white settlements in Tennessee.

April 20. Pontiac is killed in Illinois country by a Peoria Indian.

July 3. Father Junípero Serra establishes first Spanish mission in California, at San Diego. Serra will establish 10 missions, convert some 6,800 American Indians.

British crown dissolves Virginia Assembly for protesting colonial treason trials held in England. Members meet in private.

Great Famine of Bengal; millions in India die.

Cultural Progress

Dartmouth College chartered.

England's first Shakespeare festival opens at Stratford-on-Avon.

Scientific and Commercial Progress

Benjamin Franklin accurately charts the Gulf Stream.

James Watt patents improved steam engine.

Spinning frame, a water-powered spinning machine, patented by Richard Arkwright, England.

French military engineer Nicolas-Joseph Cugnot invents wheeled tractor propelled by steam engine; believed to be earliest automobile.

1770

Detroit and Michigan

June 2. Maj. T. Bruce assumes command at Detroit (to Sept.).

Sept. Capt. James Stephenson commands the fort (to Jan. 8, 1772).

Chaplain Turring performs wedding ceremony; first record of Protestant minister in Detroit.

World History

Population of 13 colonies about 2.2 million.

Jan. 19–20. Battle of Golden Hill in New York City. Skirmish between Sons of Liberty and redcoats results in first bloodshed between American colonists and British troops.

March 5. Boston Massacre: during Boston riot, 5 protesters are killed by British troops.

April 12. British Parliament repeals Townshend Act, but retains tax on tea.

Dauphin of France marries Marie Antoinette, daughter of Empress Maria Theresa of Austria.

Greeks try to overthrow Turks; though aided by Russia, move for independence fails.

Cultural Progress

Massachusetts Spy begins publication in Boston; voice for opposition to British crown.

Monticello begins to be constructed for lawyer Thomas Jefferson in Virginia.

George Frideric Handel's *Messiah* is first performed in New York.

English artist Thomas Gainsborough paints *The Blue Boy*; epitomizes 18th-century fashion and culture.

German composer Christoph Willibald Gluck's *Paride ed Elena* revolutionizes opera; places music at service of drama.

Industrial Revolution well under way in England; soon spreads.

James Cook discovers Botany Bay; claims Australia for England.

1771

Detroit and Michigan

Tax levy this year is £30, 8 shillings.

Detroit is trade center of lakes region; American Indians exchange catches for clothing, guns, ammunition, trinkets, spirits.

Small French farms and orchards are scattered on both sides of Detroit River.

World History

Battle of Alamance: North Carolina Regulators protest; British troops end the revolt.

Gustav III ascends Swedish throne upon the death of his father; regains absolute power, rousing fears of Russia and Prussia. Reigns to 1792.

Russian Cossacks conquer Crimean Peninsula.

Egyptian troops seize Damascus.

Cultural Progress

Encyclopedia Britannica is first published.

Scientific and Commercial Progress

Daniel Boone begins forging route (Wilderness Road) through Cumberland Pass.

1772

Detroit and Michigan

Maj. George Etherington assumes command; soon succeeded (to 1774) by Maj. Henry Bassett.

World History

June 22. British Chief Justice Murray rules in Sommersett case that a slave is free on landing in England.

Nov. 2. Boston patriot Samuel Adams forms American Committees of Correspondence in Massachusetts for action against Great Britain. Inspires other similar groups to form.

First Partition: Poland loses one-third its territory, half its population; divided by Russia, Prussia, Austria.

Edo (Tokyo) Japan destroyed by fire.

Scientific and Commercial Progress

Capt. James Cook begins his second voyage; becomes first explorer to cross Antarctic Circle (Jan. 17, 1773).

General Gage is launched; largest vessel built by British before 1796, its capacity is 154 tons.

Daniel Rutherford and Joseph Priestley independently discover nitrogen.

1773

Detroit and Michigan

Official documents report Detroit's population (excluding soldiers) is 1,367; there are 280 houses and 2,602 acres of land are in cultivation.

World History

March 12. Virginia House of Burgesses appoints Committee of Correspondence.

May 10. Parliament passes Tea Act.

Dec. 16. Boston Tea Party: Patriots board ships in harbor and dump tea belonging to the British East India Company overboard to protest the tax on tea and the apparent monopoly of the East India Co.

Pope Clement XIV, under pressure from European monarchs, suppresses Jesuit order; disrupts education in Europe. (Restored 1814.)

Denmark cedes Duchy of Oldenburg to Russia.

Peasant and Cossack uprising in Russia (suppressed, 1774).

Cultural Progress

Philadelphia Museum founded.

Former slave Phillis Wheatley's first book of poems is published in London.

Oliver Goldsmith's *She Stoops to Conquer* debuts at London's Theatre Royal, Covent Garden.

Scientific and Commercial Progress

First American natural history museum is established at Charleston.

English clockmaker and inventor John Harrison wins government prize (offered 1714) for developing (in 1763) marine chronometer for determining longitude at sea.

1774

Detroit and Michigan

Maj. Richard Beringer Lernoult assumes command of the fort.

June 22. Quebec Act provides first civil government for territory including Detroit, which becomes part of administration of Quebec province.

Britain sends Col. Arent de Peyster to Michilimackinac as commander and lieutenant governor.

World History

British House of Commons refuses Massachusetts petition to remove Royal Governor Thomas Hutchinson.

British Parliament passes 5 laws to assert its authority in American colonies and punish the colonies for the Boston Tea Party: Intolerable Acts (or Coercive Acts) limit colonial political power and close Boston Harbor.

May 26. Virginia's royal governor dissolves House of Burgesses, which meets secretly the next day and adopts resolution calling for intercolonial congress.

June 22. Parliament passes Quebec Act, extending provincial boundaries and invalidating western claims of Virginia, Massachusetts, Connecticut; helps secure French Canadian loyalty to British (in part because it establishes Roman Catholic Church in Canada).

Sept. 5. First Continental Congress is called to order in Philadelphia with representatives from all colonies but Georgia (which agrees to go along with outcome).

Oct. First Continental Congress declares that British Parliament has no authority over American colonies, each colony may regulate its affairs, and colonies will not trade with Britain until Parliament rescinds trade and taxation policies.

Oct. Virginia's Royal Governor Lord Dunmore leads militia against Shawnee in western Virginia; defeated, tribe yields hunting rights in Kentucky and agrees to allow colonial use of Ohio River.

Connecticut and Rhode Island prohibit importation of slaves.

English religious leader Ann Lee founds first Shaker colony in America (at Watervliet, New York).

French King Louis XV dies; he is succeeded by his grandson who reigns (to 1792) with his Austrian-born queen, Marie Antoinette, as Louis XVI.

Cultural Progress

Colonial leaders, including Thomas Jefferson and Benjamin Franklin, publish pamphlets and articles on the rise and rights of Americans.

First American painter of note, John Singleton Copely, sails for Europe.

English politician Philip Stanhope writes *Letters to His Son,* collection of advice on manners, success; among century's most popular books.

German poet Johann Wolfgang von Goethe publishes *The Sorrows of Young Werther.*

Scientific and Commercial Progress

English chemist Joseph Priestley discovers oxygen.

German geologist A. G. Werner introduces definite order and nomenclature for minerals.

1775

Detroit and Michigan

Nov. 9. Newly appointed Lt. Gov. Henry Hamilton arrives in Detroit; fort commander is Capt. Montpasant.

Inferior courts established at Detroit; superior courts in Quebec and Montreal.

World History

April 18. Paul Revere rides to warn patriots of British troops' approach.

April 19. Battles of Lexington and Concord fought between patriots and redcoats; 250 British are killed or wounded and about 90 Americans are dead. Word spreads quickly, signaling beginning of American Revolution (to 1783).

May 10. Second Continental Congress meets in Philadelphia. John Hancock is assembly's president. Continental Army is created with George Washington commander in chief (in June).

May 10. Ethan Allen leads Green Mountain Boys to seize Fort Ticonderoga (New York).

June 17. Battle of Bunker Hill is fought in Boston; more than 1,000 British are injured or dead, 400 American soldiers killed or wounded.

Oct. 13. Continental Congress establishes a navy.

First American society dedicated to freeing slaves is formed in Pennsylvania.

Britain hires 29,000 German mercenaries to fight on its side in American Revolution.

Cultural Progress

Writing in *Pennsylvania Magazine,* Thomas Paine advocates women's rights.

All colonies except Delaware and New Jersey have at least one newspaper; most are weekly and are shared by readers.

Statesman Edmund Burke delivers "On Moving His Resolutions for Conciliation with the Colonies" speech to Parliament.

Neo-Classicist movement (to 1825); painters, sculptors, architects imitate Greco-Roman art.

"Tragic muse" Sarah Siddons first performs at Drury Lane, London; leading actress to 1812.

Irish dramatist Richard Sheridan's first of 3 great comedies of manners, *The Rivals,* is performed at Covent Garden, London.

French playwright Pierre-Augustin Beaumarchais writes *The Barber of Seville*; immensely popular.

Scientific and Commercial Progress

First American submarine is built.

Daniel Boone opens Wilderness Road into Kentucky; provides route for pioneers to cross Appalachians.

King George III approves release from bondage of women and children in British coal and salt mines.

1776

Detroit and Michigan

Col. Arent de Peyster is commander of Detroit; Schuyler succeeded by Capt. Lord.

William and Alexander Macomb purchase Grosse Isle from the Potawatomi.

Citadel at Fort Pontchartrain is occupied by 200–300 British soldiers; during American Revolution (to 1783), it is used to hold American prisoners.

British Crown requires all Great Lakes vessels to be registered at Detroit.

American Indians from Detroit make raids on settlers in western Virginia (present-day Kentucky) as settlements are seen as a violation of Ordinance of 1763. Tribes demand that Lt. Gov. Henry Hamilton supply arms, ammunition, supplies to support effort. To retain their loyalty, Hamilton concedes.

First burglary occurs in Detroit: Jean Contincineau and Nancy Wiley steal furs, knives, guns. Caught, they are publicly whipped. The pair later sets fire to warehouse where the goods are stored; court judges them to be hanged.

World History

New Hampshire adopts first state constitution.

Virginia Convention incorporates religious liberty into state constitution.

Jan. Thomas Paine publishes *Common Sense,* quickly selling 150,000 copies and turning colonial public opinion in favor of independence.

March 18. Continental Congress approves use of privateers (gunboats for hire), enabling patriots to capture some 600 British ships.

July 4. Declaration of Independence is drafted by Second Continental Congress; 4 days later it is read to a crowd assembled in State House yard. Signed by members, Aug. 2.

Sept. 22. British hang Nathan Hale, accused of being a spy.

Dec. 25–26. Gen. George Washington crosses Delaware River; defeats British and Hessians at Trenton. Turns tide of war.

Delaware forbids further importation of slaves.

Father Junípero Serra establishes California missions of San Francisco de Assisi and San Juan Capistrano.

House of Commons hears first motion to outlaw slavery in Britain and colonies; slavery called "contrary to the laws of God and the rights of man." Motion fails.

Cultural Progress

Phi Beta Kappa founded at William and Mary College.

Edward Gibbon publishes the first volume of *Decline and Fall of the Roman Empire*.

Moscow's Bolshoi Theater is founded.

Scientific and Commercial Progress

Connecticut inventor David Bushnell's "Turtle" pioneers submarine warfare.

Adam Smith publishes *Wealth of Nations*, authoritative work on economics and politics.

Capt. James Cook begins his third voyage (to 1779); finds Hawaiian Islands (1778).

1777

Detroit and Michigan

Henry Hamilton makes Detroit a center of offense against American settlers in Ohio River Valley.

Maj. Richard Beringer Lernoult is commander of Detroit (to Oct. 1779).

World History

June 14. Congress adopts flag of stars and stripes.

July 8. Vermont's constitution is first to provide for manhood suffrage and the abolition of slavery.

Oct. 17. Surrender of British troops under Gen. Burgoyne at Saratoga, New York.

Nov. 15. Articles of Confederation are submitted to states by Continental Congress at York, Pennsylvania; forerunner to U.S. Constitution

Dec. George Washington leads troops into Valley Forge (to 1778).

Americans receive French aid.

Spain and Portugal sign treaty defining possessions in South America.

Cultural Progress

First American edition of John Milton's *Paradise Lost* is published.

Irish dramatist Richard Sheridan's comedy *The School for Scandal* performed at Covent Garden, London.

Scientific and Commercial Progress

George Washington gets Congressional approval to inoculate troops against smallpox.

First rails manufactured in U.S.

French chemist Antoine Lavoisier proves that air consists mainly of oxygen and nitrogen.

1778

Detroit and Michigan

March. Daniel Boone, captured by American Indians, is held at Detroit.

April 26. Census, ordered by Gov. Henry Hamilton: Detroit's population (excluding military, prisoners), 2,144.

Oct. 7. Henry Hamilton and 250 men set out from Detroit. They reach fort at Vincennes (Indiana) 71 days later, taking possession and summoning 600 residents to renew their allegiance to Britain.

World History

Feb. 6. U.S. signs alliance with France, which recognizes it as an independent country.

June. U.S. rejects British peace offer.

June 28. George Washington victorious at Battle of Monmouth (New Jersey).

Sept. 14. Benjamin Franklin is appointed minister to France.

Dec. 29. British take Savannah.

American Col. George Rogers Clark makes expedition into Illinois country; captures British posts.

British loyalists and American Indians massacre settlers at Wyoming Valley, Pennsylvania (July); Cherry Valley, New York (Nov.).

July. Prussia's Frederick the Great invades Bohemia, beginning War of Bavarian Succession (to 1779) against Austria.

Cultural Progress

Act of Congress prohibits further importation of slaves into United States.

Milan's Teatro alla Scala (La Scala) opens; becomes world's most famous opera house.

Theologian and philosopher Johann von Herder publishes collection of German folk songs.

Scientific and Commercial Progress

Capt. James Cook explores northwest coast of America; foundation for British claims to lands.

English civil engineer John Smeaton experiments with improved diving bell.

English engineer Joseph Bramah patents water closet.

Franz Mesmer practices "mesmerism" in Paris.

France charters Royal Society of Medicine; charged with studying epidemics.

George-Louis Buffon and others author (1749–1804) 44-volume *Natural History*; outlines Earth's long history.

1779

Detroit and Michigan

Maj. Richard Lernoult learns of American plan to capture fort. Also learns chieftains intend to make peace with Americans. To better defend their ground, British erect Fort Lernoult—behind Pontchartrain (on site of present-day Federal Building).

Oct. Col. Arent Schuyler de Peyster (transferred from Fort Michilimackinac) becomes British commander in Detroit (to June 1, 1784); continues practice of sending war parties into Kentucky.

March 31. Census indicates population of Detroit is 1,880 (excluding military, prisoners); figure includes 138 slaves; average price for a slave is $200.

World History

Feb. 25. American Col. George Rogers Clark leads surprise attack on Henry Hamilton (former lieutenant governor of Detroit) and British troops at Vincennes (Indiana), reclaiming fort.

June 21. Spain declares war on Britain; European powers face off in Florida and Gibraltar.

Sept. 23. In British Isles, American John Paul Jones in the *Bonhomme Richard* wins naval victory over the *Serapis*.

American Indian raids continue on American settlers; Congress dispatches troops.

Nashville (originally Nashborough) founded.

French forces take possession (to 1783) of St. Vincent and Grenada, British West Indies.

Cultural Progress

Olney Hymns published in England; popularizes hymn-singing.

Scientific and Commercial Progress

First cast-iron bridge is completed over the Severn River in Shropshire, England.

Englishman Samuel Crompton devises spinning mule.

Dutch physician and plant physiologist Jan Ingenhousz discovers photosynthesis.

Lazzaro Spallanzani proves semen is necessary for fertilization.

1780

Detroit and Michigan

April. Commander Arent de Peyster dispatches 1,200 men (British and American Indians) to attack Col. George Rogers Clark and Americans in Ohio. Expedition goes awry.

Nov. 1. Census indicates Detroit's population is 2,107 (excluding military, prisoners but including 175 slaves); 100 more inhabitants are "absent in Indian country."

Five hundred American prisoners held at Detroit.

More than 12,080 acres of land are in cultivation near Detroit.

World History

March 14. Mobile falls to Spanish governor as British prepare to take Charleston (May 12).

July 10. French troops sail to Rhode Island; British blockade of Narragansett Bay prevents landing.

Aug. 16. British troops under Charles Cornwallis victorious at Camden, South Carolina.

Sept. 23. Benedict Arnold's treason is revealed: plot to surrender West Point to British outlined in captured British spy Maj. John Andre's papers.

Oct. 7. American backwoodsmen defeat British at King's Mountain, North Carolina.

U.S. government's paper bills, called Continentals and issued to finance Revolution, are so heavily circulated that common phrase for describing something of no value is "not worth a Continental."

British engage Dutch in battles over searching ships at sea; Dutch lose some East Indies possessions.

Holy Roman Empire's Maria Theresa dies. Joseph II to rule alone; soon abolishes serfdom in Bohemia and Hungary.

Inca in Peru rebel (to 1782) against Spanish rule.

Cultural Progress

American Academy of Arts and Sciences founded in Boston.

British Gazette and *Sunday Monitor,* first Sunday newspapers, published in London.

First modern pianoforte built at Paris.

Scientific and Commercial Progress

Steel fountain pens introduced.

First hat factory established at Danbury, Connecticut.

Industrial Revolution prompts urbanization in Europe: London's population exceeds 700,000; Paris is near that mark.

1781

Detroit and Michigan

Moravians, with peaceful Delaware Indians, flock to Ohio. Delaware converted by Moravians come to be known as "Moravian Indians," who, as pacifists, attempted to avoid aligning with either the British or the Americans during the War of Independence.

World History

March 1. Articles of Confederation go into effect.

March 2. U.S. Congress (formerly Continental Congress) assembles for first time.

May 9. Spanish take west Florida from British.

Oct. 19. British under Charles Cornwallis surrender at Yorktown, ending fighting of American Revolution in the East; British continue to hold some cities (including New York) and skirmishes continue in western country.

Nov. U.S. and Britain open peace talks in Paris.

French and Spanish naval forces seize British West Indies islands (including Tobago, St. Kitts, Nevis, Montserrat).

Los Angeles is founded by Spanish settlers from Mexico who name it El Pueblo de la Reina de los Angeles.

Holy Roman Emperor Joseph II issues Edict of [religious] Tolerance; signs treaty with Russia's Catherine the Great, who is trying to drive Ottoman Turks out of Europe.

British forces take Dutch possessions on west coast of Africa, where they seized French Senegal last year.

Chinese imperial forces suppress Muslim uprising in Gansu Province.

Cultural Progress

Mother Goose's Melody issued by John Newbery publishing house; collection of popular rhymes includes "Ding Dong, Bell," "Little Tom Tucker."

Jacques-Louis David, founder of French neoclassical school of painting, exhibits 12 paintings (including *Belisarius*) in Paris Salon.

German philosopher Immanuel Kant publishes *Critique of Practical Reason*; asserts there is a moral law (calls it "categorical imperative").

Scientific and Commercial Progress

U.S. Congress establishes Bank of North America in Philadelphia.

London astronomer William Herschel uses telescope he built to discover new planet, naming it Georgium Sidus in honor of king; later renamed Uranus.

German anthropologist Johann Blumenbach separates man into 5 races: Caucasian, American, Mongoloid, Malayan, Negro.

1782

Detroit and Michigan

July 20. Census indicates Detroit's population is 2,191, including 179 slaves.

More than 13,750 acres of land are in cultivation near Detroit.

Aug. 19. Expedition from Detroit decisively defeats band of Kentuckians, including Daniel Boone.

Col. Arent de Peyster invites Moravian Indians to Michigan; they settle along Clinton River (near Mt. Clemens) where they clear land, farm, and open inland trail that becomes Gratiot Ave. Some of the Moravians eventually return to Ohio, while some settle in Ontario.

World History

Virginia authorizes manumission of slaves; some 10,000 freed over next 8 years.

British forces evacuate Savannah and Charleston.

Spain completes conquest of Florida.

Britain regains control of Caribbean islands.

Irish politician Henry Grattan demands Home Rule for Ireland.

Austria abolishes serfdom.

Cultural Progress

Philadelphia's Robert Aitken is first to publish English Bible in America.

William Cowper publishes collection of his poems; becomes leading poet of the era.

Englishman John Howard urges prison reform.

Scientific and Commercial Progress

James Watt invents double-acting rotary steam engine.

1783

Detroit and Michigan

Revolution over, Detroit is included in territory awarded U.S. in Treaty of Paris. Americans are bound by agreement to compensate exiled British for property losses. Failing to do so, British withhold surrender of Detroit (and other western forts), which remains in control of Canadian government (to 1796). Michigan continues to be administered as part of Quebec province.

Treaty of Paris specifies that Isle Royale, in Lake Superior, be given to U.S.

World History

Feb. 24. Parliament votes to abandon war against American colonies; Congress declares victory (April 19).

Sept. 3. Treaty of Paris signed by British and Americans, ending war, establishing United States, and drawing new nation's boundaries—from Atlantic Ocean to Mississippi River, north to Canada and south to Florida (claimed by Spain).

Postwar debts lead to economic depression in U.S.

Maryland forbids further importation of slaves.

Loyalists from U.S. are settled in Canada; British government gives them land, aid.

William Pitt the Younger becomes prime minister of Britain (to 1801).

British Orders in Council limit U.S. imports.

Russia annexes the Crimea; Catherine the Great expels Turks, offers lands to Mennonites.

Skaptar volcano (Laki, Iceland) erupts; among largest in history.

Volcanic eruption leads to severe famine in Japan (to1788).

Cultural Progress

Noah Webster's *American Spelling Book* is published.

Scientific and Commercial Progress

English physician Thomas Cawley makes first recorded diagnosis of diabetes.

June 5. French papermakers Joseph and Jacques Montgolfier launch first practical balloon, filled with hot air.

Oct. French scientist Jean-François Pilâtre de Rozier becomes first person to ascend in tethered hot-air balloon (made by Montgolfier brothers). Next month he joins 2 others to make first free-flight balloon ascent, over Paris.

Luigi Galvani constructs crude electric cell.

1784

Detroit and Michigan

June 1. Maj. William Ancram becomes British commander of Detroit.

World History

Jan. 14. Continental Congress, meeting at Annapolis, ratifies Treaty of Paris.

Treaty of Fort Stanwix: Iroquois (Six Nations) surrender final claims to western territory.

Methodist Church in America organized.

Parliament passes India Act, establishing constitution and government controls over colony, East India Company.

Austria's Joseph II abrogates Hungarian constitution, suppressing feudal rights.

Denmark abolishes serfdom.

Cultural Progress

First school for the blind opens in Paris; established by Valentin Hauy, who has invented a method for embossing characters on paper.

English portrait painter Thomas Rowlandson pioneers political caricature.

Scientific and Commercial Progress

Benjamin Franklin invents bifocals; proposes daylight savings time to farmers.

U.S. begins trade with China; first American ship received at Canton.

English physicist and chemist Henry Cavendish publishes *Experiments on Air*.

English mathematician George Atwood accurately determines acceleration of a free-falling body.

Scottish millwright Andrew Meikle invents threshing machine.

Scottish inventor James Small develops cast-iron plow; more durable than wood.

Swiss inventor Aimé Argand invents oil lamp; to be used in lighthouses.

1785

Detroit and Michigan

June. Capt. Bennet becomes British commander of Detroit.

British official values Detroit's fur trade at £180,000. (Some sources valued it at £150,000).

Settlement of (modern-day) Monroe County begins as French-Canadians from Detroit settle along River Raisin.

World History

Congress passes Land Ordinance of 1785: provides for orderly sale of western lands, outlines formation of townships.

Jay-Gardoqui Treaty negotiated; not ratified.

First American Unitarian church founded, King's Chapel, Boston.

League of German Princes is formed by Prussia's Frederick the Great against Holy Roman Emperor Joseph II.

Russians settle Aleutian Islands.

Cultural Progress

First state university is chartered: University of Georgia.

Land Ordinance directs that Section 16 of every township in western territory is forever reserved for public schools.

Scientific and Commercial Progress

The dollar is made the official currency of the U.S., employing decimal system devised by Thomas Jefferson.

Philadelphia Society for the Promotion of Agriculture founded; first such organization in U.S.

First American turnpike is built in Virginia.

Steam powers textile machinery for first time: Boulton and Watt rotating engine installed in Nottinghamshire, England, factory.

American Oliver Evans builds fully automated grain mill; beginning of automation of U.S. industry.

First aerial crossing of English Channel: hot-air balloonists travel from Dover to Calais.

Charles-Augustin Coulomb sets forth fundamental laws of electrical attraction.

1786

Detroit and Michigan

June. Maj. Robert Matthews becomes British commander of Detroit.

Seeing eventual control by the Americans, Moravians at Mt. Clemens abandon settlement and move to Canada.

World History

Shays' Rebellion: Daniel Shays leads Massachusetts rebellion; caused by postwar depression, public discontent.

Ohio Company organized in Boston to promote settlement in the West; shareholders purchase 750,000 acres west of Ohio River.

Bill establishing religious freedom in Virginia, written by Thomas Jefferson, becomes law.

Prussia's Frederick the Great dies and is succeeded by his nephew, Frederick William II (to 1797).

British governor of India, Warren Hastings, is removed from his office; charged with corruption and cruelty (impeached, 1788; acquitted, 1795); succeeded by Charles Cornwallis.

Cultural Progress

Robert Burns publishes *Poems, Chiefly in the Scottish Dialect.*

Wolfgang Amadeus Mozart's opera *The Marriage of Figaro* debuts, in Vienna.

Scientific and Commercial Progress

Massachusetts inventor Ezekiel Reed patents nail-making machine.

French manufacturers press for free trade measures to open up foreign markets.

Pribilof Islands, in Bering Sea, found by Russians. Soon exploited for their fur seals, which are brought nearly to extinction.

French climbers scale Mont Blanc, in French Alps, for first time.

1787

Detroit and Michigan

Under Ordinance of 1787, Michigan is included in Northwest Territory, the first organized by U.S. government. Region includes area north of Ohio River and east of the Mississippi. Nevertheless, area is still held by the British.

Maj. Wiseman becomes British commander of Detroit.

World History

May. Constitutional Convention meets in Philadelphia's Independence Hall.

July 13. Northwest Ordinance enacted, organizing Northwest Territory.

Sept. 17. U.S. Constitution is signed by convention delegates; sent to state assemblies for ratification.

Delaware, Pennsylvania, New Jersey ratify U.S. Constitution.

Second Russo-Turkish War (to 1792): Turkey declares war; attempts but fails to regain Crimea from Russia.

Rice riots in Japan; prompted by years of peasant unrest.

Cultural Progress

Ordinance of 1787 states, "Religion, morality and knowledge being necessary to good government and the happiness of mankind, schools and the means of education shall forever be encouraged."

Federalist Papers, writings of Alexander Hamilton, James Madison, and John Jay in defense of U.S. Constitution, are published in *New York Independent Journal*. (Published as book next year.)

Royall Tyler's *The Contrast* is the first comedy written by a native American and professionally produced (in New York).

Premier performance of Wolfgang Amadeus Mozart's opera *Don Giovanni*.

Scientific and Commercial Progress

Aug. 22. First workable steamboat demonstrated by inventor John Fitch on Delaware River.

Motor boat invented by James Rumsey exhibited on Potomac River.

Antoine Lavoisier pioneers quantitative chemistry; gives substances modern names.

French physicist and chemist Jacques Charles develops his law of gases; relates temperature to volume.

1788

Detroit and Michigan

Canadian authority creates judicial district of Hesse; includes Detroit, which remains (to 1796) under British law and Canadian courts despite U.S. Ordinance of 1787.

World History

Spring. Town of Marietta (Ohio) is first settlement in Northwest Territory. Also, settlement at Cincinnati.

Georgia, Connecticut, Massachusetts, Maryland, South Carolina, New Hampshire, Virginia, New York ratify U.S. Constitution.

June 21. Adoption of U.S. Constitution is secured when 9th state (New Hampshire) ratifies.

In France, wheat prices soar, causing bread riots. Economic chaos prompts Parliament of Paris to draw up grievances, present them to Louis XVI. King responds by calling for assembly of Estates-General (for first time since 1614), next year.

Spain's King Carlos III dies after 29-year reign; encouraged trade and industry, suppressed lawlessness, asserted authority of crown over state. Succeeded by his son who reigns as Carlos IV (to 1808).

Austria joins Russian war against Turkey.

Sweden invades Russian Finland; fighting with Russia continues to 1790, but prewar boundaries are preserved.

First shipload of British convicts lands at penal colony at Botany Bay, Australia.

Cultural Progress

Times of London begins publication.

1789

Detroit and Michigan

Sept. 2. Maj. Patrick Murray becomes British commander of Detroit.

World History

U.S. Constitution goes into effect (superseding Articles of Confederation).

North Carolina is second-to-last state to ratify U.S. Constitution.

New York is capital of the United States (to 1790).

Jan. 7. First national presidential election held. In March, George Washington is unanimously elected president by Electoral College; John Adams elected vice president.

March 4. First U.S. Congress meets (until Sept. 29) in New York.

April 30. George Washington inaugurated first president of the United States (to 1797).

Federal Departments of State, War, and Treasury are created. Secretaries heading each department become presidential advisors (later Cabinet members).

Judiciary Act passed by Congress, establishing federal court system, attorney general; John Jay appointed chief justice (to 1795).

U.S. declares itself an economic and customs union; declares first tariff act.

U.S. Congress adopts 12 amendments to Constitution; sent to states for ratification (10 are approved as Bill of Rights, 1791).

Episcopal Church is organized in America out of former Anglican Church.

May 5. French Revolution begins with Oath of the Tennis Court: Commoners (Third Estate) attempt to seize power from nobility, clergy, and king; insist on formation of National Assembly.

June 17. France's Third Estate forms National Assembly (to 1791).

July 14. Storming of the Bastille, Paris fortress.

Aug. 27. French Declaration of the Rights of Man and of the Citizen; proclaims man has natural and inalienable rights, including "liberty, property, personal security, and resistance to oppression."

Belgian provinces declare independence from Austria.

Cultural Progress

President George Washington proclaims first national day of Thanksgiving, Nov. 26.

Georgetown, first Catholic college in the U.S., established in Washington.

William Hill Brown's *The Power of Sympathy* (erroneously attributed to Sarah W. Morton) is first American novel.

English poet William Blake publishes *Songs of Innocence.*

Scientific and Commercial Progress

In Kentucky, bourbon is distilled from corn; soon eclipses rum in U.S. in popularity.

First steam-driven cotton factory opens in Manchester.

Antoine Lavoisier publishes first modern chemistry book.

1790

Detroit and Michigan

Nov. 14. Maj. D. W. Smith becomes British commander of Detroit.

World History

First U.S. census: population 3,929,214; area 892,132 square miles; 13 states and Ohio Territory; population per square mile, 4.5.

U.S. capital is relocated from New York City to Philadelphia (until 1800).

Washington, D.C., founded; site of capital chosen as compromise to other competing locations.

March 22. Thomas Jefferson becomes U.S. Secretary of State (to 1793).

April 17. Benjamin Franklin dies at Philadelphia; last public act was to sign an appeal to Congress calling for speedy abolition of slavery. An estimated 20,000 people attend his funeral.

May 29. Rhode Island is last of 13 original states to ratify U.S. Constitution.

Aug. 4. Revenue Cutter Service organized (origins of U.S. Coast Guard).

Settlers in Northwest Territory fall prey to American Indian raids; President George Washington orders a force to march against them but troops are defeated and turn back.

Congress passes Indian Non-Intercourse Act; forbids states to take lands from tribes without consent of Congress.

Wilderness Road (through Cumberland Gap) is principal route westward.

First Roman Catholic bishop consecrated in America: John Carroll, Bishop of Baltimore.

First session of U.S. Supreme Court.

Britain refuses to recognize Belgian independence.

Holy Roman Emperor Joseph II dies; succeeded by his brother, Leopold II (to 1792).

Cultural Progress

Premier performance of Wolfgang Amadeus Mozart's *Così fan tutte,* Vienna.

Scientific and Commercial Progress

U.S. Treasury Secretary Alexander Hamilton submits to Congress his reports on public credit and on a national bank; outlines role of strong central government in regulating nation's fiscal affairs.

More than 90% of U.S. workforce is employed in agriculture.

April 10. Congress authorizes patent office.

May 31. First U.S. copyright law passed.

Aug. 4. U.S. government authorizes its first bonds.

Dec. 20. Samuel Slater, "father of American manufactures," debuts first textile mill in America (at Pawtucket, Rhode Island).

Schweppe's founded in Geneva, Switzerland; world's first carbonated beverage company.

1791

Detroit and Michigan

Detroit and Michigan incorporated by Britain into Upper Canada. Col. John Graves Simcoe is first lieutenant governor. (*See* Canada Act, below.)

Col. Richard England is appointed British commander of Detroit; soon succeeded by Maj. John Smith.

World History

President George Washington again orders troops to march against American Indians in punishment for attacks on settlers. Army of about 2,000 men nearly destroyed.

Whiskey Tax: Congress passes legislation, promoted by Alexander Hamilton, approving excise tax on whiskey.

March 4. Vermont is first state, after original 13, admitted to Union.

June 10. Canada Act: British divide Quebec province into Lower Canada (along St. Lawrence River) and Upper Canada. Each province to have an appointed council, elected assembly, lieutenant governor. Goes into effect Dec. 26.

Dec. 15. Bill of Rights becomes law; first 10 amendments to U.S. Constitution are designed to guarantee individual liberties.

Black slaves revolt against French rule in Santo Domingo (Haiti). Begins decade of uprisings; Toussaint L'Ouverture emerges as Haitian leader.

June 25. Louis XVI, attempting to leave France with his family, is caught and returned to Paris.

Oct. 1. Legislative Assembly governs France (to Sept. 1792).

Sept. 14. Louis XVI accepts new constitution; French National Assembly dissolves (Sept. 30) after voting that no member shall be eligible for election to next assembly.

Cultural Progress

First performance of Wolfgang Amadeus Mozart's *The Magic Flute* is given in Vienna.

James Boswell publishes *Life of Johnson,* biography of English man of letters Samuel Johnson.

Scientific and Commercial Progress

First Bank of the United States chartered by Congress: 80% of stock is privately held; 20% is government.

First carpet mill opens in Philadelphia; first practical sugar refinery opens in New Orleans.

Anthracite coal discovered in Pennsylvania.

Dec 5. U.S. Treasury Secretary Alexander Hamilton presents to Congress his "Report on Manufactures"; outlines plan for stimulating trade, lists 17 viable industries to be pursued by private citizens and encouraged by government.

The Observer is founded in London; weekly gains wide readership.

English furniture designer Thomas Sheraton publishes *The Cabinet-Maker and Upholsterer's Drawing Book*; highly influential.

French physician Philippe Pinel pioneers humane treatment of the insane; considered founder of psychiatry.

1792

Detroit and Michigan

Detroit receives influx of new settlers from failed colony at Gallipolis (Ohio).

First election in Michigan history is held to select members to provincial assembly (of Upper Canada). William Macomb, Francois Baby, David W. Smith are elected. Alexander Grant is appointed to council.

Maj. Claus is British commander of Detroit; succeeded (Oct. 24) by Col. Richard England, who commands until surrender of fort to Americans (1796).

British institute trial by jury, court system, English civil law in Lower and Upper Canada, including Detroit and Michigan Marriages contracted irregularly (due to absence of clergy) are now legalized.

Peter Curry builds and manages commercial sloop *Detroit*.

World History

Two U.S. political parties formed: Democratic-Republican under Thomas Jefferson; Federalist under Alexander Hamilton.

Feb. 20. Post Office Department and Postal Service established by act of Congress.

June 1. Kentucky is admitted to the Union.

Dec. 5. George Washington and John Adams re-elected as president and vice president.

Gen. "Mad Anthony" Wayne, American Revolution veteran, leads army out of Pittsburgh, prepares to meet American Indians in Northwest Territory.

Aug. 10. Parisian mob storms Tuileries Palace; massacres some 600 guardsmen.

Sept. 21. National Convention rules France (to Oct. 1795); declares France a republic (Sept. 22).

France declares war on allied Austria and Prussia.

Sweden's Gustav III is assassinated after 21-year reign; succeeded by his son, who reigns as Gustav IV (until his forced abdication, 1809).

Holy Roman Emperor Leopold II dies; succeeded by his son, who reigns as Francis II, last Holy Roman Emperor, to 1806 (and then as Austrian emperor Francis I to 1835).

Denmark is first country to prohibit slave trade.

Cultural Progress

Alexander Placide and his wife introduce ballet to America; perform *The Bird Catcher* in New York. Pair sets up ballet company in Charleston.

In England, Thomas Paine releases *The Rights of Man*; defends cause of French Revolution.

British author-educator Mary Wollstonecraft publishes revolutionary work *A Vindication of the Rights of Woman*; charges that middle-class and upper-class women are kept in state of ignorance, trained to be useless.

Ludwig van Beethoven studies with Joseph Haydn in Vienna.

Scientific and Commercial Progress

April 2. U.S. Congress passes Mint Act, pursuant to Constitution's proclamation that federal government alone would "coin Money, regulate the Value thereof . . . ." Dollar is basic unit of money; bimetallic standard adopted (gold and silver legal tender). Congress authorizes silver half dollar, quarter, dime, and half dime (nickel).

May 17. First U.S. stock market: New York Stock Exchange is organized on Wall Street.

Farmer's Almanac is founded and published by Robert Bailey Thomas in Massachusetts.

U.S. Capt. Robert Gray explores Columbia River (Oregon); basis for U.S. claim to region.

British naval officer George Vancouver explores Pacific coast of North America (to 1794).

Illuminating gas is used for the first time in England.

1793

Detroit and Michigan

William Macomb purchases Belle Isle from the McDougall brothers.

Fort continues to be occupied by British troops.

British fleet is stationed in Detroit River; consists of the brigs *Chippewa, Dunmore, Ottawa* (6 guns each); sloop *Felicity* (with 2 swivels).

World History

George Washington sends emissaries to make peace with American Indians; negotiations fail (British induce chiefs to reject American peace offering). Gen. Anthony Wayne given go-ahead to engage tribal forces after winter.

March 4. Washington is inaugurated for 2nd term.

Yellow fever epidemic strikes Philadelphia (carried there aboard ship from West Indies): nearly all citizens afflicted; more than 4,000 die in what is called worst health disaster ever to beset an American city.

U.S. fugitive slave law requires escaped slaves to be returned to their owners.

Cornerstone of Capitol Building is laid in Washington, D.C.

United States proclaims its neutrality in European struggle; but in the Genêt Affair, French diplomat is found to be outfitting French privateers in American ports.

French King Louis XVI (Jan.) and Marie Antoinette (Oct. 16) are put to death.

Maximilien-Francois-Marie-Isadore de Robespierre's Reign of Terror begins (to July 1794): revolutionary leader guillotines thousands of nobles, other suspected loyalists, anyone believed to be against the cause.

First Coalition formed: Britain, Holland, Spain join Holy Roman Empire against France.

Napoleon Bonaparte takes Toulon.

Russia, Prussia again divide Poland (Second Partition).

First free settlers arrive in Australia.

Cultural Progress

Paris's Louvre Palace is opened to the public as an art museum.

Violin virtuoso Niccolò Paganini makes his debut.

Eli Whitney invents cotton gin, revolutionizing cotton production; becomes cash crop of southern agriculture.

Hot-air balloon debuts in U.S. before Philadelphia crowd including President George Washington.

Sir Alexander Mackenzie is the first white person to cross Canada from coast to coast; publishes account (1801).

1794

Detroit and Michigan

Aug. 20. Acting on federal orders, Gen. Anthony Wayne defeats American Indians and about 50 British volunteers from Detroit at Battle of Fallen Timbers (south of Toledo).

World History

Nov. 19. John Jay concludes treaty with Great Britain, settling issues that arose from Treaty of Paris (1783); U.S.-French relations grow hostile as result.

Unpopular excise tax sparks Whiskey Rebellion in western Pennsylvania; suppressed by federal troops.

U.S. Armory established at Springfield, Massachusetts, one of two federal arsenals (other is at Harpers Ferry, Virginia).

Toussaint L'Ouverture leads 500,000 Blacks and mulattoes in Santo Domingo (Haiti) uprising against the French colony's 40,000 whites.

French legislative assembly abolishes slavery in its colonies.

July 27. In France, Reign of Terror ends when revolutionary leader Robespierre's government is toppled by the conspiracy of 9 Thermidor; Robespierre is put to death the next day.

March. Polish patriots, led by Tadeusz Kosciuszko, rebel against Russian occupation; suppressed.

Cultural Progress

John Trumbull paints *The Declaration of Independence*; Trumbull becomes known as historical painter.

American author and educator Susanna Rowson's *Charlotte Temple* (1791) is first international best-selling novel by a woman.

English poet William Blake publishes *Songs of Experience*.

Publication of first part of Thomas Paine's *Age of Reason* creates furor.

Scientific and Commercial Progress

Lancaster Turnpike opens; stone and gravel road connects Philadelphia and Lancaster, Pennsylvania.

New York's City Hotel, on Broadway, is first building erected expressly to be a hotel.

First steam engine built entirely in America is completed at Belleville, New Jersey.

World's first technical college, École Polytechnique, opens in Paris; founded by revolutionary government for purpose of training students in applied science, mathematics.

1795

Detroit and Michigan

Detroit is included in Treaty of Greenville (*see* below).

World History

June 22. By narrow margin (due to unsatisfactory commercial provisions), Congress ratifies Jay's Treaty; agreement provides for British surrender of American posts.

Aug. 3. Treaty of Greenville (Ohio): Agreement between Ottawa, Chippewa, Potawatomi and U.S. (signed by Gen. Anthony Wayne); tribes cede all of Ohio, part of Indiana, 16 parcels of land along Michigan waterways; in exchange, U.S. makes payment of goods in amount of $20,000, plus future payments of $9,500 a year.

Oct. 27. Pinckney's Treaty (officially, Treaty of San Lorenzo) settles boundary disputes between Spain and U.S.: Spain recognizes 31st parallel (Florida border) as U.S. southern boundary, allows U.S. free use of Mississippi River.

Britain's Speenhamland Act provides relief to the poor.

White Terror in Paris; bread riots in France.

French Constitution of 1795 creates the Directory, group of 5 men who govern (to 1799).

Napoleon Bonaparte is appointed French commander in chief.

France overruns Netherlands; creates independent Batavian Republic (to 1806).

Russia, Austria, Prussia divide Poland (Third Partition); last Polish monarch, Stanislaw II, abdicates.

British forces occupy Cape of Good Hope, Africa, and other Dutch colonies.

Cultural Progress

University of North Carolina (chartered 1789) becomes first state university to enroll students.

First appearance of a black actor on American stage: William Bates plays role of Sambo in J. Murdock's *Triumph of Love.*

Joseph Haydn completes the 12 London symphonies.

German philosopher Immanuel Kant publishes *Perpetual Peace*; describes a federation that would work to prevent international conflict (idea later embodied by League of Nations, United Nations).

Ludwig van Beethoven makes public debut as a pianist.

Spanish painter Francisco de Goya paints *The Duchess of Alba.*

Paris Conservatoire de Musique is founded.

Scientific and Commercial Progress

English engineer Joseph Bramah invents the hydraulic press.

James Hutton (Scotland) pioneers scientific geology with publication of *Theory of the Earth.*

Scottish explorer Mungo Park follows (to 1796) course of Niger River.

Parisian confectioner Nicolas-François Appert experiments with food preservation in response to Napoleon's announcement of a prize to be given to developer of successful method.

1796

Detroit and Michigan

English Court of Gen. Quarter Sessions holds last sessions in Detroit.

April. William Macomb, the wealthiest merchant in Detroit and helpful in preparing for American occupation, dies. At his death he owned Belle Isle, Grosse Isle, and first farm west of town.

July 6. Father Frechette leaves for Quebec; Detroit is temporarily without a pastor as Catholic jurisdiction of parish passes from Bishop of Quebec to the Bishop of Baltimore.

July 11. British evacuate Detroit and turn it over to United States. At noon, Union Jack is pulled down and Capt. Moses Porter (in temporary command) raises American flag. Thirteen years after Treaty of Paris, Michigan is officially part of U.S. territory and under control of Territorial Gov. Arthur St. Clair.

July 13. U.S. Col. John Hamtramck and 400 men arrive in Detroit to take command.

July 14. Father Michael Levadoux arrives to take charge of parish.

Aug. 13. U.S. Gen. Anthony Wayne arrives to establish army headquarters; he is accompanied by territorial secretary Winthrop Sargent, who sets up civil government.

Aug. 15. Wayne County organized in Northwest Territory. Named for Gen. Anthony Wayne. Consists of nearly all of Michigan and parts of Ohio, Indiana, and Wisconsin.

Dec. Court of Gen. Quarter Sessions meets; divides Wayne County into 4 townships: St. Clair, Hamtramck, Detroit, Sargent. Officials (constables, overseers, highway inspectors) appointed for each.

Detroit consists of wharf, fort and Citadel, about 100 houses (with steeply pitched roofs and dormer windows), shops, taverns, and Ste. Anne's Church (also serves as a community center) crowded behind stockade. Streets are unpaved. Ribbon farms extend on both sides of town, along river as far as St. Clair River and Rouge River.

An estimated 500 people live within stockade at Detroit; 2,100 on nearby farms. Roughly 2/3 are of French extraction; Dutch, German, blacks (mostly slaves) also represented.

Some British loyalists move across river, founding Amherstburg (Ontario); British erect Fort Malden on Canadian side.

American Indians in vicinity are permitted inside Detroit stockade during day for trading; at night, gates are closed.

After American occupation, Britain's commander of the navy in the Upper Lakes, Commodore Alexander Grant, continues to live with his family at their Grosse Pointe farm. He retains command of the fleet, making trips across river as necessary (until his death, 1813).

World History

City of Cleveland founded.

June 1. Tennessee is admitted to the Union.

July 8. State Department records first passport.

George Washington refuses 3rd term in office; delivers farewell address Sept. 16.

John Adams elected president.

Napoleon Bonaparte leads French troops in Italian campaign (to 1797); conquers northern Italy.

Spain and France sign Treaty of San Ildefonso, allying them against Britain.

French fleet assembles to invade Ireland in support of rebels; landing prevented by weather.

Russia's Catherine the Great dies after 34-year reign; succeeded by her son who reigns as Paul I (to 1801).

Dutch Ceylon falls to British, who gain control of all Spice Islands except Java.

Cultural Progress

First cookbook written by an American is published in Hartford, Connecticut: *American Cookery* by Amelia Simmons.

Robert Burns publishes "Auld Lang Syne."

Scientific and Commercial Progress

English physician Edward Jenner observes that dairymaids who were sick with cowpox did not contract smallpox, suggesting they developed immunity to the disease; begins working on vaccination.

French astronomer Pierre-Simon de Laplace sets forth nebular hypothesis.

Germany's Aloys Senefelder invents lithography.

German physician Samuel Hahnemann pioneers homeopathic medicine.

1797

Detroit and Michigan

Detroit real estate boom: 188 transfers of land occur.

Maj.-Gen. James Wilkinson takes command of the fort; soon succeeded by Col. D. Strong.

World History

March 4. John Adams inaugurated 2nd U.S. president.

Oct. XYZ Affair: U.S. commissioners sent to France to settle differences encounter demand of $12 million loan and payment of $250,000 to Foreign Minister Charles-Maurice de Talleyrand.

South American earthquakes claim some 40,000 lives.

British naval commanders Horatio Nelson and John Jervis defeat Spanish and French fleets at Cape St. Vincent.

Napoleon Bonaparte forces Austrians beyond Alps; signs Treaty of Campo Formio with Austria, against orders of Directory. Returning to France, he proposes conquest of Egypt as stepping stone to India.

Frederick William II dies, leaving Prussia bankrupt and army weakened; succeeded by grandson who reigns (to 1840) as Frederick William III.

Cultural Progress

German man of letters August von Schlegel begins translation of Shakespeare.

Romantic novels by women are popular; Hannah Foster's *The Coquette* is a bestseller.

Scientific and Commercial Progress

The Medical Repository, first medical periodical in U.S., founded.

First U.S.-built frigate, the *United States*, is launched at Philadelphia.

English mining engineer Richard Trevithick constructs working model of locomotive engine.

Henry Maudslay invents carriage lathe.

1798

Detroit and Michigan

Civic and military entertainments given in Old Council House near river.

June 3. Catholic priest Father Gabriel Richard arrives to assist Ste. Anne's Father Michael Levadoux.

Northwest Territory population includes more than 5,000 free white males, warranting establishment of territorial legislature. Wayne County is entitled to elect 3 members to assembly, which will meet first at Cincinnati and later at Chillicothe.

Dec. 17–19. Wayne County election takes place to send delegates to Northwest Territory General Assembly. Only polling place is in Detroit, in John Dodemead's tavern (which doubles as courthouse). Solomon Sibley is elected.

Hudson's Bay Company completes canal allowing small vessels (canoes, other flat-bottomed boats) to traverse the St. Mary's River.

World History

Eleventh Amendment to U.S. Constitution is ratified; declares that U.S. federal courts cannot try any case brought against a state by a citizen of another state or country.

American public reaction to XYZ Affair vehement; undeclared naval war breaks out between U.S. and France; ends 1800.

Summer. Federalist-dominated U.S. Congress passes 4 Alien and Sedition Acts. Billed as patriotic response to French XYZ Affair, understood by Democrat-Republicans as attempt to quell political dissent: Naturalization Act (June 18) changes residence requirement for citizenship from 5 to 14 years; Alien Act (June 25) authorizes president to expel from U.S. any alien regarded as dangerous; Alien Enemies Act (July 6) authorizes president to arrest, imprison, or deport alien subjects of enemy power during wartime; Sedition Act (July 14) prohibits assembly or publishing when intent is to oppose government.

Opposition to Alien and Sedition Acts frames resolutions calling acts unconstitutional; not binding on states.

Irish rebellion is put down in Battle of Vinegar Hill; suppresses Irish resistance to British rule.

French occupy Rome (Feb.), annex left bank of Rhine, seize Malta, and continue to Egypt. Napoleon Bonaparte lands at Alexandria; Battle of the Pyramids (July 21).

Aug. 1. British Admiral Horatio Nelson destroys French fleet at Abukir Bay, mouth of the Nile.

Cultural Progress

English poets William Wordsworth and Samuel Taylor Coleridge publish *Lyrical Ballads*.

Johann Wolfgang von Goethe publishes epic pastoral poem *Hermann und Dorothea*.

Scientific and Commercial Progress

Eli Whitney introduces the principle of mass production by making interchangeable parts for guns.

U.S. Congress authorizes Marine Hospital Service (origins of U.S. Public Health Service).

English economist Thomas Malthus publishes *Essay on the Principle of Population*; warns that birth control measures are necessary since population otherwise increases at geometric rate while resources increase only at arithmetic rate.

English physician Edward Jenner announces his discovery of vaccinations.

French paper mill clerk invents machine that produces a continuous sheet of paper in any desired size.

1799

Detroit and Michigan

Jan. Solomon Sibley, Wayne County representative, sets out to Cincinnati to take his seat in legislative assembly.

Census results indicate 2 more Wayne County delegates are needed to Northwest Territory General Assembly. Elections are held Jan. 14–15: Jacob Visger, François Joncaire de Chabert will join Sibley (elected last year).

Dec. 17. Maj. Henry Burbeck is commander (to 1800).

Detroit becomes port of entry.

World History

Dec. 14. George Washington dies at Mount Vernon.

Napoleon Bonaparte invades Syria but is halted by British; engages British fleet at Abukir (July 25) and wins.

Second Coalition forms: Great Britain, Austria, Turkey, Russia ally against France; prepare to invade. Napoleon learns of threat and returns to France.

Nov. 9. Napoleon carries out coup d'etat of 18 Brumaire, overthrows the Directory (group of 5 men who have governed since 1795), establishes the Consulate with himself as First Consul (to 1804). French constitution (Dec.) preserves republic in name only.

Cultural Progress

Charles Brockden Brown, first American novelist to earn international reputation, publishes *Ormond,* gothic romance.

British poet Thomas Campbell publishes *The Pleasures of Hope.*

Joseph Haydn's oratorio *The Creation* performed for first time.

Rosetta Stone is discovered in Egypt; allows hieroglyphics to be deciphered. (Napoleon Bonaparte's military expeditions have awakened interest in Egyptian antiquities.)

Scientific and Commercial Progress

Harvard physician Benjamin Waterhouse gives first (smallpox) vaccine in U.S.

French chemist and civil engineer Philippe Lebon pioneers gas lighting.

German naturalist Alexander von Humboldt explores the Amazon and Orinoco Valley; part of 6,000-mile scientific journey (to 1804) through South America, Cuba, Mexico.

1800

Detroit and Michigan

Feb. 12. Memorial services for George Washington held in Detroit.

May 8. By act of Congress, Northwest Territory divided to create Indiana Territory: boundary between revised Northwest and new Indiana territories approximates present-day border between Indiana and Ohio extended north, through Michigan, to Canada.

Sept. 11. First Protestant missionary, Rev. David Bacon, arrives in Detroit; sent by Congregational Church Association of Connecticut.

Dec. 9. Wayne County Circuit Court created.

Col. Moses Porter is U.S. Commanding Officer; soon succeeded by Maj. Thomas Hunt.

World History

U.S. population, 5,308,483; area, 892,135 square miles; center of population, 18 miles west of Baltimore.

U.S. capital moves from Philadelphia to Washington, D.C.

Democratic-Republican party nominates Thomas Jefferson for office; runs against Federalist party candidate Alexander Hamilton.

Thomas Jefferson elected president.

Spain returns possession of Louisiana to France (to 1803).

European population approximately 188 million.

British capture Malta (retained by them in Treaty of Paris, 1814).

Napoleon Bonaparte establishes himself as First Consul of France; appoints committee of jurists to draw up Code Civil.

May. Napoleon Bonaparte marches across Alps to defeat Austrians, ending 8-year war.

U.S. abrogates its alliance with France.

Cultural Progress

Library of Congress established.

Ludwig van Beethoven's Symphony No. 1 performed in concert including works by Joseph Haydn, Wolfgang Amadeus Mozart.

Scientific and Commercial Progress

English astronomer William Herschel discovers infrared solar rays.

Alessandro Volta produces electricity: places saltwater-soaked cloth between piles of silver and zinc discs; basis of electric battery.

Detroit in Its World Setting
1801-1900

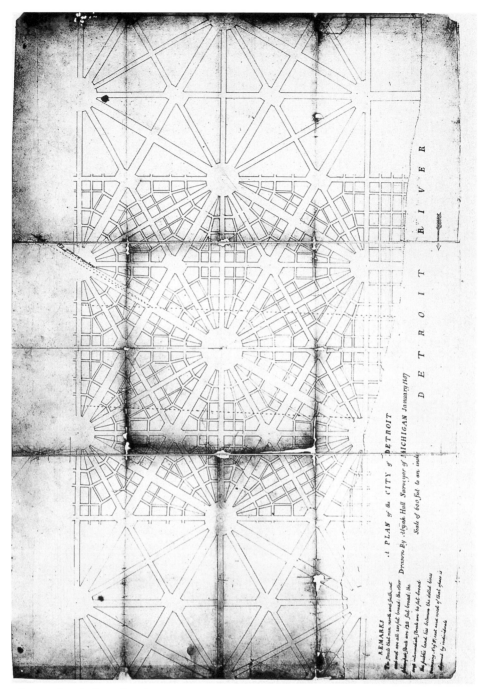

The Woodward Plan. After the disastrous fire in 1805, Judge Augustus B. Woodward drew up this plan for the city.

Tecumseh and William Henry Harrison nearly come to blows during their conference along the Wabash in 1810. They would meet again at Detroit in 1813.

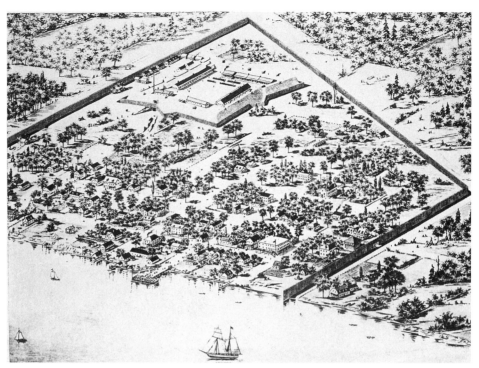

Artist's conception of the settlement of Detroit in 1818 clearly shows Fort Shelby (formerly Fort Lernoult), a typical "star" fort of the times.

Detroit's first mayor, John R. Williams. Elected in 1824, Williams had been a successful merchant.

Detroit, 1853. This view of Detroit shows the main thoroughfare—Woodward—dividing the city in half. Note the river traffic.

CENTRAL VIEW IN ~~JEFFERSON~~ AVENUE, DETROIT, MICHIGAN. 1859—1856.

Woodward Avenue, 1856. This engraving shows the first City Hall on the left. On the right is the site of the second seat of city government, which would be built in 1871.

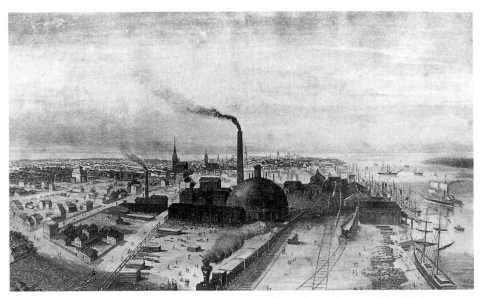

Detroit, 1860. This engraving of Detroit shows the yards and roundhouse of the Michigan Central Railroad along the river.

Elijah McCoy. Born in Canada and educated in Scotland, McCoy sought his fortune with the Michigan Central Railroad in Ypsilanti in 1865.

The Russell House, 1865. Located on Woodward Avenue near Campus Martius, this popular hotel was built in 1824, rebuilt in 1882, and finally razed in 1905.

This view of Michigan Avenue in 1872 shows the old City Hall (center, left) and the new one built in 1871 and demolished in 1956.

The Detroit Public Library. The new library at Gratiot and Farmer opened to the public on January 22, 1877. It was built at a cost of $124,000.

Woodward Avenue, 1880s. City life goes on: a newsboy hawks his papers, a woman walks her baby, and men exchange the latest news.

The foot of Woodward Avenue, 1890. Shot from mid-river, this scene looks straight up Woodward Avenue. Horse-drawn trolleys and delivery wagons are waiting for passengers and freight.

The dedication of Grand Boulevard in 1891. On horseback is Mayor Hazen S. Pingree, later governor of Michigan. At his left, also on horseback, is his daughter Hazel.

Woodward Avenue at Michigan Avenue, 1890s. Horse-drawn taxis line the street in front of City Hall. The tower in the middle of the photograph mounted streetlights that sparked and sputtered and rose over 100 feet above the street.

State Street and Woodward Avenue, 1890s. The magnificent white horse seems to know his picture is being taken and holds his head up high. Fashion of the day includes umbrellas to ward off the sun.

Woodward Avenue, 1890s. Detroiters wait to cross the avenue behind the trolley. Straw boater hats are the rage in men's—and women's—fashions.

Woodward Avenue (looking north, 1891) became the site of so many churches that it gained the nickname "Piety Hall."

1801

Detroit and Michigan

Jan. 6 & 20. Assemblies in Detroit feature fiddlers for dancing; refreshments of corned beef, bacon, bread, apples, tea, coffee, spirits.

Col. John Hamtramck returns to Detroit as commander of Department of the Lakes (to 1803).

Rev. David Bacon teaches school for boys and Mrs. Bacon teaches school for girls, in vicinity of Shelby and Larned.

World History

Jan. 1. Act of Union: Great Britain and Ireland form United Kingdom.

March 4. Thomas Jefferson inaugurated; 3rd U.S. president.

Congress repeals controversial Sedition Act (1798).

Tripolitan War: Intermittent conflict between U.S. Navy and North African Barbary States pirates (to 1815).

Toussaint L'Ouverture invades Spanish Santo Domingo (Haiti); frees slaves.

Russian Czar Paul I assassinated; succeeded by Alexander I (to 1825).

British Admiral Horatio Nelson defeats Danes off Copenhagen.

British enter Cairo; force French troops to leave. Ottoman Turks recover Egypt.

Cultural Progress

First booksellers association organized in New York City with Matthew Carey as president.

Scientific and Commercial Progress

Dec. 24. English mining engineer Richard Trevithick's road carriage first vehicle to convey passengers by steam.

Frenchman Joseph-Marie Jacquard invents pattern loom.

French astronomer Joseph-Jerome Lalande catalogs 47,390 stars.

1802

Detroit and Michigan

Jan. 18. Detroit incorporated as a town (officially Town of Detroit). Boundaries specified: from river north 2 miles (to about Warren Ave.); eastern limit between Askin and Beaubien farms; western limit between Macomb and Chene farms. Charter enacted by Northwest Territory general assembly provides for governing board of 5 trustees, secretary, assessor, tax collector, marshal.

First board of trustees: John Askin, John Dodemead, James Henry, Charles F. Girardin, Joseph Campau. After first municipal election (May 3) John Askin replaced by George Meldrum.

Feb. 23. Board of trustees adopts fire code: requires all building owners to have chimneys swept regularly; provide barrels, buckets, ladders; all citizens to turn out to fight a fire.

Other early ordinances include: prohibition of horse racing in village streets; regulation of price and weight of bread (made in large, public ovens).

April 17. First city tax levied: $150 to be paid by assessment of 25 cents upon each individual over 21 years of age and by a tax of 1/4 of 1% on houses.

May 18. Father Michael Levadoux leaves Detroit; Father Gabriel Richard in charge of Ste. Anne's parish.

At territorial assembly, Solomon Sibley, 1 of 3 Wayne County representatives, succeeds in getting an act passed making Detroit county seat.

Sept. 7. Frederick Bates appointed postmaster; 2 mail deliveries per month.

World History

April 30. Congress passes act allowing Ohio to write constitution, form state government. Boundary of new state drawn east-west from southern point of Lake Erie. Northwest Territory capital moved from Chillicothe (Ohio) to Vincennes (Indiana).

Congress allows controversial Alien and Naturalization Acts (1798) to expire.

U.S. government sells its interest in First Bank of the United States.

United States Military Academy established at West Point, New York.

France suppresses slave rebellion in Santo Domingo (Haiti) led by Toussaint L'Ouverture.

Britain and France sign Peace of Amiens, temporarily ending war that began in 1793.

Cultural Progress

System of public land grants for support of schools begins with grant to Ohio.

Scientific and Commercial Progress

U.S. Patent Office organized.

Congress passes act approving use of federal funds for road improvement.

E. I. Du Pont establishes gunpowder manufacturing plant in Delaware; origin of E. I. Du Pont de Nemours & Co.

English astronomer William Herschel discovers binary stars.

British engineer William Murdock lights factory exterior with gaslight; inventor becomes known as father of gas industry.

German naturalist Gottfried Treviranus publishes first volume of *Biologie*; coins term *biology.*

1803

Detroit and Michigan

March 1. Neighboring Ohio admitted to Union; surveyors include Toledo Strip, traditionally part of Michigan territory, as part of new state. Leads to later conflict.

March 3. Michigan becomes part of Indiana Territory.

April 11. Col. John Hamtramck dies; deeply mourned by Detroit's citizens. Maj. Zebulon Pike assumes command of post at Detroit.

World History

Marbury v. *Madison*: Supreme Court ruling establishes principle of judicial review of congressional acts to assess constitutionality.

Secretary of War Henry Dearborn orders the establishment of a fort at mouth of Chicago River, named Fort Dearborn.

May 2. U.S. purchases Louisiana from France; territory extends from Mississippi River to Rocky Mountains, from Gulf of Mexico to British America.

Cultural Progress

American artist Benjamin West paints *Christ Healing the Sick.*

English novelist Jane Porter publishes *Thaddeus of Warsaw,* popular historical romance.

Scientific and Commercial Progress

Richard Trevithick invents world's first steam railway locomotive.

English chemist John Dalton arranges table of atomic weights; first to give clear statement of atomic theory, that substances are composed of particles of matter (atoms).

English inventor Henry Shrapnel develops artillery shell; successfully used in battle next year.

German physicist Johann Ritter invents electrical storage battery.

1804

Detroit and Michigan

March 26. U.S. Land Office opens in Detroit.

First dock ordinance passed; schedule of charges prescribed to raise funds to build new public wharf.

Gates of stockade kept closed and guarded at night; no American Indians allowed in town after sunset. Curfew for townspeople enforced by night watchmen.

Father Gabriel Richard and assistant, Father John Dilhet, conduct preparatory school for boys in Detroit (next year's fire ends project).

Itinerant Methodist minister Rev. Nathaniel Bangs arrives in Detroit.

World History

Twelfth Amendment to U.S. constitution ratified; revises presidential and vice-presidential election rules.

Jan. 5. Ohio legislature passes Black Laws, designed to restrict legal rights of free African Americans.

May 14. Meriwether Lewis and William Clark set out from St. Louis on expedition (to 1806): to chart route to Pacific Ocean, trace boundaries of Louisiana Purchase, and lay claim to Oregon territory. Shoshone Indian Sacajawea is only woman guide on expedition.

July 11. Aaron Burr kills Alexander Hamilton in duel.

Thomas Jefferson reelected president.

Great Britain, Austria, Russia, Sweden form 3rd Coalition against Napoleon Bonaparte.

Dec. 2. Napoleon Bonaparte declares himself emperor of France; he has already begun European wars to gain more power. Code Civil (or Code Napoleon) in effect (as of March).

Cultural Progress

German writer Johann Schiller pens dramatic masterpiece *William Tell.*

Ludwig van Beethoven completes Symphony No. 3, *Eroica.*

Scientific and Commercial Progress

Gaslight being used in industry: 900 cotton mills in England have installed gaslights in last 2 years.

1805

Detroit and Michigan

Jan. 11. President Thomas Jefferson approves congressional act setting off Michigan Territory (includes most of Lower Peninsula, part of Upper Peninsula); to take effect June 30. Act commits Congress to carving 5 states out of Old Northwest.

March. William Hull appointed governor of Michigan Territory (to 1813); Augustus Woodward, Frederick Bates, and John Griffin, judges; and Stanley Griswold, secretary.

June 11. Detroit destroyed by fire that reportedly begins in village baker John Harvey's barn.

Judge Augustus Woodward, educated at Columbia University and Virginia, arrives to find Detroit in ruins following fire. He persuades Gov. William Hull to postpone rebuilding until comprehensive plan is drawn up; Woodward begins work on city plan.

Detroit becomes capital of newly created Michigan Territory (to 1837).

Aug. First session of governing officials takes place in Richard Smyth's tavern (on Woodward near Woodbridge).

World History

March 4. President Thomas Jefferson inaugurated; 2nd term.

Oct. 21. Battle of Trafalgar: British fleet under Admiral Horatio Nelson wins brilliant victory over combined French and Spanish fleets; Nelson mortally wounded.

Napoleon Bonaparte crowned king of Italy; defeats Austro-Russian forces at Battle of Austerlitz (Dec. 2), destroys 3rd Coalition.

Cultural Progress

Pennsylvania Academy of Fine Arts established (nation's oldest art museum).

Scientific and Commercial Progress

Yale begins offering chemistry courses.

Sir Francis Beaufort devises scale to measure wind velocity.

1806

Detroit and Michigan

Sept. 13. City of Detroit incorporated. Local affairs to be controlled by territorial governor and judges.

Territory grants charter to Bank of Detroit (first bank in Michigan); begins operation (Sept. 19) before congressional approval and is soon closed after issuing paper money of questionable value.

U.S. Congress authorizes Judge Augustus Woodward's plan for Detroit; consists of repeatable hexagon divided into 12 sections. Principal parkways are 200 feet wide; secondary (diagonal) roads 120 feet wide. Grand Circus Park northernmost boundary; Campus Martius (Latin for "military grounds") envisioned as city center—large, open space for assemblies. Landowners prevent much of plan from being realized. (Radial thoroughfares—Fort, Michigan, Grand River, Woodward, Gratiot—are part of its legacy.)

Gov. William Hull and Judge Augustus Woodward obtain grant of 10,000 acres (north of present Grand Blvd.) to be distributed to each resident over 17 years of age (lots to be no less than 5,000 square feet).

Elijah Brush, Vermont lawyer who arrived in Detroit in 1789, purchases first parcel of farmland immediately east of settlement. (Farm's boundary later marked by Brush St.)

World History

British again occupy Cape of Good Hope (Africa).

July 12. Confederation of the Rhine: Holy Roman Empire dismantled (Aug. 6); most German states under French domination, a result of Napoleonic Wars.

Oct. 14. Napoleon Bonaparte defeats Prussians; enters Warsaw.

Nov. 21. Napoleon Bonaparte issues Berlin Decree: establishes Continental System, closing off Europe from trade with Great Britain.

Prussia, Russia, Great Britain, Sweden form 4th Coalition against Napoleon Bonaparte.

Cultural Progress

English writers Jane and Anne Taylor publish *Rhymes for the Nursery*; includes "Twinkle, Twinkle, Little Star."

Noah Webster publishes his first dictionary, *A Compendious Dictionary of the English Language*.

Scientific and Commercial Progress

Congress authorizes construction of National Road (Cumberland Highway), across Appalachians into Ohio River Valley; first highway built with federal funds.

William Colgate opens New York City soap manufacturing business; origin of Colgate Co.

Zebulon Pike discovers peak in Rocky Mountain range; to be named Pike's Peak.

1807

Detroit and Michigan

Nov. 7. Treaty of Detroit: council of chiefs meets at Brownstown, below Detroit; Gov. William Hull signs treaty with 4 chieftains. American Indians cede to U.S. area that includes southeastern quarter of Michigan's Lower Peninsula; U.S. pays tribes $10,000 in goods and money plus annual payment of $2,400; tribes retain right to hunt and fish the lands. (By 1842, all tribal claims to Michigan's Lower and Upper Peninsulas relinquished by treaty.)

Gov. Hull orders new stockade built around town and fort. Work also begins on his home, on southeast corner of Jefferson and Randolph; first brick house in Detroit, considered grand mansion.

Council House completed on southwest corner of Jefferson and Randolph: unadorned stone building to be used for fairs, elections, political and religious meetings, courthouse.

World History

July 7. France compels Russia, Prussia to sign Treaty of Tilsit, ending 4th Coalition.

Sept. Aaron Burr put on trial for treason; acquitted on technicality.

Dec. 17. Napoleon Bonaparte issues Milan Decree: extends blockade of Great Britain to include neutral ships.

Parliament issues Orders in Council, requiring all vessels destined for Continent to stop in England. U.S. perceives as undue interference with trade.

U.S. frigate *Chesapeake* sails for Mediterranean; intercepted by H.M.S. *Leopard*. British demand search for deserters, fire shots, impress 4 Americans into service. Nearly precipitates war.

Dec. 22. President Thomas Jefferson signs Embargo Act, prohibiting foreign-bound U.S. ships from leaving port. Failed policy aimed to end French and British interference with neutral shipping.

Great Britain abolishes slave trade.

Scientific and Commercial Progress

Congress authorizes survey of nation's coast (origin of U.S. Coast and Geodetic Survey).

Aug. 17. Robert Fulton's vessel, "The North River Steamboat of Clermont," steams up Hudson River from New York to Albany; 32-hour inaugural run launches steamship era.

Manuel Lisa establishes trading post (Fort Manuel) on Little Bighorn, opening Louisiana Territory to fur traders. Trappers, soon known as "mountain men," begin westward migration.

American trapper John Colter discovers area to be known as Yellowstone Park.

First public street lighting with gas, London's Pall Mall.

1808

Detroit and Michigan

William Hull reappointed territorial governor. Reuben Atwater (of Vermont) succeeds Stanley Griswold as secretary of Michigan Territory; James Witherell succeeds Frederick Bates as judge.

Indians threaten village; fort occupied by only 80 soldiers.

Father Gabriel Richard establishes common school at Springwells (below Detroit) for education of American Indian and white children. Richard has also brought a printing press to Michigan to produce a spelling book for students.

World History

Jan. 1. U.S. law abolishing slave trade goes into effect, but possession of slaves remains legal.

James Madison, Democratic-Republican, elected president.

Peninsular War (to 1814): Napoleon Bonaparte struggles for control of Iberian Peninsula (Spain and Portugal).

Cultural Progress

American Academy of Fine Arts founded in New York.

First Spanish-language newspaper in U.S.: *El Misisipí* is published in New Orleans.

German writer Johann Goethe pens first part of masterwork, poetic drama *Faust* (second part 1832).

First war correspondent: *The Times* sends Henry Crabb Robinson to Spain to report on Peninsular War.

Scientific and Commercial Progress

American steamship *Phoenix* travels from New York to Philadelphia; first seagoing steamboat in world.

English artillerist William Congreve invents Congreve rocket.

1809

Detroit and Michigan

Aug. 31. Father Gabriel Richard issues Michigan's first newspaper, *The Michigan Essay* or *Impartial Observer.* Also first Catholic newspaper printed in English in U.S.

World History

Feb. 3. Illinois Territory established.

March 4. James Madison inaugurated; 4th U.S. president.

Non-Intercourse Act limits trade embargo to France and Britain; other foreign ports again open to U.S. ships.

Cultural Progress

Elizabeth Seton founds order Sisters of Charity (of St. Joseph); establishes Baltimore elementary school, laying foundations for parochial schooling in U.S.

U.S. has 30 daily newspapers.

Washington Irving publishes satirical *History of New York . . . by Diedrich Knickerbocker.*

Scientific and Commercial Progress

Mary Kies becomes first U.S. woman to receive patent; invented a method for weaving straw and silk to make bonnets.

Electric arc principle discovered by Sir Humphry Davy.

Canning (process for preserving food by heating, sealing in airtight containers) developed by French candy maker Nicolas-François Appert.

1810

Detroit and Michigan

Detroit's population, 770.

Michigan's population, 4,762.

Methodist Society organizes first Protestant church group in city.

World History

U.S. population, 7,239,881; area, 1,720,112 square miles; center of population, 40 miles northwest of Washington, D.C. (in Virginia).

Macon Act passed by Congress; another failed attempt to force warring Britain and France to allow free passage of neutral ships on high seas.

June 29. American Board of Commissioners for Foreign Missions founded; marks beginning of organized foreign missionary enterprise in U.S.

Wars begin for independence in Latin America: Spain's American colonies except Cuba and Puerto Rico declare independence by 1825. Simon Bolívar emerges as major figure in South American independence and politics.

Cultural Progress

Sir Walter Scott writes *Lady of the Lake.*

Scientific and Commercial Progress

Twenty years after first mill opened, New England now home to more than 100 cotton mills.

Nation's first silk mill established in Mansfield, Connecticut; residents begin planting mulberry trees to attract silkworms.

Passenger and freight ferry business between Staten Island and New York City founded by Commodore (Cornelius) Vanderbilt.

First American cigar factory of note established in West Suffield, Connecticut.

1811

Detroit and Michigan

Four lawyers and two doctors live in Detroit.

Value of properties (including Belle Isle) owned by Macomb brothers exceeds $24,000.

World History

Nov. 7. U.S. troops under command of William Henry Harrison defeat Tecumseh at Tippecanoe (Indiana).

War Hawks emerge in Congress: newly elected Republican representatives vote to build up military, advocate war with Great Britain. Led by House Speaker Henry Clay, eager to end maritime disputes, force British to discontinue support of American Indians in Northwest.

Charter for First Bank of the United States allowed to expire.

Britain's King George III deemed mentally unfit to rule; succeeded by his son, Prince of Wales (future George IV), as regent.

Luddite riots in northern England (sporadically to 1816): bands of laborers destroy industrial machines.

Cultural Progress

Jane Austen's *Sense and Sensibility* published; launches popular novel of manners.

Scientific and Commercial Progress

Work begins on National Road (Cumberland Highway).

First steamboat plies Ohio River: *New Orleans* is launched at Pittsburgh.

Steamboat era begins on Mississippi River; St. Louis, Memphis, New Orleans soon flourish.

Fur trading post established by American Fur Co. at mouth of Columbia River; named Astoria after John Jacob Astor, company's founder.

German industrialist Alfred Krupp opens iron works at Essen, Germany.

1812

Detroit and Michigan

Detroit's population, about 800.

Jan. Earthquake felt in Detroit.

Aug. 16. In War of 1812, Gov. William Hull surrenders Detroit to British, in whose hands it remains for a year. British accompanied by sizable force of American Indians under leadership of Tecumseh; Hull fails to put up resistance.

World History

April 30. Louisiana admitted to Union.

War of 1812: Congress, led by War Hawks, declares war (June 18) on Britain, ostensibly over interference with American shipping.

Aug. 19. U.S.S. *Constitution* defeats British *Guerriere* in naval battle.

James Madison reelected president.

British Prime Minister Spencer Perceval assassinated in House of Commons.

Sixth Coalition forms: Great Britain, Russia, Sweden, Prussia, Austria join forces against Napoleon Bonaparte.

Russia, supposedly under French control, begins trading with Great Britain, Napoleon's archenemy.

Napoleon marches into Russia to regain control.

Sept. 14. Under orders of the czar, Russians burn Moscow to prevent seizure by Napoleon; French army retreats in defeat.

Cultural Progress

Brothers Jacob and Wilhelm Grimm publish their first collection of fairy tales in Germany.

Scientific and Commercial Progress

Academy of Natural Sciences founded in Philadelphia; oldest herbarium in U.S.

John James Audubon begins classifying and describing birds of America.

English mathematician Charles Babbage conceives of calculating machine.

1813

Detroit and Michigan

Sept. 10. U.S. Commodore Oliver H. Perry defeats British fleet in Battle of Lake Erie.

Sept. 29. Americans, under Gen. William Henry Harrison, reclaim Detroit from British.

Oct. 5. Gen. Harrison defeats British Gen. Henry Proctor's army and American Indian troops at Battle of the Thames (Ontario); Tecumseh killed.

Oct. 29. Gen. Harrison appoints Lewis Cass governor and military commander of Michigan Territory (to 1831).

Fort Lernoult renamed Fort Shelby in honor of Gen. Isaac Shelby.

Citizens of Detroit honor Judge Augustus Woodward for his services during British occupation.

Successful fur trader Joseph Campau builds home on south side of Jefferson, between Shelby and Griswold.

Cholera-like epidemic kills many soldiers, townspeople.

World History

March 4. President James Madison inaugurated; 2nd term.

In War of 1812, U.S. forces capture York (Toronto) and Fort St. George, but are defeated at Chrysler's Farm near Morrisburg in what is now Ontario. British forces take Fort Niagara, burn Buffalo.

Oct. 16–19. Battle of the Nations at Leipzig (Poland): European coalition defeats Napoleon Bonaparte, who retreats to France.

Cultural Progress

Jane Austen's *Pride and Prejudice* published.

Waltz becomes popular in Europe.

Scientific and Commercial Progress

Francis C. Lowell begins building first complete American textile factory (Boston Manufacturing Co.) at Waltham, Massachusetts: combines cotton spinning and weaving in one mill; uses power looms. Operational by 1815.

1814

Detroit and Michigan

Former Territorial Gov. William Hull court-martialed for his 1812 surrender of Detroit to British and American Indians; found guilty of cowardice and neglect of duty, and sentenced to death. Sentence stayed by Pres. James Madison because of Hull's service during American Revolution.

Sept. Last Indian hostility in area occurs as Ananias McMillan is killed and his son captured.

Oct. 15. William Woodbridge appointed territorial secretary, succeeding Atwater.

In Northwest Territory, including Michigan, American Indians concede to treaties with Americans following defeat of British (with whom tribes were allied) in War of 1812.

World History

March. European allies making up 6th Coalition take Paris; Napoleon Bonaparte's generals defeated.

March 27. Andrew Jackson corners force of nearly 1,000 Creek Indians at Horseshoe Bend (present-day Alabama), killing more than 700 and ending Creek War (begun last year).

April. Napoleon abdicates and is exiled to Elba; Louis XVIII enters Paris to become king, restoring Bourbon monarchy.

Aug. 25. In War of 1812, British troops capture Washington, D.C.; burn Capitol and White House.

Sept. American fleet on Lake Champlain defeats British (in Battle of Plattsburgh), concluding War of 1812.

Dec. Hartford Convention (to Jan. 1815) marks end of influence of Federalist party.

Dec. 24. War of 1812 officially settled in Treaty of Ghent.

Cultural Progress

Emma Hart Willard organizes the first institution for higher education of women: Middlebury Female Seminary, Vermont.

Sir Walter Scott's *Waverly* a bestseller; sets tone for historical romance novels.

Francis Scott Key writes poem "Defense of Fort McHenry"; published (Sept. 20) in *Baltimore Patriot,* later set to music as "The Star-Spangled Banner."

Scientific and Commercial Progress

First practical steam locomotive built by George Stephenson in England.

London *Times* printed by steam-operated press.

1815

Detroit and Michigan

British build fort on Drummond Island; hold ground there to 1822.

March 30. Pacification Ball held at Woodworth's Hotel to celebrate Peace of Ghent (which ended War of 1812).

Oct. 24. Detroit reincorporated as City of Detroit; local governing board to be elected by residents. Solomon Sibley elected chairman of first board of trustees.

Territorial Gov. Lewis Cass and family arrive in Detroit. Their elegant carriage leaves townspeople in awe; Cass quickly and quietly sells it.

Gov. Cass buys first farm below town (southwest of Detroit) for his family's homestead.

Gov. Cass begins county system by laying out lands (most of Michigan and part of Wisconsin) ceded by American Indians. Wayne County (with seat of justice at Detroit) redrawn to near present size.

Surveyor-general of U.S. land office, Edward Tiffin, issues report based on misinformation that Michigan consists of nothing but lakes, swamps, sandy land. Erroneous account further delays development of Michigan; most westward settlers instead follow Ohio River into Ohio, Kentucky, Indiana, Illinois, Missouri.

Settlers arriving in Michigan travel Mohawk Trail as far as Buffalo, New York, where they embark on sailing vessels for remainder of trip.

World History

U.S. population, about 9 million.

Jan. 8. In New Orleans, U.S. and British troops continue fighting; news of Peace of Ghent (Dec. 1814) has not reached them. U.S. wins another battle even though War of 1812 has ended.

March 15–June 22. The Hundred Days: Napoleon Bonaparte escapes from Elba, reenters Paris to take power; King Louis XVIII flees. Napoleon defeated at Battle of Waterloo (June 18) and forced to abdicate.

April 5. Mount Tambora, Indonesia, erupts; kills some 92,000 (deadliest eruption in history).

Congress of Vienna redraws Europe after Napoleon; monarchies of France, Italy, Spain, Austria, Prussia are restored.

Holy Alliance established by Austria, Prussia, Russia; later signed by all European rulers except British monarch, Ottoman Turk sultan, Pope. Vows Christian unity in opposition to revolutionary disorder.

Quadruple Alliance created by Austria, Britain, Prussia, Russia to preserve European peace.

Oct. Napoleon exiled to St. Helena.

Cultural Progress

New England literary renaissance begins (lasts to 1860).

North American Review established.

Scientific and Commercial Progress

First steam warship built: U.S.S. *Fulton.*

British road surveyor John McAdam constructs roads of crushed stone, soon called macadam roads.

Augustin Fresnel conducts research on diffraction of light (to 1819).

1816

Detroit and Michigan

Cass Code of Michigan Territorial Laws published.

April 18. Treaty of peace concluded with American Indians in meetings at Council House. Tecumseh's brother, "The Prophet," present.

June 30. Rev. John Monteith, sent to Detroit by American Board of Commissioners for Foreign Missions, preaches his first sermon in city.

Government warehouse built at foot of Wayne St. Building soon used by army officers and their wives for amateur theatrical entertainments.

World History

Dec. 11. Indiana admitted to Union.

James Monroe, Democratic-Republican, elected president.

First protective tariff enacted by Congress.

Economic crisis in England causes large-scale immigration to U.S. and Canada.

April 9. African Methodist Episcopal Church organized; first independent black denomination in U.S.

Cultural Progress

Feb. 20. Gioacchino Antonio Rossini's *Barber of Seville* first performed in Rome.

Jane Austen's *Emma* published.

Scientific and Commercial Progress

Second National Bank of the United States chartered.

French physician and surgeon Rene T. Laennec invents the stethoscope.

First steamboats on Great Lakes; *Frontenac* and *Ontario* are launched and operated on Lake Ontario.

Philadelphia Savings Fund Society begins; first savings bank in America.

1817

Detroit and Michigan

Detroit's population, about 900.

July 25. *Detroit Gazette,* city's first regularly published newspaper, founded. Printed in English and French, it has fewer than 100 subscribers.

Aug. 13. Detroit receives first visit from a U.S. president; James Monroe stays 5 days. Procession and fireworks. City and county of Monroe named in his honor.

Sept. 15. First Evangelistic Society of Detroit organized to hold Protestant church services.

Sept. 24. Cornerstone laid for Catholepistemiad (origin of University of Michigan), on Bates, between Larned and Congress. Rev. John Monteith, president; Father Gabriel Richard, vice president.

Detroit City Library incorporated. Group of citizens sells subscriptions; books to be kept in University Building. (Library turned over to Detroit Athenaeum, 1831.)

Dec. 19. Bank of Michigan authorized by act of governor and judges.

Dec. 26. Detroit Musical Society mentioned in *Detroit Gazette* as participating in exercises at Council House.

Dec. 29. First charitable society established in Detroit, Moral and Humane Society; aims to suppress vice and report children in need of education.

Judge James Witherell and Gov. Lewis Cass determine to discard most of Judge Augustus Woodward's plan for downtown Detroit.

Hogs allowed to run in public streets if noses are ringed to prevent them from rooting up gardens.

Woodward Ave. market erected just below Jefferson; used until 1835.

George Clark is first white settler on site of Wyandotte.

Birmingham, Michigan, founded.

Barnabas Campau buys Belle Isle from heirs of William Macomb for $5,000.

World History

Era of Good Feeling (to 1823): American national pride soars.

Bonus Bill vetoed by President Madison before leaving office; was to provide funding (from $1.5 million "bonus" paid to U.S. government by Second Bank of the U.S.) for highways linking East, South, West.

March 4. James Monroe inaugurated; 5th U.S. president.

Rush-Bagot pact signed by U.S. and Britain; neither will operate armed vessels on Great Lakes. Does not apply to land defenses, soon built on both sides. Unused, they fall into decay.

Dec. 10. Mississippi admitted to Union.

First Seminole War (to 1818): Florida Indians subdued by Andrew Jackson.

American Colonization Society organized; makes West African land purchases with goal of transporting freed slaves to homeland.

Cultural Progress

First free school for the deaf (Connecticut, later American, Asylum) established in Hartford, Connecticut, by educator Thomas Gallaudet.

Scientific and Commercial Progress

July 4. Work begins on New York's Erie Canal.

National Road (begun 1811) now 130 miles long; connects Cumberland, Maryland, with Wheeling, (West) Virginia.

First gas company in U.S. established to light Baltimore's streets.

German Baron Karl von Drais de Sauerbrun develops wheeled device (draisienne); forerunner of the bicycle.

1818

Detroit and Michigan

Act of Congress extends Michigan Territory to include Wisconsin, part of Minnesota (east of Mississippi River).

Government begins offering surveyed land for sale to public.

March 31. Dedication of first Protestant church building in Michigan, near Rouge River.

June 9. Cornerstone laid for new Ste. Anne's Church at Larned and Bates.

July 4. Detroiters celebrate Independence Day in field behind Gov. Lewis Cass's house.

July 6. First auction sale of public lands in Michigan held at Council House; prices range from $2 to $40 per acre (average price $4).

July 20. Detroit Mechanics Society organized; early form of labor union.

Public whipping post erected under an ordinance passed July 27; located above market (near intersection of Woodward and Jefferson), it remains in use to 1831.

Aug. 27. *Walk-in-the-Water,* named after a Wyandotte chief, arrives in Detroit on its inaugural trip from Buffalo, launching age of steamship on Great Lakes. Entire town turns out to meet it. Begins regular service, carrying passengers and goods between Buffalo and Detroit (to 1821).

Oct. 4. First session of Protestant Sunday school held.

Regular ferry service (via canoe, later via rowboat) between Detroit and Windsor established by Edwin Baldwin.

Gen. Lewis Cass and companions follow Saginaw Indians' winter trail through present-day Oakland County, then a primeval forest. Their reports entice families to seek homesteads in area. Many newcomers are from New York, establishing towns including Rochester.

Detroit land speculators organize Pontiac Co. and purchase land tract at site of present-day Pontiac.

First settlers at site of Dearborn (first called Dearbornville).

World History

Oct. 20. U.S. and Great Britain sign convention establishing part of present-day border with Canada at 49⁰ latitude. Also agree to shared occupation of Oregon Country; leads to controversy.

Dec. 3. Illinois admitted to Union.

Cultural Progress

Mary Wollstonecraft Shelley publishes *Frankenstein*; cautionary tale of man being overpowered by what he creates.

Austrian choral director Franz Gruber composes "Stille Nacht, heilige Nacht" (Silent Night, Holy Night); words by curate Joseph Mohr.

Scientific and Commercial Progress

Anthracite coal mining begins in Pennsylvania.

First science magazine in U.S., *The American Journal of Science,* founded.

Packet service begins between New York City and Liverpool: Black Ball Line so successful that other U.S. lines soon follow.

1819

Detroit and Michigan

Detroit's population, 1,110.

Jan. 2. Bank of Michigan opens for business.

Treaty of Saginaw signed by Gov. Lewis Cass and American Indians, ceding to U.S. about 6 million acres of land diagonally across center of Michigan.

Michigan Territory authorized to send delegate to Congress. William Woodbridge elected (Sept. 2); soon resigns amidst citizens' protest (he already holds public office as territorial secretary).

Legislative Council authorizes physicians and surgeons to meet in Detroit to form medical society.

First land entry in Royal Oak is made by William Thurber.

World History

Financial panic: creditors and debtors suffer hardships; undermines confidence in federal government (Second Bank of United States).

Adams-Onis Treaty: U.S. purchases Florida from Spain.

McCulloch v. *Maryland*: Supreme Court decision, based on broad interpretation of Constitution, strengthens power of Congress, asserts legality of Bank of U.S.

Dec. 4. Alabama admitted to Union.

Military post established at Fort Snelling, later Minneapolis, Minnesota.

Simon Bolívar becomes president and military dictator of new republic of Colombia.

British settle Singapore; becomes capital of empire's Straits Settlements.

Cultural Progress

Elihu Embree begins publishing first periodicals devoted wholly to abolition: weekly newspaper in Jonesboro, Tennessee; monthly *Emancipator* (1820).

Scientific and Commercial Progress

American vessel *Savannah* (sailing ship equipped with steam-powered side paddle wheels) first steamship to cross Atlantic.

Steamboat traffic begins on Missouri River; speeds development of West.

Quaker farmer Jethro Wood builds improved cast-iron plow; moldboard design, removable pieces can be replaced after wear.

American inventor Thomas Blanchard develops lathe to mass produce rifle stocks.

1820

Detroit and Michigan

Detroit's population, 1,442.

Michigan's population, 8,927.

City limits narrowed; Gov. Lewis Cass's farm (below Detroit) now outside boundaries.

Solomon Sibley elected, replacing William Woodbridge as territorial representative to Congress.

Michigan's first highway built, from Detroit to Ohio.

May. Gov. Cass and company (including Henry Schoolcraft) set out on expedition to explore Michigan Territory, to learn about natural resources and remote inhabitants. Trace shores of Lakes Huron, Superior, Michigan, and upper reaches of Mississippi River. Cass parts company with crew in Chicago (a small settlement of fewer than 200 people), returning overland via Sauk Indian trail.

Susan Johnston, Ojibwa whose Indian name means "Green Meadow Woman" and wife of fur trader John Johnston, helps negotiate Treaty of Sault Ste. Marie between her people and U.S. government; provides land for establishment of Fort Brady (at Sault Ste. Marie).

Government-funded post roads built, from Detroit to Pontiac and Mt. Clemens; by end of decade, wagon routes fan out from Detroit and small towns develop inland.

Merchant Thomas Palmer builds first brick store in Detroit, on Jefferson Ave.

First Protestant church building in Detroit dedicated on Woodward north of Larned; Rev. John Monteith, pastor. Inter-denominational Protestant Society organized.

World History

U.S. population, 9,638,453.

Second wave of U.S. immigration begins; by 1870 nearly 7.5 million newcomers arrive. Irish (about one-third of new arrivals) settle eastern cities; German (also accounting for a third) mostly settle nation's interior farmlands.

Missouri Compromise: Maine (formerly part of Massachusetts) to be admitted to Union as free state and Missouri as slave state; slavery to be prohibited in Louisiana Territory north of 36°30' latitude (with exception of Missouri). Congressional compromise temporarily preserves Union, delicate balance between free and slave states.

March 15. Maine admitted to Union.

James Monroe reelected president with only one dissenting electoral college vote.

Revolution in Portugal.

King George IV ascends British throne upon death of George III.

Cultural Progress

Mardi Gras (Fat Tuesday) first marked in New Orleans with masked processions.

Scientific and Commercial Progress

Mary Anne Mantell discovers a tooth in a Sussex, England, quarry, leading to the identification of a dinosaur—the first ever found.

More than 60 steamboats run on Ohio River, principal westward route.

Danish physicist Hans C. Oersted discovers electromagnetism.

French physicist André Ampère develops theory of electrodynamics.

Horse-drawn cultivators begin to replace handheld hoes.

1821

Detroit and Michigan

Aug. 29. Gov. Lewis Cass negotiates Treaty of Chicago: American Indians cede all Michigan territory south of Grand River not previously ceded, except for southwestern triangle of land bound on east by St. Joseph River (in present-day Berrien County).

Furs still most important item in Detroit trade, but fur trade begins to decline this decade due to overhunting.

World History

March 4. President James Monroe inaugurated; 2nd term.

March 25. Greek War for Independence begins (to 1829).

Aug. 10. Missouri admitted to Union.

Mexican rebellion ends Spanish rule.

Cultural Progress

First free public high school in U.S. opens in Boston.

Scientific and Commercial Progress

William Underwood Co. begins canning operation in Boston.

Santa Fe Trail opens for trade; connects Independence, Missouri, to Santa Fe and becomes major commercial/settlement route to West.

Aug. 4. *Saturday Evening Post* first issued.

English inventor Thomas Hancock invents "masticator," machine to knead scraps of rubber into a mass. Origin of modern rubber processing.

German physicist Thomas Johann Seebeck discovers thermoelectricity.

1822

Detroit and Michigan

Influx of Greek settlers begins in Detroit; result of Greek War for Independence.

Fort Brady (at Sault Ste. Marie) built; Fort Saginaw also begun.

Henry Schoolcraft, now Indian agent at Sault Ste. Marie, begins intensive study of American Indian life; publishes books on subject.

Fort Mackinac doctor William Beaumont begins study of human digestion, observing process in patient with stomach wound.

March 21. First Methodist Episcopal Society of Detroit founded.

Public stagecoaches begin service from Detroit.

Superior, 2nd steamboat on Great Lakes, arrives in Detroit on maiden run from Buffalo, carrying 94 passengers.

World History

In Charleston, South Carolina, Denmark Vesey's plan is revealed to lead an estimated 9,000 slaves in an uprising. Vesey and 36 others are tried, found guilty of conspiracy, and hanged.

Florida territorial representative Joseph Hernéndez is first Latino elected to U.S. Congress.

Stephen Austin begins colonizing Texas; directs government, encourages U.S. immigration.

Brazil declares independence from Portugal.

First freed slaves are settled in Liberia (becomes independent republic, 1847).

Cultural Progress

Washington Irving's *Bracebridge Hall* published.

Franz Liszt makes debut at age 11 as pianist in Vienna.

1823

Detroit and Michigan

Sept. 22. Cornerstone laid for courthouse and territorial capitol, at Griswold and Jefferson.

Michigan granted legislative council: U.S. Congress transfers territorial government from governor and judges to governor and legislative council. People to elect 18 candidates from whom U.S. president will select 9. As Detroiters were unhappy with judges' rule, decision greeted with delight.

In bitter election, Father Gabriel Richard is elected delegate to Congress.

First white settlement at Ypsilanti, which will be named in 1825 by Judge Augustus Woodward in honor of Greek freedom fighter.

World History

Dec. 2. Monroe Doctrine announced: President James Monroe warns European nations that any interference with affairs of an independent nation in Western Hemisphere will be seen as a "manifestation of an unfriendly disposition toward the United States." Lays foundation of U.S. foreign policy.

Cultural Progress

Rugby football originates: during soccer game at England's Rugby School, a player picks up the ball and runs with it.

Scientific and Commercial Progress

Merrimack Manufacturing Co. opens in Massachusetts: textile mill incorporates latest in modern machinery, employs thousands, introduces (English) factory system to U.S., town of Lowell springs up around it.

British medical journal, *The Lancet,* first published.

Charles Babbage makes an early attempt to construct calculator.

Scottish chemist Charles Macintosh invents waterproof fabric using layers of rubber, cloth. Origin of mackintosh raincoat.

1824

Detroit and Michigan

Russell House Hotel opens in downtown Detroit.

John R. Williams elected first mayor of Detroit (to 1825); unsalaried position (to 1857).

Detroit citizen Peter Berthelet receives authorization to build a wharf on Detroit River, provided he maintain a pump from which all residents can obtain water.

June 7. First legislative council of Michigan Territory convenes in Detroit.

Aug. 5. City charter adopted; provides for local government by mayor and common council (Board of Aldermen), consisting of 5 men. Also creates offices of recorder (to perform mayoral duties in mayor's absence) and city clerk. Mayor's court to try offenses against city ordinances.

Nov. 22. First Episcopal church in Detroit organized, St. Paul's.

Nov. 25. Thanksgiving Day first observed in Detroit.

Congress appropriates $20,000 for road between Detroit and Toledo, and $10,000 for survey of Great Sauk Trail between Detroit and Chicago, to become Territorial Road (now U.S. 12).

Ann Arbor is laid out near Huron River; name honors founders' wives (both are named Ann).

World History

First women's labor organization, United Tailoresses Society of New York, founded by Lavinia White and Louise Mitchell.

U.S. signs frontier treaty with Russia: southern boundary of Russian territory in North America recognized as latitude 54°40'.

John Quincy Adams (National Republican) elected president by U.S. House of Representatives when no candidate wins majority vote.

James Bridger discovers Great Salt Lake.

Federal republic of Mexico established.

Simon Bolívar liberates Peru, becomes president (actually dictator; to 1827).

Charles X succeeds brother Louis XVIII as king of France.

Cultural Progress

Ludwig van Beethoven completes Symphony No. 9.

Scientific and Commercial Progress

Portland cement developed by English bricklayer/mason Joseph Aspdin.

Parliament strikes down laws forbidding workers to form trade unions.

1825

Detroit and Michigan

Jan. 23. First Protestant Society and church reorganized as First Presbyterian Church.

May 10. *Michigan Herald* newspaper begins publication; competes with *Detroit Gazette* for readers.

Sept. 21. Fire Engine No. 1 purchased.

All county officers, except judges, now elected to office.

Four-day steamboat service between Detroit and Buffalo maintained by ships *Superior* (built 1822) and *Henry Clay* (built 1824).

Germans begin settling in Detroit in sizable numbers.

World History

March 4. John Quincy Adams inaugurated; 6th U.S. president.

Democratic party organized by faction of Democratic-Republicans led by Andrew Jackson.

Czar Alexander I dies; succeeded by Nicholas I (to 1855).

Cultural Progress

Welsh socialist Robert Owen founds utopian cooperative colony at New Harmony, Indiana; internal dissension causes failure (by 1828).

Scientific and Commercial Progress

Oct. 26. Erie Canal opens, connecting Atlantic Ocean with Great Lakes, facilitating westward passage of settlers through New York and into Old Northwest Territory, including Michigan. Inaugural run made by barge *Seneca Chief*.

Inventor George Stephenson builds first public railroad; conveys passengers between Stockton and Darlington, England.

1826

Detroit and Michigan

Wayne County reduced to present boundaries.

Henry J. Hunt, mayor of Detroit (to next year).

Thomas L. McKenney of Indian Department and Gov. Lewis Cass journey to Lake Superior to negotiate Treaty of Fond du Lac with Chippewa.

Troops stationed at Detroit are removed. Fort Shelby, in a state of disuse since War of 1812, to be demolished next year. Congress donates site to city: Fort, Shelby, Wayne, and Cass streets are laid out.

Earth from Fort Shelby embankments deposited along riverfront.

Charles C. Trowbridge, of Bank of Michigan, builds finest frame house in territory; erected above town, only accessible via river road (Jefferson Ave. not yet expanded eastward).

First Grand Lodge of Michigan Masons organized.

World History

Panama Congress: first meeting of Pan-American nations.

Cultural Progress

Educator Josiah Holbrook founds lyceum in Millbury, Massachusetts; launches American lyceum movement (3,000 organizations founded by 1834) to improve schools, prepare teachers, set up libraries and museums, improve American culture.

James Fenimore Cooper publishes *The Last of the Mohicans.*

Scientific and Commercial Progress

Trader Jedediah Smith sets out from Great Salt Lake to chart trade route to California.

French physicist Joseph-Nicéphore Niepce produces first negative (photographic) image.

First railroad tunnel built in England, on Liverpool-Manchester line.

1827

Detroit and Michigan

John Biddle, mayor of Detroit (through 1828).

U.S. Congress authorizes construction of roads from Detroit to Chicago, Saginaw, Fort Gratiot (Port Huron). Improvements consist of clearing trees and stumps from routes, drainage, laying logs across marshy areas. Roads determine lines of Michigan settlement; towns established along routes.

Detroit city seal and motto adopted, commemorating 1805 fire: *Speramus Meliora; Resurget Cineribus,* meaning "We hope for better days; it shall arise from its ashes."

Barracks and stockade removed and Fort Shelby demolished; Fort, Cass, Shelby streets open to traffic.

Nov. 26. City Council passes ordinance requiring sidewalks; usually made of wood planks.

Logs convey water supply from pump house on wharf to wooden reservoir on Randolph St.; capacity, 9,500 gallons.

First steamboat built at Detroit: *Argo* to be used as ferry. Two hollowed logs held together by deck; has small steam engine.

Stagecoaches begin regular runs to Ohio.

Mansion House takes over stone building on south side of Jefferson, between Shelby and Wayne; among city's leading hotels for many years.

First Baptist Society organized.

World History

Oct. In ongoing Greek War for Independence, combined fleet of Greek allies (Britain, France, Russia) defeats Turk and Egyptian fleet in Battle of Navarino.

General strike in Philadelphia; workers demand 10-hour day. Marks beginning of U.S. labor movement.

Cultural Progress

John James Audubon publishes *Birds of America.*

Scientific and Commercial Progress

Baltimore & Ohio Railroad chartered.

First American Fourdrinier (printing) machine built.

German physicist Georg Ohm formulates Ohm's Law, defining electrical current potential and resistance.

1828

Detroit and Michigan

Detroit's population, 1,517.

May 5. U.S. Court House (Griswold and Jefferson) opens; houses chambers of legislative council of Michigan Territory. Remains capitol to 1847.

Treaty of Carey Mission signed with American Indians, who cede part of southwestern corner of Michigan's Lower Peninsula to U.S.

Michigan State Library created as law library for legislature.

Historical Society of Michigan founded by Lewis Cass, Henry Schoolcraft, others.

First services held by Father Gabriel Richard in new Ste. Anne's Church; twin steeples become city landmark.

World History

Congress approves protective tariff on imported goods; soon called Tariff of Abominations, leads to South Carolina Nullification Crisis (1832).

Democratic-Republican party becomes Democratic party.

Andrew Jackson, Democrat, elected president; marks ascendancy of common man in American politics. First president nominated by national political convention.

Russia declares war on Turkish Ottoman Empire.

Cultural Progress

Ladies' Magazine, first magazine for women in the U.S., founded in Boston. Edited by Sarah Josepha Hale. Moves to Philadelphia (1837) and becomes *Godey's Lady's Book.*

Noah Webster's *American Dictionary of the English Language* published; source of common usage helps build national unity and prevent provincial dialects from developing.

Scientific and Commercial Progress

July 4. Baltimore & Ohio Railroad begins service; first rail line in U.S. for passengers. Horse-drawn cars travel 14 miles of iron-covered wooden rails.

1829

Detroit and Michigan

Gen. John T. Mason becomes territorial secretary.

Jonathan Kearsley, mayor of Detroit.

Typing machine (typographer) patented by William A. Burt of Mount Vernon, Michigan. First letter written on machine sent to Secretary of State Martin Van Buren (on May 25) by John P. Sheldon, editor of *Detroit Gazette*.

Northwestern Journal founded; becomes *Detroit Journal and Michigan Advertiser* next year.

World History

March 4. Andrew Jackson inaugurated; 7th U.S. president.

President Jackson begins relying on so-called Kitchen Cabinet, unofficial advisers who meet in White House kitchen. Group disbanded when Jackson reorganizes administration in 1831.

American David Walker publishes militant anti-slavery pamphlet *An Appeal to the Colored People of the World*; circulates throughout South.

Sept. First National Negro Convention meets in Philadelphia.

Slavery abolished in Mexico.

Peace of Adrianople ends Russo-Turkish war; Turkey acknowledges Greek independence.

Cultural Progress

Karl Baedeker begins publishing his travel guides.

Frederic Chopin makes professional debut in Vienna.

Gioacchino Antonio Rossini's opera *William Tell* first performed in Paris.

Scientific and Commercial Progress

George Stephenson's locomotive engine, the *Rocket,* wins speed trial in Liverpool.

Canada completes Welland Canal, connecting Lakes Ontario and Erie. Enlarged 1845, 1887.

1830

Detroit and Michigan

Detroit's population, 2,222.

Michigan's population, 31,639.

John R. Williams, mayor of Detroit.

July 31. Territorial gov. approves first charter of incorporation for a Michigan railroad, Detroit & Pontiac Railroad; construction does not begin until 1836, by which time other rail lines have already been completed.

Aug. 21. Detroit's first substantial waterworks goes into operation. Crowd gathers to see first water flow through 3-inch pipes; Gov. Lewis Cass proclaims it "an age of progress."

Sept. 24. Stephen G. Simmons hanged for murder in Detroit; last execution in Michigan.

Irish immigration to Detroit begins; new arrivals settle west of Woodward, in Michigan-Bagley area, establishing Corktown neighborhood.

Opening of Erie Canal (5 years ago) has prompted land boom in Michigan; building boom in Detroit (to 1837).

Newspapers begin publishing articles promoting Michigan railroads.

Group of Detroiters invite scientist Douglass Houghton to town to lecture on geology, botany, chemistry, other subjects. The Rensselaer Polytechnic Institute professor gives series of talks at old Council House on Jefferson.

First temperance society in city organized.

Detroit Female Seminary incorporated by leading citizens; opens 1836, discontinued 1842.

Farmer and Mechanic's Bank organized.

World History

U.S. population, 12,866,020.

Indian Removal Act: U.S. government exchanges lands in West (Indian Territory in present-day Oklahoma, Kansas, Nebraska) for tribes' eastern holdings. Over next decade, American Indians are displaced from lands east of Mississippi River or seek refuge in Canada.

Webster-Hayne debates: Daniel Webster negates States' Rights doctrine.

Mormon Church (Church of Jesus Christ of Latter Day Saints) organized in New York.

July. Revolution in Paris: Charles X abdicates and Louis Philippe becomes constitutional monarch.

William IV succeeds his brother George IV (to 1837); last British monarch to force prime minister on Parliament.

London Protocol: Britain, France, Russia sign decree recognizing independent Greece; Ottoman Turks concede defeat in Greek War for Independence.

Cultural Progress

Barbizon School (to 1860s): During decade landscape artists portray nature as they see it, rejecting convention; forerunner to impressionism.

Poker evolves into a gambling game using a deck of 52 cards.

Scientific and Commercial Progress

U.S. has 40 miles of railroad tracks.

New England is center of nation's textiles industry.

President Andrew Jackson approves Congressional appropriation to survey, extend National (Cumberland) Road westward.

Manufacturer Peter Cooper designs, builds first American locomotive, *Tom Thumb*, for Baltimore & Ohio Railroad.

National Observatory established in Washington, D.C., by U.S. Navy.

Consumption of coffee in U.S. has increased from 1 pound per capita in 1800 to almost 3 pounds.

Cincinnati (known as Porkopolis) is nation's meat-packing center.

U.S. wheat flour consumption is 170 pounds per capita.

First graduate of veterinary medicine to practice in U.S.: Charles Grice opens veterinary hospital in New York City.

1831

Detroit and Michigan

Marshall Chapin, mayor of Detroit.

Jan. 9. Daily mail service inaugurated between Detroit and the East.

March 22. Michigan Sunday School Union organized.

May 5. *Democratic Free Press and Michigan Intelligencer* first published; issued weekly (to May 19, 1835). Origin of *Detroit Free Press.*

July. Detroit Athenaeum organized to conduct a library and reading room.

Territorial Gov. Lewis Cass resigns to become President Andrew Jackson's secretary of war.

Stevens T. Mason is appointed territorial secretary, succeeding his father, who resigns in his favor. Only 19 years of age but highly capable; also becomes acting territorial governor upon Cass's resignation.

Aug. 6. George B. Porter is appointed Michigan territorial governor. Serves until his death (1834).

French statesman Alexis de Tocqueville visits Detroit; describes it as America's "last limits of civilization."

First mention of Board of Health in Council Proceedings.

World History

Aug. 21–22. Nat Turner leads Southampton, Virginia, slave rebellion; some 60 people killed.

Poland declares independence from Russia; Russian forces defeat Poles and revolt collapses.

Belgium separates from the Netherlands.

Cultural Progress

Abolitionist paper, *The Liberator,* founded in Boston by William Lloyd Garrison.

Victor Hugo writes *Notre-Dame de Paris,* published in U.S. as *Hunchback of Notre Dame.*

Scientific and Commercial Progress

Baltimore & Ohio Railroad begins regular passenger service with locomotive the *York.*

First commercially successful reaper built by Virginia-born inventor Cyrus Hall McCormick (patented 1834; first sold 1840).

Chloroform simultaneously discovered by American Samuel Guthrie, Eugene Soubeiran of France, Baron Justus von Liebig of Germany; publicly demonstrated as anesthetic in 1847.

Scottish botanist Robert Brown discovers nucleus in plant cells.

English chemist and physicist Michael Faraday discovers electromagnetic induction; basic principle of the dynamo.

H.M.S. *Beagle* expedition (to 1836); Charles Darwin is ship's naturalist, gathering data on flora, fauna from South American coasts, Galapagos, Andes Mountains, Australia, Asia.

Sir James Clark Ross determines position of North Magnetic Pole.

1832

Detroit and Michigan

Levi Cook, mayor of Detroit.

May 24. In Black Hawk War, detachment of Detroit militia sets out to Chicago.

Legislative council petitions Congress for enabling act.

June 28. Charter granted to Detroit & St. Joseph Railroad.

July 4. Steamer *Henry Clay,* carrying soldiers to fight in Black Hawk War, docks in Detroit. Also carries passengers sick with cholera. Soon becomes epidemic, claiming many victims, including Father Gabriel Richard (Sept. 13), who dies after administering to afflicted.

Logan Female Anti-Slavery Society founded in Lenawee County; first such organization in Michigan Territory.

Belgian-born Francis Palms arrives in Detroit; amasses fortune in banking and real estate.

Royal Oak becomes separate township.

Episcopal Diocese of Michigan created.

World History

Andrew Jackson, nominated by newly styled Democratic party, reelected president.

Black Hawk War: land struggle between Sauk and Fox band and Illinois militia. Black Hawk subdued (Aug. 2).

Nullification Crisis (to 1833): South Carolina legislators declare protective tariff null and void within their state. Situation tests President Andrew Jackson, U.S. Constitution, authority of central government.

President Jackson vetoes re-charter of Second Bank of the United States.

First wagons leave Independence, Missouri, on Oregon Trail; led by Benjamin Bonneville, destination is Oregon's Columbia River region.

First British Reform Bill redistributes Parliamentary seats in interest of large cities, gives vote to middle-class men.

Cultural Progress

New England Institution for the Education of the Blind (now Perkins School for the Blind) opens in Boston; first in U.S.

National hymn "America," words by Samuel F. Smith, first sung, published.

Scientific and Commercial Progress

Ann McKim is first Baltimore clipper, small sailing vessel and basis for later clipper ships.

Soda water machine invented by John Matthews; origin of soft drink industry.

Hot Springs, Arkansas, made U.S. government reservation; first national health and recreation center.

1833

Detroit and Michigan

Treaty of Chicago (2nd) signed with American Indians, who cede last parcel of (present-day Berrien County) land, giving U.S. full possession of Michigan's Lower Peninsula south of the Grand River.

Marshall Chapin, mayor of Detroit.

Jan. Wayne County poorhouse opens; on Gratiot Ave. west of Mt. Elliott.

Jan 8. Detroit Young Men's Society organized. Douglass Houghton among leaders. Foremost literary society in Detroit, it sponsors lectures and builds sizable library.

April 22. Amendment to city charter authorizes city taxes on all real and personal property.

April 22. Erie & Kalamazoo Railroad receives charter.

June 14–15. Riot erupts when Detroit's black citizens help fugitive slaves Thornton Blackburn and his wife escape to Canada. Government troops called out to restore order. Incident gives impetus to anti-slavery movement in Detroit and Michigan.

Aug. 18. St. John's German Evangelical Church is first Lutheran Church organized in Detroit.

Father Martin Kündig arrives in Detroit to serve city's growing German and Irish Catholic populations; holds services in German in a room at Ste. Anne's Church.

Roman Catholic Diocese of Detroit created.

Act providing for common schools in Detroit is passed but little is done to carry out plan. Women organize Free School Society, raise funds, and open school over grocery store on south side of Woodbridge St. (near Shelby). Detroit has 1,350 children of school age.

Oliver Newberry, pioneer of lake transportation, builds largest steamer on Great Lakes: the *Michigan* is 156 feet long. Makes maiden voyage Oct. 11.

Erie & Kalamazoo Railroad chartered.

Chicago Rd. completed; Ten Eyck Tavern, 9 miles west of Detroit, becomes famous stopping place. Grand River Rd. authorized as northwest route.

First shoe factory established in Detroit; becomes leading industry in city.

Black Hawk, the subdued Sauk and Fox chief, arrives in Detroit; part of federal tour.

World History

March 4. President Andrew Jackson inaugurated; 2nd term.

Congress overwhelmingly approves Force Bill, giving President Jackson latitude to resolve South Carolina Nullification Crisis by whatever means necessary.

Clay's Compromise Tariff effectively ends Nullification Crisis: South Carolina legislators agree to new tariff.

Whig party takes shape as groups opposing President Jackson unify.

William Lloyd Garrison, Tappan brothers (Lewis and Arthur) found American Anti-Slavery Society.

Gen. Antonio Lopez de Santa Anna becomes president of Mexico; civil war looms.

Britain abolishes slavery throughout empire; anti-slavery campaign led by William Wilberforce.

Parliament passes Factory Act: no child under 9 can work in a factory, no one under 18 can work more than 12 hours a day.

Carlist wars (to 1839): royal struggle for power in Spain. Don Carlos challenges ascension of young Isabella II upon death of her father (Ferdinand VII).

Cultural Progress

Debut issue of daily *The New York Sun,* first penny newspaper.

Oberlin College founded in Ohio; first coeducational college in U.S. (opens to women in 1837).

April 9. First tax-supported free public library in U.S. established in Peterborough, New Hampshire.

Davy Crockett's *Autobiography* bestseller along with other adventure books.

Scientific and Commercial Progress

Canadian steamship the *Royal William* crosses Atlantic in 25 days.

Karl F. Gauss and Wilhelm E. Weber devise electromagnetic telegraph, which functions over a distance of 9,000 feet.

William Beaumont, Michigan military surgeon, publishes observations of gastric juices, digestive process.

1834

Detroit and Michigan

Detroit's population, 4,968.

Charles C. Trowbridge, mayor of Detroit; soon succeeded by Andrew Mack.

Congress rejects Michigan's petition for enabling act; extends Michigan Territory to Missouri River; now includes all of present states of Michigan, Wisconsin, Minnesota, Iowa, and part of North and South Dakota.

July 6. Michigan Territorial Governor George B. Porter dies. Territorial Secretary Stevens T. Mason serves as governor.

Holy Trinity, Detroit's second Roman Catholic church, founded to serve immigrant Irish population.

Aug.–Sept. 2nd cholera epidemic strikes city; Father Martin Kündig turns Holy Trinity Church into hospital. More than one-eighth of Detroit's citizens die.

Catholic Female Association organized for relief of Detroit's sick and poor; care for children orphaned during cholera epidemic.

Father Kündig is appointed supervisor of the poor; uses county poorhouse to care for widows and orphans of cholera epidemic. When funding is lacking, uses own money and goes into debt to provide for the needy.

Frederick Rese arrives in Detroit as first bishop of new Catholic diocese of Michigan. Brings architect Alpheus White, who makes changes to Ste. Anne's and designs new City Hall.

World History

Spain abolishes the Inquisition.

Cultural Progress

Lorenzo Delmonico opens New York restaurant (Delmonico's) serving European-style food.

English writer and statesman Edward Bulwer Lytton publishes *Last Days of Pompeii,* historical novel typical of his popular works.

Scientific and Commercial Progress

American inventor Thomas Davenport builds electrical motor; powers first electric locomotive (next year).

English mathematician Charles Babbage begins work on analytical engine; though never completed, forerunner of modern digital computer.

1835

Detroit and Michigan

Census of Michigan Territory discloses population of more than 85,000, qualifying it for statehood.

May 11. State constitutional convention assembles in Detroit.

May 19. *Democratic Free Press and Michigan Intelligencer* becomes semiweekly newspaper; on Sept. 28, begins to be issued daily (first daily newspaper in Michigan; later *Detroit Free Press*).

Oct. 5. State constitution approved by voters; state and national officials elected.

Nov. 2. First session of state legislature.

Nov. 3. Stevens T. Mason, Democrat, inaugurated as state's first governor (to 1839), despite Congressional refusal to grant statehood to Michigan until 1837.

Levi Cook, mayor of Detroit (through 1836).

Michigan adopts state seal—bald eagle (symbolizing U.S. government), elk and moose (symbolizing Michigan), and word *Tuebor* (Latin meaning "I will defend").

Michigan's admission to Union delayed (to 1837) due to Toledo War: boundary dispute with neighboring Ohio over ownership of land strip extending from southern end of Lake Michigan to Toledo and Maumee Bay; militia sent out but no casualties.

Nov. 18. Detroit's City Hall opens, east of Woodward.

Two stagecoaches a week make round trip between Detroit and Chicago.

Road improvements: First systematic street paving begins as Atwater is paved with stones between Woodward and Randolph; Griswold completed north of State St., opening area for development; Gratiot completed to Fort Gratiot (Port Huron); Saginaw Rd. reaches Flint.

Campus Martius graded and leveled.

First city bonds issued and sold to Oliver Newberry.

American Hotel built on Jefferson east of Randolph; incorporates Gov. William Hull's former residence. Considered one of Detroit's finer hostelries.

James Abbott II, American Fur Co. agent and Detroit postmaster, erects "one of the most substantial, costly, and elegant buildings" in city when he constructs gabled brick home at Griswold and Fort. Residence becomes a social center.

Timber companies in Ingham County create Biddle City, selling acreage to farmers from Lansing, New York. Farmland not a success; community (renamed Lansing) mostly abandoned.

First Baptist Church completed, northwest corner of Fort and Griswold.

Detroit's First Presbyterian Church built, at Woodward and Larned.

World History

Second Seminole War (to 1842): U.S. troops struggle to oust Indians from Florida.

New York City fire destroys some 500 buildings.

Texas declares its right to secede from Mexico.

Great Trek of the Boers (Dutch) begins to Africa's Transvaal.

Cultural Progress

Hans Christian Andersen publishes first of his 168 tales for children.

James Gordon Bennett publishes penny paper, *New York Herald.*

Alexis de Tocqueville publishes *Democracy in America.*

Scientific and Commercial Progress

Harriot Kezia Hunt of Boston is first woman to practice medicine in U.S.

Speculative boom (to 1837).

U.S. has 1,098 miles of railroad tracks.

Halley's comet reappears.

1836

Detroit and Michigan

Detroit's population, 6,927.

April 2. U.S. Congress passes act admitting Michigan to Union on condition that Ohio boundary is accepted.

Dec. 14. Convention of Assent (so-called Frost-bitten Convention) at Ann Arbor accepts congressional terms for admission to Union; terms had been denied at earlier convention (Sept. 4).

Treaties of Washington and Cedar Point: Henry Schoolcraft negotiates with tribes to secure lands in northwestern and tip of Lower Peninsula and eastern portion (roughly from

Big Bay de Noc) of Upper Peninsula; also secures triangle of land in southwestern Upper Peninsula from Green Bay west to Menomonee River.

First underground sewer (Grand Sewer) built in Detroit; follows route of Savoyard River; city purchases Hydraulic Co. Waterworks.

Signs indicating street names ordered at corners. Most of Detroit's streets are plank roads; downtown streets paved in cobblestones.

Hundreds of immigrants (mostly German or Irish) arrive in Detroit each day. Harbor, hotels, roads are jammed. Many settlers are bound for developing towns in Michigan's interior.

During May, 90 steamboats stop at Detroit's wharves.

Fall. Erie & Kalamazoo Railroad runs its first train from Port Lawrence (Toledo) to Adrian; a single coach is pulled along tracks by team of horses. First train west of Schenectady, New York.

Traveler Harriet Martineau stops in Detroit en route to Chicago via stagecoach; she writes about Detroit's choice society but notes its lack of accommodations, wooden plank roads; also mentions American Indians on road out of Detroit and poor roads along route.

Washington Allston Bacon conducts select school for boys in his residence; continues as well-known private school teacher for nearly 40 years.

Detroit Athenaeum merges with Detroit Young Men's Society, leading cultural influence.

City Theater opens (May); plays Shakespeare repertoire. First building to be called a theater in Detroit, it occupies former church at Gratiot and Farmer.

National Hotel opens at corner of Cadillac Square and Woodward.

Grand River Rd. home to new 16 Mile House; later named Botsford Tavern.

Detroit Daily Advertiser first issued, June 11 (becomes *Detroit Tribune*, 1849).

Thirteen former slaves organize Second Baptist Church, Detroit's oldest African American Baptist congregation.

Ladies' Protestant Orphan Asylum organized.

Across river, Richmond (Ontario) renamed Windsor.

On state's western shore, eastern capitalists lay out Port Sheldon on Pigeon Lake (10 miles south of Grand Haven); envisioned as great seaport of Lake Michigan. Workmen clear land, lay out streets, build houses, stores, mill, office building, lavish Ottawa Hotel.

World History

Martin Van Buren, Democrat, elected president.

Jan. Mexican Gen. Antonio Lopez de Santa Anna and troops march north to put down rebellion in Texas, now home to more than 20,000 American settlers.

Feb. 19. Texas declares its independence from Mexico.

Feb. 23–March 6. Battle of the Alamo: James Bowie, William Travis, Davy Crockett, others die in Texas War for Independence from Mexico.

April 21. Texans led by Sam Houston drive Mexicans out of Texas.

Wisconsin Territory organized.

June 15. Arkansas admitted to Union.

Charter of Second National Bank of the United States (1816) allowed to expire; wildcat banks resume unsound banking practices.

July 11. President Andrew Jackson issues Specie Circular, ordering government agents to accept nothing but gold or silver as payment for new lands.

House of Representative adopts Gag Rules to keep time-consuming anti-slavery petitions from being read on the floor. John Quincy Adams among outspoken opponents to rules; views them as violation of constitutional rights of free speech and petition. Abolished 1844.

Cultural Progress

William McGuffey publishes his first *Reader*; highly influential books become cornerstone of American public education system. More than 122 million *Reader*s will be sold by 1920; books used into 1970s.

First of *Pickwick Papers* by Charles Dickens published.

Scientific and Commercial Progress

First sleeping railcar used on Cumberland Valley Railroad in Pennsylvania.

Samuel Colt patents revolver.

1837

Detroit and Michigan

Jan. 26. Michigan admitted to Union; 26th state. Border dispute with Ohio settled by granting Toledo Strip to Ohio; Michigan gains entire Upper Peninsula. Capital at Detroit (to 1847).

Henry Howard, mayor of Detroit.

Michigan legislature develops Comprehensive State Education Plan; includes statewide system of public schools and University of Michigan. UM moves from Detroit to Ann Arbor, where a land company has donated 40 acres.

Michigan General School law: organizes public school system; John D. Pierce, state's first superintendent of public instruction. State constitution requires school in each district.

April 22. State purchases the Detroit & St. Joseph Railroad; renamed the Central Railroad.

April 26. Detroit Anti-Slavery Society organized: city becomes station on Underground Railroad; Finney barn is primary hiding place.

July 4. Michigan's first steam locomotive put into service by the Erie & Kalamazoo Railroad.

July 8. Lawyer and statesman Daniel Webster, whose son practices law in Detroit, visits while on westward trip seeking investments. Addresses large group (July 11).

Scientist Douglass Houghton secures authority to make geological survey of state.

Erie & Kalamazoo Railroad begins regular operations; also announces it will put a locomotive into operation—claimed to be first west of the Alleghenies.

Plan developed to extend Michigan's rail lines westward via 3 routes.

Grand River Rd. extends from Detroit to near Howell.

Polish settlers begin arriving in Detroit in large numbers.

In Panic of 1837, Port Sheldon (*see* 1836) and other speculative land deals collapse.

First Directory of City of Detroit published by Julius P. B. MacCabe.

Detroit has 3 fire engine companies and 1 horse company, all volunteers and keen rivals.

Bank of Michigan building erected at Jefferson and Griswold; first building of dressed stone in city.

World History

March 4. Martin Van Buren inaugurated; 8th U.S. president.

U.S. financial crisis: inflated land values, wildcat banking, paper speculation cause business panic, followed by lengthy economic depression.

U.S. recognizes independent Texas.

Abolition leader Theodore Dwight Weld writes *The Bible Against Slavery.*

Rebellion in Canada: constitutional revolts in Upper and Lower Canada.

U.S.S. *Caroline* set on fire and sunk by Canadian troops while transporting supplies to Canadian insurgents across Niagara River. Patriot War begins (to 1838).

June. Victoria ascends British throne upon death of her uncle, King William IV. She will be Great Britain's longest reigning monarch, ruling until her death in 1901.

Cultural Progress

Ralph Waldo Emerson delivers "American Scholar" speech at Harvard; Oliver Wendell Holmes Sr. hails it "our intellectual Declaration of Independence."

Mount Holyoke Female Seminary (later College) opens; first women's college.

Horace Mann, as secretary of Massachusetts Board of Education (to 1848), begins educational reforms; revolutionizes public school organization and teaching.

Educational reformer Frederich Frobel opens first kindergarten, in Blankenburg, Germany.

Scientific and Commercial Progress

John Deere develops steel plow; with McCormick's reaper (patented 1834), revolutionizes agriculture, makes possible settlement of western prairies.

American inventor John Ericsson successfully tests screw propeller he developed on commercial vessel.

Pennsylvania's Main Line Canal completed; part of canal and rail system linking Philadelphia and Pittsburgh.

In England, Charles Wheatstone and W. F. Cooke patent electric telegraph; Samuel Morse exhibits his electric telegraph at College of the City of New York.

1838

Detroit and Michigan

Augustus S. Porter, mayor of Detroit; soon succeeded by Asher Bates.

Detroiters sympathizing with patriots' cause in Canada attempt raid to furnish them with arms; U.S. Army District Commander Gen. Hugh Brady and forces thwart effort.

Detroit schools organized under state public school law: 3 school inspectors, elected in April, serve as board. First school census shows 2,097 children between ages 5 and 17; only 507 are enrolled in 7 district schools. Each district levies its own assessments; primary school fund derived from land sales. First public or tax-supported schools in Detroit; have great difficulties. Reformed in 1847.

First public school district located in 2nd-floor room of grocery store built on piles in river, on Woodbridge near Shelby.

Douglass Houghton files first report as state geologist.

Feb. Central Railroad reaches Ypsilanti; Detroit terminal is a wooden building at Michigan and Griswold. Fare to Ypsilanti $1.50; two trains daily.

Detroit & Pontiac Railroad reaches Royal Oak; spurs development.

Eaton Chemical and Dyestuff Co. founded by Theodore H. Eaton as Eaton-Clark Co.

First iron water pipes laid on Jefferson Ave.

World History

March 25. Trail of Tears begins: government-enforced western migration of as many as 17,000 Cherokee Nation Indians from tribal lands (in Georgia, Alabama, Tennessee) to Oklahoma; some 4,000 die en route.

Chartism: political reform movement in Great Britain (to 1848); demands universal male suffrage and vote by ballot.

British Afghan War (to 1842): to protect empire in India, Britain tries to assert itself in neighboring Afghanistan.

Cultural Progress

French philosopher Auguste Comte founds sociology as systematic study.

Scientific and Commercial Progress

First regularly scheduled transatlantic steamship service offered: crossing aboard British side-wheeler *Sirius* takes 18 1/2 days.

First steamship specifically for regular Atlantic crossings is launched at Bristol, England: 1,440-ton *Great Western,* designed by Isambard Kingdom Brunel, measures 236 feet and is powered by large side wheels. Arrives in New York in 15 days, setting new record for transatlantic crossing.

New York Herald is first U.S. newspaper to employ European correspondents.

First true department store opens: Bon Marché in Paris.

1839

Detroit and Michigan

De Garno Jones, mayor of Detroit.

Feb. 18. Detroit Boat Club organized; among oldest boat clubs in nation.

Act provides for Board of Aldermen (Common Council) to be composed of 2 aldermen from each ward, mayor, recorder. Detroit divided into wards (March 27); first political subdivision of city.

Sept. 1. Steamboat *Great Western* burns at Detroit.

Poorhouse on Gratiot sold by Wayne County; Torbert farm in Nankin Township purchased for poor farm. Black Horse Tavern on property used as new poorhouse. Organization becomes known as Wayne County Asylum (origin of Wayne County General Hospital at Eloise).

Caroline Stansbury Kirkland (of Pinckney) becomes first Michigan woman to publish a book: *A New Home—Who'll Follow* is released under pseudonym Mrs. Mary Clavers. Kirkland has written about trials and travails of pioneer life.

Detroit & Pontiac Railroad reaches Birmingham.

Michigan Medical Society is in existence.

World History

Slaves aboard Spanish ship *Amistad* take control of vessel and sail to Montauk, Long Island. Freedom eventually won in Supreme Court case.

Spanish courts uphold Salic law validating Isabella II's claim; rules with regent.

First Opium War (to 1842): conflict between Great Britain and China, ostensibly waged to protect foreign trade.

Cultural Progress

Educator/reformer Horace Mann founds nation's first state-supported normal school (teacher-training school), in Lexington, Massachusetts.

Philadelphia Quaker Richard Humphreys wills $10,000 to establish school for black boys. Origin of Cheyney State College (1902), later a teacher training school.

Edgar Allen Poe writes *The Fall of the House of Usher.*

Charles Dickens publishes *Oliver Twist.*

American travelers John Lloyd Stephens and Frederick Catherwood discover relics of ancient Maya culture in Central America and Mexico. Stephens's writings (1841, 1843) greatly stimulate interest in region.

Scientific and Commercial Progress

Charles Goodyear develops vulcanization process (patented 1844) for commercial applications of rubber.

Scotsman Kirkpatrick Macmillan adds pedals to *draisienne* to produce first true bicycle.

Samuel Cunard and partners launch British and North-American Royal Mail Steam Packet Co. (later known as Cunard Line).

French painter Louis-Jacques Daguerre makes direct positive image on a silver plate, soon called daguerreotype.

German-Swiss chemist Christian F. Schonbein discovers and names ozone.

Swiss physicist Carl August Steinheil builds first electric clock.

1840

Detroit and Michigan

Detroit's population, 9,192.

Michigan's population, 212,267.

William Woodbridge, Whig, governor (to 1841).

Dr. Zina Pitcher, known as father of Detroit's public school system, mayor of Detroit (through 1841).

Douglass Houghton investigates and publicizes Upper Peninsula's rich copper deposits.

Commercial lumbering of white pine begins in Michigan this decade.

Retired Detroit tradesman Joseph Campau manages real estate holdings, other investments to become wealthiest man in Michigan.

Nov. 23. Southern Railroad begins operating from Monroe to Adrian; 33 miles of track.

Tobacco manufacturing in Detroit begun by George Miller. Apprentices John Bagley and Daniel Scotten go on to become important tobacco merchants and capitalists.

Construction of homes begins on Grosse Isle. Becomes weekend and summer getaway: by 1860, 50 people own property on island.

Presidential campaign is occasion for numerous meetings, barbecues, other events in Detroit.

World History

Ernestine Rose of New York authors first petition for a law granting women the right to own property.

U.S. population, 17,069,453; national debt soars to 21 cents per capita. About 8% of Americans live in cities or towns with populations greater than 8,000.

Military hero William Henry Harrison, Whig, elected president.

Lower and Upper Canada united by Act of Parliament.

Britain's Queen Victoria marries Albert of Saxe-Coburg-Gotha (Germany). Origin of House of Windsor.

London Conference on Turko-Egyptian conflict signs Protocol des Droits; straits are closed to all powers and Black Sea closed to Russian warships.

Cultural Progress

The Dial magazine published by New England transcendentalists; edited by American critic and social reformer Margaret Fuller.

James Fenimore Cooper writes bestseller *The Pathfinder*.

Royal Botanic Gardens open at Kew, London.

Scientific and Commercial Progress

U.S. has 2,816 miles of railroad tracks; England has 1,331 miles.

More than 200 steamboats ply Mississippi River.

Agriculture engages 77.5% of U.S. workforce.

Baltimore College of Dental Surgery founded in Baltimore by American dentists Horace Hayden and Chapin Harris; world's first dental college.

1841

Detroit and Michigan

James W. Gordon, Whig, governor.

Federal government authorizes survey of Great Lakes.

Congress allocates funds for construction of Fort Wayne, to be situated about 3 miles below Detroit. Completed 1851, it is never attacked.

Sept. University of Michigan, Ann Arbor, holds first classes; school consists of 5 simple buildings—main building housing classrooms and dorms, 4 houses for professors.

Central Railroad reaches from Detroit to Chelsea; extends to Jackson by end of year.

Orleans Street Waterworks put into operation.

Cornerstone laid for St. Mary's Catholic Church (St. Antoine and Monroe), primarily German congregation.

African American Methodists who had organized a church society in 1839 reorganize as African Methodist Episcopal Church; meet in Detroit's old Military Hall.

April 20. Funeral procession and oration held in memory of President William Henry Harrison.

Sept. 12. Mt. Elliott Cemetery opens.

World History

March 4. William Henry Harrison inaugurated; 9th U.S. president.

April 4. President Harrison dies; succeeded by Vice President John Tyler, 10th U.S. president.

President Tyler's cabinet resigns.

Preemption Act passed by Congress: allows squatters to claim public lands in West. Aimed at encouraging development, superseded by Homestead Act (1862).

Slaves aboard U.S.S. *Creole* seize ship while en route from Virginia to Louisiana; redirect vessel to freedom in Nassau (Bahamas).

Social reformer Dorothea Dix tours Massachusetts state correctional institutions; becomes impassioned advocate for mentally ill.

First Canadian parliament meets at Kingston, Ontario (capital of Canada to 1844).

Treaty of Waitangi: native Maori leaders cede sovereignty of New Zealand to British; becomes crown colony.

Cultural Progress

Feb. 4. Earliest known reference to tradition of Groundhog Day appears in diary of Pennsylvania storekeeper.

James Fenimore Cooper publishes *The Deerslayer*; last of 5 "Leatherstocking Tales," vivid portrayal of American frontier.

Oberlin College becomes first U.S. school to award college degrees to women.

P. T. Barnum opens American Museum, exhibition of curios, Broadway and Ann streets, New York.

Bowling so popular in U.S. that some consider it a social evil: Connecticut outlaws game (then ninepins); enthusiasts bypass law by adding a pin (game becomes tenpins).

Unitarian minister/transcendentalist George Ripley founds Brook Farm, experimental cooperative in West Roxbury, Massachusetts.

Edgar Allen Poe publishes *The Murders in the Rue Morgue,* his first detective story.

Scientific and Commercial Progress

First screw-propelled vessel on Great Lakes, *Vandalia,* is launched at Oswego, New York.

English mechanical engineer Sir Joseph Whitworth proposes, secures standard screw threads.

Englishman W. H. Fox Talbot develops paper negative; can be used to print any number of paper positives.

Scottish missionary David Livingstone reaches Africa; explores vast continent over course of next 3 decades, publishing accounts of his discoveries.

1842

Detroit and Michigan

John S. Barry, Democrat, governor (to 1845).

Douglass Houghton, former state geologist, mayor of Detroit.

Treaty of La Pointe: western portion of Upper Peninsula cleared of Indian claims; U.S. now in full possession of entire Upper Peninsula.

Feb. 18. Legislature passes bill authorizing Detroit to organize public school system, levy taxes for support of free schools. Two people to be elected from each ward as members of Board of Education, which has power to employ teachers and manage schools. City organized as one district; schools are free to all children between ages of 5 and 17.

March 15. First Board of Education organized with 12 members.

May. Detroit's primary schools open; 6 women teachers are paid $18 a month. Middle schools open (in Nov.); here men teachers receive $30 a month.

July 8. Former President Martin Van Buren visits Detroit.

State legislature passes law requiring Detroit Board of Education to establish district library; no funding provided.

Books used in primary schools include Webster's Speller, Sander's *Readers,* Parley's *History,* Davies's *Arithmetic,* and Smith's *Geography and Grammar.*

Detroit & Pontiac Railroad builds new station at Gratiot and Farmer.

Bank of Michigan fails; building (Jefferson and Griswold) purchased by federal government for use as U.S. courthouse and post office.

Copper mining operations begin near Keweenaw Point, Upper Peninsula.

World History

Aug. U.S. and Britain sign Webster-Ashburton Treaty defining boundary between Maine and Canada.

Riots and strikes in industrial northern England.

Treaty of Nanking ends Opium War between Britain and China; cedes Hong Kong to British.

Cultural Progress

Philharmonic Symphony Society of New York founded; origin of New York Philharmonic Orchestra.

Alexander Cartwright organizes first baseball club, Knickerbocker Base Ball Club, in New York City.

Polka dance comes into fashion.

Honore de Balzac, pioneer of realistic novel, begins publishing *The Human Comedy* series of nearly 100 works, including novels, novellas, short stories.

Scientific and Commercial Progress

First wire-cable suspension bridge in U.S. is 358-foot-long span over Schuylkill River at Philadelphia.

Oregon Trail surveyed.

Anesthesia first used in an operation, by Georgia physician Crawford Williamson Long.

1843

Detroit and Michigan

Zina Pitcher, mayor of Detroit.

July 4. Detroit & Pontiac Railroad reaches Pontiac; 26 miles of track.

Sept. 25. Southern Railroad reaches Hillsdale; 68 miles of track.

Central Market opens in shed behind old City Hall.

St. Mary's Catholic Church, at St. Antoine St. and Monroe Ave., is built to serve Detroit's large German population. Third Catholic parish in the city.

Dec. 4. First Detroit Lodge of Odd Fellows chartered.

Chief state agricultural publication, *Michigan Farmer,* established.

World History

Know-Nothing political movement forms American Republican party; aims to elect only U.S.-born citizens to office. Reaction to influx of immigrants from Roman Catholic Europe. Soon dissolves (c. 1856).

Military revolt in Spain; 13-year-old Isabella II determined to be of age (rules without regent).

Maori revolt against British in New Zealand.

Cultural Progress

Dan Emmett produces first minstrel show: Virginia Minstrels perform at New York's Bowery Theater, initiating popular form of American entertainment.

Charles Dickens's *A Christmas Carol* published. Popularizes idea that Christmas day should be observed as official holiday.

World's first night club, *Le Bal des Anglais,* opens in Paris.

Skiing begins as sport, in Tromso, Norway.

Scientific and Commercial Progress

Congress grants Samuel F. B. Morse $30,000 to build telegraph line between Washington, D.C. and Baltimore.

John C. Fremont crosses Rocky Mountains en route to California.

Oliver Wendell Holmes publishes "The Contagiousness of Puerperal Fever"; influential article urges physicians to prevent spread of disease by washing hands, adhering to basic hygiene.

Missionary and pioneer Marcus Whitman crosses continent, returns to Oregon Country via Oregon Trail.

1844

Detroit and Michigan

John R. Williams, mayor of Detroit (to 1847).

Park development begins when Grand Circus area is drained, filled, raised. (In 1853, trees are planted and park is fenced.)

First Congregational Society organized; builds church at Jefferson and Beaubien (1846).

State geological surveyor William A. Burt discovers Upper Peninsula holds vast iron deposits.

Fort Wilkins built at Copper Harbor (Upper Peninsula).

World History

James Knox Polk, Democrat, elected president; first "dark horse" candidate, he campaigned on slogan "54°40' or fight" (reference to Oregon country boundary dispute with British).

U.S., China sign their first treaty of peace, amity, commerce.

Military revolts in Mexico.

Cultural Progress

Young Men's Christian Association (YMCA) founded in England by George Williams.

Alexandre Dumas publishes historical romance *The Three Musketeers.*

Scientific and Commercial Progress

Washington, D.C. and Baltimore connected by telegraph: Samuel F. B. Morse transmits (May 24) first message: "What hath God wrought!"

U.S. Navy's *Princeton* is first warship with screw propellers.

1845

Detroit and Michigan

Detroit's population, 13,065.

June 9. Wayne County Building opens at corner of Griswold and Congress.

June 9. St. Vincent's Hospital opened by Sisters of Charity in log building at Larned and Randolph; Detroit's first hospital and origin of Detroit Memorial Hospital.

July 4. Hog Island renamed Belle Isle.

Nov. 28. Catholic order Sisters of the Immaculate Heart of Mary founded near Monroe.

Horse-drawn public hacks introduced in Detroit; used mainly by hotels.

Michigan sends agent to New York City to attract newly arrived European immigrants to settle here.

Iron ore mining begins in Upper Peninsula, near Negaunee.

World History

March 1. President John Tyler signs congressional resolution annexing Texas to U.S. Mexico responds by breaking off diplomatic relations. Precipitates Mexican War (1846–48).

March 3. Florida admitted to Union.

March 4. James Polk inaugurated; 11th U.S. president.

Dec. 29. Texas admitted to Union.

New York Post editor John O'Sullivan uses term *Manifest Destiny* in article about annexation of Texas; belief spreads that U.S. has God-given right to spread influence throughout North America.

United States Naval Academy founded at Annapolis, Maryland.

Methodists and Baptists separate into Northern and Southern groups over slavery issue.

Great Irish Famine begins when potato crop fails (for 20th time since 1727); lasts to 1848. 700,000 to 1 million people die. Begins wave of U.S. immigration.

Cultural Progress

Escaped slave Frederick Douglass publishes his biography; *Narrative of the Life of Frederick Douglass* fuels abolitionist movement.

Knickerbocker Base Ball Club develops set of 20 game rules.

Tenpins (bowling) supercedes billiards as popular pastime.

Edgar Allen Poe publishes *The Raven and Other Poems*.

In Leipzig, German socialist Friedrich Engels publishes *The Condition of the Working Class in England.*

Scientific and Commercial Progress

Rainbow, designed by John W. Griffiths, is launched, begins new era of "extreme" clipper ships.

American inventor Erastus B. Bigelow builds power loom for manufacturing carpets.

First submarine cable laid across English Channel.

Pneumatic tire patented by Scottish engineer Robert W. Thomson.

1846

Detroit and Michigan

Alpheus Felch, Democrat, governor (to 1847).

Feb. 1. Central Railroad extends from Detroit to Kalamazoo; 144 miles of track.

March 28. Charter for Michigan Central Railroad approved.

May 4. Capital punishment abolished in Michigan.

Ernestine Rose becomes first woman to address state legislature; she speaks before Michigan lawmakers on behalf of woman suffrage.

Group of Detroit businessmen buys 42 acres in Hamtramck Township; establishes Elmwood Cemetery.

World History

Mexican War (to 1848): Negotiations between U.S. and Mexico for purchase of New Mexico fail; American troops move into disputed area and defeat Mexicans at Palo Alto; formal declaration of war follows.

Dispute between U.S. and Britain over Oregon Country settled by treaty. Border between U.S. and Canada established at 49° north latitude (present-day Washington's northern border).

Dec. 28. Iowa admitted to Union.

Wilmot Proviso introduced in Congress: advocates abolition of slavery in any territory U.S. gains in ongoing Mexican War; passes in House, defeated in Senate.

Cultural Progress

June. First true baseball game played at Elysian Fields, Hoboken, New Jersey: Knickerbocker Club v. New York Club.

Smithsonian Institution founded.

Belgian instrument maker Adolphe Sax patents saxophone.

Scientific and Commercial Progress

Elias Howe patents sewing machine.

Oct. 16. First hospital operation using anesthetic (ether) performed at Massachusetts General, Boston.

Hungarian obstetrician Ignaz Phillipp Semmelweis concludes that infection (puerperal fever) originates inside hospital ward; basis for use of antiseptics.

Discovery of planet Neptune by English astronomer John C. Adams and French mathematician Urbain Leverrier confirmed.

W. H. Fox Talbot's *Pencil of Nature*; first book illustrated with photographs.

1847

Detroit and Michigan

William L. Greenly, Democrat, governor.

James A. Van Dyke, mayor of Detroit.

Seat of Michigan government to move from Detroit: state legislature selects inland community Lansing as new capital; construction begins on 2-story wooden capitol with cupola. City's development aided by completion of Lansing and Howell plank road, connecting it to Detroit.

April 24. Soldiers leave Detroit for service in war with Mexico (1846–48).

Aug. 15. First U.S. postage stamps are received in Detroit.

Telegraph between Detroit and Ypsilanti first used; reaches New York and Chicago by 1848.

First regularly scheduled horse-drawn bus line begins operation on Jefferson Ave.; not successful, but others soon follow.

Campaign in Detroit for relief of Irish famine: Michigan sends more than 2,000 barrels of provisions.

Dutch settlers arrive in Michigan; found Holland, other towns.

Germans settle Frankenmuth in Saginaw Valley.

Copper mining in full swing in Upper Peninsula's Keweenaw Peninsula and Ontonagon. Operations continue to 1887.

World History

Sept. 14. U.S. forces led by Commander Winfield Scott capture Mexico City; part of ongoing Mexican War (to 1848).

Brigham Young founds Salt Lake City; Mormons begin colonization of Utah.

Cultural Progress

Charlotte Brontë publishes *Jane Eyre*.

Scientific and Commercial Progress

U.S. first issues adhesive postage stamps; previously letters were hand stamped or marked "paid" by postmaster.

American Medical Association founded.

Hermann von Helmholtz publishes paper on law of conservation of energy.

1848

Detroit and Michigan

Epaphroditus Ransom, Democrat, governor (to 1849).

Frederick Buhl, mayor of Detroit.

New Capitol at Lansing first occupied (Detroit's old capitol converted to school use).

State legislature passes Plank Road Act; provides for roadways constructed by licensed private companies who receive tolls. Tollgates placed every 10 miles.

Jan. 25. All capital stock of Erie & Kalamazoo Railroad sold; on Aug. 9 the line is leased to the Michigan Southern, who makes Toledo the main terminal.

Printers establish Detroit Typographic Union; Detroit's oldest trade union.

Barracks built at Fort Wayne; design of three-and-a-half-story stone structure credited to Lt. Montgomery Meigs.

German immigrant Frederick Ams arrives in Detroit; begins brewing and selling lager.

May 9. Fire destroys area bounded by Bates, Brush, Jefferson, river.

May 30. New Michigan Central Depot opens; riverfront begins to be acquired for rail sidetracks. Residential development of city forced farther out Fort St. and Jefferson Ave.

June 29. Saints Peter and Paul Church consecrated.

National Theater, first Detroit structure built as a theater, opens on Jefferson Ave.; renamed Metropolitan Theater (1854), later known as The Varieties.

Michigan Journal of Homeopathy, state's earliest medical publication, issued.

Sibley House, built by Judge Solomon Sibley's widow, completed next door to Christ Church; becomes one of few buildings of era to survive later demolition or disaster.

James Jesse Strang establishes Mormon settlement on Beaver Island in Lake Michigan.

World History

March 10. Treaty of Guadalupe Hidalgo officially ends Mexican War; in exchange for large indemnity, Mexico relinquishes roughly half its territory (New Mexico, California, Utah, Nevada, Arizona, parts of Colorado and Wyoming) to U.S., recognizes Rio Grande as its border with Texas.

Free Soil party organized to oppose extension of slavery into territories newly gained from Mexico. (Party absorbed by Republicans in 1854.)

May 29. Wisconsin admitted to Union.

Congress sets up Oregon Territory; Oregon Trail heavily used by settlers for next 3 decades.

July 19–20. First Women's Rights Convention held at Seneca Falls, New York. Over 240 women and men hold first public meeting on women's rights; delegates prepare Seneca Falls Declaration of Sentiments.

Former Michigan Territorial Governor and U.S. Senator Lewis Cass is Democratic candidate for president.

Nov. Zachary Taylor, Whig, elected president.

Wave of German immigration begins after failure of political uprisings in Europe.

Bourbon monarchy overthrown by revolution in France; Second Republic established (to 1852) under leadership of Louis-Napoleon.

Cultural Progress

New York City newspapers, including the *Sun,* the *Herald,* and the *Tribune,* form Associated Press (AP), first major news service in U.S.

British school representatives meet at Trinity College, Cambridge, to draw up first set of soccer rules.

Karl Marx and Friedrich Engels publish *The Communist Manifesto.*

German composer Richard Wagner's *Lohengrin* first performed.

Scientific and Commercial Progress

Jan. 24. Gold discovered at Sutter's Mill, Coloma, California.

Chicago & Northwestern Railway begins operations; first railroad west out of Chicago.

Chicago Board of Trade formed.

1849

Detroit and Michigan

Charles Howard, mayor of Detroit.

Scandinavians begin immigrating to Michigan; Finns, Swedes settle Upper Peninsula mining towns. Others arrive in Detroit to work as toolmakers.

Feb. 21. Act provides for city physician.

March 5. Detroit Savings Bank incorporated as Detroit Savings Fund Institute, origin of Detroit Bank and Trust. At end of year, total deposits are $3,287.

April 23. Michigan Central Railroad reaches New Buffalo; first railroad to cross the state.

June 1. German immigrants organize meeting for Lieder singers; group calls itself Gesang-Verein Harmonie (harmonic singing club).

June–Sept. 3rd cholera epidemic hits Detroit.

Sept. 25–27. Michigan State Fair held for first time, on grounds on west side of Woodward between Columbia and Vernor.

Nov. 19. *Detroit Daily Tribune* first issued; later merges with *Detroit News* (1915).

Nov. 26. Penny paper, *Detroit Herald,* begins publication (to 1850).

Nov. 29. Michigan Central Railroad schedules two daily trains in place of one.

Dec. 23. Mariner's Church dedicated at corner of Woodward and Woodbridge. Oldest surviving church building in city (later moved). Julia Anderson, widow of Detroit military commander, gave land and money to erect church for Great Lakes seamen.

Michigan senate committee proposes universal suffrage amendment; not acted on by legislature.

Offices of Detroit city clerk, treasurer, marshal, attorney, etc., made elective instead of appointive positions.

Eastern Michigan University founded (Ypsilanti); first state teachers' (normal school) college west of New York.

Jefferson Ave. paved with cobblestones between Third and Brush streets.

Detroit and Pontiac plank road opens. Nearly every main road to Detroit is a toll road.

New county jail occupied at Clinton and Beaubien.

City of Detroit Gaslight Co. organized.

J. E. Martin establishes first photographic studio in Detroit.

Biddle House completed at Jefferson and Randolph; for next 2 decades considered city's leading hotel; visited by President Andrew Johnson, Gen. Ulysses S. Grant, Admiral David Glasgow Farragut, other luminaries.

World History

March 5. Zachary Taylor inaugurated; 12th U.S. president.

U.S. Department of Interior established.

July. Harriet Tubman escapes slavery; becomes leading abolitionist, goes on to help more than 300 slaves to freedom via the Underground Railroad.

Cultural Progress

New Hampshire enacts law calling for first state library in U.S.

David Copperfield by Charles Dickens published as 20-part serial.

Amelia Jenks Bloomer, publisher of feminist paper *Lily,* popularizes Turkish pantaloons (full trousers), soon called bloomers. Reforms American women's dress.

Scientific and Commercial Progress

California Gold Rush; San Francisco flourishes as trade center for miners ("forty-niners").

King Cotton: U.S. cotton exports reach $66 million a year; about 40% of total exports.

American engineer Charles Ellet completes 1,010-foot wire-cable suspension bridge for Baltimore & Ohio Railroad; spanning Ohio River at Wheeling (West) Virginia, longest built so far.

French physicist Armand Fizeau measures velocity of light.

Elizabeth Blackwell graduates from Geneva Medical School of Western New York, becoming first woman to receive a medical degree. Sets up private dispensary (1853) in New York.

Mormons in Utah divert mountain streams; first American irrigation system since European settlement.

First stagecoach travels Santa Fe Trail.

1850

Detroit and Michigan

Detroit's population, 21,019; ranks 21st in size among U.S. cities.

Michigan's population, 397,654.

John S. Barry, Democrat, governor (to 1851).

John Ladue, mayor of Detroit.

One in every seven foreign-born Detroit residents is Irish.

After 2 decades of record-setting German immigration, Detroit's lower east side, north of Jefferson Ave. and along Gratiot Ave., has become known as Germantown. New arrivals settle here, setting up shops or finding work as merchants, brewers, tanners.

Fort Wayne is completed. Massive wall encloses barracks, grounds, munitions storage.

April 2. Police Court established.

June 3–Aug. 15. Michigan's constitution revised at Second Constitutional Convention.

Sept. 22. Temple Beth El, Michigan's first Jewish congregation, is founded; incorporates next year.

Oct. 6. First Unitarian Church founded.

Detroit's First Methodist Episcopal Church is erected at corner of Woodward and State.

Detroit now home to 50 churches, including 2 African American congregations.

Detroit has about 90 streets with most of the population living near river for water supply. A few houses are located as far north as Grand Circus Park, and beyond are farms. Tallow candles or lamps (burning lard or whale oil) light homes; bell rings at 6 a.m., 12 noon, 6 p.m., 9 p.m. daily (to give citizens the time).

Popular residential streets include Woodbridge, Jefferson, Congress, Larned, Fort. Main plank roads leading out of Detroit are: Detroit and Saline (Michigan Ave.); Detroit and Howell (Grand River); Detroit and Pontiac (Woodward); and Detroit and Erin (Gratiot). Taverns are located along routes.

Jefferson Ave. is Detroit's principal retail district.

Detroit attorney George Lothrop builds Grosse Pointe cottage; among first to build summer residence along Lake St. Clair. Other well-to-do Detroiters soon follow.

University of Michigan Medical School founded.

First union school, the Barstow, opens in Detroit.

Detroit Musical Association founded.

Regular steamship service begins between Detroit and Cleveland.

Stagecoach routes connect Detroit and Chicago.

German immigrant Bernhard Stroh establishes Detroit brewery.

Traub Brothers jewelry firm established as Duncan and Traub.

World History

World population reaches 1 billion.

U.S. population is 23,191,876 people. 3.2 million are African American slaves. Almost half U.S. population lives outside original 13 states.

April. Clayton-Bulwer Treaty signed by Britain, U.S. Checks British expansion in Central America; prevents Americans from building, controlling canal in region.

U.S. factory labor increasingly supplied by immigrants.

July 9. President John Taylor dies; succeeded by Vice President Millard Fillmore (Whig), 13th U.S. president.

Sept. Compromise of 1850 sponsored by Henry Clay; legislation passed by Congress provides for admission of California as free state, popular sovereignty to decide free or slave status of New Mexico and Utah, prohibition of slave trade in Washington, D.C.

Sept. As part of Compromise of 1850, Congress passes (2nd) fugitive slave law: strengthens earlier law; denies escaped slaves trial by jury, right to testify.

Sept. 9. California admitted to Union.

Cultural Progress

Nathaniel Hawthorne publishes *The Scarlet Letter*.

Elizabeth Barrett Browning's *Sonnets from the Portuguese* published.

Whist and faro are popular gambling games.

Soprano Jenny Lind, the Swedish nightingale, tours America.

Scientific and Commercial Progress

Leon Foucault successfully measures the speed of light.

German chemist Robert Bunsen invents gas burner.

United States Botanical Garden (Washington, D.C.) established.

Congress makes first federal land grants for development of U.S. railroads.

Mississippi River trade pushes New Orleans to surpass New York City in shipping volume; New Orleans's exports account for more than half U.S. total.

Henry Wells founds American Express Co.

1851

Detroit and Michigan

Robert McClelland, Democrat, governor (to 1853).

Zachariah Chandler, mayor of Detroit.

Lt. Ulysses S. Grant is commanding officer of military barracks in Detroit.

April 15. Michigan Central Depot in Detroit is destroyed by fire. Thirty-three men, landowners who oppose practices of the privately operated railroad, are arrested and charged with arson. Trial takes place over summer months; leader Abel Fitch dies in jail.

UM graduates its first doctors; 6 students complete the course of study.

June 5. St. Vincent's Catholic Female Orphan Asylum is opened by Sisters of Charity.

Sept. 24. Detroit Gaslight Co. begins operations, lighting streets with coal gas.

Firemen's Hall erected on site of old Council House (Jefferson and Randolph). Fire Dept. Society holds gala balls, concerts, lectures.

World History

Maine and Illinois begin to enforce prohibition against liquor.

Cuba declares its independence.

Dec. Coup d'etat in France: Louis-Napoleon (Napoleon III) emperor-dictator (to 1871).

Taipei Revolution in China.

Cultural Progress

Herman Melville's *Moby Dick* published; considered great American novel.

YMCA movement reaches U.S., Canada: missionary and retired sea captain Thomas Sullivan founds Boston YMCA, first in nation; YMCA also founded in Montreal this year.

Schooner *America* wins race around Isle of Wight; brings America's Cup to U.S.

Scientific and Commercial Progress

Britain's Prince Albert sponsors forward-looking Great Exhibition at London's Crystal Palace (May–Oct.); first international exposition (world's fair).

William Thompson, later Lord Kelvin, begins formulating laws of thermodynamics.

New York and Mississippi Valley Printing Telegraph Co. organized; origin of Western Union Telegraph Co.

Jordan Marsh department store opens in Boston.

Singer develops first practical sewing machine.

U.S. wheat flour consumption reaches 205 pounds per capita; 20% increase in 20 years.

William Kelly develops new method of making steel from iron.

First ice cream factory is established, in Baltimore.

Gold discovered in Australia; population almost triples over next decade.

1852

Detroit and Michigan

John H. Harmon, mayor of Detroit (to 1853).

May 21. Michigan Central Railroad reaches Chicago; 285 miles of track between Detroit and Chicago.

May 22. Michigan Southern reaches Chicago; 243 miles of track between Toledo and Chicago.

First Michigan woman earns Bachelor of Arts degree: Livonia Benedict is graduated from Hillsdale College, Lenawee County.

Art exhibition held at Firemen's Hall.

Young Men's Christian Association (YMCA) organized in Detroit.

World History

Nov. Franklin Pierce, Democrat, elected president.

Ohio is first state to pass labor law; regulates hours for working women.

Beginning of Second Empire (under Louis-Napoleon) in France. Governs to 1870.

Cultural Progress

Harriet Beecher Stowe publishes *Uncle Tom's Cabin*; popular novel helps gain widespread public support for abolition.

Massachusetts is first state to pass compulsory school attendance law.

Roget's *Thesaurus* is first issued in England.

Scientific and Commercial Progress

Wells, Fargo & Co. founded.

First practical fire engine invented by Alexander Latta; built in Cincinnati.

First horse-drawn streetcars (called horsecars), in New York City.

In response to steamboat boiler explosions that have claimed more than 700 lives in past year, Congress passes (2nd) Steamboat Act to improve safety of nation's waterways.

National Road is completed: originates in Cumberland, Maryland; reaches Vandalia, Illinois.

Sept. First power-driven airship, built by French engineer Henri Giffard, is flown 17 miles from Paris to Trappes, France.

1853

Detroit and Michigan

Andrew Parsons, Democrat, governor (to 1854).

Detroit Board of Water Commissioners established to manage the water supply.

April 3. *Daily Free Democrat* is first issued.

Free Press begins publishing Sunday edition, among nation's first papers to do so.

Oct. 13. Reformer Amelia Bloomer visits Detroit, lectures on women's rights.

Michigan State Normal College (founded 1849) opens at Ypsilanti; oldest teacher training school west of the Alleghenies.

Congregational Unitarian Church erected at Lafayette and Shelby; structure is culmination of Greek Revival church architecture in Detroit.

German immigrant Traugott Schmidt establishes furrier/tannery on Monroe St. in Detroit's Germantown.

George B. Russel organizes Detroit Car and Manufacturing Co. to produce railroad cars.

Wyandotte Rolling Mills, later Eureka Iron and Steel Co., established by E. B. Ward and associates.

John J. Bagley opens tobacco business; manufactures chewing tobacco called Mayflower.

World History

March 4. Franklin Pierce inaugurated; 14th U.S. president.

Gadsden Purchase: U.S. acquires southern Arizona from Mexico; U.S. now owns all territory of contiguous (48) states.

July 8. U.S. Commodore Matthew Perry arrives in Japan to negotiate trade treaty.

Antoinette Louisa Brown is ordained; first woman minister in U.S.

Crimean War (to 1856): Russia fights allied forces of Britain, France, Ottoman Empire, Sardinia over control of strategic Black Sea region.

Cultural Progress

German composer Richard Wagner completes text of *Der Ring des Nibelungen* (The Ring Cycle).

World's largest tree, *Wellingtonia gigantea,* discovered in California.

New York Central Railroad is organized.

Henry Steinway and sons begin New York piano manufacturing firm.

American inventor Samuel Colt opens armory at Hartford, Connecticut; revolutionizes manufacture of small arms.

Bavarian immigrant Levi Strauss begins making, selling sturdy clothing to San Francisco area miners.

Queen Victoria allows chloroform to be administered to her during birth of her 7th child; promotes use of chloroform as an anesthetic.

Vaccination against smallpox compulsory in Britain.

1854

Detroit and Michigan

Oliver M. Hyde, mayor of Detroit.

Jan. 17. Celebration is held in Detroit for completion of Canadian Great Western Railway's Buffalo-to-Windsor line, linking Detroit by railroad to the East. Ferries carry freight and passengers across river.

June–Aug. Fourth cholera epidemic strikes Detroit.

July 6. Organizational meeting held in Jackson for what becomes national Republican party. Preliminary conference held by anti-slavery leaders in Detroit who call for Convention of Free-Soilers. Jacob M. Howard and Zachariah Chandler are among leaders.

Over next 11 years intense opposition to railroads results in arson destruction of various Detroit railroad buildings.

Shipping magnate Oliver Newberry constructs 5-story warehouse in Detroit; for a time, it is the largest and tallest structure west of Buffalo.

World History

More than 1.3 million Irish have immigrated to U.S. since 1846 (due to famine in Ireland).

Republican party is founded by opponents of extension of slavery into new territories; absorbs Free Soil party, Whigs, Know-Nothings. During 1880s becomes known as Grand Old Party (GOP).

Kansas-Nebraska Act: Kansas and Nebraska apply for statehood; Congress officially repeals Missouri Compromise (1820); leaves slavery question in new states to popular sovereignty. Nebraskans vote for freedom; Kansas becomes staging ground (to 1858) between pro-slave forces and abolitionists.

Susan B. Anthony crusades for women's rights in U.S. and abroad.

Britain and France ally with Turkey, declare war on Russia; Allies land unopposed in Crimea and begin siege of Sebastopol.

Japanese agree to trade treaty negotiated last year by U.S. Commodore Perry.

Cultural Progress

Henry David Thoreau writes *Walden, or Life in the Woods.*

Scientific and Commercial Progress

Ferdinand de Lesseps is awarded contract to build Suez Canal.

Florence Nightingale organizes relief work, nurses wounded after Battle of Inkerman, part of Crimean War.

Canadian geologist Abraham Gesner develops process for distilling fuel from petroleum; kerosene illumination widespread by 1860s.

1855

Detroit and Michigan

Kinsley S. Bingham, Republican, governor (to 1858).

Henry Ledyard, mayor of Detroit.

Influx of Italian immigrants to Michigan begins; many settle on Detroit's east side.

Detroit Light Guard is established as a militia unit.

Nation's first land grant college, Michigan Agricultural College (later Michigan State University), is founded in East Lansing. Becomes model for land grant colleges.

Michigan Female College is founded at Lansing; first Michigan college for women.

Feb. 13. Michigan Southern R.R. receives state approval to consolidate with the Northern Indiana R.R., forming the Michigan Southern & Northern Indiana line; incorporated on April 25.

Sault (Soo) Canal is completed and opens to traffic; facilitates shipment of iron and copper ores from Upper Peninsula, prompting increase in Michigan's mining production.

John F. Nichols is appointed first superintendent of Detroit schools. Known as a strict disciplinarian.

Fort Street Presbyterian Church, Gothic structure modeled on King's College Chapel (Cambridge, England), is built on corner of Third St.

World History

Castle Garden, New York, becomes principal immigration center.

First Amana colony settled in Iowa.

Temperance movement has results in liquor bans in 31 states; but no national policy.

Czar Nicholas I of Russia dies; succeeded (to 1881) by Alexander II.

Russians surrender Sebastopol; Allies occupy.

Cultural Progress

"Poet of democracy" Walt Whitman self-publishes collection *Leaves of Grass*; regarded as first truly American verse.

Henry Wadsworth Longfellow writes *Hiawatha*; most famous literary work set in Michigan.

Frank Leslie's Illustrated Newspaper first published.

Scientific and Commercial Progress

First iron Cunard steamer crosses Atlantic Ocean in 9.5 days.

English inventor David E. Hughes patents printing telegraph.

Henry Bessemer patents process to remove impurities from molten iron to produce (Bessemer) steel.

Florence Nightingale introduces hygienic standards to military hospitals.

Paris International Exposition opens; displays technical and economic progress.

1856

Detroit and Michigan

Oliver M. Hyde, mayor of Detroit (to 1857).

Aug. 27. Abraham Lincoln speaks at political rally in Kalamazoo.

Federal Act grants 3.8 million acres of public land in Michigan to railroads for further development. State of Michigan adds nearly 1.7 million acres to the grant.

Detroit buys site for new City Hall for $18,816.

Railway connection between Detroit and Toledo is completed.

Detroit Board of Trade is organized.

Frederick Stearns begins to manufacture drug specialties as a sideline to his retail drug store; beginning of Detroit's great pharmaceutical company.

Daniel Scotten starts tobacco business with George Lovett; manufactures Hiawatha chewing tobacco.

Factory built by D. M. Richardson begins to manufacture matches.

World History

May 24. Bleeding Kansas: Abolitionist John Brown leads massacre of 5 pro-slavery men, retribution for earlier killings of freemen at Lawrence, Kansas.

Nov. James Buchanan, Democrat, elected president.

Treaty of Paris ends Crimean War (begun 1853); requires Russia to surrender Ottoman lands, abolishes Russian navy/military presence in Black Sea region.

Second Opium War (to 1858).

Cultural Progress

Aug. 30. Ashmum Institute (chartered 1854) opens in Oxford, Pennsylvania; origin of Lincoln University, oldest historically black college in nation.

Landscape architect Frederick Law Olmsted designs New York's Central Park.

Scientific and Commercial Progress

Neanderthal Man is discovered near Düsseldorf, Germany; workers find what appears to be human skull, skeletal remains.

1857

Detroit and Michigan

Feb. 5. New city charter created; official name is City of Detroit. Recorder's Court is established and mayor becomes salaried position.

May 13. Michigan Agricultural College (Michigan State University) opens in East Lansing.

July 16. First telegraph cable is laid across Detroit River.

July 22. J. C. Kershaw leaves Detroit, sails for Liverpool, England.

Nov. 30. Marine Hospital (Jefferson and Mount Elliott) opens.

New water reservoir on Dequindre St. is used; capacity, 9 million gallons.

First railroad in Upper Peninsula begins operation from Marquette to Ishpeming.

David Whitney arrives in Detroit from Massachusetts; over next several years he operates wholesale lumber and industrial interests to become one of Midwest's most influential businessmen.

Jacob Beller opens concert hall on the site of present county building.

World History

March 4. James Buchanan inaugurated, 15th U.S. president.

March 6. U.S. Supreme Court rules in Dred Scott case; effectively ends Missouri Compromise, deepens North-South political divide over slavery.

Hinton Helper's *Impending Crisis* published; attacks slavery. Banned in some southern states.

Financial and economic panic in Europe; caused by speculation in U.S. railroads.

Giuseppi Garibaldi forms Italian National Association for unification of country.

Czar Alexander II begins emancipation of Russian serfs.

Cultural Progress

Cooper Union opens in New York; offers free day and evening classes to men and women.

J. S. Pierpont writes popular song "Jingle Bells" or "The One-Horse Open Sleigh."

Atlantic Monthly founded; edited by noted American poet James Russell Lowell.

French novelist Gustave Flaubert publishes *Madame Bovary.*

National Association of Baseball Players; first governing body of baseball.

Scientific and Commercial Progress

Louis Pasteur proves fermentation is caused by living organisms.

American civil engineer Elisha Otis installs first safety elevator.

Comstock Lode, rich deposit of silver, discovered at Mount Davidson, western Nevada.

First overland stagecoach line begins operation to California.

Borden Co. founded; American inventor Gail Borden has developed method for condensing, preserving milk in a can.

1858

Detroit and Michigan

John Patton, mayor of Detroit (to 1859).

First session of high school is held in upper story Broadway St. building; 23 boys are enrolled.

Detroit & Milwaukee Railroad reaches Grand Haven on Lake Michigan.

Berry Brothers open their first varnish factory.

World History

Lincoln-Douglas debates.

May 11. Minnesota admitted to Union.

Young Women's Christian Association (YWCA) founded in New York City to promote welfare of women and girls through spiritual, social, intellectual, physical development. (World organization established 1894.)

Ottawa is made the capital of Canada.

War of Reform in Mexico (to 1861); federalist government collapses, civil war ensues.

British proclaim peace in India.

Treaty of Teintsin ends Second Opium War.

Cultural Progress

New York Symphony Orchestra gives its first public concert.

American artist Albert Bierstadt joins expedition to survey wagon road to Pacific; inspires him to capture western landscape in series of popular paintings.

Scientific and Commercial Progress

Anatomy of the Human Body, Descriptive and Surgical by English physician Henry Gray is first published; later commonly known as *Gray's Anatomy.*

American inventor John Landis Mason develops glass jar and lid suited to home canning.

R. H. Macy's founded in New York City; becomes known for creative advertising.

Suez Canal Co. is formed.

1859

Detroit and Michigan

Moses Wisner, Republican, governor (to 1860).

Jan. 25. Centennial celebration for Robert Burns is held in Detroit.

March 12. Abolitionist John Brown arrives in Detroit with 14 slaves to smuggle across the river; Frederick Douglass delivers lecture that same night.

April 12. First national championship billiards match is held in Detroit. Michael Phelan defeats John Seereiter.

Committee in Michigan's House of Representatives considers granting voting rights to black males.

Walter Harper and Nancy Martin announce gift of his estate for establishment of Detroit hospital to care for the sick and poor.

Dr. Herman Keifer becomes one of Detroit's city physicians.

Michigan's first public asylum for mentally impaired is founded by Sisters of Charity.

State and plank roads crisscross Michigan.

Railroad from Detroit to Port Huron completed, in connection with Grand Trunk Railway.

Thomas Edison, 12-year-old from Port Huron, gets job as newsboy on train route to Detroit. During layovers downtown, future inventor goes to library where he later claims he read not a few books, but the entire collection.

Merrill Block, northeast corner of Woodward and Jefferson, is completed as a retail and office center.

World History

Feb. 14. Oregon admitted to Union.

Oct. 16. Abolitionist John Brown leads raid on armory at Harpers Ferry, Virginia (now part of West Virginia); attempt to emancipate slaves by force fails. Tried for treason, Brown is hanged Dec. 2.

Cultural Progress

Charles Dickens publishes *A Tale of Two Cities.*

Richard Wagner writes *Tristan und Isolde*.

Rubaiyat of Omar Khayam is translated by Edward Fitzgerald.

French tightrope walker Charles Blondin crosses Niagara Falls on a tightrope.

Scientific and Commercial Progress

English naturalist Charles Darwin publishes *On the Origin of the Species*; evolutionary theory sets off storm of controversy.

First U.S. zoo founded: Philadelphia Zoological Society. Due to Civil War, does not open until 1874.

Aug. 27. Oil industry begins with Drake's Folly: retired railroad conductor Edwin Drake drills Titusville, Pennsylvania, well and discovers "black gold." By 1900 more than 64 million barrels will be produced annually.

Tailor Ebenezer Butterick invents standardized patterns for shirts, suits, dresses.

George Gilman and George Huntington Hartford found Great Atlantic & Pacific Tea Co. in New York City; origin of A&P. Becomes first true chain store.

Pikes Peak gold rush in Colorado.

1860

Detroit and Michigan

Detroit's population, 45,619; ranks 19th in size among U.S. cities.

Michigan's population, 749,113.

Christian H. Buhl, mayor of Detroit (to 1861).

Jan. 30. Custom House and Post Office open in Detroit, at corner of Griswold and Larned.

July 1. American operatic soprano Adelina Patti gives Detroit recital.

Sept. 4. William Seward gives speech at large Republican gathering and torchlight procession in Detroit.

Oct. 15. Stephen A. Douglas speaks at large Democratic meeting.

Nov. Michigan's 6 electoral votes go to Abraham Lincoln for president.

Detroit contracts for its first steam fire engine.

High school moves into its own building on Gratiot St.; girls are allowed to enroll for first time. 85 pupils.

American reformer Dorothea Dix inspects Wayne County Poor House and Asylum at Eloise; finds conditions deplorable, claims it is worst she has seen.

With her husband, preacher Ellen Gould Harmon White cofounds 7th Day Adventist Church, in Battle Creek, Michigan.

Michigan's first Jewish congregation, Beth El, adopts Reform practices and quickly grows to become one of Midwest's largest temples.

Rail lines link many Michigan cities this decade; most important line is Michigan Central Railroad, running from Detroit, through Ann Arbor, Dexter, and Chelsea, and to St. Joseph River.

Steamer *Dove* carries passengers to and from Grosse Isle during warm months.

Total value of Detroit manufactured products exceeds $5 million for first time.

Detroit's retail operations and other businesses begin to migrate up Woodward from Jefferson Ave. area, which for past 3 decades has been city's principal retail district.

Salt mining industry begins in Saginaw.

Former Gov. Lewis Cass donates land to city; becomes Detroit's Cass Park.

About this time, the Campau family, who own and live on Belle Isle, begin hosting annual fall picnic; considered a fashionable event among Detroit society.

World History

U.S. population, 31,443,321, including about 4,000,000 slaves.

Since 1850, 424,000 British and 914,000 Irish have immigrated to U.S.

Average U.S. workweek, 66 hours.

Slavery divides nation and political party system is in disarray: Southern political leaders threaten to secede from Union if Republican candidate Abraham Lincoln is elected.

Nov. Newly formed Republican party candidate Abraham Lincoln is elected president.

Dec. South Carolina secedes from Union.

Cultural Progress

Skiing becomes a competitive sport.

Scientific and Commercial Progress

Florence Nightingale founds training institution for nurses in London; publishes *Notes on Nursing,* first textbook for nurses.

April 3. Pony Express begins delivery service between St. Joseph, Missouri (western terminus of nation's rail system) and Sacramento. Route covered by riders in about 10 days.

U.S. has 30,000 miles of railroad.

Oliver F. Winchester introduces Henry repeating rifle.

Longhorn cattle, a breed descended from cows and bulls left by early Spanish settlers, exist in great numbers; roam open range of West, especially Texas.

More than 1,000 steamboats service Mississippi River.

First practical internal combustion engine patented by Frenchman Étienne Lenoir.

1861

Detroit and Michigan

Austin Blair, Republican, governor (to 1864).

March 12. First Detroit police commission is created; consists of mayor and 2 others and is authorized to employ policemen.

May 2. In response to President Abraham Lincoln's call for troops, First Michigan Infantry Regiment is mustered into service; departs for Washington May 13 after being presented with the colors in Campus Martius ceremony. Second Michigan Infantry Regiment leaves Detroit June 16.

Union officer Gen. George Custer leads Michigan cavalry; Fort Wayne serves as a training center for Union soldiers.

July 6. House of Corrections completed in Detroit.

Aug. First Michigan Infantry suffers heavy losses in Battle of Bull Run.

Sept. 27. Shaarey Zedek Jewish Society is organized; first orthodox Jewish synagogue and second oldest Jewish congregation in Detroit.

Temple Beth El congregation erects temple building on Rivard.

Michigan Supreme Court ruling provides for penal fines to be credited to library fund, allowing Detroit Board of Education to proceed with plans to establish a public library.

Nation's first Ladies Aid Society is organized in Detroit; group aids Civil War soldiers in hospitals, camps, and on the battlefield.

At outbreak of Civil War, Detroit's buildings are a mix of federal, classical, romantic, and Gothic styles. Signs of industry are present but relatively unobtrusive; skyline is punctuated predominately by church spires.

Young Men's Society building is opened on Woodbridge. Hall seats 1,500 people; becomes leading theater for next decade.

World History

Jan. 29. Kansas admitted to Union.

Feb. Mississippi, Florida, Alabama, Georgia, Louisiana join South Carolina in seceding from Union. In Feb., the 6 states hold Congress of Montgomery to set up Confederate States of America; Jefferson Davis, president. Joined by Texas (March); Virginia, Arkansas, North Carolina, Tennessee (April).

March 4. Abraham Lincoln inaugurated, 16th U.S. president.

April 12. Confederate troops fire on Fort Sumter, U.S. military post in Charleston, South Carolina. Begins U.S. Civil War (to 1865).

May. Residents of western Virginia vote against ordinance of secession; government loyal to Union organizes at Wheeling (June). Population votes to create new state.

Dec. Banks suspend specie payments (payments in gold or silver coins for paper currency).

Morrill Tariff Act raises duties.

Italian unification movement results in most of Italy being unified this year; nationalist reformer Giuseppe Garibaldi a prominent leader. Struggle continues (to 1870) to annex remaining states—Venetia, Rome.

Prussia's Frederick William IV dies; succeeded by William I.

Russia emancipates serfs.

Cultural Progress

Charles Dickens publishes *Great Expectations*.

New York brewer Matthew Vassar donates large sum of money to found Vassar College, dedicated to providing higher education for women. Generates widespread interest in women's education.

Mrs. Isabella Beeton publishes *Beeton's Book of Household Management*.

British Open Golf Championship held for first time.

Scientific and Commercial Progress

French chemist and microbiologist Louis Pasteur first puts forth germ theory.

Wanamaker's department store founded in Philadelphia; implements fixed pricing.

March. Transcript of President Abraham Lincoln's first address to Congress delivered to Sacramento via Pony Express in record 7 days, 17 hours.

Oct. 24. First transcontinental telegraph line in U.S. is completed; messages can be sent cross-country in matter of minutes.

Oct. 26. Pony Express service ends.

Gold discovered in New Zealand; population doubles over next 6 years.

1862

Detroit and Michigan

William C. Duncan, mayor of Detroit (to 1863).

U.S. Congress's passage of Morrill (Land-Grant) Act provides additional funding for Michigan Agricultural College.

Twenty-fourth Michigan Infantry is recruited chiefly from Detroit and Wayne County and leaves for the front in July.

July 8. *Detroit Daily Advertiser* and the *Detroit Daily Tribune* consolidate.

World History

March 9. First battle between two ironclad ships: Union's *Monitor* confronts Confederacy's *Virginia*; though outcome is indecisive, U.S. Navy soon begins production of fleet.

July 17. Congress allows enlistment of African Americans into Union Army. More than 186,000 blacks serve; 38,000 die in service.

Aug. 29–30. Second Battle of Bull Run: Union troops defeated by Confederates in northeastern Virginia.

Aug.–Sept. Sioux Uprising: in southwestern Minnesota, tribes rebel against harsh policy, treatment by U.S. Hundreds of settlers killed; hundreds of Sioux captured and 38 are publicly hanged (Dec. 26). Reservation lands are broken up; remaining Sioux dispersed. Some observers sympathetic to American Indian plight.

Sept. 17. Battle of Antietam: Union troops force Confederates to withdraw across the Potomac into Virginia.

To finance war effort, Congress sets up Bureau of Internal Revenue to administer first U.S. income tax; workers and businessmen required to pay between 3 and 5% of earnings. Program phased out after Civil War.

Legal Tender Act suspends specie payments; $150 million in national notes (greenbacks) issued.

Congressional Medal of Honor authorized.

Congress passes Homestead Act: settlers can buy cheap land or farm a tract for 5 years to claim ownership of up to 160 acres; promotes westward expansion.

Morrill Act sets aside government land, funds to establish (land grant) colleges; origin of agricultural and mechanical (A&M) universities.

Mexican army defeats French in Battle of Puebla (May 5); French nevertheless seize and occupy Mexico (to 1867).

Otto von Bismarck becomes Prussian prime minister.

France acquires Cochin-China and begins colonization of Indochina. Monaco sells Menton and Roquebrune to France.

Cultural Progress

Wilberforce University (Ohio), founded in 1856 to grant baccalaureate degrees to African American students, becomes nation's first college to be controlled by blacks.

Julia Ward Howe publishes "Battle Hymn of the Republic" in *Atlantic Monthly*.

Actress Sarah Bernhardt debuts in Paris.

Victor Hugo writes *Les Miserables*.

Scientific and Commercial Progress

U.S. Department of Agriculture is established.

Chicago surpasses Cincinnati as nation's meatpacking center.

Union Pacific and Central Pacific Railroads chartered.

International Exposition held in London.

German engineer August Otto invents four-stroke cycle engine; with internal combustion engine (1860), leads to development of liquid fuel engines.

1863

Detroit and Michigan

Jan. 1. Detroit's African American community gathers at Second Baptist Church (Monroe Ave. and Beaubien St.) to celebrate President Abraham Lincoln's Emancipation Proclamation.

Dec. 26. Clinton Street jail is completed.

May 15. Brotherhood of the Footboard (later Brotherhood of Locomotive Engineers) founded in Detroit; first lasting railroad union in nation.

African American Detroit resident William Faulkner is wrongly convicted of rape; innocence later demonstrated but not before rioting occurs, with white citizens burning homes of black people. Troops called out to restore order.

Fannie Richards founds a private school for African American children in Detroit.

Detroit High School graduates its first class including girls.

Aug. 4. Detroit City Railway is incorporated to run horse-drawn streetcars on Jefferson Ave.; typical fare is 5 cents. Streetcars operate on Woodward, Gratiot, and Michigan by the end of the year.

First National Bank opens under new national banking act.

Detroit Bridge and Iron Works is established.

World History

Jan. 1. President Abraham Lincoln issues Emancipation Proclamation, freeing slaves in rebel states.

First wartime conscription bill adopted by Union, provoking anti-draft riots in New York and other cities.

National Bank Act creates national banking system, floats federal war loans, creates $300 million in national currency.

Arizona, Idaho organized as territories.

June 20. West Virginia admitted to Union.

July 1–3. Battle of Gettysburg: Union troops under Gen. George Meade defeat advancing Confederates; victory effectively stops Gen. Robert E. Lee's invasion of North. Turning point in Civil War.

Nov. 19. President Lincoln delivers Gettysburg Address upon dedication of battlefield as national cemetery.

U.S. Congress establishes mail delivery service in cities.

Oct. Red Cross founded in Switzerland.

Cultural Progress

President Abraham Lincoln calls for national observance of Thanksgiving on last Thursday in Nov.

Representatives of English soccer clubs found Football Association.

French painter Édouard Manet exhibits groundbreaking works *Déjeuner sur l'herbe* and *Olympia*; pioneers impressionism.

Scientific and Commercial Progress

National Academy of Sciences founded in Washington, D.C.

Travelers Insurance Co. established in Hartford, Connecticut.

World's first subway begins operation in London; passengers call it the "underground" or "tube."

English geologist Henry Clifton Sorby discovers microstructure of steel; leads to development of science of metallurgy.

Gasoline created as a distillate of oil.

Manufacture of paper from wood pulp (instead of rags) introduced; increases paper supply.

Sod houses begin to dot Great Plains: in absence of lumber, other building materials, homesteaders build homes using bricks of turf.

Work begins on coast-to-coast U.S. railroad: in next 6 years Central Pacific Railroad will lay 689 miles of track eastward from Sacramento; Union Pacific Railroad will lay 1,086 miles of track westward from Omaha.

1864

Detroit and Michigan

K. C. Barker, mayor of Detroit (to 1865).

April 24. Shakespeare tercentenary celebration is held at Young Men's Society Hall.

Sept. 27. First draft is called to fill Detroit's quota for Union Army.

Oct. 12. Harper Hospital opens; Detroit's second hospital, it begins care of soldiers wounded in battle. Named in honor of merchant Walter Harper, who endowed the public health facility, it is in part situated on acreage donated by Nancy Martin, Mr. Harper's housekeeper, who operated a market stall to accumulate a small fortune.

Oct. Free mail delivery by carrier begins in Detroit.

Detroit Trades Assembly organized; coalition of unions soon boasts 5,000 members. Richard Trevellick, leader. Employers respond by forming association to resist movement.

Pere Marquette Railroad enters Detroit.

Detroit businessmen James McMillan and John S. Newberry organize Michigan Car Co. to manufacture railroad freight cars; leads to organization of numerous ironworks.

Jeremiah Dwyer organizes Detroit Stove Works.

Bessemer steel first produced in U.S. at Wyandotte, Michigan, by Eureka Iron and Steel Works; uses Kelly pneumatic process.

World History

May–June. Wilderness Campaign: Gen. Robert E. Lee ravages Union forces in northern Virginia. 60,000 Union dead.

Gen. Sherman begins march through Georgia; reaches coast by Dec.

Confederate agents set fire to Barnum Museum and Astor House; attempt to burn New York City.

Montana organized as a territory.

Cheyenne and Arapahoe Indians are massacred at Sand Creek, Colorado.

Lincoln vetoes Wade-Davis Bill.

Oct. 31. Nevada admitted to Union.

Nov. Abraham Lincoln reelected president.

"In God We Trust" first appears on U.S. coins.

French exert control of Mexico; install Maximilian as emperor.

First International Workingmen's Association organized in London; Karl Marx instrumental in founding.

Geneva Convention sets forth rules of war; establishes neutrality of battlefield medical facilities.

Scientific and Commercial Progress

English surgeon Joseph L. Lister begins working with antiseptics to stave off infection.

Italian archeologist Giovanni de Rossi publishes results of exploration and maps of Rome's catacombs.

U.S. steel manufacturing industry begins using Bessemer process (*see* Detroit and Michigan entry); lowers costs, increases output. Soon accounts for 90% of steel output.

1865

Detroit and Michigan

Henry H. Crapo, Republican, governor (to 1868).

March 25. With a collection of 5,000 books, Detroit Public Library opens in a room in the old Capitol High School (corner of State and Griswold).

April 3 & 10. Detroit citizens celebrate news of the fall of Richmond and the Confederacy's surrender.

During Civil War, 90,747 Michigan men joined the Union Army. Wayne County sent 9,213, of which 6,000 were from Detroit. 14,343 Michigan men died in service.

April 15. Detroiters gather in Campus Martius to mourn death of President Abraham Lincoln.

April 25. Memorial services held in Detroit for President Lincoln.

May 10. Fourth Michigan Cavalry captures Confederate President Jefferson Davis near Irwinville, Georgia.

July 4. Union workers hold first parade in Detroit.

Aug. 12. Gen. Ulysses S. Grant visits Detroit; reception held at Biddle House.

State legislature creates Detroit Metropolitan Police Department. Permanent force is managed by 4-man commission appointed by the governor.

Detroit pharmacist James Vernor returns from Civil War to discover concoction he'd experimented with before he left is "deliciously different"; his ginger ale stored in charred oak barrel soon becomes popular.

Richard H. Fyfe establishes shoe store by purchasing C. C. Tyler's store.

World History

March 4. President Abraham Lincoln inaugurated; 2nd term.

April 9. Confederates under Gen. Robert E. Lee surrender to Union under Gen. Ulysses S. Grant at Appomattox Courthouse, Virginia, ending Civil War.

Ku Klux Klan organized by Confederate Army veterans in Pulaski, Tennessee.

April 12. Ku Klux Klan leader Nathan Bedford Forrest leads massacre of 300 African American Union soldiers at Fort Pillow, Tennessee.

April 14. President Lincoln assassinated by actor John Wilkes Booth. First U.S. president to be assassinated. Vice President Andrew Johnson sworn in as 17th U.S. president.

April. Steamboat *Sultana* explodes on Mississippi River, killing 1,653 of 2,300 people on board, many of them Union soldiers.

Dec. 6. 13th Amendment to U.S. constitution is ratified; outlaws slavery.

Reconstruction, 12-year period of rebuilding, follows Civil War.

Congress approves 10% tax on notes issued by banks, making it unprofitable for banks to print money.

English preacher William Booth organizes Christian Revival Association; origin of Salvation Army (renamed 1878), charitable program for social reform.

Cultural Progress

The Nation is first published as a liberal weekly newspaper (later becomes a magazine).

Lewis Carroll publishes *Alice's Adventures in Wonderland.*

Mary Mapes Dodge writes *Hans Brinker and His Silver Skates.*

English alpinist Edward Whymper is first to climb Switzerland's Matterhorn.

Leo Tolstoy begins writing *War and Peace* (to 1869).

1866

Detroit and Michigan

Merrill I. Mills, mayor of Detroit (to 1867).

Jan. 2. Harper Hospital, opened 1864 as military facility, begins treating civilians.

Feb. 7. Civil War Gen. William Sherman visits Detroit.

June 20. Funeral of former Gov. Lewis Cass is held in Detroit.

Sept. 4. President Andrew Johnson visits Detroit.

Michigan's first bill on woman suffrage defeated by 1 vote.

Detroit Daily Post begins publication; city's first 8-page daily.

Wayne County Medical Society is organized.

Druggist Samuel P. Duffield and Hervey C. Parke form partnership, Duffield, Parke and Co. Manufacturing company opens pharmacy at corner of Cass and Henry streets. George Davis joins company next year; origin of Parke, Davis and Co. (incorporated 1871).

James Vernor and Co. is organized.

Hazen S. Pingree and Charles H. Smith found boot and shoe factory in Detroit, which soon becomes one of nation's largest shoe manufacturing centers.

World History

Feb. James Gang robs its first bank: outlaw Jesse James and band hold up Missouri's Clay County Savings Association for $60,000; begin crime spree in West.

May 5. Waterloo, New York, citizens close shops, fly flags at half-staff, decorate soldiers' graves in honor of Union dead; generally accepted as first observance of Memorial (Decoration) Day.

Congress passes Civil Rights Act, extending citizenship to freed slaves and guaranteeing them equal protection under the law; President Andrew Johnson vetoes, but for first time in American history, Congress musters enough votes to overturn.

Race riots in the South.

Indian Wars: U.S. military wages campaign (to 1891) against American Indian tribes; series of conflicts in West.

National Labor Union organized; Richard Trevellick, president.

Cholera epidemic strikes U.S. for 18th consecutive year; part of worldwide epidemic.

Seven Weeks' War begins between Austria and Prussia; Prussia emerges as strongest German state. Under Prime Minister Otto von Bismarck, Prussia leads campaign for German unification.

Cultural Progress

U.S. reformer Henry Bergh founds American Society for the Prevention of Cruelty to Animals.

English actor Henry Irving has first London success in *Hunted Down*, beginning brilliant international career.

Croquet becomes popular.

Scientific and Commercial Progress

French chemist and microbiologist Louis Pasteur explains that heating is necessary to kill bacteria in certain foods.

Transatlantic cable laid between Newfoundland and Ireland; successfully operated.

Texas rangers Charlie Goodnight and Oliver Loving blaze cattle trail from Belknap, Texas, to Fort Sumner, New Mexico. Route becomes 1 of 4 principal cattle trails in West.

Alfred Nobel invents dynamite.

English engineer Robert Whitehead invents self-propelled underwater torpedo.

1867

Detroit and Michigan

March 26. Detroit Board of Fire Commissioners is created.

July 10. Michigan Mutual Life Insurance Co. organized.

Central Police Station is first occupied on Woodbridge east of Woodward.

Women taxpayers are given right to vote for school trustees but Michigan legislature fails to grant total suffrage to women.

Central Methodist Church is completed at Woodward and Adams.

D. M. Ferry and Co. is founded; seed manufacturer becomes one of Detroit's most prominent businesses.

Canadian Great Western Railway begins running railroad car ferry across Detroit River.

World History

March 1. Nebraska admitted to Union.

Tenure of Office Act.

U.S. purchases Alaska from Russia for $7,200,000.

American agriculturalist Oliver Hudson Kelley founds National Grange of the Patrons of Husbandry to advance political, economic interests of nation's farmers.

New York is first state to adopt legislation addressing poor conditions of tenement housing.

Rebels expel French from Mexico; execute Maximilian. President Benito Juárez resumes full control.

British Parliament passes Second Reform Bill, doubling number of men able to vote in national elections.

British Parliament passes North America Act, establishing Dominion of Canada.

Austria-Hungary dual monarchy created.

Cultural Progress

Ragged Dick series by American clergyman Horatio Alger Jr. first published; with *Luck and Pluck* (1869) and *Tattered Tom* (1871), the basis for rags-to-riches stories (soon called "Horatio Alger stories").

Paris World's Fair introduces Japanese art to the West.

Feb. 15. Johann Strauss's "Blue Danube" waltz first performed, in Vienna.

Karl Marx publishes first volume of *Das Kapital* (Capital); with subsequent volumes (1885, 1894), predicts failure of capitalist system.

Englishman John Graham Chambers devises set of 12 rules for boxing; basis of modern sport.

Baseball is becoming American national pastime.

Scientific and Commercial Progress

In medical journal *Lancet*, English surgeon Joseph L. Lister publishes favorable results of his work with antiseptics.

Joseph Monier patents reinforced concrete; French inventor used iron to strengthen concrete.

Railcar manufacturer George Pullman invents sleeping car.

Abilene, Kansas, is first cow town.

Diamond field discovered near Orange River, South Africa.

1868

Detroit and Michigan

William W. Wheaton, mayor of Detroit (to 1872).

Detroit's wards divided into polling precincts.

Cornerstone laid for new City Hall.

Detroit Medical College is founded at Harper Hospital; forerunner of Wayne State University College of Medicine.

Detroit and Cleveland Navigation Co. is incorporated.

William Davis of Detroit obtains patent for an "icebox on wheels," a refrigerator car he uses to ship fruit and fish by rail; next year, he develops refrigerated car for shipping meat.

Department store Newcomb, Endicott and Co. is founded in Detroit.

World History

Feb. Articles of impeachment are brought against Andrew Johnson over political and ideological differences between president and Congress. Upheld by House of Representatives, fails to pass Senate by 1 vote on May 16.

July. 14th Amendment to U.S. constitution is ratified; defines U.S. citizenship and gives all citizens equal protection under law. Makes former slaves citizens of U.S. and of state where they live; forbids states from denying equal rights to any person.

Nov. Ulysses S. Grant, Republican, elected president.

U.S. and China sign Burlingame Treaty.

Ten Years' War begins: Cuba fights Spain for independence.

Benjamin Disraeli becomes British prime minister but soon resigns; succeeded by William Gladstone (to 1874).

Revolution in Spain; Queen Isabella II flees to France.

Cultural Progress

Johannes Brahms composes *German Requiem.*

Louisa May Alcott writes *Little Women.*

Scientific and Commercial Progress

Skeleton of Cro-Magnon man found in southern France by archeologist Edouard Lartet, founder of paleontology.

James Oliver invents modern steel plow.

Industrialist Philip Armour opens pork packing operation in Chicago; renamed Armour & Co. (1870).

1869

Detroit and Michigan

Henry P. Baldwin, Republican, governor (to 1872).

Feb. 2. Detroit Medical College opens.

March 29. Detroit Opera House opens, across Campus Martius from City Hall.

May 29. Memorial Day is first observed in Detroit with a parade of Civil War veterans, orations, scattering of flowers on graves of war dead.

April 6. Michigan Southern & Northern Indiana Railroad merges into the Lake Shore and Michigan Southern.

June 5. Women's Hospital and Foundlings' Home incorporated.

Nov. 25. Detroit's first symphony concert is given by Theodore Thomas Orchestra at Detroit Opera House.

African American children are first admitted to Detroit public schools.

Providence Hospital founded.

Tobacco products manufacturer John J. Bagley builds home on Washington (and Park Ave.); Italian villa style residence is first Michigan residence to have plate glass windows and is called a "monument of elegance" by the *Free Press.*

World History

March 4. Ulysses S. Grant inaugurated, 18th U.S. president.

Sept. 24. Black Friday: gold prices rise sharply in response to attempts by robber baron Jay Gould to corner market; causes panic. U.S. government responds by selling $4 million of gold reserves, causing prices to tumble. Market crash sets off severe depression.

Joseph H. Rainey, South Carolina, is first African American elected to Congress; serves in U.S. House of Representatives to 1879. Nineteen more black men will be elected to the House before 1900; all from southern states.

Elizabeth Cady Stanton and Susan B. Anthony organize National Woman Suffrage Association; Lucy Stone and Henry Brown Blackwell found American Woman Suffrage Association.

John Stuart Mill publishes *The Subjection of Women*.

Knights of Labor, first national union of note, founded by Philadelphia garment workers.

U.S. National Prohibition party forms in Chicago.

Red River Rebellion in Canada.

Cultural Progress

Russian novelist Fyodor Dostoevsky publishes *The Idiot*.

Cincinnati Red Stockings organized; first professional baseball team, make barnstorm tour around the country, playing nonprofessional club teams.

Nov. 6. First game of American football played, in New Brunswick, New Jersey: Rutgers defeats College of New Jersey (Princeton).

Scientific and Commercial Progress

May 10. At Promontory, Utah, last tracks are laid of first cross-country railroad, making North America the first continent spanned coast to coast by rail. Last spike driven in is connected to telegraph, signaling great event.

American George Westinghouse invents railroad airbrake. (Establishes Westinghouse Electric Co. 1886.)

Suez Canal opens to shipping.

Famous clipper ship *Cutty Sark* is launched.

American businessman P. A. Pillsbury buys small Minneapolis flour mill; Pillsbury & Co. becomes world's largest flour producer.

American Museum of Natural History founded, New York City.

Russian chemist Dmitri Mendeleyev formulates periodic table of elements by atomic weight.

1870

Detroit and Michigan

Detroit's population, 79,577; ranks 18th in size among U.S. cities. Almost half Detroit's population is foreign-born.

Michigan's population, 1,184,059.

Nov. 8. Michigan voters approve removal of the word "white" from state constitution; first African American residents (males) are eligible to vote.

Germans are Detroit's largest ethnic group.

Michigan State Woman Suffrage Association is formed; Michigan legislature passes woman suffrage amendment but the governor vetoes the bill.

University of Michigan becomes first state university to admit women; Madelon Louisa Stockwell is first woman to officially enroll, graduating 2 years later. UM also becomes first U.S. university to open medical school to women students. Amanda Sanford is the first female graduate.

Lucy M. Arnold becomes first woman physician in Detroit.

Fire alarm system is installed in Detroit.

Poem "Curfew Must Not Ring Tonight," written by American Rose Thorpe, age 16, is published in Detroit; becomes internationally famous—recited by schoolchildren at home and abroad.

New steam vessels shorten Atlantic crossing to 9 days; the well-to-do, including prosperous Detroiters, travel to Europe. Experiences of these leading citizens begin to influence Detroit's cultural life and architecture.

Department store Mabley and Co. is founded in Detroit.

Detroit industries respond to wealth of ores being mined in Upper Peninsula; large-scale manufacturing keeps pace with production of raw materials.

Campus Martius area begins to shift from residential to business use.

R. L. Polk and Co. incorporated.

World History

U.S. population, 39,818,449; 20% of Americans are illiterate.

Congress sets up new Department of Justice under attorney general.

Fifteenth Amendment to U.S. Constitution is ratified; right of U.S. citizens to vote cannot be denied or abridged on account of race, color, or previous condition of servitude. Extends suffrage to African American men.

Farmers' Alliance movement is under way; organizations form to counter effects of agricultural crisis; alliances run cooperatives, collectively market crops, support political candidates.

Hiram Rhoades Revels (Mississippi) is first African American elected to U.S. Senate.

Union is fully restored when last southern states (Georgia, Mississippi, Texas, Virginia) comply with requirements for statehood.

Harper's Weekly, New York Times expose corruption of New York City's Tweed Ring, group of politicians headed by former New York Senator William Marcy "Boss" Tweed (convicted, 1873).

Canada's Red River Rebellion ends; Manitoba becomes a province.

Franco-Prussian War is fought (to 1871); German states lay siege to Paris.

Second Empire overthrown in bloodless French revolution precipitated by Franco-Prussian War. Third Republic established.

Unification of Italy completed when Rome is annexed.

Cultural Progress

Former Detroit newspaper writer Bronson Howard has first success with the play *Saratoga*. Virtually creates new theater genre—dramas about American life; inspires other playwrights.

New York's Metropolitan Museum of Art opens.

McCall's magazine first published.

Jules Verne writes *Twenty Thousand Leagues Under the Sea*.

Scientific and Commercial Progress

U.S. has 49,168 miles of railroad.

U.S. Weather Service authorized by Congress.

B. F. Goodrich begins rubber manufacturing operation in Akron, Ohio.

John D. Rockefeller founds Standard Oil.

U.S. canning industry has increased annual output from 5 million cans a decade ago to 30 million cans.

English inventor James Starley devises bicycle (Ariel) with large front wheel, small rear wheel. Popularly called penny-farthing, high-wheeler, or the ordinary.

Longhorn cattle industry thriving.

German archeologists Heinrich and Sophia Schliemann begin to excavate Troy.

Swedish geologist Nils Adolf Nordenskjold explores interior of Greenland.

1871

Detroit and Michigan

June. Gov. Henry Baldwin appoints State Board of Building Commissioners to determine design for a much needed new capitol building in Lansing.

July 4. Detroit's new City Hall is dedicated at Campus Martius. At base of its cupola are sandstone sculptures of civic virtues Justice, Art, Industry, and Commerce, carved by noted local artist Julius Melchers.

Nannette B. Gardner of Detroit votes in city and state elections.

Michigan's first compulsory school attendance law is passed: all children ages 8 to 14 are required to attend school at least 12 weeks a year.

Fannie Richards, first African American teacher in Detroit's integrated school system, establishes Michigan's first public school kindergarten (at Everett School).

Sarah Killgore Wertman is the first woman to graduate from University of Michigan Law School and becomes the first woman to practice law in Michigan.

At citizens' meeting, Detroiters raise $25,000 to help victims of Chicago fire.

Chicago fire affects building practices in Detroit; more brick is used.

Detroit Car and Manufacturing Co. is purchased by George Pullman; Detroit becomes center for Pullman car manufacture until he builds plant near Chicago.

Mutual Gaslight Co. established on Detroit's east side.

Michigan Stove Co. is founded in Detroit.

Detroit and Windsor manufacturers, including distillery owner Hiram Walker, found Globe Tobacco Co. to produce tobacco products, including cigars.

Fires in Holland and Manistee cause great damage to cities; forest fires destroy timber from Lake Michigan to Lake Huron.

World History

Oct. 8–9. Chicago Fire; 3.5 square miles of city destroyed, 250 deaths.

U.S. Congress passes Force Bill, giving President Ulysses S. Grant authority to direct federal troops against Ku Klux Klan.

U.S., Britain sign Treaty of Washington; settles American Civil War–related disputes between countries, legitimizes U.S. claim to Washington's San Juan Islands, resolves coastal fishing rights.

British Columbia joins Dominion of Canada.

Prussia victorious over France in Treaty of Frankfurt, ending Franco-Prussian War.

Jan. 18. German empire is announced; created through unification of several smaller states. Prussian King William I is proclaimed emperor of Germany (reigns to 1888).

March 1. French National Assembly deposes Louis-Napoleon.

151

English mountaineer Lucy Walker becomes first woman to successfully climb Switzerland's Matterhorn.

Cultural Progress

P. T. Barnum opens his *The Greatest Show on Earth* in Brooklyn, New York.

Scientific and Commercial Progress

American engineer Andrew Smith Hallidie invents cable car: street railway system runs on underground moving ropes.

White Star Line launches S.S. *Oceanic,* first modern luxury liner.

Norwegian physician Gerhard A. Hansen discovers leprosy bacillus.

1872

Detroit and Michigan

Hugh Moffat, mayor of Detroit (to 1876).

April 9. Soldiers and Sailors Monument, Civil War memorial designed by Randolph Rogers, is unveiled in Campus Martius, opposite City Hall.

Michigan's Board of Building Commissioners unanimously selects plans prepared by Illinois architect Elijah Myers: his were among some 20 proposals for the new capitol, which is completed under budget—a point much celebrated in the press.

Circulation at Detroit Public Library exceeds 100,000 volumes annually. Plans are made to construct a dedicated facility for the library (founded in 1865 in a schoolroom).

Moffat Building is finished; features Detroit's first passenger elevator.

Jewelry firm of Roehm and Wright is established. In 1886, John Kay becomes Henry Wright's partner in firm Wright, Kay and Co.

Detroit Boat Club builds clubhouse on Detroit River, in front of Parke, Davis headquarters.

World History

U.S. General Amnesty Act pardons most ex-Confederates.

Nov. 5. Susan B. Anthony and 14 other women vote in Rochester, New York, national elections. Three weeks later, all are arrested for violating federal laws regarding voting. Anthony is tried (June 1873), found guilty, and fined.

Nov. Ulysses S. Grant reelected president.

Credit Mobilier of America scandal uncovered: financial wrongdoings of Union Pacific Railroad shareholders prompt congressional investigation.

Civil war in Spain: Carlists are defeated; Don Carlos flees to France.

Compulsory military service is introduced in Japan.

Cultural Progress

Yellowstone National Park established.

American painter James McNeill Whistler exhibits *Portrait of the Artist's Mother.*

American writer/reformer Julia Ward Howe suggests celebration of Mother's Day in U.S.

Jules Verne publishes *Around the World in Eighty Days.*

French artist Claude Monet paints *Impression, Fog (La Havre)*; becomes source of art movement's name, impressionism.

Scientific and Commercial Progress

Popular Science Monthly founded.

Mail-order business pioneered by retailer Montgomery Ward & Co., founded in Chicago; sends catalog of bargains to farmers.

Northern Pacific Railroad reaches Fargo, North Dakota.

British engineer Willoughby Smith conceives of "visual telegraphy" (television).

1873

Detroit and Michigan

John J. Bagley, Republican, governor (to 1876).

Board of Public Works established in Detroit.

Board of Estimates is created to replace citizens' meetings in matters of Detroit city expenditures.

Superior Court is established for civil actions.

Michigan State Board of Health established.

Cornerstone is laid for Michigan's new Capitol Building in Lansing. Five railroads, constructed over last 10 years, now service state capital.

July 31. Detroit & Bay City Railroad is completed to Bay City.

Aug. 23. *Detroit Evening News* is first issued; founded by James E. Scripps.

Frances Newberry Bagley founds Detroit Woman's Club for cultural studies; first of its kind in the city.

Depression of 1873 sets back labor movement; ends Detroit Trades Assembly.

Detroit's stagecoach lines cease operations. (City now serviced by rail.)

Commercial lumbering is Michigan's 2nd largest industry (behind agriculture).

Keweenaw Peninsula's Portage Lake canals completed.

St. Aloysius Roman Catholic Church acquires the Presbyterian church and rectory on Washington Boulevard.

World History

March 4. President Ulysses S. Grant inaugurated; 2nd term.

Sept. 18. Panic of 1873: stock prices fall on news of investment banking firm Jay Cooke & Co.'s failure; begins depression that lasts through most of decade and stems tide of European immigration. Silver demonetized.

Spain captures the *Virginius* off Jamaica; war between U.S., Spain narrowly averted.

Prince Edward Island joins Dominion of Canada.

Spain is proclaimed a republic.

Germans evacuate France.

Cultural Progress

English sportsman Maj. Walter Wingfield publishes rule book for lawn tennis.

Scientific and Commercial Progress

Andrew Carnegie founds nation's first large-scale steel plant (Braddock, Pennsylvania).

Big Bonanza, super-rich silver vein, tapped in western Nevada.

1874

Detroit and Michigan

April 16. Detroit Scientific Association is organized.

June 2. American Medical Association holds 25th meeting in Detroit.

Michigan voters reject proposed amendment to state constitution that would give women the vote; ballot measure is defeated 135,957 to 40,077; Michigan State Woman Suffrage Association disbands.

Detroit chapter of the Woman's Christian Temperance Union is founded; WCTU is largest women's organization in U.S.

"Kalamazoo decision" by Justice Thomas M. Cooley upholds right of school boards to use taxes collected in support of primary schools for high schools.

Michigan State School for underprivileged children opened at Coldwater; first of its kind in the world.

Webster School built, 21st St. near Howard.

Detroit Conservatory of Music established.

World History

Greenback party founded; members (mostly farmers) advocate government issue of paper money to alleviate economic constraints.

Free Silver movement begins; advocates U.S. government's unlimited coinage of silver to put more money into circulation, allow payments of debts.

Woman's Christian Temperance Union (WCTU) founded.

Belva Ann Lockwood is first woman admitted to practice before U.S. Supreme Court.

Chautauqua movement founded by Methodist pastor John H. Vincent and Lewis Miller, who set up Sunday school teachers' assembly at Lake Chautauqua, New York.

Beginning of decade-long drought in American West.

Benjamin Disraeli again British prime minister.

Cultural Progress

German composer Richard Wagner completes the *Ring* cycle (begun 1848).

Society for the Prevention of Cruelty to Children founded in New York.

English sportsman Maj. Walter Wingfield patents lawn tennis equipment.

American sportswoman Mary Ewing Outerbridge observes British officers playing tennis in Bermuda; soon introduces game in U.S., establishing first tennis court at Staten Island Cricket and Baseball Club, New York.

Scientific and Commercial Progress

Barbed wire is commercially developed by American inventor Joseph Glidden; soon used by Great Plains farmers to construct fences.

Cable cars installed in San Francisco; success prompts other cities to implement the system.

Sophia Jex-Blake founds London School of Medicine for Women.

Norwegian physician Gerhard Henrik Hansen discovers leprosy bacterium.

1875

Detroit and Michigan

Jan. 2. Capt. Eber Brock Ward dies in Detroit; shipowner and steel magnate was Michigan's wealthiest man and Detroit's first millionaire.

May 29. Cornerstone is laid for Centre Park Library.

Aug. 11. American Association for the Advancement of Science meets in Detroit.

Sept. 13. Whitney Opera House opens (at corner of Fort and Shelby) in Detroit.

Statewide Woman's Christian Temperance Union is formed (at Grand Rapids).

New high school building is erected in front of old Capitol Building.

Evening schools are first maintained for children unable to attend during the day.

Fred Sanders establishes confectionery store at corner of Michigan and Woodward; among first in U.S. to serve ice cream sodas.

Grosse Pointe's heyday as popular summer resort: sandy shores of Lake St. Clair are lined with cottages (some on a large scale), boathouses, docks.

World History

March 1. Congress passes Civil Rights Act of 1875; protects all citizens from discrimination in places of public accommodation. (Later struck down by U.S. Supreme Court.)

Blanche Kelso Bruce (Mississippi) is first African American to serve full term in U.S. Senate.

Whiskey Ring scandal exposed: distillers have bribed public officials and retained tax proceeds. Eventually $3 million in taxes recovered; 10 men convicted.

Molly Maguires, Irish-American coal miners in eastern Pennsylvania, incite strike, which is soon broken by company detectives. The following year, Molly Maguires are tried and convicted for murders of 9 Philadelphia and Reading Coal and Iron Co. foremen.

National Grange movement peaks; 21,000 regional organizations boast total membership of 860,000.

Christian Science Church founded by Mary Baker Eddy.

Great Britain gains control of Egypt's Suez Canal.

Cultural Progress

Leo Tolstoy begins writing *Anna Karenina*.

First Kentucky Derby is run; Aristides wins.

Aug. 24–25. Matthew Webb is first to swim English Channel, from Dover to Calais; takes 21 hours, 45 minutes.

Scientific and Commercial Progress

June 3. First voice communication transmitted over telephone: Alexander Graham Bell calls to assistant, "Watson, come here. I want you." (Telephone patented 1876.)

Western Pennsylvania pipeline is built to carry oil to Pittsburgh.

American horticulturalist Luther Burbank moves to California; begins breeding new varieties of plants.

Rotary perfecting press is developed: prints on both sides of paper sheet, delivers cut-and-folded newspaper.

Boston printer Louis Prang begins making engraved Christmas cards for export to England, where custom of sending greeting cards is already established.

1876

Detroit and Michigan

Alexander Lewis, mayor of Detroit (to 1877).

July 4. Centennial of nation's independence celebrated in Detroit with procession, street decorations, boat races, illuminations.

Fire devastates Fort St. Presbyterian Church structure is rebuilt according to original plans.

Competition is held for the design of Detroit Waterworks. Joseph E. Spark's plan is selected and construction begins on East Jefferson building next year.

Hewn-log Brush house, east of town's center, is torn down. For 70 years dwelling was home to Elijah Brush and his wife Adelaide, prominent citizens of Detroit. Distinguished visitors to Northwest Territory, Michigan state governors were later guests at Brush house.

Michigan Building at Philadelphia's Centennial Exposition draws much attention; "showy structure" reflects Michigan's rich natural resources and industrial growth.

Russel Wheel and Foundry Co. established by George H. and Walter S. Russel. Their father, George B. Russel, founded Hamtramck's Iron Works to manufacture first car wheels in the West.

First practical carpet sweeper patented by Melville Rueben Bissell of Grand Rapids; becomes great commercial success.

World History

Greenback party active in American politics (to 1884).

June 25. Custer's last stand: defeat of Gen. George Custer at Battle of Little Bighorn; his troops are outnumbered, badly beaten by Sitting Bull's Sioux.

Aug. 1. Colorado admitted to Union.

Presidential election: Democratic candidate Samuel Tilden receives about 250,000 more votes than Republican opponent Rutherford B. Hayes. Republicans dispute outcome; Electoral Commission forms to examine returns.

Cultural Progress

Centennial Exposition held in Philadelphia.

American writer Mark Twain publishes *The Adventures of Tom Sawyer.*

Johannes Brahms's Symphony No. 1 is performed.

U.S. now boasts more than 200 museums.

American Library Association founded.

National League of Professional Baseball Clubs founded; includes teams in Boston, Chicago, Cincinnati, Hartford, Louisville, New York, Philadelphia, St. Louis; first major league.

Polo is first played (indoors) in U.S.

Scientific and Commercial Progress

German physician Robert Koch identifies bacteria that causes anthrax.

Safety bike developed by Englishman H. J. Lawson: bicycle has wheels of equal size, bike chain.

F. & J. Heinz Co. founded to make and sell pickles, other prepared foods (reorganized 1888 as J. J. Heinz Co.).

Charles E. Hires introduces new soft drink, root beer, at Philadelphia's Centennial Exposition; soon begins business on national scale.

1877

Detroit and Michigan

Charles M. Croswell, Republican, governor (to 1880).

Jan. 22. Over 5,000 people attend grand opening of Centre Park Library (Gratiot and Farmer), now the downtown branch of Detroit Public Library. Three-story building holds 34,000 books and includes reading room, gallery.

Feb. 9. Reformer and clergyman Henry Ward Beecher lectures at Detroit Opera House.

Sept. Jesuit priests open Detroit College (renamed University of Detroit, 1911).

Oct. 14. *Detroit Post and Tribune* first issued; consolidation of *Detroit Daily Post* and *Detroit Daily Tribune.*

Dec. 15. New waterworks on Jefferson at foot of Cadillac Ave. begins supplying water to Detroit.

First telephones are installed in Detroit; Fredrick Stearnes Co. is first business to be connected.

Two-day rowing regatta held on Detroit River; rowing and boating have become popular sports.

World History

Electoral Commission elects Hayes to presidency. Tilden does not contest.

Last federal troops are withdrawn from the South.

Rutherford B. Hayes inaugurated; 19th U.S. president.

In *Munn* v. *Illinois,* U.S. Supreme Court rules state boards can regulate railroads.

July 17. Great Strike begins when Baltimore & Ohio Railroad workers walk off the job; sets off series of sympathy strikes and work stoppages, national crisis.

Porfirio Diaz becomes president of Mexico.

Russia wages war with Turkey (to 1878).

Cultural Progress

Swan Lake, first of Tchaikovsky's great ballets, debuts in Moscow.

Henry James publishes *The American.*

All England Croquet Club changes name to All England Croquet and Lawn Tennis Club; sponsors first major tennis tournament at its Wimbledon headquarters. Spencer Grove is champion.

Scientific and Commercial Progress

Thomas Edison invents the phonograph.

Robert Koch develops method to stain, identify bacteria.

Italian astronomer Giovanni Schiaparelli observes markings (calls them canals) on Mars.

First public telephones in U.S.

Gustavus Swift begins slaughterhouse operation in Chicago, shipping ready-packed meat via refrigerated railcars to eastern markets.

1878

Detroit and Michigan

George C. Langdon, mayor of Detroit (to 1879).

Detroit Association of Charities is formally organized.

June 16. Detroiters get their first glimpse of the phonograph, exhibited in the city.

Nov. 16. *Detroit Evening Telegraph* ceases publication.

Michigan State Capitol is dedicated in Lansing.

Centre Park Library is expanded to include 2nd gallery.

Detroit Home and Day School (later known as Liggett School), a private girls' school, is founded by educator Ella Liggett.

Virginia Watts is the first African American woman to enroll at University of Michigan, graduating in 1885 with a medical degree.

Detroit uses 26 lamplighters to ignite its gas street lamps.

First telephone exchange opens; Detroit telephone directory is issued listing 124 customers.

Detroit Athletic Club is organized.

World History

Congress passes Bland-Allison Act over Hayes's veto; U.S. Treasury to buy silver bullion, coin $2–4 million of silver dollars/month. Attempt to lift economy out of depression.

Greenback party unites with workers to form Greenback Labor party; gains 14 Congressional seats in election. Dissolves 1884.

Outlaw Billy the Kid (William Bonney) joins Lincoln County War, New Mexico range conflict.

Congress of Berlin meets to address Eastern Question: Balkans, other territories controlled by declining Ottoman Empire are at issue.

Two-year drought in Asia causes death of as many as 20 million Chinese. (Worst famine in history.)

Cultural Progress

Joseph Pulitzer buys St. Louis *Dispatch*; merges it with the *Post* to form St. Louis *Post-Dispatch*, first Pulitzer journal.

Gilbert and Sullivan's comic opera *H.M.S. Pinafore* first produced, in London.

New Scotland Yard established in London.

Paris World Exhibition.

German historian Heinrich Treitschke begins anti-Semite movement.

Scientific and Commercial Progress

Albert A. Pope founds Hartford, Connecticut, bicycle factory; first in U.S.

U.S. has about 3,000 telephones.

First home (glass bottle) milk delivery, in Brooklyn.

German engineer Carl Benz begins building his first gasoline engine.

1879

Detroit and Michigan

April 27. Tent of the Knights of the Maccabees established in Detroit.

May. Universalist Church is organized in Detroit.

Sept. 18. President Rutherford B. Hayes and First Lady attend Michigan State Fair.

Nov. 17. Michigan College of Medicine opens in Detroit.

New State Capitol Building is dedicated at Lansing.

Act passes providing for Poor Commission to administer programs aiding the needy.

State legislature passes bills providing for the construction of Grand Blvd., planned as a 12-mile-long residential drive running the periphery of Detroit, and for purchase of Belle Isle as a public park.

Knights of Labor begins organizing Detroit workers.

Campau family sells Belle Isle to city of Detroit for $200,000; parcel of land in Detroit River is a wilderness of forest and marshland. Park commissioners call on noted landscape architect Frederick Law Olmsted (designer of New York's Central Park) to plan the public recreation facility.

Six-story Newberry and McMillan Building is completed at Griswold and Larned, becoming Detroit's tallest and most luxurious office building.

Ferry Building, constructed of cast iron, erected on Woodward, north of Cadillac Square; occupied by department store Newcomb, Endicott and Co.

Electric lights first exhibited in Detroit.

World History

Jan. U.S. Treasury begins paying gold for greenbacks.

Congress passes Gold Resumption Act; revokes bimetallic standard (adopted 1792).

Pope declares philosophical works of St. Thomas Aquinas are the official Catholic doctrine.

Cultural Progress

Henry James publishes *Daisy Miller.*

Henry George publishes *Progress and Poverty.*

Scientific and Commercial Progress

Russian physiologist Ivan Pavlov demonstrates conditioning, result of studies of dog behavior.

Thomas Edison invents incandescent electric lamp.

McCormick Harvesting Machine Co. founded (origin of International Harvester, Navistar Corp.).

W. P. Woolworth founded; beginning of Five-and-Dimes.

New York inventor George Selden applies for first U.S. patent for a gasoline-driven car ("road engine"); granted 1895 even though he probably did not have a functioning model.

First electric tramway exhibited by Ernst and Karl Siemens at Berlin Trade Exhibition.

Cincinnati firm Proctor & Gamble begins making Ivory soap.

Chemical standardization of pharmaceutical products introduced by Parke, Davis & Co.

1880

Detroit and Michigan

Detroit's population, 116,342; ranks 17th in size among U.S. cities. More than 40 nationalities represented in Detroit: German population (17,292), largest; Greek population (1), smallest.

Michigan's population, 1,636,937.

William G. Thompson, mayor of Detroit (to 1884).

City's manufactured products total more than $33 million, produced by more than 900 factories. Leading industries include iron and steel, tobacco products, foundries, and machine shops. Immigrants supply growing need for labor.

Common Council adopts ordinance prohibiting cattle from running at large in parks and other public places.

Detroit Council of Trades and Labor Unions is formed by representatives of city's leading trade unions. Reorganized and renamed Detroit Federation of Labor in 1906.

Detroit's Central Market Building is built on Cadillac Square.

German-owned Kanter Block, on Campus Martius, flourishes this decade; home to popular Detroit restaurant Considine's.

Seed firm Dexter M. Ferry and Co. constructs office and warehouse building on Brush St. between Lafayette and Monroe; warehouse is equipped with automatic sprinkler system, a new invention, in case of fire.

Streetcar line is extended out East Jefferson to the city limits, at Grosse Pointe.

Broad, tree-lined East Jefferson Ave. is home to many of Detroit's most magnificent residences, but with improvements in transportation, year-round residences begin to be built in Grosse Pointe.

The Flats, group of islands in St. Clair River delta, become popular destination this decade; during warm months, excursion steamers run twice a day from Detroit. Described by a Detroit journalist as a "Western Venice," the Flats' recreation facilities include tennis, croquet, boating, swimming. Hotels and cottages spring up to accommodate visitors.

World History

U.S. population, 50,155,783.

Nov. James A. Garfield, Republican, elected president.

"Jim Crow" laws in effect in American South: states enact legislation discriminating against African Americans.

Benjamin Disraeli resigns as British prime minister; succeeded by William Gladstone (to 1885).

Capt. C. C. Boycott, land agent in Mayo, Ireland, is "boycotted" when he refuses to accept rents fixed by his tenants.

Boer rebellion in South Africa; British and Afrikaners (Dutch descendants) fight over Kimberley area, site of newly discovered diamond field.

Cultural Progress

American writer Lewis Wallace publishes *Ben Hur*.

Vaudeville reaches American stages.

James Bailey and P. T. Barnum combine shows to form Barnum & Bailey Circus.

French novels, issued in inexpensive American editions, become popular with U.S. readers.

Scientific and Commercial Progress

Louis Pasteur discovers cholera vaccine.

American mining magnate George Hearst uses Comstock Lode fortune to buy *San Francisco Examiner*; son, William Randolph Hearst, takes over operation (1887).

Sherwin Williams Co. of Cleveland is first manufacturer to produce paint from standard formulas.

Andrew Carnegie develops first large steel furnace.

Miriam Leslie takes over operation of late husband Frank Leslie's publishing business; becomes great success under her guidance.

World Exposition held in Melbourne, Australia.

1881

Detroit and Michigan

David H. Jerome, Republican, governor (to 1882).

March 8–9. Sarah Bernhardt performs at Whitney Opera House; Fanny Davenport performs at Detroit Opera House.

April 2. Joseph L. Hudson, 35, opens men's and boys' clothing store in rented space on 1st floor of Detroit Opera House, competing with his former employer, C. R. Mabley mercantile.

May 26. First provision is made for Detroit Board of Health.

Aug. 14. First train from St. Louis (Wabash Railroad) arrives in Detroit.

Latino population growing; result of need for labor in railroads and other industries.

Forest fires in the Thumb destroy timber.

Detroit Board of Estimates is abolished; replaced by Board of Councilmen. Twelve men are elected from among citizens to levy and control city expenditures.

New law abolishes unwieldy 26-member school board, provides for a 12-member board elected at large. School suffrage is granted to all parents and guardians of school-age children.

Board of Education turns over administration of Detroit Public Library to newly created Library Commission.

Emma Hall is named superintendent of the Reform School for Girls at Adrian; first woman to head a Michigan institution (run by an all-female staff).

Detroit Normal Training Class founded to train teachers (becomes Detroit Teachers College, 1921).

U.S. government completes Weitzel Lock; assumes administration of Sault (Soo) Canal.

Michigan Central Railroad reaches Mackinaw City.

Railroad car ferry service begins between Lower and Upper Peninsulas.

James Dwyer organizes Peninsular Stove Co.; Detroit becomes center of nation's stove industry.

Russell House, called "the most complete and elegant hostelry in Michigan," reopens in downtown Detroit. Distinguished guests will include Prince of Wales and Grand Duke Alexis of Russia.

Detroit Baseball Club, organized in 1880, begins professional play as new member of National League.

World History

March 4. James A. Garfield inaugurated, 20th U.S. president.

Sept. 18. President James Garfield dies 80 days after being shot by Charles J. Guiteau. Chester Arthur is sworn in as 21st U.S. president, leaving vice presidency vacant.

Third wave of U.S. immigration begins; by 1920 more than 23 million newcomers arrive, many from eastern and southern Europe.

Federation of Organized Trade and Labor Unions formed in Pittsburgh by trade union leaders representing some 50,000 members in U.S. and Canada. Origin of American Federation of Labor (*see* 1886).

Three-Emperors' League established by Otto von Bismarck: Germany, Russia, Austria-Hungary agree to remain neutral if any of them goes to war with another country. Also recognizes Austria-Hungary's, Russia's zones of authority in Balkans.

Reformist Russian Czar Alexander II is assassinated in St. Petersburg; succeeded by his son (to 1894), anti-reformist Czar Alexander III.

Jews are persecuted in Russia.

Cultural Progress

Booker T. Washington founds Tuskegee Institute, pioneering industrial and agricultural school for African Americans.

Boston Symphony Orchestra founded.

United States National Lawn Tennis Association (later renamed United States Tennis Association) established; sponsors first U.S. men's open championship tournament in Newport, Rhode Island. Richard Sears wins (claims victory each year through 1887).

Scientific and Commercial Progress

Humanitarian Clara Barton founds American Red Cross.

Cuban physician Carlos Finlay publishes paper suggesting mosquitoes transmit yellow fever.

Standard Oil trust formed; monopolizes 90% of U.S. oil market.

Canadian Pacific Railway Co. founded.

Southern Pacific Railroad completed between New Orleans and California.

Marshall Field Department Store founded in Chicago.

1882

Detroit and Michigan

Woodward Ave. between Campus Martius and Grand River is so crowded that by year end policemen are posted at crosswalks to escort people across the street.

Centre Park Library is expanded to include 3rd gallery.

Park Commissioners engage Detroit Opera House orchestra to perform weekly band concerts at Belle Isle.

Detroit theatergoers see Edwin Booth in *Hamlet* (March 15) and "Tom Thumb" and his troupe perform Dec. 12.

Detroit Club founded by city's political and industrial leaders.

Brothers Ira and Clayton Grinnell open Detroit music store.

Detroit diners can have a well-cooked meal for 30 cents. Typical menu: soup, beef, pork, mutton, fish, three kinds of vegetables, bread and butter, pies, pudding, coffee.

Solid rock salt is discovered at Marine City.

World History

Chinese Exclusion Act: U.S. bans Chinese immigrants for 10 years.

German immigration to U.S. peaks.

Sept. Labor Day first commemorated in U.S.: New York's Central Labor Union organizes workers' parade, political speeches, fireworks, picnics.

Overproduction of cotton in South causes price to plummet.

Triple Alliance formed by Germany, Austria-Hungary, Italy. Serbia (1882) and Romania (1883) also join. Nations agree to help one another in case of attack by 2 or more great powers. Alliance lasts until World War I.

British occupy Cairo.

Cultural Progress

Carlo Collodi publishes *The Adventures of Pinocchio* in Italy.

American Baseball Association founded.

Scientific and Commercial Progress

Viennese physician Josef Breuer uses hypnosis to treat hysteria; origin of psychoanalysis.

International polar stations established.

Nevada's Comstock Lode has yielded $397 million in ore and produced half U.S. silver output since 1857. Soon abandoned.

U.S. secures trading rights in Korea.

World Exposition held in Moscow.

1883

Detroit and Michigan

Josiah W. Begole, Democrat and Greenback, governor (to 1884).

Jan. 27. Incandescent lights are first used in Detroit, at Metcalfe's dry goods store.

June 5. Revised Detroit city charter is enacted.

July 3. Barnum & Bailey Circus, featuring Jumbo the elephant, appears in Detroit.

Sept. 1. *Detroit Evening Journal* first issued.

Sept. 1–Nov. 10. Detroit's first official art exhibit is held in a temporary gallery on Larned. During 10-week run, show attracts 134,924 visitors at 25 cents each, making it a popular and financial success; the *Free Press* hails it as the "first step" toward the community's "artistic education." Local patrons inspired to subscribe $100,000 for construction of permanent building, founding Detroit Museum of Art (to become Detroit Institute of Arts).

Sept. 5. Detroit Zoological Garden is established on Michigan Ave. near 10th St. when a traveling circus auctions its menagerie in Detroit. Animals are purchased; spectators may view exhibit for admission fee.

Charlotte Kawbawgam ("Laughing Whitefish"), daughter of Negaunee (Chippewa) chief, wins Michigan Supreme Court battle to regain mine rights that had been granted to her father. Case sets standard (based on tribal law) for rights of inheritance for American Indians.

Construction begins on new Michigan Central Railway depot (Third and Woodbridge); previous depot destroyed by arson.

Detroit's YMCA Building is completed at Grand River and Griswold.

First electric street lighting in Detroit is installed on Jefferson Ave. at Woodward.

Henry B. Ledyard becomes president of the Michigan Central Railroad.

Lloyd's Parker Block, fashionable retail center at Woodward and State, is completed; Detroit's shops continue to move out Woodward Ave.

John Wallace Page erects fence of horizontally and vertically woven wires on his farm in Lenawee County, Michigan. Due to demand, soon opens Adrian factory to manufacture fencing.

World History

Pendleton Act creates U.S. Civil Service Commission.

Aug. Krakatau, Indonesia, volcano erupts; claims 36,417 lives.

Cultural Progress

Robert Louis Stevenson writes *Treasure Island*.

Oct. 22. Metropolitan Opera House, New York, opens; first performance is Charles Gounod's *Faust*.

Royal College of Music, London, founded.

Ladies' Home Journal first issued.

Scientific and Commercial Progress

Robert Koch describes method of preventive inoculation against anthrax.

English scientist Sir Joseph Swan produces synthetic fiber.

Orient Express makes its first run.

May 24. Brooklyn Bridge inaugurated; suspension bridge celebrated as feat of modern engineering.

Northern Pacific Railroad is completed.

Joseph Pulitzer buys *New York World*.

William "Buffalo Bill" Cody organizes his "Wild West Show."

1884

Detroit and Michigan

S. B. Grummond, mayor of Detroit (to 1886).

June 19. Harper Hospital opens in new facility on John R St.

Oct. 14. Republicans gather in Detroit with national leaders James G. Blaine and John C. Fremont present.

Detroit police move into new headquarters at Bates and Randolph.

Michigan Equal Suffrage Association is formed.

Centre Park Library is expanded.

Belle Isle, a 2.5 mile-long and half-mile wide parcel of land situated in the narrows of the Detroit River, opens. Belle Isle Casino is completed.

Grosse Pointe Club is founded (later reorganized as Country Club of Detroit).

Average daily wage for males in Detroit is $1.74 skilled, $1.45 unskilled; women, $0.78.

World History

Bureau of Labor established as part of U.S. Department of the Interior.

Michigan Senator Thomas W. Palmer makes first speech in U.S. Senate in support of woman suffrage.

National Equal Rights party nominates lawyer Belva Ann Lockwood for U.S. president (nominated again in 1888).

Nov. Grover Cleveland, Democrat, elected president.

London Conference meets to discuss Transvaal; representatives of 14 nations attend Berlin Conference to discuss African affairs.

Standard time introduced; international agreement divides world into 24 standard time zones. Necessitated by expansion of industry.

Cultural Progress

Mark Twain publishes *The Adventures of Huckleberry Finn*; seminal American novel, national biography.

Swiss author Johanna Spyri's *Heidi* is published in the U.S.

Oxford English Dictionary begins publication.

Ringling Brothers (Albert, Otto, Alfred, Charles, and John) organize a circus.

Scientific and Commercial Progress

First long distance telephone call is made between Boston and New York.

Sir Charles Parsons invents first practical steam turbine engine.

Improved fountain pen patented and manufactured by American Lewis Waterman.

Montgomery Ward catalog is 240 pages, offers almost 10,000 products including household items, fashions.

1885

Detroit and Michigan

Jan. 1. Russell A. Alger, Detroit Republican, inaugurated governor (to 1886).

June 6. "Buffalo Bill" Cody and his Wild West Co. perform in Detroit.

Detroit receives its first Ukrainian settlers. Influx at turn of the century.

Michigan passes law limiting child labor.

Detroit Museum of Art is incorporated.

Detroit College of Medicine is incorporated by merger of Detroit Medical College and Michigan College of Medicine.

Lumber baron David Whitney erects Grand Circus Building (retail and office space) on Park at Woodward. Formerly residential area is becoming increasingly business oriented.

Frank Hecker and Charles Freer found the Peninsular Car Co. in Detroit to manufacture railcars.

Roller skating becomes popular in Detroit.

World History

March 4. Grover Cleveland inaugurated, 22nd U.S. president.

Social Gospel movement under way (to early 1930s): adherents, mostly Protestants, believe capitalism's ills can be cured by teaching religious values to working class. Reform movement credited with starting new era of Christian thought.

Cultural Progress

Johannes Brahms's Symphony No. 4 first performed (his last).

Bare-knuckled boxer John L. Sullivan, the "Boston strong boy," becomes first heavyweight champion; retains title to 1892.

Scientific and Commercial Progress

July 6. Louis Pasteur administers rabies vaccine to boy bitten by rabid dog; treatment is a success.

Sir Francis Galton proves individuality of fingerprints; devises method for identification.

Chicago's 10-story Home Insurance Building is completed; generally regarded as first skyscraper. Designed by American architect William Jenney.

German inventors Carl Benz and Gottlieb Daimler, working independently of each other, develop forerunners of modern gas engine. Benz builds motorized three-wheel car with top speed of 7 mph; vehicle has electric ignition, water-cooled engine, and differential gear.

Bicycles go into mass production.

Canadian Pacific Railroad is completed.

American inventor George Eastman manufactures coated photographic paper.

American Telephone and Telegraph Co. (AT&T) organized.

1886

Detroit and Michigan

M. H. Chamberlain, mayor of Detroit (to 1888).

April 6. Snow begins falling just after midnight, continues throughout day. Record daily snowfall of 24 inches blankets city, stopping streetcar and train traffic, halting business.

Sept. 1. Electric streetcars introduced in Detroit, operating on Dix. Ave. (Vernor) from 24th to city limits at Livernois.

Sept. 18. The Highland Park electric streetcar begins operating on Woodward Ave. from Baltimore to Manchester.

Dec. 31. In spite of state-of-the-art sprinkler system, D. M. Ferry Co. office and warehouse building (on Brush St.) catches fire and quickly burns. *Free Press* reporter describes scene as "almost terrifying in its grandness."

Firemen's Hall is sold to Water Board.

John J. Bagley Memorial Armory is built in Detroit; includes drill room for Light Guard Infantry.

Helen Jenkins, founder of woman suffrage societies in other states, becomes first president of Detroit Equal Suffrage Association.

Michigan College of Mines, founded last year, opens at Houghton (later Michigan Technological University).

Ste. Anne's Church (built 1828) is torn down to make way for commercial interests in downtown Detroit; new church is constructed (1887) at 19th and Howard streets.

German immigrant Albert Kahn begins working in offices of noted architectural firm Mason & Rice, launching 10-year training period.

Belle Isle Zoo originates with the establishment of a deer park.

Detroit sportsmen found Lake St. Clair Fishing and Shooting Club (later called the Old Club); build shingle-style club on edge of St. Clair River's main channel at Lake St. Clair.

World History

Presidential Succession Act passed.

In *Wabash Railroad* v. *Illinois,* U.S. Supreme Court reverses 1877 decision (in case of *Munn* v. *Illinois*), proclaims only Congress has the right to regulate interstate commerce.

May 4. Workers demonstrating (for 8-hour day) in Chicago's Haymarket Square attract crowd of 1,500; police arrive to disperse them as bomb explodes and rioting ensues. Eleven killed; more than 100 injured.

Knights of Labor reaches peak membership.

Federation of Organized Trade and Labor Unions reorganizes to form American Federation of Labor (AFL); elects Samuel Gompers president. Represents 140,000 skilled laborers.

Sept. 4. Apache Chief Geronimo surrenders to U.S. Gen. Nelson Miles in Arizona, ending sensational campaign against whites.

Oct. 28. Statue of Liberty is dedicated, Bedloe Island, New York Harbor.

Decade of intermittent drought begins in Great Plains; loss of livestock, crops and failure, foreclosure of numerous farms.

Cultural Progress

Robert Louis Stevenson publishes *Dr. Jekyll and Mr. Hyde.*

Scientific and Commercial Progress

Coca-Cola is invented by Atlanta pharmacist.

Hydroelectric installations are begun at Niagara Falls.

Peak of open-range livestock (cattle, sheep) boom in West.

Richard Sears enters mail-order business, opening operations in Minneapolis.

Gold discovered in South Africa; spurs development of Johannesburg.

1887

Detroit and Michigan

Cyrus G. Luce, Republican, governor (to 1890).

New Ste. Anne's Church is finished on Howard St.; Detroit's first church, the Roman Catholic congregation has had numerous homes in the city.

Detroit Opera House is remodeled.

Centre Park Library is expanded to include a 4th gallery.

Detroit Athletic Club builds Woodward facility.

John J. Bagley Memorial Fountain, built through bequest of Detroit businessman and former governor, is unveiled in Campus Martius. Eighteen-foot-tall white granite fountain discharges drinking water, which Bagley envisioned would be chilled by city-supplied ice (held in base).

East Ferry Ave., off Woodward, is platted by Detroit businessman Dexter M. Ferry as fashionable residential area.

Grand Hotel opens on Mackinac Island; resort is financed by railroad and steamship companies. Extension of rail lines to northern Michigan has given birth to tourism as new state industry.

In Lansing, Ransom E. Olds builds and drives 3-wheeled vehicle self-propelled by steam.

Detroit Wolverines baseball team wins National League pennant. Goes on to defeat St. Louis Browns (American Association champs) in a 15-game World Series.

World History

Centennial of U.S. Constitution celebrated.

Congress passes Dawes Act; allots land to American Indians in individual holdings under certain conditions.

President Grover Cleveland and Congress struggle over tariff and surplus.

Interstate Commerce Commission established by act of Congress to control certain practices of U.S. railroads.

Severe winter (1886–87) nearly wipes out range-cattle industry in American West.

Queen Victoria celebrates her Golden Jubilee.

Indochina is organized by France.

Flooding in China kills an estimated 900,000.

Cultural Progress

Sir Arthur Conan Doyle publishes *A Study in Scarlet,* first Sherlock Holmes story.

Polish pianist and composer Ignacy Paderewski makes professional debut in Vienna.

Baseball championship series between St. Louis and Detroit attracts 51,000 spectators (*see also* Detroit and Michigan entry).

Scientific and Commercial Progress

American inventor Emile Berliner develops gramophone talking machine and method of duplicating records.

Thomas Edison and Joseph Swan combine to produce Ediswan electrical lamps.

American Hannibal Goodwin invents celluloid (flexible photographic) film.

1888

Detroit and Michigan

John Pridgeon Jr., mayor of Detroit (to 1890).

Peak year for Michigan lumber: state produces more than 4 million board feet.

Sept. 1. Detroit Museum of Art opens its doors at Jefferson and Hastings.

April 17. Hotel Cadillac opens.

Detroit businessman and Michigan politician Russell A. Alger vies for Republican presidential nomination.

Detroit businessman James McMillan, cofounder of the Michigan Car Co. and developer of the Duluth, South Shore & Atlantic Railroad (which opened Michigan's Upper Peninsula to development), is elected to U.S. Senate.

Dec. 2. Detroit milkmen meet to try to raise milk prices to 7 cents per quart.

Dec. 6. Grace Hospital opened to patients.

Lake Erie, Essex, and Detroit River Railway (owned by whiskey magnate Hiram Walker) opens, connecting Detroit/Windsor with rich agricultural fields of Ontario's interior.

Beecher, Peck and Lewis Paper Co. is established.

World History

March 12–14. Northeastern U.S. hit by blizzard dubbed Great White Hurricane.

Secret ballot is introduced at local American elections.

Nov. Benjamin Harrison (grandson of William Henry Harrison), Republican, elected president.

William II becomes emperor (kaiser) of Germany upon the death of his grandfather, William I. Rules to 1918.

"Jack the Ripper" murders 6 London women.

Cultural Progress

Collier's Magazine established.

American actor DeWolf Hopper recites poem "Casey at the Bat" for first time at Wallack's Theater, New York; soon popularized.

Walter Camp becomes coach of Yale football team (to 1892); revises rules to shape American game.

Scientific and Commercial Progress

Institute Pasteur (contagious disease research center) established in Paris.

American inventor George Eastman introduces Kodak camera: box-shaped device uses rolled film rather than plates. Soon popularizes photography.

Scottish inventor John B. Dunlop patents pneumatic tire; organizes Dunlop Rubber Co. (next year).

Norwegian explorer Fridtjof Nansen leads expedition across Greenland's ice fields on foot.

National Geographic Society founded; becomes world's largest scientific and educational organization.

Lobengula, last king of South African Ndebele Nation, accepts British protection and grants mining rights to Cecil Rhodes.

1889

Detroit and Michigan

Jan. 3. Detroit City Railway receives grant for new trackage; tickets for workingmen cost 25 cents for 8 tickets.

May 12. First Belle Isle Bridge opens to traffic.

Michigan Federation of Labor organized; printer and outspoken reformer Joseph Labadie, president.

Raise in teacher pay favored: Current salary is $30 per month to start, increasing to maximum of $70 per month after 9.5 years.

Projected strike of streetcar conductors and drivers postponed: men work 14.5 hours for 2 days and 9 hours on 3rd day, 7 days per week. Reduction to 11 hours daily for 6 days is advocated.

Detroit College of Medicine Building (on St. Antoine) is completed.

Detroit Business University opens on East Grand River.

Detroit News publisher James Scripps donates a number of old master paintings to Detroit Museum of Art, providing foundation for new museum's permanent collection, launching its European collection.

Detroit hosts International Fair and Exposition; elaborate, temporary exposition hall is designed by young German-American architect Louis Kamper. Fair is held on 70-acre Delray site along Detroit River. Visitors reach event by steamer service from Detroit. Fair is so successful that it reopens each year for next 3 years.

Canadian whiskey magnate Hiram Walker develops Lake Erie resort near Kingsville, Ontario, 30 miles from Detroit: Mettawas is situated on Walker's railroad and offers golf, tennis, casino; quickly becomes popular with excursionists.

Michigan is nation's leading copper and iron ore producer.

Following trip to Japan, Frederick Stearns (founder of the Stearns Drug Co.) writes series of articles about the country for the Detroit *Free Press.*

First Presbyterian Church is built at Woodward and Edmund Place.

Village of Highland Park is incorporated.

World History

March 4. Benjamin Harrison inaugurated; 23rd U.S. president.

Department of Agriculture created.

April 22. Federal government opens unsettled region of Indian Territory (Oklahoma) to white settlers; sets off first of 3 major land rushes by homesteaders.

May 31. Johnstown flood: South Fork Dam on Conemaugh River gives way; more than 2,000 people die.

North and South Dakota (Nov. 2), Montana (Nov. 8), and Washington (Nov. 11) admitted to Union.

Reformers Jane Addams and Ellen Gates Starr found Hull House in Chicago. Settlement house serves neighborhood poor, becomes center for social reform.

Pan-American Conference.

Cultural Progress

Congress establishes National Zoological Park in Washington, D.C. (opens 1890).

Scientific and Commercial Progress

Insulin discovered by German physiologist Oskar Minkowski and German physician Joseph von Mering.

Mayo Clinic is founded in Rochester, Minnesota.

Alexander Gustave Eiffel designs 1,056-foot Eiffel Tower for Paris World Exposition.

Electric elevator is successfully operated by Otis Brothers and Co. in New York's Demarest Building.

Dow, Jones and Co. begins publishing the *Wall Street Journal.*

1890

Detroit and Michigan

Detroit's population, 205,876, or more than 4 times what it was 3 decades ago. Growth has been fueled by growing industry. Ranks 15th in size among U.S. cities.

Michigan's population, 2,093,889.

Hungarians begin arriving in Detroit/southeastern Michigan in significant numbers.

Michigan elects Edwin B. Winans, first Democratic governor in 40 years (inaugurated Jan. 1, 1891).

Hazen Pingree takes office as mayor of Detroit; becomes leading civic reformer.

Mayor Pingree suggests civic center be built at foot of Woodward, along riverfront, which has been used primarily for commercial purposes since Detroit's founding.

Dec. 1. Detroit City Railway becomes the Detroit Street Railway.

Dec. 7. American Federation of Labor's national convention held in Detroit; Samuel Gompers presides. Mary Burke of Detroit is first woman delegate to a national labor convention.

Bike riders complain city's roads are impassable; leads to enactment of county road law (1893).

David Whitney builds the Garrick Theater.

Detroit pharmaceutical manufacturer Frederick Stearns donates to Detroit Museum of Art 16,000 objects from China, Japan, Korea, India, and Persia; the institution's first antiquities.

Grand opening of Detroit's first skyscraper: 10-story Hammond Building, at corner of Fort and Griswold streets, is owned by financier Ellen Barry Hammond (widow of meatpacker George H. Hammond, originally of Hammond, Indiana). Among nation's first skyscrapers.

Interurban rail lines carry workers between home and factory.

Michigan is nation's leading lumber producer.

Union Trust Co. bank founded in Detroit.

Midland Chemical Co. is organized (becomes Dow Chemical Co.).

Roast pork is 8 cents per pound, butter is 25 cents per pound in local stores.

Golf becomes a popular pastime; courses are soon laid out beyond Detroit city limits in Grosse Pointe.

World History

U.S. population, 62,974,714.

Average U.S. workweek, 60 hours, a 9% decline over the last 30 years.

Jan. 25. American Journalist Nellie Bly completes around-the-world trip in a record 72 days; traveling for *The World* newspaper, she departed Hoboken, New Jersey, Nov. 14, 1889, and journeyed by boat, train, handcar, and burro.

Congress passes Sherman Anti-Trust Act; outlaws restraints on trade, conspiracy to monopolize market.

Congress repeals Bland-Allison Act, passes Sherman Silver Purchase Act to double government purchase of silver and increase money in circulation.

Félix Martínez Jr. founds El Partido del Pueblo Unido (United People's Party), first Latino political party in U.S.

Idaho (July 3) and Wyoming (July 10) admitted to Union.

McKinley Tariff Act of 1890.

Dec. 29. U.S. Army's 7th Cavalry massacres 300 Sioux at Wounded Knee (South Dakota); tragic event memorialized by American poet Stephen Vincent Benet's "Bury My Heart at Wounded Knee."

(2nd) Morrill Act adds monetary gifts to states for use in A&M college programs.

National Woman Suffrage Association and American Woman Suffrage Association join forces to form National American Woman Suffrage Association.

United Mine Workers founded; affiliate of American Federation of Labor.

American journalist and reformer Jacob Riis publishes *How the Other Half Lives*; exposes living conditions in New York's slums.

Otto von Bismarck dismissed by German Kaiser William II.

German Social Democrats adopt Marxist program at Erfurt Congress.

Hungarians begin emigrating; 1.5 million arrive in U.S. over next 20 years.

Cultural Progress

Tchaikovsky writes *The Sleeping Beauty*.

First collection of poems by Emily Dickinson published posthumously; she died unknown in 1886. Soon regarded as great American poet.

Yosemite National Park is established.

Daughters of the American Revolution founded in Washington, D.C.

Scientific and Commercial Progress

German bacteriologist Emil von Behring announces discovery of principle of antitoxic immunity.

Louise Blanchard Bethune is first woman elected to membership of American Institute of Architects.

St. Louis's Wainwright Building completed; first skyscraper designed by modern architecture pioneer Louis H. Sullivan.

W. Duke Sons and Co. organizes merger with its competitors; founds American Tobacco Co. to control nearly 90% of domestic cigarette market.

1891

Detroit and Michigan

Edwin B. Winans, Democrat, governor (to 1892).

April 21–24. Streetcar employees strike against Detroit Street Railway. Agree to return to work while demands are being arbitrated, agreement reached May 12: conductors to be paid 18 cents an hour for 10-hour day, drivers $1.50 a day.

June. Detroit Boat Club dedicates new clubhouse on Belle Isle.

Aug. Construction begins on Grand Blvd., envisioned as a "gravel road where gentlemen with fast horses could let out the reins."

Sept. Grand Army of the Republic holds national convention in Detroit.

Sept. 16. Detroit Street Railway becomes the Detroit Citizens Street Railway.

Sept. 17. J. L. Hudson Co. Department Store opens new 8-story building at Gratiot and Farmer in Detroit. Redbrick trimmed brownstone structure was designed by H. H. Richardson, who also designed the Marshall Field Store in Chicago.

James Scripps purchases *Detroit Tribune*. (Since 1878 he and his brother Edward Scripps have started or acquired papers in Cleveland, St. Louis, Cincinnati.)

Detroit College building completed on Jefferson, east of Saints Peter and Paul Church.

YMCA establishes vocational education classes.

Elmwood Cemetery's board of trustees commissions landscape architect Frederick Law Olmsted to outline plan for management of cemetery, envisioned as "welcoming retreat" from hustle and bustle of Detroit. Elmwood becomes final resting place of many of Michigan's most prominent citizens.

First building completed at Parke-Davis Pharmaceutical Co.'s riverfront complex.

John B. Ford successfully drills for salt at Wyandotte.

New quarters of Detroit Club, at Cass and Fort, open to city's leaders (men only).

Detroit barbers raise price of a shave from 10 to 15 cents.

Grand Trunk Railway Tunnel opens under St. Clair River at Port Huron.

World History

Fifty-second Congress is first to appropriate $1 billion.

Populist (or People's party) organized by farmer and labor groups. (Dissolves by 1908.)

Baltimore crisis with Chile: *Baltimore* sailors attacked in Valparaíso after U.S. gives political asylum to supporters of former Chilean president, José Manuel Balmaceda, following Chilean Civil War.

American explorer Robert E. Peary leads Arctic expedition to try to reach North Pole. Returns 1892, unsuccessful.

Widespread famine in Russia.

Japanese earthquake kills 10,000.

Cultural Progress

May 5. Tchaikovsky conducts concert of his works at opening of Carnegie Hall.

American painter Mary Cassatt has first solo exhibit.

Chicago Symphony Orchestra founded.

Chicago's Monadnock Building is completed; early example of modern architecture.

Dec. Basketball invented by Canadian-American educator James Naismith at YMCA College, Springfield, Massachusetts.

Scientific and Commercial Progress

Ape-man of Java, *Pithecanthropus erectus* (*Homo erectus*), discovered by Eugene Dubois.

Thomas Edison invents the motion picture machine (kinetoscope).

William Morrison builds first successful American electric car, 6-passenger vehicle is powered by batteries under the seats.

Traveler's checks devised by Marcellus Berry, general agent of American Express Co.

1892

Detroit and Michigan

Jan. 12. Polish pianist and composer Ignacy Paderewski performs at Detroit Opera House.

Detroit's Trinity Episcopal Church is completed. Design was commissioned by *Detroit News* publisher James Scripps and his wife Harriet: Gothic Revival church includes stained glass windows by Tiffany of New York.

Only 4 Detroit streets are paved with asphalt: Jefferson, Lafayette, Cass, Second. Woodward is paved with cedar blocks.

Aug. 22. Jefferson streetcar line is electrified, followed by Woodward Ave. on Dec. 15 and Mack Ave. in early 1893.

Charles B. King applies for a patent on his new invention, a pneumatic hammer.

Henry Ford produces his first (2-cylinder) car in a workshop behind his home at 58 Bagley Ave. in southwest Detroit.

World History

Jan. 1. Federal Immigration Station opens on Ellis Island; becomes country's chief immigration facility.

July. AFL strike at Carnegie Steel plant in Homestead, Pennsylvania, turns into riot; militia called out. Strike ends in failure for union.

Oct. Dalton Boys (brothers Robert, Grattan, and Emmet) are killed in bank robbery attempt in Coffeyville, Kansas.

Nov. Grover Cleveland, Democrat, again elected president; will serve second, nonconsecutive term.

Gladstone again British prime minister (to 1894).

Dual Alliance formed by France, Russia.

Cultural Progress

Boston Symphony Orchestra and New York Symphony Orchestra perform first works by a woman composer, Amy Marcy Cheney Beach.

June 4. Naturalist John Muir founds Sierra Club to protect the Sierra Nevada; nation's first environmental group.

Sept. 7. "Gentleman" Jim Corbett defeats John L. Sullivan in first heavyweight championship boxing match fought by Marquis of Queensbury rules; origin of controversial American spectator sport.

Scientific and Commercial Progress

German mechanical engineer Rudolph Diesel patents his internal combustion (diesel) engine.

French company Panhard et Levassor builds front-engine, rear-wheel drive automobile.

First automatic telephone switchboard introduced.

1893

Detroit and Michigan

John T. Rich, Republican, governor (to 1896).

Jan. 21. First train arrives at new Fort Street Union Station.

Jan. 27. Detroit's High School, in Old Capitol Building, destroyed by fire. Enrollment has surpassed 1,000 students.

Jefferson Ave. dry goods wholesaler Edson, Moore and Co.'s iron building, considered fireproof, is consumed by flames in less than an hour; claims 7 lives.

March 16. Grace Whitney Evans founds Detroit branch of Young Women's Christian Association (YWCA).

June 30. Detroiters line riverbank to watch replicas of Columbus's ships sail up the river en route to Chicago Columbian Exposition.

Economic depression prompts organizers to cancel state fair this year.

Sept. 18. People's Outfitting Co. opens.

Nov. 7. Hazen Pingree is elected mayor for 3rd time.

Dec. 19. Adelina Patti gives Detroit concert.

Detroit College of Law chartered.

Belle Isle Police Station is completed.

Marie Owen, first U.S. policewoman, is appointed by Detroit Bureau of Police.

Physicians Sarah Gertrude Banks and Florence Huson establish (in connection with Woman's Hospital) the Free Dispensary for women and children in Detroit.

Union Station, corner of Fort and Third, begins operation as terminus of the Pennsylvania, Wabash, and Pere Marquette railroads.

Wayne County passes road law requiring local governments to assume road maintenance.

Detroit Public Lighting Commission created.

Long-distance telephone service from Detroit to New York and Chicago is introduced. Detroit has about 4,000 telephones.

Detroit Gas Co. is created through a merger of Detroit and Mutual Gaslight companies.

Senator and Mrs. Thomas W. Palmer donate 130 acres of their 725-acre estate (along Woodward Ave.) to Detroit for park development.

Virginia Park, an area west of Woodward Ave. now accessible by streetcar, is laid out as a neighborhood of architect-designed houses for businessmen and their families. Construction begins in earnest in 1900.

Development of Indian Village begins: east side land formerly farmed by Abraham Cook is subdivided by his heirs to make way for "first class residential district."

Detroit Driving Club, which used land of former Cook farm as a racetrack for trotters, moves from Detroit to Grosse Pointe Township.

Detroit Boat Club on Belle Isle is destroyed by fire.

Belgian National Alliance founded in Detroit; Charles Goddeeris among leaders.

Mackinac Island has become summer home to many of Detroit's most prominent families.

World History

March 4. Grover Cleveland inaugurated, 24th U.S. president.

Congress repeals Sherman Silver Purchase Act; U.S. returns to gold standard (to April 1933).

July 12. University of Wisconsin Professor Frederick Jackson Turner delivers paper (at Chicago exposition) declaring American frontier is "closed." Lecture emphasizes importance of frontier to nation's expansionist character.

American Railway Union (ARU) founded by radical labor leader Eugene V. Debs.

Financial panic causes economic depression (to 1896).

Hawaiian monarchy overthrown.

German Kaiser William II begins opposition to growth of socialism.

New Zealand is first nation to grant women the right to vote.

Widespread cholera epidemic.

Cultural Progress

First college extension courses granting college credits offered by University of Chicago's Home Study department.

Chicago hosts World's Columbian Exposition (world's fair); includes George Ferris's "pleasure wheel," other amusements. Fair also launches City Beautiful movement, renewing interest in urban planning and improvement throughout U.S.

Scientific and Commercial Progress

Johns Hopkins University Medical School founded.

Carl Benz builds his 4-wheel car, the Victoria. Soon for sale in Germany.

First movie studio is built in West Orange, New Jersey, for Edison Co.; the Kinetographic Theater.

175

Richard Sears and Alvah Roebuck found Sears, Roebuck and Co. in Chicago; issues catalog, soon known as "Wish Book."

Ready-to-eat breakfast food industry begins when machine for shredding wheat is patented by Henry Perky and William Ford of Watertown, New York; they make shredded wheat biscuits.

1894

Detroit and Michigan

Mayor Hazen Pingree sponsors vegetable gardens to provide work and food for the poor and unemployed during economic depression.

New federal building opens at Fort and Shelby, housing Post Office and U.S. Courthouse.

Hurlburt Memorial Gate, at entrance of Detroit's Waterworks Park (East Jefferson), is constructed; funded by bequest of Water Commissioners board member Chauncey Hurlburt.

American Electric Co. founded in Detroit to make electric soldering irons.

Detroit's first building constructed with steel (frame) is new headquarters of Detroit Bank and Trust.

Lumberman and industrialist David Whitney and his wife complete Woodward Ave. home; has 42 rooms, 218 stained glass windows, and 20 fireplaces, the *Free Press* describes it as "the most pretentious modern home in the state."

Large, single-family homes begin to be built in Indian Village. Prominent Detroiters commission architects to design residences.

Detroit Boat Club gets new Belle Isle clubhouse (previous clubhouse destroyed by fire last year).

Detroit Yacht Club founded.

William W. Ferguson is first African American elected to state legislature, serving two terms of two years each, 1894–1896.

World History

Congress again passes income tax law, charging 2% on all incomes over $4,000. Part of Wilson-Gorman Tariff Act.

May. American businessman and politician Jacob Coxey leads unemployed men (Coxey's Army) in march on Washington, D.C., to protest unemployment and advocate for public improvement projects to create jobs.

Workers at Pullman Palace Car Co. (Pullman, Illinois) strike to protest significant reduction in wages; leads to general rail strike, paralyzing nation's transportation.

July 2. Federal court order demands all striking rail workers return to work; American Railway Union refuses to comply. Troops are called out to break strike (cited as interfering with the mails); situation turns deadly.

National observance of Labor Day signed into law.

Alianzo Hispano Americana (Hispanic American Alliance) founded in Tucson; civil rights organization soon spreads throughout Southwest.

Boll weevil beetles spread into Texas from Mexico; soon devastate cotton crops and spread to other states.

Dreyfus Affair begins: French army captain Alfred Dreyfus is arrested on treason charges, convicted and sentenced to life imprisonment on Devil's Island, French Guiana. Dreyfus' innocence brought to light (1898) but controversy reveals European anti-Semitism.

Czar Alexander III dies; succeeded by his son, Nicholas II (to 1917), Russia's last czar.

Sino-Japanese War (to 1895) fought over control of Korea.

Cultural Progress

Amateur Golf Association of the United States (later the United States Golf Association) founded.

French sports enthusiast Baron Pierre de Coubertin founds a committee to organize modern Olympic Games.

Scientific and Commercial Progress

German physician Arthur Nicolaier discovers tetanus bacillus.

French brothers Auguste and Louis Lumière invent the Cinematographe, early motion picture camera.

1895

Detroit and Michigan

April 1. Power is first supplied to streetlight system and public buildings from a municipal power station.

July 8. Three-cent crosstown streetcar line begins operation; built by Detroit Railway Co. and organized by the Pack brothers under Mayor Hazen Pingree's sponsorship. Pingree serves as motorman on opening day.

Nov. 6. Disastrous explosion and fire destroy Detroit Journal Building.

Proposed state constitutional amendment to grant woman suffrage is defeated in the House.

Elizabeth McSweeney is first woman to graduate from Detroit College of Law and first woman attorney to practice in Wayne County.

Kindergartens are organized in Detroit public schools.

Centre Park Library is expanded.

Michigan State Federation of Women's Clubs founded; Clara Avery of Detroit is organization's first president.

Oakland Railway electric interurban begins regular service to Detroit.

Union Trust Building and Chamber of Commerce Building, Detroit's first metal skeleton skyscrapers, are completed.

Hellas Cafe founded in Greektown by Demetrios Antonopoulos. Detroit landmark restaurant.

Masonic Temple is completed at Lafayette and First to house association of fraternal organizations.

Harmonie Club, on East Grand River in Detroit, is built as a meeting place for German singing group Gesang-Verein Harmonie; triangular-shaped Harmonie Park (along Randolph St.) takes its name from the organization.

World History

Supreme Court ruling in *United States* v. *E. C. Knight Co.* undermines Sherman Anti-Trust Act (1890).

President Grover Cleveland broadly applies Monroe Doctrine to resolve Venezuelan boundary dispute between U.S. and Britain.

Anti-Saloon League of America is organized to advocate national prohibition.

Good Roads movement gains impetus.

Beginning of Cuban War for Independence.

Jameson Raid into Boer colony of Transvaal.

April 17. Treaty ends Sino-Japanese War; provides for independent Korea (to 1910), for Chinese surrender of Taiwan and Liaodong Peninsula to Japan. China seriously weakened by conflict, opening it to European incursion.

Cultural Progress

Cincinnati Symphony Orchestra founded.

New York Public Library chartered; city- and state-funded with large private endowment.

March 22. First in-theater showing of a motion picture, in Paris: National Society for the Promotion of Industry members view film about Lumière factory workers.

First U.S. Open Golf Championship is played (at Newport Golf Club); won by Horace Rawlins.

First professional football game is played in U.S. at Latrobe, Pennsylvania.

Volleyball is invented by William G. Morgan, YMCA director in Holyoke, Massachusetts.

Scientific and Commercial Progress

Sigmund Freud publishes his first work on psychoanalysis.

German physicist Wilhelm Roentgen discovers x rays.

Radio ("wireless") is developed by Italian physicist and inventor Guglielmo Marconi.

Bicycle improved with addition of air-filled (pneumatic) tires.

Duryea Motor Wagon Co. places the first auto ad, in magazine *Horseless Age*.

First American auto race is held in Chicago; winning car is built by Duryea Co. Event makes national headlines.

Baltimore & Ohio Railroad establishes world's first electric mainline service in Philadelphia.

Canada begins construction of Sault Canal on its side of St. Mary's River (between Ontario and Michigan).

King Gillette invents safety razor; organizes manufacturing co. (1901).

Ernest Kimball opens first cafeteria, in Chicago.

1896

Detroit and Michigan

March 6. Charles Brady King and assistants trundle his automobile out of St. Antoine machine shop in the middle of the night; King drives the vehicle through city's streets—the first car driven in Detroit.

June 4. Early a.m. Young mechanic Henry Ford test drives his car (buggy chassis mounted on 4 bicycle wheels); drives Grand River and Washington Blvd. before returning home. An assistant rides a bicycle ahead to warn carriage drivers of vehicle's approach.

July 1. Thomas Edison's Vitascope is demonstrated to Detroit newspapermen at Opera House.

Summer. Detroit Opera House exhibits several reels of film (of a bullfight in Mexico).

Sept. 8. New Central High School (Old Main on Wayne State Univ. campus) opens at Cass and Warren avenues.

Nov. 5. Detroit Mayor Hazen Pingree, Republican, is elected governor of Michigan.

Nov. 9. Last horse-drawn streetcar operates on Detroit streets.

Professor Eliza Mosher becomes University of Michigan's first Dean of Women and the first woman on the faculty.

James Vernor opens downtown Detroit plant to brew his signature ginger ale.

Chamber of Commerce Building loses its claim to title of Detroit's tallest building when the 14-story Majestic Building is completed at Woodward and Michigan avenues, overlooking Campus Martius. Considered a monument to Detroit commerce, it was planned by C. R. Mabley, who abandoned it mid-project due to financial problems.

Salt mining begins in Detroit.

World History

Jan. 4. Utah admitted to Union.

In *Plessy* v. *Ferguson,* Supreme Court upholds constitutionality of Louisiana's separate-but-equal law regarding public facilities.

At Democratic National Convention, William Jennings Bryan delivers "Cross of Gold" speech, securing presidential nomination.

Nov. William McKinley, Republican, elected president.

Klondike gold rush (to 1899); influx of precious metal lifts nation out of economic depression.

Cultural Progress

Nobel Prize established in Swedish chemist/inventor Alfred Nobel's will; awards to be given annually (beginning 1901) recognizing accomplishments in peace, chemistry, physics, physiology or medicine, literature.

April 20. First motion picture showing in U.S.: New York screening uses Thomas Edison's Vitascope, Thomas Arnat's projector.

April. First modern Olympic Games held in Athens, Greece. Thirteen nations participate.

First Alpine ski school founded at Lilienfeld, Austria.

First women's intercollegiate basketball game in U.S.: Stanford University defeats University of California at Berkeley.

Scientific and Commercial Progress

French physicist Antoine-Henri Becquerel discovers natural radioactivity.

Radio inventor Guglielmo Marconi transmits telegraph signals through the air from Italy to England.

Duryea Motor Wagon Co. sells first American-built, gas-powered car.

May. Samuel P. Langley tests his airplane; makes 3,000-foot unmanned flight over Potomac River.

U.S. Postal Service expands into remote areas with Rural Free Delivery (RFD); boon to mail-order businesses.

1897

Detroit and Michigan

Hazen S. Pingree, Republican, governor (to 1900).

Michigan Supreme Court rules Hazen Pingree cannot hold offices of mayor of Detroit and governor of Michigan at same time; he resigns as mayor.

April 5. William C. Maybury is elected mayor.

Oct. 7. Detroit Opera House is destroyed by fire.

Oct. 29. Ernst Kern's Department Store opens.

Sebastian S. Kresge opens Detroit store in partnership with J. G. McCory; slogan is "Nothing over 10 cents."

Nov. 27. New Post Office and Federal Building are occupied.

Former Michigan governor Russell A. Alger becomes U.S. secretary of war (to 1899).

Wayne County Jail is built at Clinton and Beaubien.

Florence Crittenton Mission begins work in Detroit.

Detroit's first branch library: Detroit Water Commission establishes Hurlburt Library in Water Works Park to house book collection of former water commissioner Chauncey Hurlburt. Detroit Public Library agrees to supply facility with books for circulation.

"Childhood Memories of Life in Detroit," by Electa Maria Bronson Sheldon, is published in Detroit *Free Press*. Memoirs of the author's youth in Detroit, where she moved with her family in 1824.

Olds Motor Vehicle Co., Inc. is established in Lansing; first automobile company in the state.

World History

March 4. William McKinley inaugurated; 25th U.S. president.

Dingley Tariff passed by Congress: increases duties on sugar, salt, tin cans, glassware, tobacco, iron, steel, petroleum, lead, copper, locomotives, matches, whisky, leather goods. Raises cost of living by almost 25% in next 10 years.

Queen Victoria celebrates Diamond Jubilee amidst outpouring of public support; considered Britain's first modern monarch, prime ministers (Benjamin Disraeli and William Gladstone) have been allowed to secure more power during her reign.

First World Zionist Convention is held in Switzerland; beginning of Zionism, political movement to establish independent Jewish state.

Severe famine in India.

Cultural Progress

Steeplechase Park opens at Brooklyn's Coney Island; amusement park includes roller coaster, Ferris wheel.

Scientific and Commercial Progress

British physician Ronald Ross discovers malaria bacillus.

Japanese bacteriologist Kiyoshi Shiga discovers dysentery bacillus.

English physicist Joseph John Thomson discovers the electron.

Cathode-ray tube developed by German physicist Karl Ferdinand Braun for radio use; later makes television possible.

Stanley Motor Co., producers of "Stanley Steamers," established in U.S.

First municipal subway in U.S. opens in Boston.

Dow Jones Industrial Average (DJIA) first printed in the *Wall Street Journal*.

1898

Detroit and Michigan

Average wage for Michigan workers, $1.62 per day.

Bread prices increase; 1-pound loaf rises from 4 to as much as 6 cents, 2-pound loaf rises from 7 to 10 cents.

Feb. 8. Society for the Prevention of Cruelty to Children organizes Detroit chapter.

Feb. 14. First Church of Christ Scientist organized in Detroit.

April 6. William Jennings Bryan speaks in Detroit.

April 19. First Michigan troops leave for Cuba; state raises 5 infantry regiments plus naval brigade for service in Spanish-American War.

June 20. Bob-Lo Excursion Co. is born. Steamers carry passengers to Canada's Bois Blanc island (18 miles downstream from Detroit) for picnics, carousel rides, dancing.

Light Guard Armory is completed at Brush and Larned Streets.

Michigan Association of Colored Women's Clubs is founded; co-founder Mary E. McCoy of Detroit becomes organization's first vice president.

New Detroit Opera House is built.

State Savings Bank, the largest financial institution in Detroit, commissions New York architectural firm McKim, Mead and White to design its new headquarters.

Detroit Automobile Co. is organized by local capital to produce Ford-designed cars. Ford withdraws after 3 years, during which time only 2 cars are built.

William Metzger establishes first independent automobile dealership at 274 Jefferson Ave.

World History

April 25. Spanish-American War begins over liberation of Cuba.

July 1. Battle of San Juan Hill: Theodore Roosevelt leads Rough Riders to defeat Spanish.

July 17. Spanish surrender Santiago, Cuba.

Aug. 12. Armistice signed by Spain and U.S. ends Spanish-American War.

Dec. 10. Treaty of Paris provides for Cuba's full independence from Spain, grants U.S. control of Guam and Puerto Rico. U.S. to pay Spain $20 million for Philippine Islands.

Hawaii annexed in Treaty of Paris, signed by U.S., Spain.

Pollock v. *Farmers' Loan and Trust Co.*: U.S. Supreme Court declares income tax law (1894) unconstitutional.

Cultural Progress

H. G. Wells writes *The War of the Worlds*.

Scientific and Commercial Progress

Pierre and Marie Curie discover radium; first radioactive element later proves effective weapon against cancer.

Radio communication lines established between England and France.

First American automobile show held in Boston; 4 exhibitors.

First automobile insurance policy is issued by Travelers Insurance Co. of Hartford to Dr. Truman J. Martin of Buffalo.

1899

Detroit and Michigan

Edgar A. Guest begins writing occasional verse for Detroit *Free Press*.

University Club is founded as an organization of Detroit's college graduates.

Frank Hecker and Charles Freer, who founded Peninsular Car Co. in 1885, retire; they are millionaires several times over and have been instrumental in Detroit's industrial growth. Freer devotes himself to art, amassing impressive collection of contemporary American art and Oriental paintings, later given to Smithsonian Institution in Washington, D.C.

Ransom E. Olds opens his first automobile factory in Detroit; Olds Motor Works is on East Jefferson near Belle Isle.

First Detroit auto show is held when auto dealer William Metzger and hardware merchant Seneca Lewis lease Light Guard Armory and organize the Tri-State Sportsman's and Automobile Association exhibit; 2 steam and 2 electric cars are displayed.

Dec. 30. Excursion steamer *Tashmoo* is launched.

Rabbi Leo M. Franklin begins serving Temple Beth El congregation (to 1950); becomes highly influential community leader.

River Rouge is incorporated as a village.

World History

Zealous temperance leader Carrie Nation begins Kansas wrecking expeditions ("hatchetations") in protest of alcohol consumption.

Cigar workers in Tampa (Ybor City), Florida, go on strike.

Filipinos rebel (to 1901) against U.S. control.

Open Door policy advanced by U.S. Secretary of State John Hay, asking major powers to uphold free use by all nations of treaty ports in China.

Boer War (to 1902): Afrikaner republics, Orange Free State and Transvaal, join forces against Britain.

International Peace Conference at The Hague; initiated by Russian Czar Nicholas II's peace proposals (1898).

Cultural Progress

Educator and reformer John Dewey publishes *School and Society*; sets forth influential ideas on progressive education.

American writer Kate Chopin pens *The Awakening*. Harshly criticized for realistic depiction of social, moral restrictions placed on women; becomes influential later.

Scott Joplin begins playing, popularizing ragtime.

Scientific and Commercial Progress

Motor Age first published.

British physicist Ernest Rutherford discovers and names alpha and beta rays in radioactive atoms.

President William McKinley becomes first U.S. president to ride in a car—a Stanley Steamer.

J. A. Packard builds his first car.

Canned condensed soup originates with Dr. John T. Dorrance and is marketed by the Joseph Campbell Preserve Co. of Camden, New Jersey.

United Fruit Co. is incorporated.

Drought-resistant wheat introduced in U.S.

1900

Detroit and Michigan

Michigan's population, 2,420,982.

Detroit's population, 285,704, 6-fold increase since 1860; ranks 13th in size among U.S. cities. Expansion of industry has prompted growth. (Combined population of Detroit, Highland Park, Hamtramck, about 300,000.)

Detroit has largest percentage of non-English-speaking population in nation—11.98%.

Beginning of peak immigration periods for many Detroit nationality groups.

Detroit consists of 23 square miles of territory along Detroit River; extends northward (inland) roughly 2 miles.

April 2. Henry M. Utley Library, first Detroit Library branch fully staffed and operated by Library Commission, opens in Central High School, Rm. 18. Another branch opens in Harris School (April 16); 3rd branch opens at Western High (Oct.).

Detroit Tigers become charter members of newly formed American Baseball League; first league game played April 19.

Sept. 29. Detroit Golf Club links formally opened.

Dec. 31. Detroit United Railway consolidates city's streetcar lines.

Side-wheeler *Tashmoo* (White Star Lines) begins taking Detroiters on excursions to Harsens Island, where amusement park occupies 60 acres with picnic grounds, casino.

Alice Chaney (Detroit) is first woman to be licensed as Great Lakes ship's pilot.

Grand residences for Detroit's leading industrialists begin to be built in Boston-Edison neighborhood (between Woodward and Linwood avenues). Over next 3 decades, about 900 homes will be built.

State Savings Bank, white marble beaux arts classical building, completed at corner of Fort and Shelby.

Bicentennial Memorial project launched: supporters hope to raise $1 million to build elaborate monument with viewing tower on lower Belle Isle; plan fails to gain public support.

Twentieth Century Club, founded by Clara Arlette Avery, builds Century Association Building, first in Detroit financed by women.

Joseph Boyer, founder of Boyer Machine Co. (pneumatic hammer manufacturer), moves business from St. Louis to Detroit; commissions Albert Kahn to design factory. Small mill on Second Ave. is Kahn's first factory.

Grand Army of the Republic Building, designed by Detroit architect Julius Hess, completed at 1924 Grand River Ave. Fortress-like structure provides meeting place for Michigan Civil War veterans.

Jerome H. Remick becomes sole owner of Detroit music publishing firm he built into world's largest.

Dry goods wholesaler Crowley Brothers (forerunner of Crowley, Milner and Co.) occupies Palms Block; one of many wholesale operations along Jefferson, whose former retailers have steadily moved up Woodward.

Detroit, center for production of iron, brass, copper, and hub of great railroad network, positioned to become center of auto industry, now just a fledgling concern. Local capitalists turn attention to new enterprise.

Detroit is nation's largest producer of heating and cooking stoves; city also center for shipbuilding, cigar and pharmaceutical manufacturing. Other major products are rail cars, paints, foundry and machine shop products, and beer.

World History

World population, 1.6 billion. Most populous cities are London, New York, Paris.

U.S. population, 75,994,575.

Average U.S. life expectancy, 47; median age, 23.

Infant mortality per 1,000 live births (U.S.), 140.

U.S. unemployment, 5%.

Average weekly earnings (U.S.), $9.70; average workweek, 52 hours.

U.S. postal rate for first-class mail, 2 cents.

U.S. has 5.7 million farms; 42% of American workers are employed in agriculture.

Estimated 8,000 cars on U.S. roads.

Sept. 8. Galveston, Texas, struck by powerful hurricane; at least 8,000 die. Worst recorded natural disaster in American history.

Nov. 6. Radical labor leader Eugene Debs makes unsuccessful run for U.S. presidency. President William McKinley is reelected over rival William Jennings Bryan.

Aug. 14. Boxer Rebellion (began May) in China suppressed by international forces.

Cultural Progress

Number of American newspapers peaks this decade; about 2,600 dailies, 14,000 weeklies in print.

Best-selling book in U.S., *To Have and to Hold,* historical novel by American Mary Johnston.

Frank L. Baum writes *Wonderful Wizard of Oz.*

John Singer Sargent paints *The Three Graces* (*The Wyndham Sisters*); among his finest portraits.

Jean Sibelius composes *Finlandia.*

Philadelphia Orchestra founded.

Scott Joplin's "Maple Leaf Rag" (recorded 1899) is a breakout hit.

Vaudeville is rapidly becoming popular form of entertainment in U.S.; Americans also enjoy baseball, ragtime music, the cakewalk (dance), poker, table tennis (Ping-Pong). Dream books, palm reading, fortune-telling also popular.

April 2. First motion picture theater showings, in Los Angeles; admission 2 cents.

More than 10 million Americans own bicycles.

Baseball's American League founded.

Olympics (2nd) held in Paris.

Scientific and Commercial Progress

Ferdinand von Zeppelin builds, pilots first successful rigid airship.

Max Planck develops quantum theory of light; with Einstein's theory of relativity (1905), forms basis of modern physics.

U.S. army surgeon Walter Reed confirms Cuban physician Carlos Finlay's suggestion that yellow fever is transmitted by mosquitoes.

Sigmund Freud publishes *Interpretation of Dreams.*

Wireless telegraphy inventor Guglielmo Marconi establishes American Marconi Company.

First operating escalator used in New York City train station.

National Automobile Manufacturers Association organized; reaches 112 members by 1902.

Nov. 3. National automobile show held at New York's Madison Square Garden; 31 exhibitors display cars.

Mission furniture becomes popular in U.S.

Detroit in Its World Setting

1901-2001

The morning trip to Bois Blanc Island and Amherstburg cost thirty-five cents for adults and twenty-five cents for children in this turn-of-the-century photograph.

Fannie Richards, the first African American schoolteacher in Detroit and an early opponent of segregated schools.

The operators of the Michigan State Automobile School pose for a formal group photograph in the early 1900s. There are an estimated 8,000 automobiles in the U.S. in 1900.

These members of the Department of Public Works pause from their labors for a photograph.

The AME Zion Church on Catherine Street shows members of its Sunday school class in all their finery.

Chief Andrew J. Blackbird at age 98, in Harbor Springs, Michigan.

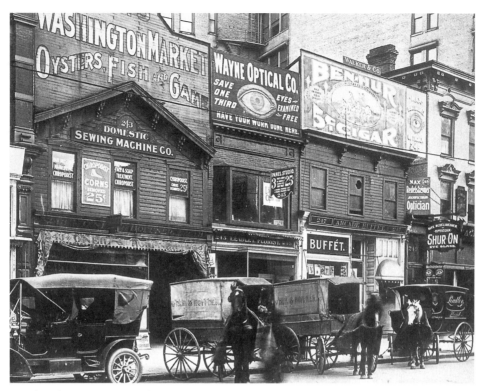

Woodward Avenue, 1907. Delivery wagons line the west side of Woodward, but the automobile is starting to make its appearance.

Chippewa Indian Chief David Shappenagon, dressed in traditional tribal garb.

Campus Martius, 1909. The heart of the city throbs with activity as electric streetcars, horse-drawn delivery wagons, and automobiles all move people and freight throughout.

Woodward Avenue, 1911. A man waits patiently for the photographer to get his shot as horses share Woodward Avenue with automobiles.

Campus Martius, 1915. Women wear their finest while strolling down Woodward Avenue. Across the street, the Soldiers and Sailors Monument stands guard next to the Pontchartrain Hotel.

Woodward Avenue, 1918. This view looking north shows Hudson's department store not yet soaring up into the sky. World War I was in its last year.

The world's largest flag. First unfurled in 1923, the Hudson's flag measures 90 feet tall by 230 feet long, and weighs 900 pounds.

The Ambassador Bridge, 1928. A shot from the U.S. tower toward Canada shows the suspension cables in place on the world's longest international suspension bridge.

The Fox Theater, 1928. The last of the lavish movie palaces built in Detroit, the Fox Theater opened in 1928. It could seat just over 5,000.

The Housewives League of Detroit was founded in 1930 and aimed to strengthen the economic base of the African American community by directing families to spend money with African American-owned businesses.

Hudson's Thanksgiving Day Parade, 1930s. This float, representing Goldilocks and the Three Bears, is pulled by hand.

The All-Time Tiger Team, as chosen by the voice of the Detroit Tigers, Ernie Harwell.

The Tigers win the pennant! An aerial view of Brigg's Stadium shows the crowd in the field as the home team captures the American League pennant on October 5, 1940.

Passengers get a close-up of river traffic from the deck of the Bob-Lo boat during the 1940s.

On the home front, 1940s. Home on furlough, a young woman takes time to pose with her friends at the USO Club.

Detroit Red Wing All Star Gordie Howe admires the Stanley Cup, which spent more time in Detroit than anywhere else during the 1950s.

The Corner at night. Briggs Stadium is lit up for a night game during the 1950s.

Grand Boulevard and Second Street, c. 1951. Traffic is heavy along West Grand Boulevard near the Fisher Building, with five busses in sight.

Mayor Albert E. Cobo trowels mortar in the dedication ceremony for the new City-County Building in 1953.

The Corner, 1953. Fans flock to the ballpark early in mid-season to see if their Tigers can win another pennant race.

Santa Claus arrives at the J. L. Hudson Building flanked by toy soldiers at the end of another Thanksgiving Day Parade.

The 1953–54 National Hockey League Stanley Cup Winners, the Detroit Red Wings.

Riverfront parking, 1954. Pleasure steamers are at their berths along the riverfront. One of the Bob-Lo boats and two steamers of the Detroit and Cleveland line await their passengers.

The riverfront, 1959. This aerial view of Detroit's riverfront shows the ongoing construction of Cobo Hall and Convention Arena.

The riverfront, 1959. The Penobscot and Guardian Buildings dominate Detroit's skyline.

A view of Detroit from Canada, 1980. The Detroit skyline as seen from Windsor, Ontario, displays its latest addition—the Renaissance Center.

Soon to be a memory, Old City Hall stands empty and nearly windowless awaiting the wrecker's ball in 1961.

The Hudson's Parade, late 1960s. What a contrast to earlier parades where the floats were man-powered.

Jefferson Avenue, 1973. The riverfront along Jefferson Avenue depicts Mariners Church and the Detroit-Windsor Tunnel on a summer day.

The 1984 World Champion Detroit Tigers.

1999 DETROIT LIONS
National Football Conference Central Division

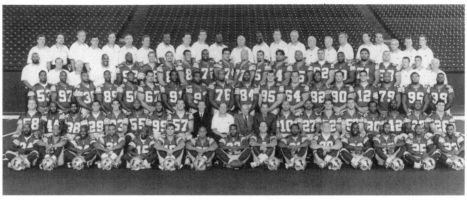

1999 Detroit Lions team photo. Courtesy Detroit Lions.

NBA Championship celebration in the Detroit Pistons locker room (1990). Photo by Allen Einstein.

1901

Detroit and Michigan

Aaron T. Bliss, Republican, governor (to 1904).

Feb. 2. Fire in *Free Press* building.

Feb. 28. Detroit Olds plant burns; Detroit factory rebuilt and a second plant opens in Lansing.

May 4. Ripper Act places single commissioner as head of Detroit public works, parks, boulevards, and police department.

May 30. Memorial Day observances include strewing flowers from Belle Isle bridge in memory of naval heroes.

June 18. Hazen Pingree, Detroit's great reform mayor and former Michigan governor, dies.

July 24. Detroit celebrates its bicentennial. Leaders recreate Cadillac's arrival; 2 parades are held. "Chair of Justice" erected in Cadillac Square.

Dec. 18. Eastern High School dedicated.

Dedication ceremony held for Merrill Fountain, in front of Detroit Opera House on Campus Martius. Built in honor of Detroit lumberman Charles Merrill, his son-in-law, Senator Thomas Palmer, speaks at event.

Interurban rail lines consolidated as Detroit United Railway System.

Fire claims Detroit Boat Club on Belle Isle; Detroit architect Alpheus Chittenden commissioned to design fireproof structure.

Henry Ford Co. organized.

Oldsmobile produces first American car to be manufactured in quantity; Curved Dash Oldsmobile has a top speed of 18 mph and sells for around $650.

Michigan Pioneer Museum founded in Lansing.

World History

American Federation of Labor now 1 million strong.

Jan. 22. Queen Victoria dies; succeeded by oldest son, Edward VII (to 1910).

July 29. Socialist party founded in U.S.

Sept. 6. President William McKinley is shot by anarchist Leon Czolgosz; dies Sept. 14. Succeeded by Vice President Theodore Roosevelt, 26th U.S. president.

Civil government established in Philippines following rebellion.

Cultural Progress

Booker T. Washington's *Up from Slavery* published.

Chicago's Tribune Building erected after design contest.

Scientific and Commercial Progress

First state automobile legislation is Connecticut's speed limit law.

First transatlantic message sent via radio.

American engineer Reginald Fessenden patents high-frequency alternator; first successful radio transmitter.

Spindletop oilfield in eastern Texas produces nation's first gusher.

Feb. J. P. Morgan founds U.S. Steel.

Hershey chocolate bar debuts.

1902

Detroit and Michigan

There are 74 millionaires in Michigan, including 44 in Detroit.

Feb. 27. First annual automobile and sportsman show held at Detroit Armory.

Detroit union carpenters propose 30 cents/hour minimum wage; painters, $2.50/day.

April 29. Voigt Farm (30,000 feet frontage in vicinity of Woodward, Calvert and Chicago Blvd.) sells for $800,000. Eighteen years earlier, Voigt paid $55,000 for property.

May 3. Prohibitionist Carrie Nation lectures in Detroit.

June 6. Protest against proposed $3 license fee for auto owners.

Aug. 17. Marie Dressler appears at Avenue Theater.

Sept. 21. President Theodore Roosevelt addresses Spanish-American War Veterans Convention in Detroit.

Oct. 11. Wayne County Building dedicated.

Wayne County Courthouse completed at eastern end of Cadillac Square: portico decorated with relief of Gen. Anthony Wayne conferring with American Indians, flanked by bronze sculptures symbolizing Progress and Victory; on building's 4 corners are figures symbolizing Law, Commerce, Agriculture, and Mechanics.

Detroit Boat Club inaugurates its third clubhouse (in Spanish colonial style) on Belle Isle; previous structures consumed by fires.

Henry Ford Co. reorganizes to form Cadillac Automobile Co.

Pierce-Arrow Automobile Co. founded.

Jonathan Maxwell and Charles King design running boards for their Silent Northern Car.

Detroit businessman Joseph Boyer becomes president of Arithmometer Co. (later Burroughs Adding Machine Co.); lays plans to move operations from St. Louis to Detroit.

Detroit's Dexter Ferry donates acreage to University of Michigan for new athletic fields; Regents Field renamed Ferry Field, home of the Wolverines.

World History

May 9. United Mine Workers strike of anthracite coal mines begins; far-reaching effects. Resolved by presidential commission, Oct. 21.

Republic of Cuba established.

Maryland is first state to enact workmen's compensation law; by 1920 all but 5 states have such laws.

Aug. 30. Martinique's Mount Pelee erupts; claims 29,000 lives.

Cultural Progress

Jan. 1. First Rose Bowl played: University of Michigan defeats Stanford, 49-0.

Black writer Paul Laurence Dunbar publishes novel *The Sports of Gods*; Dunbar's poetry (published mid- to late-1890s) has gained him a national reputation.

Rhodes scholarships for Oxford study established by will of Cecil Rhodes.

Scientific and Commercial Progress

J. C. Penney founded: originally called Golden Rule, by 1946 it will open 1,612 stores.

Teddy bear introduced.

1903

Detroit and Michigan

Jan. 20. Detroit Edison Co. incorporated.

Feb. First automobile sections appear in Detroit newspapers.

May 5. Booker T. Washington speaks in Detroit on race problem in South.

June 16. Ford Motor Co. incorporated in Detroit by 40-year-old Henry Ford. $28,000 in capital put up by 12 shareholders; Henry Ford owns 25% of stock. First factory located at Bellevue and Mack.

June 30. Detroit Board of Commerce formally organized.

Oct. 25. Belle Isle Horticultural Building opens to public.

Nov. 13. Price of milk increases to 7 cents per quart.

Clara B. Arthur founds Detroit's first playground; instrumental in establishing 138 playgrounds before her death in 1929.

Mary Chase Perry, with funding from businessman Horace J. Caulkins, founds Pewabic Pottery in Detroit; iridescent glazed tiles and pottery become one of city's artistic trademarks. Pewabic tiles are installed in Detroit Public Library, St. Paul's Cathedral Church; in homes, banks, other buildings in area. (Perry names pottery company after Pewabic Copper Mine near her hometown of Hancock in Michigan's Upper Peninsula.)

Palms Apartment Building on East Jefferson (Detroit) and UM's Engineering Building (Ann Arbor), both by Albert Kahn and George Mason, completed; Michigan's first buildings of reinforced concrete.

Engineer Julius Kahn (brother of Albert) invents "Kahn system"; makes construction of concrete buildings practical. To manufacture concrete bars, he founds Trussed Concrete Steel Co. (later renamed Truscon) in Detroit.

Buick Co. organized in Flint by Benjamin Briscoe to manufacture cars designed by David Buick.

Packard Motor Car Co. founded by Detroiter Henry Joy; Russell A. Alger among several prominent owners.

Construction begins on Packard Motor Car Co. factory on East Grand Blvd. Detroit's first large automobile plant, *Motor Age* praises it as one of "new style of factories" and calls it part of "movement toward rational working places." Facility (designed by Albert Kahn) will be added to over next several years to remain Packard's chief manufacturing plant until 1956.

World History

July. Mary "Mother" Jones leads child workers in demanding 55-hour week.

Hay-Bunau-Varilla Treaty grants Panama Canal to U.S.

Twenty-year Belgian genocide in Africa's Congo prompts human rights campaign.

W. E. B. Du Bois's *The Souls of Black Folk* predicts problem of the twentieth century will be "the problem of the color line."

June 16. Norwegian explorer Roald Amundsen sets out on voyage (to Sept. 1906) to completely navigate Northwest Passage; first to succeed.

U.S. Department of Commerce and Labor created.

McClure's magazine serializes Ida Tarbell's *History of Standard Oil*, exposé of monopoly; runs series by Lincoln Steffens on urban corruption in U.S. (later published as *The Shame of Cities*). Launches journalism movement dubbed "muckraking"; impetus for political, social, commercial change in Progressive Era.

Cultural Progress

Alfred Stieglitz publishes *Camera Work*; helps establish photography as valid form of artistic expression.

Jack London's *Call of the Wild* and Kate Douglas Wiggins's *Rebecca of Sunnybrook Farm* among bestsellers.

New York's 21-story, triangular Flatiron Building completed.

Edwin S. Porter's 12-minute film *The Great Train Robbery* is first motion picture to tell complete story.

Oct. First World Series: Boston Red Sox (AL) defeat Pittsburgh Pirates (NL), 5 games to 3.

First professional ice hockey league forms in Houghton, Michigan, called International Hockey League.

Scientific and Commercial Progress

American industrial engineer Frederick Winslow Taylor puts forth scientific management theories.

First national bird reservation in U.S. created on Pelican Island, Florida.

July 3. American Pacific cable reaches from San Francisco to Manila (via Honolulu).

July 26. Dr. Horatio Jackson and mechanic Sewall K. Crocker complete first transcontinental trip in gasoline automobile, a Winton. Departed San Francisco May 23; arrive New York City this day.

Dec. 17. Wright brothers make first airplane flight at Kitty Hawk, North Carolina.

1904

Detroit and Michigan

April 22. City ordinance requiring licensing of automobiles is upheld by Supreme Court.

May 30. Gov. Pingree statue unveiled in Grand Circus Park.

Aug. 18. Belle Isle Aquarium opens.

Detroit's first exhibition of handicrafts held at Detroit Museum of Art.

Michigan's Anna Howard Shaw (Big Rapids) elected president of National American Woman Suffrage Association.

Penobscot Building erected; names for river in Maine where Detroit lumberman and builder Simon Murphy grew up.

Detroit News publisher George Booth and wife Ellen (Scripps) Booth purchase large farm in Bloomfield Hills and names it Cranbrook, after Booth family's ancestral home in England.

Detroit loses *Free Press* journalist Frank Cobb (and the paper's leading editorial writer) to the *New York World*. Cobb was handpicked by Joseph Pulitzer to succeed him at the New York paper where he becomes famous for his "fighting" editorials.

Leland-Faulconer Manufacturing Co. (producer of marine and auto motors, machinery, tools) and Cadillac Automobile Co. merge to form Cadillac Motor Car Co.; headed by Henry Leland, who implements assembly with interchangeable parts.

Maxwell-Briscoe Manufacturing Co. founded to make 2-cylinder cars.

Detroit, becoming known as automobile manufacturing center of America, produces nearly 20,000 cars this year.

Burroughs Adding Machine factory begins operation in Detroit.

Olds Motor Works, founded 1897, has grown to become largest producer of automobiles. Founder Ransom E. Olds leaves company and organizes his second self-named auto-manufacturing endeavor, REO Motor Car Co.

Ford Motor Co. outgrows original Mack Ave. factory, moves into new quarters at Piquette Ave. and Beaubien St.

Salt mining begins in Detroit Rock Salt Co. mine near Rouge River.

National Ski Association of America formed at Ishpeming.

World History

Construction of Panama Canal begins. U.S. army officer and physician William Gorgas enforces strict policy of mosquito destruction, greatly reducing instances of yellow fever; key reason for U.S. success.

First survey of U.S. roads reports there are more than 2 million miles of rural public roads; less than 154,000 miles are surfaced in gravel, stones, or planks.

Feb. 10. Russo-Japanese War begins over interests in China and Korea.

Northern Securities case becomes symbol of trust-busting.

Nov. 8. Theodore Roosevelt, Republican, reelected president.

Cultural Progress

Feb. 17. Giacomo Puccini's *Madame Butterfly* first performed, in Milan.

Little Johnny Jones a Broadway hit; features popular songs "Give My Regards to Broadway" and "Yankee Doodle Dandy." Stars George M. Cohan (who also wrote it). Anton Chekhov's play *The Cherry Orchard* and Sir James Barrie's adaptation of fantasy *Peter Pan* also performed this year.

May 5. Cy Young pitches baseball's first perfect game.

Olympics held in St. Louis; first Games hosted by U.S.

Scientific and Commercial Progress

New York subway begins operation.

Ice cream cone debuts at St. Louis World's Fair when vendor serves scoop in wrapped-up waffle.

1905

Detroit and Michigan

Fred M. Warner, Republican, governor (to 1910).

George P. Codd, mayor of Detroit.

May 1. Detroit adopts standard time instead of sun time.

June 4. Remains of Gov. Stevens T. Mason (died 1843) brought to Detroit and interred in Capitol Square.

Aug. 30. Ty Cobb begins major league baseball career with Detroit Tigers.

First Glidden tour held; overland competition (covering 870 miles this year) helps establish auto industry.

Western Michigan College of Education (later Western Michigan University) opens at Kalamazoo.

Michigan State Highway Department established; becomes national leader in highway development.

Detroit Orchestral Association formed to bring orchestras to city; concerts held at Arcadia Theater to 1920.

Detroit Library Commission given authority to operate and staff Hurlburt Library at Water Works Park.

Casino, Detroit's first movie theater, opens on Monroe Ave.

First trucks introduced by Packard, Mitchell, and Maxwell.

Packard Building Number 10 completed; launches building boom in Detroit. Albert Kahn–designed structure is first reinforced concrete factory in city. Automakers recognize advantages of reinforced concrete over mill construction: stronger and more rigid, it allows for increased floor space, greater expanses of windows (for natural lighting); also fireproof. Cheaper and easier than steel construction.

Shortly after Packard's Building Number 10 completed, work finished on Cadillac's reinforced concrete plant on Cass.

Packard and Cadillac plants are served by Michigan Central Belt Line railroad; congestion along line prompts plans for development of outer belt line.

World History

Jan. 22. Bloody Sunday in St. Petersburg. Russian Revolution begins (to 1917); ends war with Japan.

March 4. President Theodore Roosevelt inaugurated; 2nd term.

April 17. Supreme Court ruling declares New York law limiting workweek to 60 hours unconstitutional.

Sept. 5. President Roosevelt mediates settlement of Russo-Japanese War; Korea becomes Japanese protectorate.

International Workers of the World (IWW), "Wobblies," founded to organize workers regardless of craft, skill, sex, or race; advocate socialism. Led by Mother Jones, Bill Haywood, the union eschews politics and advocates general strikes, boycotts, and sabotage.

Niagara movement founded; lead by W. E. B. Du Bois, advocates total integration of blacks into mainstream society.

Rotary Club founded in Chicago.

German sociologist Max Weber writes "The Protestant Ethic and the Spirit of Capitalism": essay asserts Protestant principles contribute to growth of industry, commerce; help build capitalist economy.

Irish nationalist movement Sinn Fein (Ourselves Alone) forms under leadership of Arthur Griffith.

Cultural Progress

George Bernard Shaw's *Major Barbara* produced in London.

Franz Lehar's operetta *The Merry Widow* debuts in Vienna; reaches U.S. next year for first of thousands of performances.

Claude Monet paints *Water Lilies*.

Fauvism art movement begins: Henri Matisse and others stage salon exhibit in Paris; critic decries colorful paintings are *fauves* (wild beasts).

First theater devoted exclusively to screening motion pictures opens": Pittsburgh's Nickelodeon; other nickel-admission theaters soon open.

Scientific and Commercial Progress

Einstein puts forth theory of relativity.

Robert Koch wins Nobel Prize for medicine for work on tuberculosis.

U.S. produces 25,000 cars, 450 trucks this year.

First pizzeria in U.S. opens in New York City.

1906

Detroit and Michigan

June. *Detroit News* founder and publisher James Scripps dies; son-in-law George Booth becomes president of news company; Scripps wills $50,000 to Detroit for beautification projects.

Sept. 4. Estimated 115,000 Detroiters jam fairgrounds to hear William Jennings Bryan speak.

Detroit River is world's busiest inland water channel.

Henry Ford now owns 51% of Ford Motor Co.

Detroit's Library Commission constructs its first branch building: Gray Branch, on Field Ave. near East Jefferson, opens June 1.

Society of Arts and Crafts founded; promotes ideal that practical objects should be inherently beautiful.

Detroit Fine Arts Society founded.

Shrine Circus begins in Detroit.

Construction finished on Detroit home of architect Albert Kahn at Mack Ave. and John R.

Henry Ford buys 60-acre tract in Highland Park, about 10 miles northwest of downtown Detroit; future site of manufacturing complex.

England's Rolls Royce introduces Silver Ghost; car sets new standard in auto design.

World History

Jan. Upton Sinclair publishes *The Jungle,* exposing deplorable health standards of U.S. meatpacking industry. Leads way to reforms.

April 18. Earthquake rocks San Francisco; fire burns 3 days to claim two-thirds of city, including business district; 3,000 are killed.

June 30. Congress passes Pure Food and Drug Act, Meat Inspection Act.

Hepburn Act strengthens Interstate Commerce Commission.

Cultural Progress

Zane Grey first enters ranks of bestsellers with *Spirit of the Border,* as does Robert W. Chambers with *The Fighting Chance.*

O. Henry's *The Four Million* gains popularity.

John Galsworthy begins publishing *Forsyte Saga* trilogy: *A Man of Property* is first to appear; becomes popular in Britain and U.S.

Henry O. Tanner paints *Disciples at the Tomb.* African American artist's religious and earlier works depicting slavery gain him international reputation.

Henrik Ibsen's *Hedda Gabler* among Broadway hits this year.

John Philip Sousa is "march king."

Feb. 24. Tommy Burns of Detroit becomes world heavyweight champion.

Scientific and Commercial Progress

First gasoline automobile fire engine with hose wagon produced in U.S.

Dec. 24. First radio broadcast of voice and music originates from Brant Rock, Massachusetts.

1907

Detroit and Michigan

William B. Thompson, mayor of Detroit.

March 2. *Detroit Saturday Night* begins publication.

July 29. First session of Juvenile Court (division of Wayne County Probate Court).

Detroit Tigers win American League pennant.

Oct. 29. The 10-story Pontchartrain Hotel completed at Woodward on Cadillac Square; replaces old Russell House to become Detroit's premier hostelry, setting for social events.

Police try to establish auto speed limit of 8 miles per hour in business district; 12 mph elsewhere.

Seven people are killed in auto accidents in Detroit this year.

High school for practical training opens in Cass Union School (origin of Cass Tech).

St. Florian Church founded in response to Detroit's growing Polish population.

Hopkin Club founded to promote arts in Detroit.

Pewabic Pottery works built on East Jefferson.

Clara B. Arthur founds first public swimming pool in Detroit.

Annual auto show organized by city's 16 dealers, who form what becomes Detroit Auto Dealers Association.

Edward Murphy begins building the Oakland car (later renamed Pontiac).

International Salt acquires rights to mine formerly operated by Detroit Salt Co.

Russian immigrants Perry and Ben Feigenson found Faygo soft drink company.

World History

March 21. U.S. Marines land in Honduras to protect U.S. interests.

Nov. 16. Oklahoma admitted to Union.

Second Hague Conference held.

Cultural Progress

Robert Baden-Powell of Britain starts Boy Scouts when he organizes camp for 20 boys, publishes first Boy Scout manual 1908.

American psychologist William James publishes *Pragmatism,* founding philosophic movement by same name.

Pablo Picasso's *Les Demoiselles d'Avignon* heralds cubism art movement.

Ziegfeld Follies a Broadway hit.

Vaudeville features Salome dancers after U.S. performance of Richard Strauss's opera *Salome* created stir.

Gibson Girl style is popular among fashion-conscious women.

Oct. Chicago Cubs defeat Detroit Tigers 4 games to 0 in World Series.

Scientific and Commercial Progress

Albert A. Michelson is first American to win Nobel Prize for physics, for his design of precise optical instruments.

Lee De Forest invents radio vacuum tube.

Bell & Howell Co. founded in Chicago to improve motion picture photography, projection equipment.

First complete, self-contained electric washing machine, brand name Thor, is marketed by Hurley Machine Co. of Chicago.

1908

Detroit and Michigan

April. Common Council passes ordinance for systematic collection of garbage throughout city.

Sept. 16. Flint businessman William Durant (founded Buick Motor Car Co., 1905) unifies several Michigan-based automakers as General Motors Co.; acquires Lansing-based Olds Motor Works.

Detroit Tigers win American League pennant for second year in a row.

Oct. 8. First automobile taxicabs appear on Detroit streets with automatic fare registers.

Motorcycles replace bicycles on Detroit's police cycle squad.

State constitutional convention: woman suffrage defeated 57 to 38, but women who pay taxes can vote on local bonding and tax issues.

New Michigan constitution adopted (state's third; goes into effect 1909).

New casino erected on Belle Isle to replace original structure.

Ford builds first Model T; sells 10,000 this year.

Packard introduces rumble seat.

Fisher Body Co. organized.

Paige-Detroit Motor Car Co. incorporated.

Crowley, Milner and Co. founded.

Improvements begin to Grand River—U.S. Highway 16.

World History

U.S. Department of War contracts Orville and Wilbur Wright to build first military airplane.

July 6–24. Young Turk Revolution: revolt against Ottoman sultan Abdülhamid II; culminates in establishment of constitutional government.

Aug. Three days of racial violence in Springfield, Illinois, lead to call for "conference on the Negro"; origin of NAACP (*See* 1910).

Nov. 3. William Howard Taft, Republican, elected president.

Cultural Progress

L. M. Montgomery writes *Anne of Green Gables*.

"Shine On, Harvest Moon," and "Take Me Out to the Ball Game" (both by Jack Norworth) are popular songs.

Olympics held in London.

National Hockey League founded.

Oct. Chicago Cubs defeat Detroit Tigers in World Series.

Dec. 26. Jack Johnson is first black to win world heavyweight championship, defeating Tommy Burns.

Scientific and Commercial Progress

U.S. produces 50,000 motor cars this year.

Glenn H. Curtiss makes first official public flight of more than 1 kilometer in U.S.

1909

Detroit and Michigan

Philip Breitmeyer, mayor of Detroit.

Pay scale in auto factories (Oct.) ranges from 9 cents per hour for unskilled to 40 cents for skilled workers.

Jan. 1. New Y.M.C.A. building at Witherell and Adams first occupied.

Feb. 20. Hudson Motor Car Co. founded by J. L. Hudson and other investors.

May. Common Council creates City Plan and Improvement Commission.

July 3. First Hudson motor car comes off line.

July 7. GM acquires Cadillac Motor Car Co.

Summer. New bathhouse and bathing beach open on Belle Isle.

Detroit Tigers win American League pennant for third year in a row.

Dec. 31. In first full year of production, Ford delivers 17,500 Model Ts.

Construction begins on Ford's Highland Park plant, first large auto manufacturing facility in city. In operation 1910. Over next decade, building continues on 30-acre site along Woodward Ave., with complex completed in 1920.

Ford Building (18 stories), designed by Chicago architect Daniel Burnham (who has gained prestige for his skyscrapers), completed on northwest corner of Griswold and Congress.

Nation's first mile of concrete pavement laid in Detroit over stretch of Woodward Ave. (between 6 and 7 Mile roads).

Booths plan art academy at Cranbrook; to be modeled on American Academy in Rome—students independently pursue courses of study under guidance of master artists.

World History

March 4. William Howard Taft inaugurated; 27th U.S. president.

April 6. Robert E. Peary reaches North Pole; accompanied by African American explorer Matthew A. Henson, 3 Inuit. Credited as first expedition to do so.

Nov. 22. Women shirtwaist laborers strike.

Payne-Aldrich Tariff: Taft's efforts to reform tariffs thwarted.

Lynchings result in numerous deaths in U.S.

Cultural Progress

American feminist and Socialist Charlotte Perkins Gilman founds monthly *Forerunner* (published to 1916).

Girl Guides organized in England.

Arnold Schoenberg composes atonal work *Three Pieces* for piano; vehemently criticized by establishment, work is later hailed by many as century's most important.

Sergey Diaghilev founds Ballets Russes in Paris; lavish productions revolutionize ballet.

Frank Lloyd Wright builds Robie House in Chicago; influences international architecture.

U.S. has 9,000 film theaters.

Oct. Pittsburgh Pirates defeat Detroit Tigers in World Series.

Scientific and Commercial Progress

Airship inventor Ferdinand von Zeppelin cofounds world's first commercial airline.

Bakelite plastic introduced; launches synthetics industries.

1910

Detroit and Michigan

Michigan's population, 2,810,172.

Detroit's population, 465,766; ranks 9th in size among U.S. cities. City is 40.8 square miles in area.

Chaldeans (from northwest Iraq) begin immigrating; settling in Detroit.

Michigan has 9,100 miles of railroad tracks.

Jan. Ford's Highland Park plant begins producing cars: main structure is 4 stories, 75 feet wide, and 865 feet long—largest building under one roof in Michigan. Albert Kahn–designed building becomes model for other auto manufacturing plants.

June 20. Detroit Industrial Exposition opens.

July 14. Arch Hoxsey pilots biplane at fairgrounds; first airplane flight in Detroit.

Aug. 1. Jessie Bonstelle Stock Co. opens first theatrical season in Detroit's Garrick Theater; presents *The White Sister*. Bonstelle becomes known as maker of stars, helping launch careers of stage notables Katharine Cornell, Ann Harding, Frank Morgan, Melvyn Douglas, William Powell.

Sept. 5. First primary election in Michigan.

Sept. 18. Michigan Central Railroad tunnel under Detroit River to Windsor opens to freight train traffic; opens to passenger trains Oct. 15.

Sept. Detroit schools organize Department of Special Education; among earliest in nation to do so.

Oct. 28. Detroit Rotary Club organized.

Detroit Mayor Philip Breitmeyer founds City Plan Commission, which invites Chicago architects Daniel Burnham and Edward Bennett to make tour of city; Bennett is asked to develop beautification plan for Detroit.

Virginia Park homeowners, in neighborhood of Woodward and Second avenues, form association to protect community from deterioration caused by encroachment by commercial Woodward Ave.

Paradise Valley, entertainment hot spot in African American neighborhood (bounded by Brush, Gratiot, Hastings, Vernor), begins to thrive. Over next 4 decades, becomes home to black-owned stores, restaurants, hotels, bowling alleys. Its nightclubs, including 606 Horseshoe Lounge, Club Plantation, B&C Club, become nationally known.

Between middle belt line and (under-construction) outer belt line of Detroit's rail system, rows of frame houses are erected to accommodate growing number of factory workers in city.

Improvements in transportation prompt Detroit businessmen to convert summer homes in Grosse Pointe to year-round use.

Chicagoan Daniel Burnham completes work on Detroit's 24-story Dime Building (northwest corner of Griswold and Fort).

Steamer *Ste. Claire* put into service (with *Columbia*, launched 1902) will ferry excursion-ists to popular Bob-Lo Island. Vessels include dance floors and beer gardens.

Cadillac begins offering enclosed, weatherproof bodies as standard equipment.

Maxwell-Briscoe Manufacturing cofounder Benjamin Briscoe combines company with several other auto companies to form United States Motor Co.

Parke, Davis & Co. pioneers profit sharing and old age pension plan.

World History

U.S. population, 91,972,266.

U.S. unemployment, 5.9%.

U.S. workforce includes 9 million women; 75% earn less than $8 per week.

Ballinger-Pinchot controversy raises questions about President Taft's support of conserva-tion. Department of Agriculture's chief forester forced to resign.

April. National Urban League founded.

July 4. Boxer Jack Johnson's knockout of "Great White Hope" James J. Jeffries sets off race riots in many U.S. cities.

Nov. 8. First Socialist elected to Congress; Victor Berger represents Wisconsin.

NAACP (National Association for the Advancement of Colored People) founded by black and white leaders. Official journal, *The Crisis,* advocated by "crusader for justice" Ida Bell Wells Barnett.

Mann-Elkins Act strengthens Interstate Commerce Commission.

Britain's King Edward VII dies; succeeded by son, George V (to 1936).

British combine holdings in Africa to form Union of South Africa.

Cultural Progress

William D. Boyce founds Boy Scouts of America.

The Fundamentals is published; sets forth ideas of philosophical movement by same name.

Newspaper cartoonist John Randolph Bray pioneers animated motion pictures, using "cel" system.

Jan. 13. New York's Metropolitan Opera is broadcast over radio for first time: "father of radio" Lee De Forest airs performance by tenor Enrico Caruso.

John Philip Sousa's band begins triumphal U.S. tour.

March 1. Russian ballet dancer Anna Pavlova makes New York debut; kicks off company tour of U.S., Canada that renews public interest in classical ballet.

First newsreel is screened: Pathé Weekly by French cinematographers Charles and Emil Pathé.

Detroit's Ty Cobb wins his first American League batting title; wins it every season through 1919 (except 1916).

Scientific and Commercial Progress

U.S. steel production has increased by factor of 20 since 1880.

Electric laundry machine introduced by National Sewing Machine Company.

1911

Detroit and Michigan

Chase S. Osborn, Republican, governor (to 1912).

William B. Thompson, mayor of Detroit.

Jan. 10. Detroit College reorganized as University of Detroit.

Jan. 15. Detroit Tuberculosis Sanatorium dedicated.

March. Juvenile Detention Home opens.

May 1. Herman Kiefer Hospital for infectious diseases opens.

June 17. Steamer *Put-in-Bay,* hailed as biggest excursion boat yet built for Detroit River, takes maiden voyage from Wyandotte.

Sept. 18. President William Howard Taft visits Detroit.

GM stock sells on New York Stock Exchange; first auto securities to be listed on NYSE.

Nov. 3. Chevrolet Motor Co. founded as joint venture of American auto racer and designer Louis Chevrolet and GM's William Durant.

Dec. Detroit Zoological Society formed; Horace Rackham first president.

State flag adopted, bearing Michigan seal.

Cathedral Church of St. Paul (Episcopal) dedicated at Woodward and Warren in Detroit.

St. Peter Claver Mission, African American Catholic congregation, is organized in meeting room at St. Mary's School (on St. Antoine).

White traffic lines painted on River Rd. near Trenton, Michigan, under direction of Wayne County Road Commissioner Edward N. Hines to provide "center line safety stripe"; first in U.S.

Michigan's Harriet Quimby (Branch County) becomes first woman in nation, second in world, to receive pilot's license.

Cadillac begins installing electric starters on its cars; eliminates hand cranking.

Headlights and horns become standard equipment on Model T.

World History

March 25. Triangle Shirtwaist factory fire (New York City) kills 146; gives impetus to labor movement, workplace safety reforms.

May 15. Standard Oil Trust broken by U.S. Supreme Court. With court-ordered dissolution of James B. Duke's American Tobacco, decision sets precedent for enforcement of Sherman Anti-Trust Act (1890), demonstrates new intolerance for monopolies—forms "rule of reason" doctrine.

Dec. Roald Amundsen leads Norwegian expedition to South Pole; first to reach it.

Mexican President Porfirio Diaz overthrown by rebels led by Francisco Madero; Mexican Revolution begins.

Cultural Progress

Song "Everybody's Doing It" and turkey trot dance popular.

American songwriter Irving Berlin's "Alexander's Ragtime Band" sweeps nation.

May 30. Indianapolis 500 first held. Ray Harroun runs his car at speed of 74 mph to win.

Scientific and Commercial Progress

Efficiency expert Frederick Winslow Taylor publishes landmark work *The Principles of Scientific Management*; doctrine soon embraced by American industry.

First transcontinental airplane flight: Calbraith P. Rogers leaves New York Sept. 17; arrives Pasadena Nov. 5. Actual flying time, 3 days, 10 hours, 4 minutes.

1912

Detroit and Michigan

U.S. Census Bureau places Michigan first in nation in manufacture of automobiles.

Feb. 5. Detroit Boy Scouts honor founder Sir Robert Baden-Powell.

March 15. Workman's Compensation Act passed by Michigan legislature.

April 20. Navin Field dedicated for baseball.

William Scripps backs promotional voyage of 35-foot boat *Detroit,* powered by gasoline marine engine manufactured by his company. Vessel gets under way July 2; destination, St. Petersburg, Russia. Scripps hopes publicity will boost public confidence in ocean travel after *Titanic* disaster (April 15).

July 22–26. Cadillaqua: Detroit celebrates its founder and river with parades. Festivities end when several Detroit city council members are arrested and charged with accepting bribes.

Oct. 19. Livingstone Channel in lower Detroit River opens after more than 4 years of work; it is 11 miles long and cost $10 million.

Nov. Gov. Osborn convinces state legislature to put question of woman suffrage before all-male electorate. Clara Arthur (Detroit) leads campaign and proposal appears to gain favor but is ultimately defeated in general elections.

First class for blind established in Detroit public schools.

Detroit Library Commission selects Woodward Ave. property (at Kirby) for new site of main library. New York architect Cass Gilbert selected to design facility.

Detroit businessman J. L. Hudson dies in Europe; department store taken over by his 4 nephews, Webber brothers. J. L. Hudson Co. Department Store, at Gratiot Ave. and Farmer St. in Detroit, completes its first site expansion.

Dance pavilion added to Tashmoo Park on Harsens Island at mouth of St. Clair River. Destination continues to be popular with weekend excursionists from Detroit.

Idlewild, 2,700-acre tract in Lake County, develops as resort for Detroit's and Chicago's growing African American middle class.

Detroit Business Woman's Club founded.

Overalls manufacturer William Muir Finck builds 18-room residence on Van Dyke near Jefferson, beginning long history of "Van Dyke Place."

World History

Jan. 6. New Mexico admitted to Union.

Feb. 14. Arizona admitted to Union (last of contiguous states to be admitted).

April 15. Luxury liner R.M.S. *Titanic,* en route from Southampton, England, to New York Harbor, hits an iceberg in North Atlantic and sinks just after 2 a.m. There are 1,513 dead; 711 survivors, mostly women and children traveling as first-class passengers. Disaster prompts lawmakers to pass legislation making sea travel safer: ships must carry enough lifeboats to save all passengers, lifeboat drills must be conducted, shipping lanes are moved farther south (away from ice fields).

Radio Act: In *Titanic* aftermath, Congress passes act requiring ship radios be manned 24 hours, have minimum 100-mile range; licensed operators must adhere to bandwidth regulations, observe protocol for distress signals. (Paves way for Federal Communications Commission.)

Nov. 5. Woodrow Wilson, Democrat, elected president.

Tibet regains independence following overthrow of China's Ch'ing (Manchu) dynasty.

Cultural Progress

Camp Fire Girls organized by national recreational leader Halsey Gulick and his wife, Charlotte Vetter Gulick.

Italian educator Maria Montessori publishes *The Montessori Method* in English; instant U.S. bestseller. Advocates method to "develop and set free [a child's] personality in a marvelous and surprising way."

Juliette Gordon Low establishes Girl Guiding (holds first meeting in her Savannah, Georgia, home March 12); name soon changed to Girl Scouting.

Zane Grey's *Riders of the Purple Sage* begins run of bestsellers for the Ohio native.

W. C. Handy's "The Memphis Blues" is a hit.

Olympics are held in Stockholm, Sweden. American Indian Jim Thorpe wins pentathlon and decathlon but is later disqualified for not being an amateur athlete.

Scientific and Commercial Progress

Carl Gustav Jung publishes revolutionary work *Psychology of the Unconscious*.

Oreo cookie first produced.

1913

Detroit and Michigan

Woodbridge N. Ferris, Democrat, governor (to 1916).

Oscar B. Marx, mayor of Detroit.

March 26. Himelhoch Brothers open new store.

April 7. Detroit elections: voters favor charter providing for municipal ownership of street railways after state constitution was amended to permit city operation; approve city charter amendment establishing Civil Service Commission.

July 22. Workers in the Copper districts of the Upper Peninsula initiate a strike that lasts until April 14, 1914. Workers seek 8 hour day, better working conditions, $3.50 minimum a day, and right to unionize. They are only partially successful.

Sept. 12. Detroiters celebrate centennial of Commodore Perry's 1813 victory over British on Lake Erie.

Dec. Copper strike turns tragic when 73 women and children from miners' families are trampled to death fleeing upon a false cry of "Fire!" in hall at Calumet where they are attending a Christmas party. Miners blame management.

Dec. 26. New Michigan Central Railroad Station opens on West Vernor in Detroit. Public building was designed by architects responsible for New York's Grand Central Station.

Amendment to Michigan constitution provides for principles of initiative, referendum, recall.

State legislature passes act providing for school board of 7 inspectors elected at large. Adopted by Detroit electors Nov. 7, 1916.

Woman suffrage proposal, again on state ballot, defeated a second time.

Royal Shakespeare Company gives Detroit performances of Shakespeare plays at Detroit Opera House.

United States Motor Car Co. reorganized as Maxwell Motor Co.

Ford inaugurates first moving assembly line at company's Highland Park plant.

Michigan Historical Museum organized out of Michigan Pioneer Museum (Lansing).

World History

Federal Reserve Act passed to establish central banking system; creates 12 regional federal reserve banks (Boston, New York, Philadelphia, Cleveland, Richmond, Atlanta, Chicago, St. Louis, Minneapolis, Kansas City, Dallas, San Francisco), to begin operation next year.

Jan. 1. Parcel post service begins in U.S. (authorized 1912).

Feb. 3. The 16th Amendment to U.S. Constitution ratified; gives federal government authority to levy, collect income taxes.

The 17th Amendment to U.S. Constitution ratified; provides for direct election of senators.

March 3. Suffragists march on Washington, D.C.

March 4. Woodrow Wilson inaugurated; 28th U.S. president.

July. International Workers of the World lead unsuccessful silk strike.

Dec. 23. Congress creates Federal Reserve Board.

U.S. Department of Commerce reorganized; Department of Labor created as separate entity.

Cultural Progress

Marcel Proust publishes *Swann's Way,* first novel in acclaimed *Remembrance of Things Past* series.

American author Winston Churchill again tops bestseller list with *The Inside of the Cup;* his historical and political novels have been popular since early 1900s.

Feb. Groundbreaking modern art exhibit held at New York Armory; cubism, futurism, post-impressionism introduced to Americans. Marcel Duchamp's *Nude Descending a Staircase* among sensations.

May 29. Composer Igor Stravinsky's radical *Rite of Spring* first performed, in Paris at Ballets Russes. Audience reaction nearly erupts into riot. Later widely considered first piece of truly modern music.

George Bernard Shaw's *Pygmalion* a success.

July. *Queen Elizabeth,* starring Sarah Bernhardt, is shown at New York's Lyceum Theater; first feature-length motion picture seen in America.

New York World begins publishing crossword puzzle as regular feature.

Knute Rockne's pass receiving critical to Notre Dame's (35-13) upset of Army; game brings national attention to Fighting Irish and to the forward pass, which becomes common to football by 1920s.

Scientific and Commercial Progress

Danish physicist Niels Bohr explains atomic structure.

Inventor Igor Sikorsky flies his *Russian Knight* ("The Grand"), first 4-engine (multi-motored) plane.

Summer. Ford introduces moving assembly line in Model T manufacturing plants; heralds beginning of consumer age.

Lincoln Highway, coast-to-coast paved road, is laid out; construction to begin next year. The brainchild of auto manufacturer Carl Fisher, U.S. automakers back project.

1914

Detroit and Michigan

Women employed in offices in Michigan earn average of $1.81 per day.

Jan. 5. Henry Ford institutes $5 day. (Most skilled workers earn $2.50/day; unskilled, just $1/day.); automaker explains move, which heads off unionization, saying, "This is neither charity nor wages, but profit sharing and efficiency engineering."

Jan. 14. First complete endless chain conveyor for assembly line production installed in Ford Motor Co.'s Highland Park plant.

Feb. 26. Detroit Orchestra has first performance, conducted by Music Director Weston Gales. Detroit Symphony Society also founded. (Origins of Detroit Symphony Orchestra.)

March. Clarence M. Burton deeds his collection of research materials on Detroit, Michigan, and Old Northwest to Detroit Public Library; becomes known as Burton Historical Collection.

July 17. John and Horace Dodge found Dodge Brothers Co.

Winter (to 1915). Economic downturn causes regional unemployment.

Connors Creek Generating Station, large-scale fossil fuel plant operated by Detroit Edison, gces into operation; 7,227-foot-tall smokestacks become known as Seven Sisters.

Detroit's rebuilt Gothic style Fort St. Presbyterian Church (1855, 1876) again destroyed by fire and again rebuilt according to original plans.

Orpheum Theater opens in Detroit.

More housing built in Highland Park: 270 homes, including bungalows in craftsman, arts and crafts styles, go up in Medbury/Grove Lawn residential area.

Construction wraps up on original buildings at Ford's Highland Park plant complex; visualized by Henry Ford as early as 1906, now includes power plant (5 smokestacks become Woodward Ave. landmark), office building (Ford headquarters), machine shop, foundry. More buildings planned for site.

Ford Motor Co. produces 248,000 cars this year; typical price is $490.

Last section of outer belt line (Detroit Terminal Railway) completed, opening city's outer area to industrial development. Route begins east of downtown near Waterworks Park and extends in arc, crossing Woodward 6 miles north of City Hall; it joins Michigan Central line on west. Already positioned along outer belt are Chalmers (1908) and Hudson (1910) plants on East Jefferson; and Ford Highland Park plant on Woodward.

World History

Mother's Day becomes official U.S. holiday; to be celebrated 2nd Sunday in May.

April 20. Striking coal miners in Colorado massacred; women and children are among victims.

June 28. Archduke Francis Ferdinand of Austria-Hungary is assassinated by Serbian nationalist in Sarajevo.

July 28. World War I (called the Great War) begins when Austria-Hungary makes declaration against Serbia. Germany throws support behind Austria-Hungary; soon joined by Ottoman Empire, Bulgaria to form Central Powers. Allies France, Britain, Russia, Japan, and Italy back Serbia.

Aug. 15. Panama Canal opens to traffic.

Sept. 26. Congress creates Federal Trade Commission (FTC).

Oct. 15. Clayton Anti-Trust Act strengthens Sherman Anti-Trust Act (1890).

Nov. 13. Western Federation of Miners strike in Butte, Montana, suppressed by militia.

Revolutionaries Emiliano Zapata and Pancho Villa attack Mexico City.

Cultural Progress

Vanity Fair begins publication.

W. C. Handy writes "St. Louis Blues"; introduces new style of music soon labeled jazz.

Fannie Brice, Marx Brothers—Julius (Groucho), Leonard (Chico), Arthur (Harpo), Milton (Gummo)—among Vaudeville favorites.

Dancers Vernon and Irene Castle popularize the tango.

Roxy's Strand in New York heralds heyday of deluxe motion picture houses—movie palaces.

Milton Work's *Auction Bridge Today* a bestseller; testimony to card game's popularity.

Scientific and Commercial Progress

Theodore W. Richards is first American to win Nobel Prize for chemistry, for determining atomic weights of many elements.

Destruction of habitat, other factors have contributed to extinction of passenger pigeon, once among America's most numerous birds. Last known passenger pigeon dies in Cincinnati Zoo.

Brassiere patented; replaces corset.

1915

Detroit and Michigan

Feb. 1. *Detroit News* and *Tribune* merge.

Feb. 6. Statler Hotel opens at Grand Circus Park and Washington Blvd. The 18-story building holds 800 guest rooms, each with its own bath. Chain hotel, situated in a fashionable retail area, sets new standard for Detroit's hotels.

April 27. Belle Isle bridge burns.

Oct. 1. Henry Ford Hospital opens (completed after World War I).

Oct. 12. Municipal Receiving Hospital opens.

Postgraduate high school training first offered by Board of Education at Central High School (forerunner of Detroit Junior College).

Fire breaks out in Detroit's Majestic Building, one of Detroit's earliest skyscrapers; effective fireproofing prevents its destruction. Firemen bring blaze under control in 2 hours.

Architect Edward Bennett completes Detroit beautification and growth management plan (commissioned by city); includes system of parks and outer boulevards, continuous park extending from Lake Erie to Lake St. Clair. Much of scheme fails to materialize.

Construction begins on new Detroit Public Library building on Woodward, but progress is delayed by funding problems and war effort.

State Savings Bank, at corner of West Fort and Shelby streets, enlarged to accommodate bank's 1907 merger with Peoples State Bank.

David Whitney Building completed at Grand Circus Park; office space for Detroit's professional community.

Detroit Athletic Club completed on tree-lined Madison Ave.; meeting place for automobile industry elite.

Fair Lane, estate of Henry and Clara Ford, completed along Rouge River in Dearborn.

Building begins in Palmer Woods at 7 Mile and Woodward. By 1940, upscale neighborhood consists of some 300 residences, many designed by noted architects (including Frank Lloyd Wright and C. Howard Crane). Chief executives of auto industries call Palmer Woods home.

Chevrolet Motor Co., founded 1911, bought by General Motors.

Roy A. Fruehauf and son Harvey build trailer with open slat sides and hard rubber tires; first modern truck trailer in Detroit. Origin of Fruehauf Trailer Co.

Vernor's Ginger Ale begins bottling operation in Detroit.

Reinhold Niebuhr becomes pastor at Bethel Evangelical Church in Detroit; in this capacity (to 1928) he becomes an outspoke critic of capitalism and advocate of socialism, publishing political and theological works in this vein.

World History

U.S. unemployment, 8.5%.

Typhoid Mary Mallon, first known carrier of typhoid fever in U.S., is institutionalized; though recovered, New York health officials discover she has spread disease to some 50 others since 1900.

Jan. 25. Supreme Court ruling upholds legality of yellow dog contracts forbidding workers from joining unions.

April. Turks begin Armenian genocide.

May. German U-boat sinks British passenger ship S.S. *Lusitania* off Irish coast; 1,200 civilians, including 128 Americans, killed.

June 9. U.S. Secretary of State Bryan resigns; statement of opposition to President Woodrow Wilson's leaning toward American involvement in World War I.

Sept. 9. Carter G. Woodson establishes Association for Study of Negro Life and History.

Nov. 19. American labor leader and songwriter Joe Hill, convicted of murder on circumstantial evidence, is put to death. Becomes hero of labor movement.

Nov. Ku Klux Klan is revived in South.

Cultural Progress

Kiwanis club is founded in Detroit; becomes Kiwanis International, community service organization for men and women. By end of the century it has more than 300,000 members in about 8,000 clubs in countries around the world.

W. Somerset Maugham's *Of Human Bondage* published.

Dada: international "anti-art" movement gets under way (to 1923).

Movies come of age with D. W. Griffith's *Birth of a Nation*: despite negative stereotypes, provides model for narrative films.

Charlie Chaplin makes *The Tramp*.

April 5. Great White Hope knocks out Jack Johnson.

Scientific and Commercial Progress

Transcontinental phone service begins between New York City and San Francisco.

Transatlantic radio telephone demonstrated.

Germany's Richard Willstatter wins Nobel Prize for chemistry for his research on chlorophyll and other coloring matter in plants.

1916

Detroit and Michigan

The 31st Regiment of Michigan Infantry departs for Texas to guard Mexican border against raids by Pancho Villa. (*See* World History.)

July. President Woodrow Wilson visits Detroit.

Sept. 10. Evangelist Billy Sunday (baseball star turned all-star preacher) opens 2-month Detroit revival; preaches against "demon rum" and beer.

Oct. 25. Henry Ford Trade School opens.

Nov. Voters approve statewide prohibition (to take effect May 1918); Detroit and other major cities vote against it, but rural Michigan carries dry vote.

General Motors reincorporates in Delaware (various holdings become divisions of parent firm); William Durant is named president.

Frances Elliott Davis (Detroit) is first African American nurse officially accepted into American Red Cross.

Detroit chapter of Urban League founded.

First registered Girl Scout troop in Michigan organized in Detroit.

Detroit Zoological Society purchases 100-acre site in Royal Oak.

Scarab Club founded in Detroit; as heir to Hopkin Club, organization promotes arts in Detroit.

Society of Arts and Crafts building completed on Watson St.; Detroit organization celebrates its 10th anniversary.

New movie house, Madison Theater, opens on Grand Circus Park.

Woodward Highway paved to Pontiac.

Municipal Court Building completed at Macomb and St. Antoine.

Detroit News Building completed.

Washington Blvd. refurbishment (between Michigan Ave. and Grand Circus Park): 15-year-long project backed and promoted by Book brothers, whose vision is to transform run-down area into upscale shopping/office district equal to New York's Fifth Ave.

Five stories are added to Pontchartrain Hotel, which boasts nearly 400 hotel rooms, but only half of them with baths.

Car windshield wipers and slanted windshields are introduced.

World History

Estimated 2.5 million cars in U.S.

Pancho Villa's revolutionaries attack trains, make raid along U.S.-Mexico border, killing 16 Americans. President Woodrow Wilson sends General John Pershing and troops after him.

April 24. Easter Rebellion in Dublin suppressed by British; Sinn Fein leader Michael Collins's Irish Republican Army (IRA) emerges as dominant nationalist group in Ireland.

July–Nov. Allies wage Somme offensive; 794,000 of their men die and little ground is gained as World War I rages in Europe.

Sept. 3. Rail workers win 8-hour day.

Sept. 7. Congress passes Workmen's Compensation Act for federal employees.

Nov. 7. Woodrow Wilson reelected president.

Dec. David Lloyd George becomes British prime minister.

Dec. Notorious czarist adviser Rasputin killed by Russian aristocrats.

Dec. 21. U.S. stock market soars on news that American involvement in World War I is imminent.

Reformer Margaret Sanger opens birth control clinic in Brooklyn; nation's first. Arrested; upon release (1 month later), Sanger founds American Birth Control League. Origin of Planned Parenthood Federation of America.

Olympics are canceled due to World War I.

Cultural Progress

Carl Sandburg's *Chicago Poems* a critical and popular success.

James Joyce publishes *A Portrait of the Artist as a Young Man*; redefines modern novel.

Professional Golf Association (PGA) founded.

Scientific and Commercial Progress

Lee De Forest transmits first radio news broadcast.

Igor Sikorsky develops twin engine airplane

Popular race car driver Ralph De Palma establishes De Palma Manufacturing Co. in Detroit to build racing cars and auto and aircraft engines.

1917

Detroit and Michigan

Albert E. Sleeper, Republican, governor (to 1920).

Detroit automobile production tops 1 million vehicles.

Kathleen McGraw Hendrie (Detroit) and 3 other Michigan women join Alice Paul of National Woman's Party to picket White House in support of suffrage.

Feb. 3. Saxon Motor Plant destroyed by fire.

May 8. Gov. Albert E. Sleeper signs bill granting Michigan women right to vote in presidential elections.

July. Detroit Board of Commerce discusses housing to accommodate influx of African Americans.

July. Selfridge Field opens in Macomb County to train pilots and mechanics for U.S. Army Air Corps.

Oct. 3. Detroit's first meatless day.

Nov. 2. Cornerstone laid for new main public library on Woodward at Kirby.

Nov. Fuel shortage in Michigan; as conservation measure, on Dec. 22 all manufacturing plants (except munitions factories) suspend operations.

Dec. 28. Ossip Gabrilowitsch makes debut as guest conductor of Detroit Symphony.

Fort Wayne heavily garrisoned due to World War I.

Michigan sends about 175,000 men into armed forces during war, of whom about 65,000 are from Detroit and Wayne County.

Michigan National Guard organizes into 32nd Division of U.S. Army. Called Red Arrow Division, reaches France Feb. 1918; returns to U.S., May 5, 1919.

Michigan State Constabulary organized to guard strategic war points around state; origin of state police.

Fort Wayne serves as an induction center for World War I military (to 1918).

Millions subscribe to Liberty Loans and Red Cross; Detroit consistently oversubscribes quotas in all drives.

Detroit school system allows married women to teach.

Children's Museum opens under sponsorship of Detroit Museum of Art and Board of Education.

Detroit Junior College (2-year course) authorized by legislature.

Detroit College of Medicine and Surgery admits first women students.

Book Building, centerpiece of Book brothers' Washington Blvd. renovation, completed. Limestone faced 13-story structure, designed by Detroit architect Louis Kamper; mostly offices, but some retail at ground level.

Madison Theater, Adams Theater open to accommodate growing number of Detroit moviegoers.

Detroit Golf Club, designed by Albert Kahn, completed on Hamilton Rd. (off Woodward).

Highland Park and Royal Oak Railway begins service along Stephenson Highway.

Maxwell Motor Co. expands manufacturing facilities by leasing part of East Jefferson plant of Chalmers Motor Co.

Henry Leland and son Wilfred form Lincoln Motor Co. to manufacture Liberty engines.

Building B completed at Ford's Rouge River plant in Dearborn. Albert Kahn–designed facility a massive, single-story structure made of steel and glass; half-mile-long structure to house assembly line for manufacturing Eagle boats for war effort. Manufacturing improved by eliminating need to move raw materials, parts between floors.

First 7 stories of Telephone Building are erected.

World History

Germany resumes attacks on unarmed ships in Atlantic.

March 4. President Woodrow Wilson inaugurated; 2nd term.

March. Zimmerman note published in U.S.; reveals German attempt to incite Mexico to declare war on U.S.

March. Russian troops stationed on eastern front mutiny; French troops mutiny (April) on western front.

March 15. Russian Czar Nicholas II loses all political influence; abdicates.

April 6. U.S. joins World War: Congress issues war declaration; President Woodrow Wilson declares "world must be made safe for democracy."

Jones Act confers U.S. citizenship on Puerto Ricans.

Britain's King George denounces family ties to Germany; establishes House of Windsor.

April. Lenin arrives in Petrograd (St. Petersburg).

Nov. Bolshevik Revolution topples provisional government in Russia.

July 31–Nov. 10. Battle of Passchendaele (northwest Belgium); 400,000 British troops die as World War I rages.

Oct. 15. Mata Hari, charged with espionage and held responsible for deaths of some 50,000 Allied soldiers, is killed by firing squad.

French munitions carrier *Mont Blanc* is struck by relief ship and explodes in Halifax, Nova Scotia, harbor; 1,635 dead and some 1,000 injured.

American Federation of Labor has 2.5 million members; includes 111 national unions, 27,000 local unions.

Great migration begins: Southern blacks resettle in North.

Suffragists picket White House; arrested.

U.S. purchases Virgin Islands from Denmark.

Mexico adopts new constitution.

Cultural Progress

American actor and playwright George M. Cohan writes WWI song, "Over There."

Birth of the international film star: Charlie Chaplin featured in *Easy Street*; Mary Pickford in *Rebecca of Sunnybrook Farm* and *Poor Little Rich Girl.* Movie actors become world famous.

1918

Detroit and Michigan

Jan. War bread is distributed in Detroit.

Jan. 21. First of 10 consecutive heatless Mondays; wartime fuel conservation measure.

Jan. 22–26. All Detroit businesses except hotels, restaurants, drug stores, close to save fuel.

Feb. Coal shortage causes Detroit schools to close.

Feb. 20. Detroit Patriotic Fund organized for centralized war work.

March 27. Central Standard Time adopted in Michigan (*see also* Oct.).

April 24. Women employed as mail carriers.

May 18. Michigan becomes dry (2 years before national prohibition goes into effect).

May 20. Katharine Cornell appears with Jessie Bonstelle Stock Co. in Detroit. Actress later goes onto Broadway (biggest success is 1931's *Barretts of Wimpole Street*).

May. Some 200,000 Wayne County women over age 16 are registered for work.

May 14. Ossip Gabrilowitsch becomes music director of DSO; internationally known Russian pianist brings instant credibility to orchestra.

June 7. Fort Shelby Hotel opens.

June 25. Detroit voters approve new city charter.

Aug. 10. Detroit United Railway raises streetcar fare to 6 cents; on Aug. 13 city council passes ordinance returning fare to 5 cents.

Sept. The 339th Infantry Regiment, composed mainly of Detroit men, departs for service in Siberia. Nicknamed Polar Bears, return to U.S. July 4, 1919.

Oct. Flour sells for as much as $2.10/sack; cold storage eggs cost up to 65 cents/dozen.

Oct. Eastern Standard Time adopted in Michigan.

Oct. Flu epidemic prompts closure of theaters, churches, schools to prevent further spreading.

Sept. Detroit United Railway begins employing women.

Nov. 5. Detroit holds first non-partisan election. Voters abolish war system and elect 9 members to Common Council.

Nov. 11. Unprecedented civic demonstration over Armistice.

Nov. 18. Bishop Michael J. Gallagher arrives in Detroit to serve Catholic Diocese.

Michigan voters approve state constitutional amendment granting suffrage to women.

Auto factories are converted to wartime manufacturing, producing aircraft engines, tanks, tractors, military vehicles, guns, other materials.

Board of Education takes over Detroit College of Medicine and Surgery, which becomes municipal institution. Origin of Wayne University School of Medicine.

Detroit branch of Federal Reserve Bank opens.

Detroit Museum of Art becomes city institution.

Tracy W. and Katherine Whitney McGregor donate parcel of land to Highland Park for a library.

Meeting House completed at Cranbrook.

Michigan Federation of Business and Professional Women's Clubs founded; Lena Lake Forrest (Detroit), first president.

World History

Espionage and Sedition Acts passed by Congress: criticism of war effort or of administration illegal.

Wartime conservation efforts result in meatless, wheatless, heatless days across U.S.

Jan. 8. President Woodrow Wilson announces his Fourteen Points, formulation of peace program for Europe after World War I.

March 3. Russia withdraws from World War I (Brest-Litovsk Treaty).

June 3. Supreme Court rules child labor laws are unconstitutional. First federal law was passed 1916.

Sept. Lenin rises to absolute power in Russia; begins Red Terror to suppress opposition.

Nov. 11. Germany signs armistice, ending World War I.

Flu pandemic kills 20 million people worldwide, including 500,000 Americans.

Cultural Progress

First Pulitzer Prize for drama is awarded to *Why Marry?*—American comedy by Jesse Lynch Williams.

James Joyce's *Ulysses* first published in serial form; modernist novel causes controversy, inspires bans.

Zane Grey's *U.P. Trail* tops bestseller lists.

Cleveland Orchestra (later Cleveland Symphony) founded.

At conclusion of 1917–18 season, NHL teams compete for Stanley Cup for first time: Toronto Arenas defeat Vancouver Millionaires, 3 games to 2.

Scientific and Commercial Progress

American Railway Express Co. consolidates rail lines as wartime measure.

March 31. Daylight savings time first put into effect in U.S.

Max Planck wins Nobel Prize for physics for developing quantum theory.

1919

Detroit and Michigan

Average wage paid to skilled workers in Detroit, $6.26/day.

Jan. James Couzens, mayor of Detroit.

March 5. Michigan women vote in statewide (primary) elections for first time.

March 20. Michigan's first all-woman jury seated in county court in Detroit.

June 10. Michigan is second state to ratify National Suffrage Amendment (19th Amendment) to U.S. Constitution.

July. Red Scare reaches Detroit; 25 aliens deported amidst hysteria.

Orchestra Hall completed in under 4 months (designed by noted architect C. Howard Crane). Over next 2 decades it will host performances by such noted musicians as Pablo Casals, Sergei Rachmaninoff, Arthur Rubinstein.

Oct. 23. Grand opening of Orchestra Hall: Music Director Ossip Gabrilowitsch leads DSO in performance of Weber's overture to *Oberon,* Mozart's Concerto in E-flat for 2 pianos and orchestra, Bach's Concerto in C Major for 3 pianos and orchestra, and Beethoven's Symphony No. 5 in C Minor.

Dec. 18. World War I hero General Pershing visits Detroit.

State Police organized by law.

$50 million bond issue approved for Michigan road building.

Dora Hall Stockman, of Lansing area, elected to State Board of Agriculture; first woman voted into Michigan state office and first American woman to serve on board of land grant college.

Josephine S. Davis (Detroit) is first woman police officer in Michigan authorized to make arrests.

Remembrance Rings presented by city to each Detroit man who served in armed forces during war.

Florence Belle Swickard Brotherton (Detroit) becomes first president of Michigan League of Women Voters.

Merrill-Palmer School (later Merrill-Palmer Institute) opens; school uses interdisciplinary approach to train students in all aspects of child development. Made possible through $3 million donation of Lizzie Pitts Merrill Palmer.

Dunbar Hospital, Detroit's first African American hospital, opens.

Building B, at Ford's Rouge River plant, reconverted from wartime (boat) assembly to auto assembly.

Lincoln engine plant on West Warren and Livernois retooled to produce cars.

General Motors announces plans for its new headquarters: Durant Building, after company founder William Durant, to be built in Detroit on West Grand Blvd.; site selected since it is geographical center of city and is removed from downtown congestion.

GM acquires major share of Fisher Body Co.

Dodge Brothers Co., parts suppliers for Ford, are bought out by Ford for $25 million.

Ford Motor Co. recapitalized; Ford family now owns all stock.

The 14-story building for Fyfe's Shoe Store erected on Grand Circus Park; Gothic tower a new landmark in busy area of Detroit.

Construction begins in 10-block neighborhood of Dearborn where Henry Ford has planned a residential community for workers at nearby Henry Ford and Son Tractor Plant. Seven models are distributed throughout subdivision.

Henry Ford sues *Chicago Tribune* for libel, asking for $1 million in damages; after 4-month trial, jury awards him 6 cents in damages and costs.

World History

Jan. Paris Peace Conference convenes; led by President Woodrow Wilson, British Prime Minister David Lloyd George, French Premier Georges Clemenceau, Italian Premier Vittorio Orlando.

Jan. 2. Red Scare begins with U.S. Department of Justice raid of radical organizations; 6,000 Americans believed to be communist sympathizers detained.

Jan. 16. The 18th Amendment to U.S. Constitution ratified; makes prohibition legal.

Congress passes National Prohibition Act (Volsted Act) to enforce constitutional amendment banning manufacture, transportation, sale, consumption of alcohol.

May Fourth movement fans fires of revolution in China; Sun Yat-sen emerges as leader.

June 28. Treaty of Versailles dissolves Austro-Hungarian monarchy, severely punishes Germany for World War I; with other peace agreements, redraws Europe, establishes League of Nations.

July. Race riots erupt in 26 U.S. cities.

Sept. 1. U.S. Communist Party founded.

President Woodrow Wilson proclaims Nov. 11 as Armistice Day (1938 law makes it a federal holiday; name changed to Veterans Day, 1954).

Nov. 11. International Workers of the World strike in Centralia, Washington, turns deadly.

Nov. 19. Senate votes down U.S. membership in League of Nations.

As nation considers national suffrage for women, 15 states (mostly in West) now allow women to vote; 12 other states allow voting in presidential elections; 2 states allow voting in primary elections.

U.S. Army makes first transcontinental convoy of military vehicles; due to lack of good roads, trip from Washington to San Francisco takes about 2 months.

New York City hotel owner Raymond Orteig offers $25,000 to first aviator to fly nonstop across Atlantic. (*See* 1927.)

Mahatma Gandhi begins passive resistance movement against British rule in India.

Cultural Progress

Booth Tarkington's *The Magnificent Ambersons* wins Pulitzer Prize for fiction.

V. Blasco Ibañez's *Four Horsemen of the Apocalypse* heads bestseller lists. Joseph Conrad, Zane Grey, Mary Roberts Rinehart among other top-selling authors.

Walter Gropius founds Bauhaus, German educational center for art and design; exerts strong influence on modern style and functional architecture.

Irene a hit musical.

Los Angeles Philharmonic Orchestra founded.

July 4. Jack Dempsey wins heavyweight crown from Jess Willard.

Oct. Cincinnati Reds defeat Chicago White Sox in World Series. (*See also* 1920, World History.)

Scientific and Commercial Progress

U.S. completes fourth lock at Soo Canal connecting Lakes Superior and Huron; tonnage passing through American and Canadian channels at Sault Ste. Marie exceeds any other canal in world.

British fliers John Alcock and Arthur Whitten Brown make first transatlantic crossing in an airplane, flying 1,950 miles from St. John's, Newfoundland, to Clifden, Ireland.

RCA, Radio Corporation of America, founded at behest of U.S. Navy to provide American-based wireless communication.

1920

Detroit and Michigan

Michigan's population, 3,668,412.

Detroit's population, 993,078 (double 1910); ranks 4th in size among U.S. cities. Includes nearly 2 million foreign-born residents. Growth fueled by auto industry.

Detroit's African American population has grown 600% over past decade.

Detroit has expanded geographically (now 77.9 square miles) to surround cities of Highland Park and Hamtramck.

Detroit metropolitan area population, 1,165,153.

First census to show more urban than rural residents in Michigan.

Hamtramck's population reaches 45,000; community's growth largely due to influx of Polish immigrants, many of whom find jobs in nearby auto plants.

Detroit's foreign-born population accounts for 29% of total; natives of Canada, Poland, Germany, and Russia predominate.

Scots, Irish, Norwegians, Swedes, and Slovaks are nationality groups whose peak immigration occurs during this decade.

Detroit area has 134,491 telephone subscribers; 150% increase since 1900.

Jan. Red Scare continues: 500 radicals rounded up, held for deportation in Detroit.

Jan. 31. Pontchartrain Hotel, once considered city's premier hostelry, closes; destroyed to make way for First National Bank.

April 5. Voters approve a $15 million bond issue to build a street railway system; referred to as the Municipal Operation.

April. Railroad strike worsens economic situation in Detroit; many factories close due to general downturn.

May 23. Pennsylvania Railroad begins service from Detroit.

June 11. Detroit Motorbus Co., Detroit's first large bus company, begins operating double-deck buses from Water Works Park to City Hall.

Aug. 17. Detroit receives first airmail delivery (from Cleveland).

Aug. 20. WWJ begins broadcasting; joins Pittsburgh's KDKA in being nation's first regular commercial radio stations.

Dec. 1. Wayne County Library system established by Detroit Public Library; operates under Detroit Library Commission (until Nov. 30, 1943).

Detroit policeman William Potts invents electric red-amber-green traffic light; first installed at intersection of Michigan and Woodward.

House numbering system on Detroit streets is revised according to block-and-plat plan.

Our Lady of Guadeloupe Mission, Hispanic Catholic congregation, organized in meeting room at St. Mary's School (on St. Antoine).

Normal Training School renamed Detroit Teachers College.

Sarah Schooten is first woman admitted to Detroit College of Medicine (later Wayne State University).

Detroit millionaire Gar Wood (inventor of hydraulic lift) begins series of powerboat race wins; *See* Cultural Progress.

Detroit Department of Recreation created.

Detroit purchases 147 acres of former Thomas Palmer estate to add to Palmer Park, now a 300-acre tract along Woodward, between McNichols and 7 Mile Rd.

Grosse Pointe develops into thriving suburb this decade.

GM ousts William Durant; company founder has fallen out of favor with Du Pont family, which now owns controlling interest. Pierre S. Du Pont becomes president.

Duesenberg introduced.

First Lincoln produced.

Laurens Hammond, a Detroit auto engineer, independently develops original devices including a soundless clock; goes on to invent the Hammond organ.

Maxwell Motor Co. production comes to a standstill; former GM Vice President Walter P. Chrysler called in to turn ailing company around.

Detroit Edison Co. builds office on Second Ave.

World History

U.S. population, 105,710,620.

U.S. unemployment, 5.2%.

Average week for U.S. manufacturing workers, 47 hours.

Majority of Americans, 51.4%, live in urban areas.

Jan. League of Nations founded; headquartered in Geneva.

Jan. 19. American Civil Liberties Union (ACLU) founded.

Feb. 14. League of Women Voters founded.

The 19th Amendment to U.S. Constitution ratified; grants women the right to vote.

Aug. 1. Universal Negro Improvement Association (founded by pan-Africanist Marcus Garvey) holds first national convention in Harlem.

Nov. 2. American women vote for first time in presidential election.

Nov. 2. Warren G. Harding, Republican, elected president.

Black Sox scandal: Chicago White Sox players indicted for throwing last year's World Series.

Parliament passes Government of Ireland Act offering home rule to Ireland; 6 out of 9 Ulster counties form Northern Ireland.

Treaty of Sèvres dissolves Ottoman Empire; agreement gives Britain control of Palestine. British policy encourages Jews to immigrate. Fighting breaks out with Arabs opposed to resettlement.

Cultural Progress

Saturday Evening Post, McClure's magazines important vehicles of nationwide communication

Roaring Twenties get under way; characterized by speakeasies, flappers, roadsters, optimism, iconoclasm.

Flapper style popular.

Art Deco popular (to 1930s).

Modern architecture takes firm hold; height of movement to come in works of Gropius, Le Corbusier, Mies van der Rohe, Frank Lloyd Wright.

Olympics held in Antwerp, Belgium.

Rogers Hornsby wins first of 6 National League batting titles.

Bill Tilden wins U.S. National Tennis Championship; holds title through 1925. Regarded as greatest male tennis player for several decades.

Ouija boards popular pastime.

Gar Wood wins first of 9 Harmsworth trophies with his boat *Miss America* in race off Isle of Wight.

Scientific and Commercial Progress

Nov. 2. Westinghouse station KDKA (Pittsburgh) makes first commercial radio broadcast; announces election results.

Prosperity this decade bolstered by American investment in stock market.

1921

Detroit and Michigan

Alexander J. Groesbeck, Republican, governor (to 1926).

Edwin Denby, a Detroit lawyer, is named secretary of the navy in President-Elect Warren Harding's cabinet.

Eva McCall Hamilton (of Grand Rapids) elected to Michigan senate, first woman to serve in state legislature.

Feb. 1. First municipal streetcar operates on St. Jean and Charlevoix lines.

June 3. Detroit new Main Library building opens: white marble edifice on Woodward Ave. is heart of city's Cultural Center; houses 439,000 books.

July 27. Memorial fountain dedicated in Grand Circus Park in honor of Gen. Russell A. Alger.

Oct. 6. William R. Hearst purchases *Detroit Times*.

Nov. 7. World War I (French) hero Ferdinand Foch visits Detroit.

Goodwill Industries begins operating in Detroit (originated in Boston, 1895).

Harry Heilman of Detroit Tigers wins first American League batting title (also wins in 1923, 1925, 1927).

Gar Wood wins second of 9 Harmsworth trophies with *Miss America II* in Detroit River race.

After 2 years of construction in Dearborn neighborhood developed by Henry Ford, building stops: slump in agriculture prompts Ford to close nearby tractor plant; interest in community, now consisting of 250 houses and elementary school, wanes.

Cadillac Motor Car Co. consolidates manufacturing operations at new facility (2680 Clark St.) in southwest Detroit.

Robert Frost is writer in residence at University of Michigan to 1923; while in Ann Arbor the poet works on volume that wins him a Pulitzer Prize (1931).

World History

March 4. Warren Harding inaugurated; 29th U.S. president.

March. American labor leader Big Bill Haywood, sentenced to 20 years for sedition, jumps bail and escapes to Russia.

May 31–July 14. Murder trial of Italian immigrants Nicola Sacco and Bartolomeo Vanzetti: active anarchists are sentenced to death and executed (Aug. 23, 1927). International observers conclude pair were killed because of radical views.

George Washington Carver, developer of 300 peanut-based products, testifies before Congress on behalf of National Association of Peanut Growers; helps secure future of African American farmers.

Anglo-Irish Treaty signed, ending civil war in southern Ireland; the 26 Catholic counties form Irish Free State (Republic of Ireland).

Cultural Progress

Edith Wharton is first woman to receive Pulitzer Prize for fiction, for best-selling *The Age of Innocence*.

Sinclair Lewis's novel *Main Street* a bestseller; uncompromising attack on conformity ushers in new literary age, introduces realism into American fiction, which has long been dominated by romance and adventure.

H. G. Wells's *The Outline of History* a nonfiction bestseller; renews public interest in historical works.

National Football League (NFL) organized.

Kenesaw Landis, U.S. district court judge renowned for his fairness, is hired as baseball's first commissioner; charged with cleaning up game in wake of 1919's Black Sox scandal.

U.S. heavyweight champion Jack Dempsey defeats Georges Carpentier in first boxing match to draw $1 million gate; also first major fight to be broadcast over radio.

Scientific and Commercial Progress

Albert Einstein wins Nobel Prize for physics.

First drive-in restaurant opens in Dallas.

1922

Detroit and Michigan

Jan. City Tuberculosis Sanitarium in Northville begins receiving patients.

Jan. 4. Ford purchases Lincoln Motor Car Co. from Lelands for $8 million.

March 20. First National Bank and Central Savings Bank occupy new 24-story building on Woodward and Cadillac Square.

April 10. Horse-drawn fire engines make last run in Detroit.

May 4. Radio station WJR licensed.

May 15. City takes over Detroit United Railway operation; voters approved purchase on. Company named Department of Street Railways.

July 21. *Detroit Journal* absorbed by *Detroit News.*

Aug. 30. Dodge Brothers Co. donates 11 parks (627 acres) to state.

Sept. 22. Michigan Steel Corporation chartered to make steel sheets in plant planned near Ecorse Creek. Reorganized as Great Lakes Steel, 1929.

New Temple Beth-El at Woodward and Gladstone dedicated; Leo Franklin is named rabbi for life.

Dec. 5. Detroit Mayor James Couzens resigns; appointed by Gov. Groesbeck to replace Truman Newberry as U.S. Senator; John C. Lodge assumes office of mayor.

Dec. 8. Dancer Isadora Duncan performs at Orchestra Hall.

Detroit police department staffed by numerous female cops.

Detroit among first cities to use police broadcasting system and radio-equipped police cars for receiving messages.

Sunday morning services at St. Paul's Cathedral are first broadcast over WWJ.

Merrill-Palmer nursery school opens.

World's first radio broadcast of a complete symphony concert given by Detroit Symphony Orchestra with guest pianist Artur Schnabel.

Detroit Historical Society founded. Opens museum, 1928.

Streets radiating from Grand Circus Park become home to more movie palaces; Capitol Theater opens this year.

Work completed on General Motors Building in New Center: 15-story building and 5-story annex house some 1,800 offices for headquarters of what is now world's largest manufacturing corporation. Building itself is second largest in capacity in world (after New York's Equitable Building).

Ford passes million mark, delivering 1,216,792 Model Ts this year.

Forty-hour week adopted by Ford Motor Co.

Regular airplane service established from Detroit to Chicago and Cleveland; primarily for airmail.

World History

Coal strike lasts 6 months, cripples U.S. industry.

Teapot Dome scandal revealed; Secretary of Interior Albert Fall secretly transferred government land to private use, accepted bribe.

Fascist leader Benito Mussolini takes power in Italy; institutes economic, social regimentation. Opposition to dictatorship forcibly suppressed.

Soviet Union officially created when Russia joins with Ukraine, Belorussia, Transcaucasian Federation (later Armenia, Azerbaijan, Georgia).

Cultural Progress

May 30. Lincoln Memorial, sculpted by Daniel Chester French, dedicated in Washington, D.C. Chief Justice and Committee Chair William Howard Taft presents monument to President Warren Harding, who accepts it on behalf of American people.

Harlem Renaissance: African American literature, art, and music flourish. Upper Manhattan a hotbed of creativity (to 1929).

Sinclair Lewis coins new word with best-selling *Babbitt* (which comes to mean unthinking conformist or boor).

T. S. Eliot publishes *The Waste Land*; A. E. Houseman publishes *Last Poems*.

Player pianos and phonographs have heyday.

Charles Atlas wins title "world's most perfectly developed man."

Knute Rockne and Four Horsemen keep Notre Dame on top of American college football.

Mahjongg game craze.

Scientific and Commercial Progress

Niels Bohr wins Nobel Prize for physics for studies of atomic structure.

Insulin begins to be used to treat diabetics. Discovery of insulin by Frederick G. Banting, John J. R. Macleod awarded Nobel Prize for medicine (1923).

Archeologist Howard Carter discovers Egyptian King Tut's tomb, relics.

Eskimo pie (chocolate-coated ice cream) patented by C. K. Nelson of Iowa.

1923

Detroit and Michigan

Feb. 4. Dr. Emil Coué, who has developed popular system for self-help through auto-suggestion, lectures in Detroit.

April 9. Frank E. Doremus, mayor of Detroit.

April 21. Marathon dance at Majestic Institute; lasts 96.5 hours. National craze.

June 14. Ku Klux Klan initiates 1,000 novices in public ceremony in Detroit. First in series of demonstrations this year: Burns cross in front of City Hall, Nov. 6, in front of County Building, Dec. 25. (*See also* Oct. 21.)

Detroit Police get new headquarters in 9-story building on Beaubien, site of old Wayne County Jail (1897).

Sept. First traffic school for motorcar drivers held in police auditorium.

Sept. 2. Streetcar fare raised from 5 to 6 cents, or 9 tickets for 50 cents.

Sept. 10. College of City of Detroit (4-year school) opens, replaces Detroit Junior College.

Oct. 21. Ku Klux Klan demonstration draws mob; dispersed by Detroit Police.

Nov. 11. To commemorate Armistice Day, Hudson's hangs giant American flag, 90 by 123 feet, on side of its downtown Detroit store, beginning a patriotic tradition.

Nov. 1. New Belle Isle bridge opens.

Nov. 28. Detroit-Windsor ferry buildings destroyed by fire.

Dec. 22. New water filtering plant begins operation in Water Works Park. Water treated with chlorine since 1913 but not filtered.

Detroit Free Press Building completed.

Pioneering concert series for children begun in Detroit Public School System.

Construction begun on Law Quadrangle at University of Michigan; consisting of 4 highly dignified Gothic buildings around central courtyard, it is completed 10 years later.

New Country Club of Detroit built in Grosse Pointe.

World History

Equal Rights Amendment proposed by National Woman's Party.

Aug. 2. Warren Harding dies; succeeded by Vice President Calvin Coolidge, 30th U.S. president.

Nov. 8–9. Adolf Hitler's beer hall putsch: Nazi leader and 9 co-conspirators arrested, tried for treason. (*See* 1924.)

Speakeasies operate around U.S.

Cultural Progress

Time magazine founded.

Edna St. Vincent Millay is first woman to receive Pulitzer Prize for poetry.

Willa Cather's *One of Ours* wins Pulitzer Prize for fiction.

Top non-fiction bestseller is *Etiquette* by Emily Post; becomes perennial favorite.

Freer Gallery opens at Smithsonian Institution in Washington, D.C.; collection of Oriental art was donated by Detroit industrialist Charles Freer and includes famous Peacock Room he acquired in 1877.

Popular song, "Yes! We Have No Bananas."

The charleston becomes popular dance; hallmark of jazz age. Marathon dances are the rage.

Bobby Jones wins National Open Golf Championship for first time; wins again 1926, 1929, 1930.

Helen Wills wins National Women's Tennis Championship; holds it to 1931 (except for 1926 and 1930 losses).

Scientific and Commercial Progress

Three years after first commercial radio broadcast, U.S. has more than 500 radio stations.

Vladimir Zworykin, working for Westinghouse Electronic Corp., invents iconoscope (first successful television camera tube).

First nonstop transcontinental flight made by U.S. Army pilots: New York to California in 26 hours, 50 minutes.

Akron's Firestone Tire and Rubber commercially produces balloon tires.

1924

Detroit and Michigan

May 29. Paul Whiteman and George Gershwin perform at Arcadia.

Nov. 4. Incumbent Mayor Frank E. Doremus forced by illness to step down midterm, Detroit voters go to polls: John W. Smith, who has garnered support of Catholics, blacks, and immigrants, elected mayor in bitter contest—narrowly defeating KKK-backed write-in candidate Charles Bowles. (Final tally is 116,775 to 102,602, with some 15,000 ballots deemed illegible by election officials.) Smith's term will expire in 1 year.

Newly elected John W. Smith takes office as mayor of Detroit.

Nov. Hudson's sponsors its first Thanksgiving Parade. Department store display director Charles Wendel spearheads event, which becomes annual tradition.

Dec. 8. Book-Cadillac Hotel opens; luxury hotel boasts elegant lobby and dining rooms, grand ballroom, 1,200 guestrooms (each with its own bath).

Eliel Saarinen, architect and visiting professor at University of Michigan, draws up plan for Detroit riverfront civic center; lack of funding prevents development.

Master plan of thoroughfares drawn up for Detroit; results in widening of all major highways.

Father Solanus Casey begins ministry in Detroit; Capuchin friar's life work is to serve the poor.

College of Pharmacy established in Detroit; classes are held at Cass Tech.

Detroit Repertory Theater organized.

Detroit College of Music opened.

Construction begins on Detroit Zoo in Royal Oak.

Rouge River Park purchased by Detroit.

On-the-field brawl between Yankees and Tigers inspires 18,000 Detroit fans to riot; Tigers forfeit game.

Ford Motor Co. produces its 10 millionth car.

First Chrysler car produced, in old Chalmers Motor Co. plant on East Jefferson.

Detroit Auto Show held at new Convention Hall, Woodward and Warren.

Steamship *Greater Detroit* completed.

World History

Jan. 21. Lenin dies. Joseph Stalin rises to power.

Feb. In beer hall putsch trial, Adolf Hitler takes stand to indict German government, gains great support of people in highly publicized oration. Found guilty of treason, he is sentenced to 5 years in prison; spends only 9 months but writes *Mein Kampf* (My Struggle), putting forth racial supremacy theories, asserting superiority of Third Reich.

Congress passes Johnson-Reed Act: effectively ends Asian immigration, severely restricts immigration from southern, eastern Europe.

Sept. 10. Sensational murder trial of Nathan Leopold and Richard Loeb ends in guilty verdict; each is sentenced to life in prison plus 99 years for kidnapping.

Nov. 4. Calvin Coolidge reelected president. Progressive candidate Robert La Follette polled 5 million votes.

J. Edgar Hoover appointed director of FBI.

Cultural Progress

Ernest Hemingway publishes first major work, *In Our Time,* collection of Nick Adams stories set in northern Michigan.

A. A. Milne introduces Winnie the Pooh in *When We Were Very Young;* children's literature classic. Tops U.S. bestseller lists next year.

George Gershwin writes American jazz/orchestral work *Rhapsody in Blue.*

Surrealism flourishes in artwork of Rene Magritte, Salvador Dali, Joan Miró.

Approximately 2.5 million households have radios.

Jan. 25–Feb. 4. First Winter Olympics held in Chamonix, France.

Summer Olympics held in Paris.

All-American running back Red Grange, "the Galloping Ghost," turns in spectacular performance in game against University of Michigan: he scores 5 touchdowns (4 on long runs during first 12 minutes) to secure victory for his Fighting Illini.

Scientific and Commercial Progress

Two U.S. Army planes make first round-the-world flight; complete 26,345-mile journey in 6 months.

At annual New York Auto Show, only cars displayed are powered by gas engines; for first time, no electric or steam cars are exhibited.

International Business Machine (IBM) organized; originally Tabulating Machine Co. (founded 1896).

Wirephotos first appear: newspapers transmit photographs via fax.

1925

Detroit and Michigan

Jan. 1. Department of Street Railways begins first regular bus service on Mack Ave.

Chrysler sells 32,000 of new Phaeton model, best-selling new car yet.

May 31. Scott Fountain unveiled on Belle Isle. Designed by Cass Gilbert, terraced structure of polished white marble was funded by bequest of Detroit businessman James Scott, who died 15 years ago.

June 3. Radio station WXYZ licensed.

June 6. Chrysler Corp. founded: Maxwell Motor Corp. reorganized and renamed for chief executive who turned company around. Maxwell plant in Highland Park becomes Chrysler Highland Park plant; Chrysler calls on Albert Kahn to expand East Jefferson plant manufacturing facilities.

Aug. 10. Airplane crash at Packard Field claims life of passenger Austin A. Nelson and (a week later) pilot Walter Kemp; aviator Nelson had just been named chair of Detroit Aviation Society committee to investigate safety.

Late summer. African American gynecologist Ossian Sweet and family move into bungalow in all-white neighborhood on Detroit's east side, provoking violent reaction from residents, who mob home at 2905 Garland St. Shots fired from within house; its inhabitants are charged with murder. Dr. Sweet and his brother stand trial, with noted attorney Clarence Darrow (hired by NAACP) defending them. Dr. Sweet's trial ends in hung jury; he and brother are later acquitted.

Sept. 29. Airplane Reliability Tour of 1,900 miles begins from Ford Airport.

Detroit mayoral election: incumbent John W. Smith wins, defeating opponent Charles Bowles, roughly 140,000 to 111,000.

Cora Reynolds Anderson (of L'Anse) is first woman elected to state house of representatives.

Bertha Hansbury School of Music founded in Detroit; city's first school (and possibly first in nation) to bring together African American music teachers and students.

Igor Stravinsky conducts DSO.

Jessie Bonstelle founds professional theater company (reorganized in 1928 as Civic Players; origin of Civic Theater).

Detroit gets new movie houses: State Theater, Michigan Theater, Palms Theater.

Grand Riviera Theater completed at Grand River and Joy Rd. (near junction of 3 streetcar lines). "Atmospheric theater" creates ambience by projecting images (clouds, stars, birds) onto ceiling.

The 26-story Buhl Building erected at Griswold and Congress.

Bankers Trust Building erected at Congress and Shelby.

Steel manufacturing facilities at Ford's Rouge River plant expanded: Henry Ford sees Detroit as logical center for booming steel industry, since it is midway between Upper Peninsula's iron mines and the South's coal fields.

Detroit and Michigan Stove Works merge; continue in business to 1957.

Apartment-building begins along streets of former Palmer estate. Over next decades, Palmer Park becomes home to eclectic mix of apartments, including Whitmore Plaza, El Dorado, La Vogue.

Poet Robert Frost is again writer in residence (to 1926) at University of Michigan; some readers later note a Midwestern quality in his works. Frost writes a friend that he has "got to be a good deal more Ann Arboreal than I should suppose I could have at my age," saying he likes the landscape and the "folks."

World History

U.S. unemployment, 3.2%.

March 4. President Calvin Coolidge inaugurated.

July 10–21. Scopes "monkey" trial: Clarence Darrow defends Tennessee educator John Thomas Scopes, charged with violating state law prohibiting teaching evolution in public schools; state's case argued by William Jennings Bryan. Showdown between scientific thought and religious fundamentalism. Guilty verdict later reversed on technicality.

Brotherhood of Sleeping Car Porters organized by black labor leader A. Philip Randolph.

Aug. 8. Ku Klux Klan marches in Washington, D.C.

Oct. 28–Dec. 17. Court-martial of Billy Mitchell: Brigadier general is charged with insubordination and "conduct of a nature to bring discredit upon the military service" for his outspoken criticism of U.S. military's failure to develop air service. Later hailed as a visionary, Mitchell is found guilty and suspended from service.

Cultural Progress

The New Yorker begins publication.

F. Scott Fitzgerald publishes *The Great Gatsby*; with earlier works, defines American jazz age.

Countee Cullen publishes *Color*.

Theodore Dreiser's *An American Tragedy* epitomizes naturalism movement in American literature.

France hosts International Exhibition of Modern Decorative and Industrial Art; makes headlines around globe.

Jan. 28. Igor Stravinsky conducts New York Philharmonic in program of his works during his first U.S. tour.

Trumpeter and singer Louis Armstrong begins fronting own band, the Hot 5; transforms jazz into improviser's art.

Nov. 28. At height of jazz age, *The WSM Barn Dance* is broadcast on radio; becomes known as *Grand Ole Opry,* puts country music on map.

Soviet director Sergei Eisenstein's *Potemkin* pioneers *montage,* a film editing technique.

The Phantom of the Opera, starring Lon Chaney, among classic 1920s horror movies.

Scientific and Commercial Progress

American physicists Gregory Breit and Merle A. Tuve bounce short radio pulses off ionosphere to determine height of ionosphere; considered first practical use of radar.

In one day Ford produces a Model T every 10 seconds. Tin Lizzie now retails for $295, affordable for most working-class families.

System of standard road markers adopted in U.S.

Clarence Birdseye develops successful method for quick-freezing foods.

1926

Detroit and Michigan

Feb. 1. New Central High School opens on Tuxedo Ave.

Feb. First contract airmail service from Detroit to Cleveland takes place in Ford plane designed by William B. Stout, Detroit's foremost airplane designer.

Feb. 13. First dial telephones are installed in residences.

Feb. 22. First concert held in new Masonic Temple, overlooking Cass Park. Complex to include cathedral, 4,600-seat auditorium, 2 ballrooms. Meeting place for Detroit's fraternal orders and venue for entertainment. (Completed 1928.)

Record seasonal snow accumulation: 78 inches, almost twice annual average.

March 27. City Plan Commission adopts zoning ordinance.

May 9. Admiral Richard E. Byrd uses Detroit-built plane, *Josephine Ford,* in historic North Pole flight.

May 19. Sebastian S. Kresge establishes $25 million foundation for education, charity, religion.

June 8. Babe Ruth clubs 626-foot home run out of Navin Field off Tiger hurler Lil Stoner; ball lands 2 blocks from park.

Tiger great Ty Cobb goes to Philadelphia Athletics.

Sept. 5. Cass Theater opens in refurbished auditorium of Detroit's old Board of Commerce Building.

Sept. Mine shaft at Ironwood collapses, trapping 43 men for more than 5 days.

Oct. 15. Dirigible *Los Angeles* moors at Ford airport.

Nov. 18. Detroit's new NHL team begins first season with game against Boston Bruins; Detroit Cougars lose (and end season in last place). Team plays at Border Cities Arena in nearby Windsor.

Father Coughlin, commissioned by Bishop Gallagher to establish Royal Oak parish, buys radio time and begins his Radio Shrine of the Little Flower. Listeners send in money.

Society of Arts and Crafts establishes art school.

McGregor Library completed on Woodward Ave. in Highland Park.

The 36-story, Louis Kamper–designed Book Tower completed on Washington Blvd. in Detroit. Book brothers now plan second tower—rising 70 stories and towering over all other buildings in city.

First buildings (designed by Eliel Saarinen) open at Cranbrook Academy of Art.

Car heaters (which draw heat from engine's cooling system) first appear in American cars.

World History

Textile strike in Passaic, New Jersey; lasts 1 year.

Florida land development scheme; investors lose thousands of dollars.

Philadelphia hosts Sesquicentennial Exposition.

Cultural Progress

Carter G. Woodson and the Association of the Study for Negro Life and History (ASNLH) begin promoting a Negro History Week; becomes Black History Month.

Scholastic Assessment Test (SAT) first given.

Amy Lowell's *What's O'clock* wins Pulitzer Prize for poetry.

Langston Hughes publishes *The Weary Blues.*

Sinclair Lewis publishes *Elmer Gantry.*

Kalamazoo-born Edna Ferber wins Pulitzer Prize for novel *So Big.*

Book-of-the-Month Club founded; influences American literary tastes.

New Orleans pianist "Jelly Roll" Morton begins recording with Red Hot Peppers (to 1930).

Parisian fashion maven Coco Chanel introduces the little black dress; establishes new style for women.

Don Juan offers moviegoers a synchronized musical score; first sound picture.

Contract bridge originates; card game becomes popular by 1930 (superseding predecessor, auction bridge).

Scientific and Commercial Progress

Nov. 11. RCA president David Sarnoff founds National Broadcasting Company (NBC).

May 9. American explorers Richard E. Byrd and Floyd Bennett claim first airplane flight over North Pole.

May 21. Detroit-born Charles Lindbergh becomes international hero; *See* World History.

1927

Detroit and Michigan

Fred W. Green, Republican, governor (to 1930).

Detroit reaches (present) geographical size of 139 square miles—6 times bigger than at turn of century.

Feb. 2. J. L. Hudson Co. acquires Newcomb-Endicott store to become third largest department store in U.S.

April 19. First Tiger broadcaster Ty Tyson announces 8–5 win.

May 26. Last Model T rolls off assembly line; more than 15 million had been made since its introduction.

Aug. 10. Tablet placed on wall of Charles Lindbergh's birthplace, at 1120 West Forest Ave., in honor of his transatlantic flight.

Oct. 6. Detroit Museum of Art renamed Detroit Institute of Arts; moves into new building on Woodward; with Detroit Public Library, anchors Cultural Center.

Oct. 24. Detroit City Airport opens; dedication, Nov. 5.

Nov. 2. Stout Air Service begins regular passenger airline service from Detroit to Cleveland. Detroit-Chicago service begins next year.

Nov. 22. Cougars play first game in newly built Olympia Stadium; Detroit's NHL team manages to make playoffs this year.

Dec. Ford introduces Model A.

Dec. 8. A 60-mph gale blows passenger steamer *Tashmoo* free of anchorage at foot of Griswold; vessel found upstream, knocking against Belle Isle bridge. Tugs manage to tow boat to safety and repairs are made. No one injured.

State gasoline tax authorized to provide funds for highway construction, maintenance.

University of Detroit expands from downtown campus to new facility at McNichols and Livernois.

Detroit Law School established.

Marygrove College founded (outgrowth of St. Mary's College, Monroe).

Having outgrown Ferry Field athletics facility, University of Michigan regents authorize construction of Michigan Stadium to seat 72,000 fans.

Cranbrook School opens in Oakland County; Cranbrook Foundation created by George and Ellen Booth.

The 14-story Maccabees Building completed, on Woodward south of Detroit Public Library.

Detroit Leland Hotel opens on corner of Cass and Bagley, at edge of city's new theatrical and shopping district; adds 720 hotel rooms to Detroit.

Miller-Storm Co. begins building neighborhood of bungalows south of Plymouth Rd. in southwest Detroit; Mark Twain Development intended as affordable housing; price range, $5,000–$15,000.

Chrysler acquires American Body Corp. plant across East Jefferson from its manufacturing facilities; ceases production of Maxwell model.

World History

Average industrial wage in U.S., $1,304 annually; poverty level for family of 4 is $2,000.

U.S. designates system of numbering routes, highways.

May 21. At 10:21 p.m. (local time) American Charles A. Lindbergh lands single-engine monoplane *Spirit of St. Louis* at Le Bourget Air Field, Paris, after completing first solo non-stop transatlantic flight. Took off from Long Island's Roosevelt Field over 33 hours earlier, May 20 at 7:52 a.m., just clearing telephone wires (plane carried 450 gallons of fuel). Wins Orteig prize (*See* 1919).

Cultural Progress

Ask Me Another quiz book sells 100,000 copies in first month; begins quiz craze.

Duke Ellington's Washingtonians become house band at Harlem's Cotton Club.

Lindy hop, American dance craze.

Composer George Antheil's *Ballet mécanique* debuts.

Dec. *Show Boat* opens on Broadway; epic musical by Jerome Kern and Oscar Hammerstein becomes highly influential.

First full-length talking picture: *The Jazz Singer*, with Al Jolson; by 1932 all movies talk.

Academy of Motion Picture Arts and Sciences founded.

Tennis great Helen Wills Moody wins her first Wimbledon singles championship; over next decade wins title 7 more times.

Gene Tunney retains heavyweight title in second match with Jack Dempsey after infamous "long-count." Fight broadcast to millions; sets new record for gate.

Ty Cobb, of Philadelphia Athletics, gets his 4,000th major league hit in game against Bengals.

Sept. 30. Babe Ruth hits 60th home run this season; 714 runs in career—new record.

Sonia Henie wins first of 10 consecutive world figure-skating championships.

Scientific and Commercial Progress

New York's Holland Tunnel completed after 7 years of construction; first long underwater tunnel in nation designed specifically for auto traffic.

First coast-to-coast paved highway is completed: paved Lincoln Highway (U.S. 30) runs from New York City to San Francisco.

German physicist Werner Heisenberg develops quantum mechanics; leads to discoveries in hydrogen. (Awarded Nobel Prize for physics, 1932.)

Television publicly demonstrated.

Commercial transatlantic telephone service inaugurated between New York and London.

1928

Detroit and Michigan

U.S. Coast Guard stations armored craft along river to deter Canadian liquor coming into Detroit.

Jan. 10. John C. Lodge, mayor of Detroit.

April 19. *Cadillac* goes into service, ferrying passengers between Detroit and Windsor.

June 6. *Detroit News* payroll department held up by 5 armed men, who get away with about $15,000. Rival publication *Detroit Times* scoops *News,* publishing full account of robbery.

July 30. Chrysler Corp. purchases Dodge Brothers Co.

Aug. 1. Detroit Zoo opens: among first U.S. zoos to extensively use exhibits without bars; animal habitats are moated or enclosed by simulated rock.

Oct. 25. State supreme court upholds city's ordering of jitneys off Detroit streets; citizens had demanded their return due to poor service by Detroit Street Railway.

Fall. Fisher Theater opens, last of great movie palaces built in Detroit.

Fisher Building, with famed golden tower, completed in Detroit's New Center; granite and marble structure rises 28 stories above bustling West Grand Blvd. Center for business, banking, shopping, dining, entertainment. Interior is lavishly ornamented by noted craftsmen of day. Though 3 towers are planned for site, only 1 built.

Water Board Building opens.

St. Florian Church built among Hamtramck's working-class houses.

Tigers draw smallest crowd ever, 404, for game against Boston.

Detroit Symphony Orchestra makes first appearance at Carnegie Hall in NYC.

Henry Ford Museum and Greenfield Village (named for Ford's birthplace) founded. Dearborn facility will exhibit automaker's collection of Americana—tools, utensils, other everyday items. Complete historical structures are moved to museum for public view.

Wilson Theatre (Madison Ave. at Brush) built at cost of $1.5 million; small performance space was vision of Detroit philanthropist Matilda (Dodge) Wilson.

United Artists Theater opens on Bagley; exotic, Spanish-inspired interior.

Fox Theatre completed on Woodward Ave.: lavish structure, designed by local architect C. Howard Crane, testament to Golden Age of movie palaces; seats 5,000.

Towering Penobscot Building completed at Griswold and Fort in Financial District; at 47 stories, claims title of Detroit's tallest building for next 5 decades. (*See* 1977 entry about Renaissance Center.) Original Penobscot building erected 1902.

Chrysler launches Plymouth Motor Corp. Steel and glass Lynch Rd. Assembly Plant is one-half mile long; houses longest assembly line in industry.

Chrysler Corp. sets up De Soto division; assembly at East Jefferson plant.

Union Trust Co. and National Bank of Commerce merge to form Union Commerce Corp.

Better Made Potato Chip Co. established by Detroiters Peter Cipriano and Cross Moceri.

Detroit architect Albert Kahn is commissioned by Soviet government to design industrial structures.

Elizabeth Nelson Elliott (Detroit) founds Elliottorian Business Women's Club, Michigan's first African American business women's club.

World History

Aug. 27. Kellogg-Briand Pact signed by 15 nations (eventually 62), who agree to settle conflicts by peaceful means.

Nov. 6. Herbert Hoover, Republican, elected president.

U.S. Customs Court lists James Joyce's *Ulysses* as obscene.

Joseph Stalin begins 5-year plan: collectivization of Soviet industry, agriculture. Resulting famine claims 25 million lives.

Chiang Kai-shek leads Nationalists in capturing Beijing; China reunited under one government.

Cultural Progress

Louis Armstrong and Earl "Fatha" Hines record jazz classics "West End Blues" and "Weather Bird."

Walt Disney's *Steamboat Willie* is first animated movie with sound.

Winter Olympics held in St. Moritz, Switzerland.

Summer Olympics held in Amsterdam, the Netherlands; women compete for first time, in field events.

Americans travel to Europe in record numbers.

Scientific and Commercial Progress

U.S. auto production tops 4 million this year.

Scottish bacteriologist Alexander Fleming discovers penicillin.

Dogs first trained as "seeing-eye" companions.

Sept. 26. Columbia Broadcasting System (CBS) founded by William S. Paley.

U.S. cigarette production doubled in last decade (to over 100 billion); in part due to social acceptance of smoking by women.

1929

Detroit and Michigan

June 2. Woman's Hospital at Hancock and Brush opens.

Aug. 26. Dirigible *Graf Zeppelin* visits Detroit on world tour.

Aug. 28. Common Pleas Court of Detroit established superceding justice courts.

Detroit ranks third nationally (behind New York and Chicago) in new construction over past decade. Building spate includes public buildings, hotels, movie palaces, skyscrapers—transforming downtown skyline.

The 23-story David Stott Building completed above Capitol Park, downtown.

Detroit Union Produce Terminal completed; cost $5 million.

Headquarters of Guardian Group (formerly Union Trust Co.), a 36-story skyscraper, completed at corner of Griswold and Congress (extending to Larned).

Guardian Group and Union Commerce Corporation merge to form Guardian Detroit Union Group, city's largest banking institution.

Vanity Ballroom completed in fashionable shopping district along East Jefferson (at Newport Ave.); last public ballroom constructed in Detroit. City's youth crowds Vanity's "floating" maple floor to dance to tunes of Benny Goodman, Duke Ellington, Dorsey Brothers.

Scarab Club building completed on corner of Farnsworth and John R streets in Detroit's Cultural Center.

Construction completed on Meadow Brook Hall, Oakland County estate of Alfred and Matilda Wilson.

Eleanor and Edsel Ford family moves into new home on Lake Shore Rd. in Grosse Pointe Shores; idyllic grounds equipped with swimming pool, lagoon, boathouse, 3/4-scale dollhouse.

Tourism has become leading source of income in Michigan.

Tiger George Uhle pitches victory in 21-inning contest with White Sox; Uhle pitched 20 innings before being removed for a pinch runner.

Henry Ford Museum opens. Incorporated in exterior are facades of Philadelphia's Independence Hall, Congress Hall, and old City Hall.

Oct. 21. Edison Jubilee, celebration of semicentennial of Edison's invention of incandescent light, hosted by Henry Ford; President Herbert Hoover among guests. Greenfield Village's Edison Institute opens during event.

Oct. Market crash brings to a halt building boom of 1920s; among projects canceled is proposed 70-story (second) Book Tower along Washington Blvd.

Nov. Father Solanus Casey opens Capuchin Kitchen, a soup kitchen on Mt. Elliott to serve Detroit's needy.

Nov. 15. Ambassador Bridge opens to traffic. Spans 9,602 feet across Detroit River.

In less than 3 years, Father Coughlin's religious radio broadcasts have raised enough money from listeners that building begins on Shrine of Little Flower church and tower on Woodward in Royal Oak.

Children's Fund of Michigan begins operations.

First station wagon offered for sale to consumers, a version of Ford Model A.

Hudson Motor Car Co. has peak year; third in sales, behind Ford and Chevrolet.

World History

March 4. Herbert Hoover inaugurated; 31st U.S. president.

Sept. 3. U.S. stock market hits new high.

Oct. 24. Black Thursday: U.S. stock market crashes, ending speculative boom. Stock sell-off peaks Tuesday, Oct. 29.

Great Depression begins: decade of worldwide economic hardship.

League of United Latin American Citizens (LULAC) founded in Texas; becomes largest Hispanic civil rights organization in U.S.

Cultural Progress

William Faulkner publishes *The Sound and the Fury.*

Stephen Vincent Benet wins Pulitzer Prize for poetry for popular epic *John Brown's Body.*

All Quiet on the Western Front, portrayal of action in World War I, a bestseller.

Dramatist, actor, composer Noel Coward hits stride with musical *Bitter Sweet.*

Robert Ripley's *Believe It or Not* is popular book and newspaper feature.

New York's Museum of Modern Art (MOMA) founded.

April 14. Martha Graham Dance Group debuts; ushers in modern dance.

First Academy Awards are held; columnist Sidney Skolsky dubs them Oscars.

Scientific and Commercial Progress

Blue Cross first offers form of prepayment insurance to help patients pay hospital bills.

Dirigible *Graf Zeppelin* circumnavigates globe before beginning passenger service between Europe and South America.

Commander Richard Byrd and crew fly over South Pole.

U.S. farmers have stepped up wheat production to meet increased demand; wheat acreage is 3 times what it was 10 years ago.

Business Week magazine established.

Eastman Kodak introduces 16-millimeter film for motion picture cameras.

Vladimir Zworykin, working for Westinghouse Electronic Corp., invents kinescope (television picture tube).

U.S. advertising volume is $3 billion; doubled in last decade.

1930

Detroit and Michigan

Michigan's population, 4,842,325.

Detroit's population, 1,568,662; ranks 4th in size among U.S. cities. Immigrant population (est.), 400,000; includes thousands from Eastern Europe.

Jan. 14. Charles Bowles, mayor of Detroit.

Jan. Detroit's new traffic court hears 4,810 cases in its first month in operation.

May 2–31. Detroit Institute of Arts holds one of largest Rembrandt exhibitions ever assembled.

June 22. First recall in major U.S. city: Detroit Mayor Charles Bowles is recalled in special election for poor handling of city's unemployment problems.

Sept. 9. Frank Murphy elected mayor of Detroit; takes office Sept. 23.

Nov. 3. Detroit-Windsor vehicular tunnel completed beneath Detroit River. The tunnel is 5,135 feet long and provides motorists with quick access to Canada from downtown (access on American side at foot of Randolph St.).

Detroit Metropolitan Airport opens.

Jennings Memorial Hospital erected on East Jefferson; facility was made necessary by city's rising population and its spread eastward toward city limits.

During this and next decade, nightclubs in Detroit's Paradise Valley, an entertainment Mecca in African American neighborhood, are venues for performances by Ella Fitzgerald, Pearl Bailey, Billy Holiday, Bill "Bojangles" Robinson, and other internationally known and up-and-coming musicians. Blacks and whites alike are in audiences.

Contest held to rename Detroit Cougars: hockey team to be called Falcons.

Brodhead Naval Armory completed on East Jefferson at entrance to Belle Isle Bridge. Over next decade, its interior is decorated by Federal Arts Project (WPA) employees.

General Motors plans technical center; acquires suburban land to build facility. Eliel Saarinen and son Eero are commissioned to design complex.

Michigan's copper mining industry declines; Upper Peninsula ore lies too deep underground to make extraction cost-efficient. Unemployment results.

Covered Wagon Co. of Detroit begins manufacturing mobile homes.

Mecca-born Wallace D. Fard establishes the Temple of Islam in Detroit, founding the Nation of Islam (also called Black Muslim).

World History

World population reaches 2 billion.

U.S. population, 122,775,046.

U.S. unemployment, 8.9% (4.5 million workers unemployed).

Average annual wage for U.S. workers drops to $1,288.

U.S. Veterans Administration founded (renamed Department of Veteran Affairs, 1988).

March. Mahatma Gandhi leads 200-mile march.

Cultural Progress

Children's Charter: White House Conference on Child Health and Protection draws up Bill of Rights for childhood.

Sinclair Lewis wins Nobel Prize for literature; first American author to win the prize.

Mystery writers popular with readers; fictional characters Charlie Chan, Sam Spade, The Saint, Ellery Queen well known.

Grant Wood paints *American Gothic.*

New York's 75-story Chrysler Building (William Van Alen, architect) completed; world's tallest.

Golfer Bobby Jones makes history: wins British Amateur, British Open, U.S. Open, U.S. Amateur.

Miniature golf popular.

Scientific and Commercial Progress

American Karl Landsteiner wins Nobel Prize for medicine for discovering 4 main types of human blood.

Advertising Age and *Fortune* begin publication.

Beauty is big business: cosmetics now widely accepted.

Great Plains farmers stop sowing expansive wheat fields due to Great Depression; leaves topsoil vulnerable to extreme weather conditions. (*See* dust bowl, 1933.)

Frozen foods first marketed by Postum Co. (later General Foods Corp.); not widely popular until 1950s (when freezers become common in the home).

257

1931

Detroit and Michigan

Wilber M. Brucker, Republican, governor (to 1932).

Jan. 2. Unemployed workers hold city hall protest.

Wickersham Commission report discloses Detroit as leader in Prohibition law violations.

Ford builds 20 millionth car; Ford plant at Rouge River recognized as one of world's largest industrial establishments.

DIA's first auxiliary group, Friends of Modern Art, founded by W. Hawkins Ferry.

Gar Wood in *Miss America* defends his Harmsworth trophy for unlimited powerboat racing in contest on Detroit River. Results are disputed, but Wood puts to rest any doubt next year when he defeats contender Kaye Don in *Miss England*.

New Center Building completed near Fisher Building, adding 10 stories of office space to uptown.

Kingswood School for girls opens.

Attorney Charles Roxborough first African American elected to state senate, serving one term, 1932–1933.

World History

Some 8 million American workers unemployed; corporate losses top $800 million.

May 4. Miners strike in Harlan County, Kentucky. More violent labor disputes in southeastern Kentucky over next several years—"Bloody Harlan."

Oct. 6–24. Notorious mobster Al "Scarface" Capone is tried in federal court for income tax evasion. Sentenced to 11 years in prison, payment of various fines and court costs.

April. First trial of "Scottsboro boys" makes national headlines. Nine black men are tried for raping white women in Alabama; 8 are convicted despite overwhelming evidence and testimony supporting their innocence. Case deepens racial divide.

American Jane Addams is awarded Nobel Prize for peace for her work with Women's International League for Peace and Freedom. Shares honor with Nicholas M. Butler of Carnegie Endowment for International Peace.

Cigar factory laborers in Ybor City (Tampa), Florida, strike.

Japan invades Manchuria.

Cultural Progress

Robert Frost wins his second Pulitzer Prize for poetry for *Collected Poems*.

Salvador Dali paints *Persistence of Memory*.

Dec. 26. *Of Thee I Sing*, with music by George Gershwin, opens on Broadway. Wins Pulitzer Prize next year; first musical to win the coveted drama award.

New York's 102-story Empire State Building (Shreve, Lamb, and Harmon, architects) completed; surpasses Chrysler Building as tallest in world.

Bill Tilden turns pro; gives professional tennis boost in popularity.

Scientific and Commercial Progress

Auguste Picard ascends to 52,000 feet in hot-air balloon; first ascension into stratosphere.

Hugh Herndon and Clyde Pangborn make first nonstop flight across Pacific—from Tokyo to Wenatchee, Washington.

American pilot Wiley Post and navigator Harold Gatty fly monoplane around the world in record 8 days, 15 hours, 51 minutes.

1932

Detroit and Michigan

Jan. 1. Department of Street Railway takes over Detroit Motorbus Co. lines. Suburban lines on the west side become Dearborn Coach; Lake Shore Coach on the east side.

March 7. "Union peace march" at Ford Rouge plant turns violent; five are killed.

May 14. About 40,000 people attend Detroit parade against Prohibition

July 25. Diego Rivera begins work on frescoes in Detroit Institute of Arts.

Oct. 2. Franklin Delano Roosevelt speaks at giant political rally in Detroit.

State Prohibition amendment repealed; national Prohibition still in effect.

Detroit fiscal crisis caused by heavy tax delinquency; salaries of city workers sharply reduced; and welfare expenditures drastically cut.

Unemployment means thousands are on public welfare in Detroit.

Architect Eliel Saarinen becomes president of Cranbrook Academy of Art.

James "Pops" Norris, former Montreal Winged Wheeler, buys Detroit Falcons for $100,000 and pays tribute to his former team by renaming Detroit's NHL franchise the Red Wings.

Gar Wood sets new speedboat record in *Miss America X*.

World History

American workforce includes 10 million women.

Estimated 13 million American workers unemployed.

Average annual wage for U.S. workers drops to $843.

March 1. Lindbergh kidnapping: toddler son of Charles and Anne Morrow Lindbergh is abducted from family's New Jersey home. Charles Jr.'s body found (May 12) in nearby woods.

May 21. American aviator Amelia Earhart is first woman to make solo transatlantic flight; sets speed record. Made 2,026-mile crossing from Harbor Grace, Newfoundland, to Londonderry, Northern Ireland, in 14 hours 56 minutes.

Nov. 8. Franklin Delano Roosevelt, Democrat, elected president.

Benjamin Nathan Cardozo is first Hispanic named to U.S. Supreme Court.

Cultural Progress

Pearl S. Buck's *The Good Earth* wins Pulitzer Prize for fiction.

Aldous Huxley's science fiction novel *Brave New World* describes terrifying future society.

Duke Ellington's band records "It Don't Mean a Thing If It Ain't Got That Swing."

Winter Olympics held in Lake Placid, New York.

Summer Olympics held in Los Angeles.

Detroit athlete Eddie Tolan sets an Olympic record, winning the 200-meter in 21.2 seconds; in 100-meter race he narrowly wins in 10.3 seconds but manages to set a world record. He is the first African American athlete to win two Olympic gold medals.

Scientific and Commercial Progress

Amelia Earhart is first woman to make both a transatlantic solo flight (from Newfoundland to Ireland; May 21) and transcontinental nonstop flight (Aug. 24).

Germany's autobahn opens; first modern highway system.

1933

Detroit and Michigan

William A. Comstock, Democrat, governor (to 1934).

Feb. 14. Gov. Comstock declares Michigan bank holiday; some Detroit banks never reopen.

March 29. Some 10,000 Detroiters meet at Naval Armory to protest German persecution of minorities.

April 3. Michigan is first state to vote for repeal of national Prohibition.

Michigan Liquor Control Commission created.

Detroit defaults on its debts.

April 27. Detroit issues $8 million in scrip to city employees.

May 6. Detroit Mayor Frank Murphy resigns; appointed by President Franklin D. Roosevelt to governor-general of Philippines.

May 10. Frank Couzens takes office as mayor of Detroit.

June 1. State sales tax passed by Michigan legislature.

Red Wings land on top of standings in American Division, tied with Boston, at the end of the 1932–33 season: fans rally behind the team, go "hockey crazy," as Wings make steady climb over next few years. (*See* 1936.)

Aug. 8. Colleges of City of Detroit organized under Board of Education, merging schools of medicine (Detroit College of Medicine and Surgery), education (Detroit Teachers College), liberal arts (Colleges of City of Detroit), and pharmacy (College of Pharmacy). Full engineering and graduate school programs are added.

Sept. 24. Widening of Woodward Ave. begins; trees removed between Kirby and Ferry avenues.

Diego Rivera completes *Detroit Industry* murals, painted on walls of interior courtyard of Detroit Institute of Arts.

Under Civil Works Administration, additional construction projects are undertaken at Detroit Zoo.

Detroit News sponsors trip aboard luxury steamer *City of Detroit III* to Chicago World's Fair.

Tigers trade catcher Johnny Pasek and $100,000 for Philadelphia Athletics catcher Mickey Cochrane; also obtain Goose Goslin from Washington (paving way for glory years to come).

World History

Since beginning of Great Depression (Oct. 1929), almost 6,000 banks have closed; 100,000 businesses have failed, corporate profits have fallen from $10 billion to $1 billion; about 25% of U.S. labor force (13 million workers) unemployed. Hoovervilles, bread lines common sights.

Jan. 30. Adolf Hitler is appointed chancellor of Germany.

March 4. Franklin Delano Roosevelt inaugurated; 32nd U.S. president. Begins work restoring American confidence; in address proclaims, "The only thing we have to fear is fear itself."

March 5. President Roosevelt declares national bank holiday; begins Hundred Days of sweeping reforms.

New Deal gets underway; dubbed "alphabet soup" by critics, recovery and relief programs include Civilian Conservation Corps (CCC), Federal Deposit Insurance Corp. (FDIC), Public Works Administration (PWA), Tennessee Valley Authority (TVA).

March 12. FDR gives first fireside chat; 60 million Americans tune radios to hear president's message.

June. National Industrial Recovery Act authorizes president to institute industry-wide codes to eliminate unfair trade practices, curb unemployment, establish minimum wage, set maximum workweek, guarantee collective bargaining.

The 20th ("lame duck") Amendment to U.S. Constitution ratified; moves congressional terms of office, date of presidential inauguration closer to election (March 4 to Jan. 20).

Frances Perkins named secretary of labor; first woman cabinet member in U.S. history.

The 21st Amendment to U.S. Constitution ratified; repeals 18th Amendment, ending Prohibition.

U.S. Customs' ruling that James Joyce's *Ulysses* is obscene is challenged in court; Judge John Woolsey decides book can be openly admitted into U.S. Ruling is a turning point in reducing government censorship.

Screen Actors Guild (SAG) formed; Hollywood actors establish self-governing organization.

Dust bowl (to 1939). Great Plains farmlands destroyed by drought, high winds. Some 350,000 ruined farmers, families (dubbed "Okies" and "Arkies") begin migration west to "promised land" of California.

Cultural Progress

Newsweek magazine published.

May. Chicago World's Fair ("Century of Progress Exhibition") begins; Ford Motor Co. Rotunda part of 2-year exhibit seen by millions.

School of American Ballet founded.

Ballet Russe de Monte Carlo makes first American tour.

Wireless part of everyday American life; chief source of news, entertainment (dramas, variety shows, live music), sporting events.

Dec. 1. Benny Goodman's "Let's Dance" is broadcast on network radio; launches swing era.

Dec. 4. *Tobacco Road* opens on Broadway; goes on to record-breaking run.

Hollywood debuts special effects: *King Kong* features stop-motion and rear-projection photography. Marx Brothers' *Duck Soup* also in movie theaters. Marx Brothers now made up of Groucho, Chico, Harpo, and Zeppo (Gummo left act c. 1916).

First drive-in movie theater opens (June 6) outside Camden, New Jersey.

Jigsaw puzzle fad.

Scientific and Commercial Progress

American Thomas H. Morgan wins Nobel Prize for medicine for studies of chromosomes' function in heredity.

Wiley Post is first person to make solo flight around the world: in single-engine Lockheed Vega (named *Winnie Mae*), equipped with autopilot, he covers 15,596 miles in 7 days, 18 hours, 49 minutes.

1934

Detroit and Michigan

Jan. 23. Colleges of City of Detroit adopt name Wayne University.

April 23. New federal building and post office open on Lafayette.

Red Wings make it to Stanley Cup finals for first time; defeated by Chicago Blackhawks, who take 3 games to Detroit's 1.

June. Billy Sunday opens second Detroit revival.

Botsford Tavern renovated by Henry Ford and opened to public.

Babe Ruth hits his 700th career home run over right field wall off Tommy Bridges in Detroit.

Mickey Cochrane leads Detroit Tigers to first American League pennant in 25 years.

Lions football team comes to Detroit.

Nov. In first Thanksgiving Day game, Detroit Lions narrowly lose to Chicago Bears at University of Detroit stadium; sell-out crowd of 26,000 watches them play while thousands more spectators are turned away at the gates.

Joe Louis wins his first fight against Jack Kracken.

At Chicago's Century of Progress Exposition, DSO (under name Ford Symphony) performs two concerts a day for 94 days and is heard by total of 1 million people.

Ford Symphony Hour radio broadcast begins; DSO becomes nation's first official radio broadcast orchestra.

Detroit area's interurban trains cease operation; with proliferation of automobile, light rail service no longer in demand.

Built-in radios introduced in some automobiles.

World History

Federal Communications Commission (FCC), Federal Housing Administration (FHA), Securities and Exchange Commission (SEC) founded; part of New Deal.

First Lady Eleanor Roosevelt begins radio program to address American public; soon called "first lady of radio."

Joseph Stalin begins Great Purge, reign of terror to suppress opposition.

Oct. Mao Tse-tung leads Long March; 100,000 communists set out on walk across China.

Cultural Progress

Rhumba is popular dance.

Radio personality Alexander Woollcott gains popularity.

Shirley Temple a box office hit.

Max Baer knocks out Primo Carnera to win heavyweight championship.

Oct. St. Louis Cardinals defeat Detroit Tigers in World Series.

Scientific and Commercial Progress

Enrico Fermi splits the atom.

Burlington *Zephyr*, first streamlined passenger train powered by diesel-electric locomotive, begins service in U.S.

Mutual Broadcasting System founded; joins NBC, CBS on radio airwaves.

1935

Detroit and Michigan

Frank D. Fitzgerald, Republican, governor (to 1936).

Average wage for auto workers, 76 cents per hour.

Local labor leaders help organize UAW, to be headquartered in Detroit. (*See* World History)

School of Social Work added at Wayne University.

Father Coughlin's National Union for Social Justice claims 5 million members.

Summer. Following Depression-related hiatus, Bob-Lo resumes excursions to popular downriver island.

City of Champions: after winning second straight American League pennant, Tigers go on to claim their first World Series championship by defeating Chicago Cubs in Oct.; Detroit holds downtown ticker-tape parade in their honor. Within weeks, Lions beat New York Giants 26-7 for National Football League championship. Red Wings wrap up (1935–36) season with first Stanley Cup victory.

Nov. Frank Navin dies; Walter O. Briggs becomes sole owner of Detroit Tigers.

World History

U.S. unemployment, 20.3%.

Jan. 2–Feb. 13. Bruno Richard Hauptmann is tried for murder of Charles Lindbergh Jr. amidst circuslike atmosphere. Found guilty, he is electrocuted (1936) despite appeals he was framed.

March 19. Harlem riot sparked by rumors that police had killed a 16-year-old African American suspect in a department- store basement.

May 27. Supreme Court invalidates 1933's National Industrial Recovery Act.

June 10. Alcoholics Anonymous founded.

Powerful hurricane strikes Florida Keys.

Congress of Industrial Organizations (CIO) officially founded by former AFL member unions. CIO sets up industrial unions of skilled and unskilled workers; stages sit-down strike at Akron, Ohio, rubber plant, popularizing protest method.

United Automobile Workers (UAW) organized in Detroit as part of CIO; will become one of nation's most powerful labor unions.

Second New Deal begins: More government programs launched to counter labor unrest, effects of ongoing Depression. Social Security Administration (SSA), National Labor Relations Board (NLRB), Works Progress Administration (WPA, later Work Projects Administration) among initiatives.

Cultural Progress

Popular Front Culture (to 1940): American art, literature, music, film focus on American life; convey political message.

Sept. George Gershwin's American opera *Porgy and Bess* opens; soon admired internationally.

George Balanchine choreographs *Serenade* (music by Tchaikovsky); considered his signature work.

Becky Sharpe, first full-length technicolor movie, is released.

May 24. Major league baseball plays first night game in Cincinnati.

Oct. Detroit Tigers claim their first World Series victory.

Detroit Lions win National Football League championship.

Scientific and Commercial Progress

Jan. 1. Amelia Earhart is first woman to fly solo across Pacific, from Honolulu to Oakland (California).

British team of physicists led by Robert A. Watson-Watt refine radar pulse techniques to locate aircraft at distances up to 17 miles.

U.S. has 1 international airline—Pan American World Airways (flies to Latin America); 4 major domestic airlines—-American, Eastern, United, and Transcontinental and Western Air (later Trans World Airlines). Regional airlines include Braniff, Delta, Northwest.

Parking meters first used, in Oklahoma City.

1936

Detroit and Michigan

May 14. Ford Rotunda, reassembled after debut at Chicago World's Fair, opens to visitors in Dearborn. Showcases auto industry.

June 18. Excursion steamer *Tashmoo* sinks at dock after striking submerged rock; passengers and crew safely disembarked.

July 8–14. Severe heat wave cripples Detroit. Some survive sweltering weather by taking refuge on Belle Isle, which resembles campground. Seven days of 100+ degree temperatures take their toll, claiming 364 lives in city. Statewide death toll 570.

Tiger pitchers Eldon Auker and Tommy Bridges score biggest double shutout win ever with 12-0 and 4-0 triumphs over St. Louis Browns.

Oct. 15. President Franklin D. Roosevelt visits Detroit during his run for second term; whistlestop draws large crowd.

Oct. Detroit Institute of Arts holds Van Gogh exhibition; great success.

Common Council approves construction of Chandler Park low-cost government housing.

Neurosurgeon Elizabeth C. Crosby is first woman to be full professor at University of Michigan.

Ford Foundation established by gift from Edsel Ford.

Chrysler moves De Soto division to old La Salle plant at Wyoming and Michigan, originally built for Saxon Motor Car Co.

Natural gas from Texas piped to Detroit.

World History

Axis Powers: Italy, Germany, Japan ally.

July 17. Spanish Civil War begins; becomes popular cause among left-leaning Americans. Germany and Italy throw support behind Generalissimo Franco.

First Lady Eleanor Roosevelt begins writing syndicated daily column "My Day."

Mary MacLeod Bethune becomes first African American woman to head federal agency (National Youth Administration's Division of Negro Affairs).

Nov. 3. Franklin Delano Roosevelt reelected president, defeating Alf Landon.

Britain's George V dies; son Edward VIII soon abdicates throne to marry American heiress Wallis Simpson and George VI (second son of George V) ascends to power (to 1952).

Italy conquers Ethiopia.

Life magazine begins weekly publication.

Cultural Progress

American dramatist Eugene O'Neill wins Nobel Prize for literature.

Margaret Mitchell's Civil War saga *Gone with the Wind* a bestseller; 1 million copies sold in 6 months.

John Dos Passos writes last volume of *USA* trilogy.

Robert Johnson records *King of the Delta Blues Singers*; overlooked for next 2 decades but later recognized as landmark blues album.

WPA's Federal Arts Project puts 5,000 artists to work in U.S.

Feb. Charlie Chaplin's *Modern Times* opens in movie theaters.

Winter Olympics held in Garmisch-Partenkirchen, Germany.

Detroit Red Wings close 1935–36 season by taking home their first Stanley Cup—completing sweep of Detroit sports franchises. (*See* 1935.)

Summer Olympics held in Berlin: African American athlete Jesse Owens wins 4 gold medals.

Scientific and Commercial Progress

Medicine begins using sulfa drugs.

Rural Electrification Act results in 90% of American rural homes having electrical service.

Boulder Dam completed (renamed Hoover Dam, 1947).

John Maynard Keynes publishes *General Theory of Employment, Interest and Money*; lays theory of modern macroeconomics.

British ocean liner *Queen Mary* launched.

1937

Detroit and Michigan

Frank Murphy, Democrat, governor (to 1938).

Michigan enacts civil service law.

Jan. Detroit celebrates centennial of Michigan statehood.

Jan. 13. WXYZ begins *Lone Ranger* radio program; tremendously popular, program is carried by more than 400 U.S. stations by 1940.

Jan.–Feb. UAW strikes Fisher Body and Chevrolet plants in Flint; union demands a closed shop. Settled Feb. 11 when union is recognized by GM, receives collective bargaining rights.

March. UAW President Homer Martin addresses one of largest crowds ever assembled in Cadillac Square during labor union rally.

April 6. One-month UAW sit-in strike at Chrysler ends.

May 26. Battle of Overpass at Ford's Rouge River complex: Demonstration by UAW turns bloody when Ford "Service Department" men brutally beat union members; Walter Reuther emerges as UAW leader. Ford refuses to concede to demands in spite of bad publicity, which turns tide of public opinion to pro-union.

William S. "Bunky" Knudson becomes president of General Motors.

May. New Greyhound bus terminal opens on Washington Blvd.

Detroit cheers Red Wings repeat championship: Stanley Cup winners two years in a row, defeat New York Rangers 3 games to 2.

June 22. Detroit celebrates Joe Louis's boxing victory; heavyweight champ grew up on Detroit's east side, where his mother still lives. Mrs. Lilly Reese Brooks becomes neighborhood hero.

Aug. Tiger catcher Rudy York hits 17th and 18th home runs; sets new 1-month record.

Sept. First seeing-eye dog in Detroit aids blind Ellsworth Smith.

Tigers score 36 runs in a doubleheader with St. Louis Browns, a Major League offensive record.

Oct. 21. Detroit's baseball park renamed Briggs Stadium; previously Bennett Field (1900–12), Navin Field (1912–37).

Charles C. Diggs Sr. (Detroit) is Michigan's first black Democratic state senator.

Detroit Roman Catholic Diocese made Archdiocese; the Most Rev. Edward Mooney arrives to replace Bishop Gallagher.

Detroit Law School merged into Wayne University.

Chrysler opens Dodge truck plant on Mound and 8 Mile roads in Warren; massive steel-and-glass structures at plant rank among architect Albert Kahn's most famous.

Indian Village homeowners form residents association to enforce preservation of neighborhood's homes; many industrialists fled area in 1920s in favor of suburbs.

World History

Jan. 20. President Franklin D. Roosevelt inaugurated; begins 2nd term.

Feb. 11. General Motors recognizes United Auto Workers after sit-down strike in Flint.

May 26. German passenger airship *Hindenburg* explodes while landing at Lakehurst, New Jersey.

May 26. Battle of the Overpass at Ford Rouge River plant. (*See* Detroit and Michigan.)

July 2. American aviator Amelia Earhart and navigator Fred Noonan make last radio contact before disappearing. Pair had set out May 20 from California on around-the-world flight along equator; reached New Guinea June 30; last seen July 1.

Sino-Japanese War begins; later absorbed by World War II.

Britain reverses Jewish resettlement policy in Palestine; attempt to gain Arab support in event of war in Europe.

Cultural Progress

Dale Carnegie's self-help book *How to Win Friends and Influence People* a bestseller.

Zora Neale Hurston publishes highly acclaimed novel *Their Eyes Were Watching God.*

Twenty-five cent paperbacks popular with American readers.

George S. Kaufman and Moss Hart win Pulitzer Prize for drama for *You Can't Take It with You.*

June. Sociopolitical playwright Marc Blitztein's musical *The Cradle Will Rock* opens.

Dimitri Shostakovich writes Symphony No. 5.

Billie Holiday releases *The Quintessential Billie Holiday,* Vol. 4.

Pablo Picasso paints *Guernica*; portrayal of German attack on Basque village widely regarded as his masterpiece.

June 22. Joe Louis knocks out opponent Jim Braddock in 8 rounds, claiming boxing heavyweight championship; New York sports columnist calls boxer "a credit to his race—the human race." Louis remains on top for next 12 years.

Scientific and Commercial Progress

American bacteriologist Max Theiler develops 17-D vaccine, effective in combating yellow fever.

British inventor Frank Whittle builds first successful jet engine; soon copied by Germans.

San Francisco's Golden Gate Bridge completed.

In Los Angeles, first drive-through bank opens.

1938

Detroit and Michigan

Jan. 4. Richard Reading, mayor of Detroit.

Feb. Peak welfare load: 30,000 families.

June 22. Heavyweight champion and Detroit native Joe Louis enters ring to fight former champion Max Schmeling, only man who had ever beaten him. Louis reigns victorious—the win even more important to American fans as Schmeling is symbol of Germany's Nazi government.

July 18. Detroit-Windsor ferry discontinued.

Oct. First units of Brewster and Parkside housing projects are occupied.

Oct. 8. International Blue Water Bridge opens; connects Port Huron with Sarnia (Ontario).

Nov. 20. Detroiters join nationwide prayer service of protest against Nazi persecution of religious minorities, especially Jews.

Secret party ballots are used at primary elections for first time.

Michigan Consolidated Gas Co. formed by combining gas companies in Detroit, Grand Rapids, Muskegon, Ann Arbor.

Ford's Rouge River complex in Dearborn consists of more than 2 dozen steel-and-glass manufacturing facilities. Henry Ford achieves goals of self-sufficiency, vertical integration: property has powerhouse, steel mills, metal-stamping works, engine plant, tire plant, glass-manufacturing facility; 24-mile network of railroad tracks services buildings.

Hank Greenberg hits 57th and 58th home runs of season in nightcap of twin bill against Browns.

World History

Fair Labor Standards Act establishes national minimum wage, length of standard work-week for most U.S. employees.

March. Germany takes over Austria (to 1945).

May 26. House Committee on Un-American Activities formed.

June 25. Congress passes Wages and Hours Act, banning child labor and establishing 40-hour workweek.

Sept. 20. British Prime Minister Neville Chamberlain signs Munich Agreement with Adolf Hitler, Joseph Stalin.

Sept. 21. Hurricane strikes Long Island and New England.

Nov. 9. *Kristallnacht* (Night of Broken Glass): Nazi crowds burn synagogues, break windows of Jewish businesses; begins German campaign of anti-Semitic violence.

Cultural Progress

American Pearl S. Buck wins Nobel Prize for literature.

Thornton Wilder's *Our Town* wins Pulitzer Prize for drama.

African American artist Jacob Lawrence begins his *Frederick Douglass* series; paintings portray struggle of oppressed to win justice.

King of swing Benny Goodman and orchestra perform landmark Carnegie Hall concert.

Ella Fitzgerald records her first hit, "A-Tisket, A-Tasket," with drummer Chick Webb's big band.

Kate Smith's version of Irving Berlin's "God Bless America" becomes unofficial national anthem.

The jitterbug a popular dance; hallmark of big band era.

Information Please a popular radio quiz show.

Oct. 30. Orson Welles's radio production of H. G. Wells's science fiction novel *The War of the Worlds* creates sensation.

Screwball comedy *Bringing Up Baby* in movie theaters.

Disney releases *Snow White and the Seven Dwarfs*; first full-length animated film is among most popular movies in history.

Scientific and Commercial Progress

Enrico Fermi wins Nobel Prize for physics for discovering radioactive elements beyond uranium.

First xerographic image made.

Du Pont Co. introduces nylon.

1939

Detroit and Michigan

Frank D. Fitzgerald, Republican, governor.

March 16. Gov. Fitzgerald dies in office; succeeded by Lt. Gov. Luren D. Dickinson, Republican (to 1940).

March 7. Branch of UAW led by Homer Martin secedes from CIO; reaffiliates with AFL (June 4).

Detroit chapter of NAACP sends representatives to organization's convention in Richmond, Virginia.

Act 147 of Michigan Public Act authorizes development of Huron-Clinton Metropolitan Park system, to be built around area's two longest inland rivers.

Detroit Symphony Orchestra moves from Orchestra Hall to Masonic Temple.

Campaign begins for a Medical Center in Detroit.

Buick introduces flashing turn signal on its cars.

Macomb County's Selfridge Field expanded to 5 times original size.

World History

Jan. 2. Michigan's Frank Murphy is sworn in as U.S. attorney general.

Feb. Daughters of the American Revolution bar Marian Anderson from Constitution Hall concert on account of race. Prompts Eleanor Roosevelt's resignation from DAR. Anderson performs before audience of 75,000 at Lincoln Memorial (April 9).

Feb. 27. Supreme Court ruling declares sit-down strikes illegal.

March 28. Generalissimo Franco, Nationalists capture Madrid; begin era of extreme rule (to 1973).

April. Italy takes Albania.

June 12. Inter-Allied Declaration: leaders of Belgium, Czechoslovakia, France, Greece, Luxembourg, Netherlands, Norway, Poland, Yugoslavia, British Commonwealth vow to work together for a free world.

Sept. 1. World War II begins when Germany invades Poland. Great Britain, France declare war on Germany (Sept. 3).

Oct. 11. President Franklin D. Roosevelt receives letter from Albert Einstein warning him of German development of atomic bomb, advising U.S. development and study of nuclear energy.

Nov. 30. Russia invades Finland.

Cultural Progress

Jan. American composer Charles Ives's *Concord* piano sonata premieres; bucks convention.

April 30. Roosevelt's speech opening New York World's Fair is first televised presidential talk. NBC's fair coverage initiates weekly television programming but TV network development is thwarted by WWII.

May 17. NBC televises Princeton v. Columbia baseball game; first televised sporting event.

Oct. Bluegrass music makes national debut: Bill Monroe and the Blue Grass Boys perform on country music radio's *Grand Ole Opry.*

Nov. 8. *Life with Father* opens on Broadway; goes on to record run.

John Steinbeck's *The Grapes of Wrath* a bestseller; story of westward journey of Oklahoma farm family devastated by dust bowl.

Height of Hollywood's golden age: *Gone with the Wind, The Wizard of Oz, Wuthering Heights, Stagecoach, Mr. Smith Goes to Washington,* and *Gunga Din* among releases.

Scientific and Commercial Progress

German scientist Otto Hahn splits uranium atom (awarded Nobel Prize, 1944).

WPA projects undertaken to date include building 75,000 bridges and constructing or improving some 650,000 miles of roads in U.S.

First jet airplane takes flight in Germany.

July 10. Pan American's *Yankee Clipper* makes first transatlantic passenger flight; inaugurating regular passenger service to Europe.

Igor Sikorsky develops first practical helicopter.

1940

Detroit and Michigan

Michigan's population, 5,256,106.

Detroit's population, 1,623,452; ranks 4th in size among U.S. cities.

City's African American population accounts for 9% of total.

Jan. 2. Edward J. Jeffries, mayor of Detroit.

March 25. Detroit Public Library celebrates its 75th anniversary.

April 3. *Detroit Free Press* purchased by John S. Knight.

April 6. Ford Motor Co. builds 28 millionth automobile.

June 16. Peace Carillon dedicated on Belle Isle.

Aug. 15. Work begins on Chrysler's $20 million tank plant on Van Dyke in Warren. Six months later, facility turns out first tank as Detroit's automakers turn to wartime production.

Sept. 6. Michigan Supreme Court rules women doing equal work must be paid wages equal to those of men.

Detroit Tigers win American League pennant; lose series to Cincinnati in 7 games.

Oct. 15. Michigan National Guard mobilized for active service, including nearly 1,500 Detroiters.

Oct. 16. Half million Detroiters register for first selective service. (State quota for initial call just 627.)

Oct. 16. Granite statue of Father Gabriel Richard unveiled in Gabriel Richard Park.

Dec. 8. Women clerks at Neisner Brothers strike.

Dec. 12. Hudson Motor Co. and UAW sign contract; first union shop in a major automobile plant.

Chinatown begins to develop this decade, near Third and Michigan avenues; moves to Cass and Peterboro neighborhood later.

GM's William S. Knudson is named head of U.S. National Defense Council.

Fifteen Detroit brewers supply beer, some nationally; Strohs, Tivoli, Von, Cadillac, Pfeiffers, Goebel's Banner among labels.

Passenger steamer S.S. *South American* offers vacation cruises of Great Lakes.

World History

U.S. population, 131,669,275.

U.S. unemployment, 14.6%.

U.S. workforce is 25.3% female.

Feb. 5. Michigan's Frank Murphy (former U.S. attorney general) takes seat on U.S. Supreme Court (to 1949).

The 2,800-foot bridge over Washington's Puget Sound is hit by high winds, causing bridge to undulate and suspension cable to break.

May 10. Britain's King George VI names Winston Churchill prime minister; asks for new government after failure of Neville Chamberlain's.

June. European Jewish refugees on board S.S. *St. Louis* are turned away from New York Harbor.

Nov. 5. Franklin Delano Roosevelt reelected president; to serve unprecedented 3rd term.

President Roosevelt appoints GM President William "Bunky" Knudsen director of industrial production for National Defense Research Committee. Continues to direct production of war materials as head of U.S. Office of Production Management (1941) and in his role in War Department (1942–45).

Benjamin O. Davis Sr. is first black general in U.S. Army.

Olympics are canceled due to World War II.

Cultural Progress

Richard Wright publishes *Native Son.*

How Green Was My Valley is best-selling novel.

American Ballet Theatre (ABT) first performs; with New York City Ballet, one of America's major ballet companies. Develops repertory including works by choreographers George Balanchine, Agnes de Mille, Jerome Robbins, Antony Tudor.

New York's Rockefeller Center is completed.

About 30 million U.S. households have radios.

Frank Sinatra begins touring with Tommy Dorsey's band; gains teen following.

Folksinger Woodie Guthrie writes anthem "This Land Is Your Land"; releases *Dust Bowl Ballads.*

Oct. Detroit Tigers lose World Series to Cincinnati Reds.

Scientific and Commercial Progress

U.S. has 245,740 miles of railway.

CBS's Peter Carl Goldmark develops color television.

1941

Detroit and Michigan

Murray D. Van Wagoner, Democrat, governor (to 1942).

April 14. Ford Motor Co. recognizes UAW; signs contract after 10-day strike. Union now represents workers of all large auto companies.

May. WWJ establishes first FM radio station in Michigan.

Red Wings lose Stanley Cup finals to Boston Bruins.

Detroit hosts its first All Star baseball game; American League wins on Ted Williams's 9th inning home run.

In his last game before induction into Army, first baseman Hank Greenberg hits 2 home runs as Tigers beat Yankees at home.

Nov. 11. International peace monument dedicated on Belle Isle; commemorates 126 years of peace between U.S. and Canada.

Dec. 8. Army guards are stationed at Detroit-Windsor tunnel and Ambassador Bridge after attack on Pearl Harbor.

Dec. 10. State Defense Council launches training programs for emergency police, firemen, air raid wardens.

Dec. 24. Orchestra Hall, former home of DSO, reopens as Paradise Theatre, jazz venue.

Rosa Slade Gragg (Detroit) is only black person on President Franklin D. Roosevelt's National Volunteers Participation Committee of Civilian Defense.

Fort Wayne becomes ordnance depot during war.

Lila M. Neuenfelt (Dearborn) is first woman circuit court judge in Michigan; on Wayne County Circuit Court.

Mayor Edward Jeffries asks City Plan Commission to develop master urban plan; resulting scheme divides Detroit into 150 neighborhoods.

Wayne University Press founded.

World History

By acts of Congress, American Independence Day (July 4) becomes legal holiday; 4th Thursday in Nov. is set aside for Thanksgiving.

Jan. 6. Four Freedoms: President Franklin D. Roosevelt extols freedom of speech and worship, freedom from fear and want.

Jan. 20. President Roosevelt inaugurated; begins 3rd term.

March 11. Lend-Lease is passed by Congress; approves $50 billion in aid to Britain, Allies.

June 20. Ford recognizes UAW.

June 25. President Roosevelt signs executive order barring discrimination in government and defense industries.

Aug. 14. Atlantic Charter: Franklin D. Roosevelt and Winston Churchill outline aims for peace.

Dec. 7. Japanese launch surprise attack on U.S. military installations at Pearl Harbor.

Dec. 8. President Roosevelt addresses Congress, calling Dec. 7 "a date which will live in infamy"; U.S. issues declaration against Japan, entering World War II.

Dec. 15. In recognition of war effort, American Federation of Labor vows no-strike policy in defense plants.

Second great migration (to 1945): more southern blacks, drawn to work in defense plants, move North.

Rosie the Riveter: as more men go off to war, 3.5 million more American women join work-force (by 1945).

Cultural Progress

Billy Strayhorn composes "Take the 'A' Train"; becomes theme song of Duke Ellington's band.

American artist Edward Hopper paints *Nighthawks*.

Presidential sculptures carved out of Mount Rushmore (South Dakota) completed after 14 years of work.

National Gallery of Art dedicated in Washington, D.C.

Arsenic and Old Lace opens on Broadway.

Citizen Kane, written, directed by, starring Orson Welles, is in movie theaters.

Joltin' Joe DiMaggio hits safely in 56 consecutive games (May 15–July 16), setting major league record.

June 18. Joe Louis works to defend title: knocks out Billy Conn in 13th round.

Gin rummy a popular card game.

1942

Detroit and Michigan

Jan. 28. Horace H. Rackham Educational Memorial Building, built for Engineering Society of Detroit and University of Michigan Extension Service, opens on Farnsworth in Detroit; first new Cultural Center building since 1927.

Feb. 25. Belle Isle Bridge renamed Douglas MacArthur Bridge.

Feb. 28. Racial clash at Sojourner Truth housing project: confrontation came as black residents began moving into their new homes in heavily Polish and all white north Detroit neighborhood.

May 3. Wayne County holds first blackout drill.

May 4. Detroit receives its first ration books.

May. Ford's Rouge River plant converted to war production; as part of war effort, a record 120,000 people are employed at complex. Car production halted; automakers retool to produce tanks, jeeps, aircraft, other war materials. (*See also* Aug. 15, 1940; 1945, following Aug. 14 entry.)

Red Wings lose Stanley Cup finals to Toronto Maple Leafs.

June 30. Detroit School Superintendent Frank Cody resigns after 50 years as schoolmaster; succeeded by Warren Bow.

July 2. Max Stephan of Detroit found guilty of treason for aiding Nazi prisoner of war in escape; sentenced to death (Aug. 6). First U.S. treason conviction and sentence of execution since Whiskey Rebellion (1794). President Franklin D. Roosevelt later (July 1943) commutes sentence to life imprisonment.

July 17–24. Department of Street Railway strike cripples city transportation.

Aug. *Life* magazine runs article titled "Detroit is Dynamite"; points to riot at Sojourner Truth project (Feb.) and details other incidents showing deep-seated racism in city.

Sept. 18. President Franklin D. Roosevelt tours Detroit's war plants.

Nov. Herman Gardens housing project opens for occupancy.

Dec. 8. Renowned architect Albert Kahn dies at age 72.

Fort Wayne serves as induction center for military (to 1945).

College of Medicine of Wayne University staffs 36th General Hospital in Europe (until 1945).

Selfridge Field becomes training center for military personnel.

Wayne University, which has been holding classes in makeshift facilities near Woodward and Warren, holds competition for campus plan; winning scheme developed by architect Suren Pilafian.

Ford Symphony Hour, national radio broadcast featuring DSO, goes off air.

Davison Freeway built across Highland Park; thoroughfare answers need for more east-west arteries in Detroit.

GM fences in 900-acre Tech Center site in Warren; construction delayed by war effort.

World History

Jan. 1. "Declaration by the united nations" signed by 26 Allied countries who pledge to fight Axis powers, not make separate peace agreements.

Jan. Nazis hold conference in Germany to plan genocide of European Jews.

Feb. FDR signs executive order authorizing removal and internment of Japanese Americans on West Coast.

Japan claims the Philippines; by midyear also claims Guam, Wake Island, Hong Kong, Singapore, Malaya, Dutch East Indies.

Bataan Death March: Japanese soldiers in Philippines force already weak American and Filipino prisoners on 65-mile walk; 10,000 die.

May. Battle of the Coral Sea; U.S. carrier planes halt Japan's advance toward Australia.

May 14. Women's Army Auxiliary Corps (WAAC) founded.

June 4–6. Battle of Midway: American forces weaken Japan's naval strength.

Aug. 23. Battle of Stalingrad (to Feb. 2).

African campaign: U.S. Generals Dwight Eisenhower and George Patton cooperate with British General Montgomery to push back Rommel's combined German and Italian forces.

Nov. Casablanca, Morocco, is surrendered to Allies.

U.S. government authorizes Manhattan Project to develop atomic bomb.

Cultural Progress

The Robe by Lloyd C. Douglas begins long stay on bestseller lists.

Dec. Bing Crosby's "White Christmas" is best-selling single.

Scientific and Commercial Progress

Red Cross begins nationwide collection of blood.

First self-sustaining nuclear chain reaction conducted by Enrico Fermi's team at University of Chicago.

First U.S. built jet-propelled airplane is tested Oct. 1.

Alcan (Alaska) Highway completed.

1943

Detroit and Michigan

Harry F. Kelly, Republican, governor (to 1946).

May 26. Edsel Ford dies at age 49.

June 20. Sunday evening: fights break out between white and black youths on Belle Isle; word of fracas spreads through city and in predawn hours of June 21, full-scale rioting occurs, with white mobs attacking black pedestrians and angry blacks lashing out at white motorists en route to work Monday morning. Gov. Kelly requests federal troops; order is restored late in day, but 34 people die (25 of them black), more than 1,000 people are injured, 1,800 are arrested. Property damage in the millions.

Sept. 27. Detroit's First Grand Opera Festival.

Detroit Symphony Orchestra is revived with financial support from Henry Reichold and with Karl Krueger as conductor.

Singer and guitarist John Lee Hooker moves to Detroit where he earns his reputation as a blues musician.

Dec. Flu epidemic affects 10% of Detroit's population.

Gas ration stickers issued as part of wartime conservation efforts on home front.

Ford's Willow Run bomber plant begins assembling airplanes using mass production techniques; huge factory covers 70 acres and assembly line extends 3,000 feet.

Mayor Edward Jeffries's Street Improvement Committee proposes system of freeways in Detroit.

Detroit radio station WWJ hires newscaster Fran Harris; first woman in city to hold such a job.

Some 350 armed troops guard ballpark as Tigers and Indians play doubleheader (home team wins opener; loses second).

All American Girls Professional Baseball League, formed while players on men's (farm) baseball teams are in military service; includes Grand Rapids Chicks, Battle Creek Belles, and Muskegon Lassies.

Detroit Red Wings defeat Boston Bruins to win Stanley Cup.

World History

Jan. 17–27. Franklin D. Roosevelt and Winston Churchill hold Casablanca conference; Allied leaders call for Axis powers to surrender unconditionally.

Feb. 2. Soviet victory at Stalingrad a turning point in World War II.

March. U.S. begins rationing meat, butter, cheese.

Navajo Code-Talkers transmit Allied messages that cannot be broken by the enemy; key to war effort.

April 19. Warsaw Ghetto uprising begins; 60,000 confined Jews rebel. Most are killed by German troops.

May 13. Some 250,000 German and Italian troops surrender to Allied forces in Tunisia. North African coast becomes basis for Allied invasion of Italy.

June 3–6. Zoot suit riot in Los Angeles. After 9 young Mexican American men were falsely accused of murder and sentenced to life, 11 sailors claimed they were jumped by Mexican Americans. Sailors and servicemen went on a rampage attacking men of Mexican American descent.

Sept. 9–18. U.S. troops land at Salerno, Italy. Captured after severe fighting.

Nov. Franklin D. Roosevelt, Winston Churchill meet with China's Chiang Kai-shek in Cairo.

Nov.–Dec. Roosevelt, Churchill, Stalin hold Teheran Summit; agree to launch operation OVERLORD (invasion of Europe from English Channel) early next year.

Cultural Progress

Wendell Willkie publishes *One World,* about his world tour.

Norman Rockwell paints the *Four Freedoms.*

Jazz pianist and singer Nat "King" Cole has first hit, "Straighten Up and Fly Right."

Bela Bartok writes *Concerto for Orchestra*; considered masterpiece of 20th-century music.

March 31. *Oklahoma!* begins long Broadway run; first musical with integrated cast.

African American actor Paul Robeson stars in *Othello.*

Casablanca a box office favorite.

Lena Horne's "Stormy Weather" emerges from movie by same name.

Stanley Cup claimed by Detroit Red Wings, who tromp Boston Bruins, 4 games to 0.

Scientific and Commercial Progress

American microbiologist Selman Waksman discovers powerful antibiotic streptomycin; used to treat tuberculosis, typhoid fever, bubonic plague, bacterial meningitis. (Waksman wins Nobel Prize for medicine, 1952.)

First use of DDT as standard insecticide.

Pentagon building is completed in Arlington, Virginia.

U.S. railroads jammed with passengers due to wartime gas rations.

Government orders RCA to give up radio network; sells NBC Blue. Origin of American Broadcasting Corporation (ABC).

1944

Detroit and Michigan

Michigan's 32nd Division serves in Philippines.

Jan. 11. First season of Civic Light Opera performances opens.

Jan. 13. Inter-Racial Relations Committee appointed by Mayor Edward Jeffries.

Feb. 1. Detroit industrial area, including plants in Wayne and Oakland counties, leads nation in war contracts with total of $12,745,525,000.

World History

June 6. D-Day for Operation OVERLORD: U.S. General Dwight Eisenhower leads 200,000 Allied troops in landing at Normandy, France; claims beaches and begins push inland. Total of 4,000 ships, 3 million American, British, Canadian, French troops participate in invasion; largest amphibious landing in history.

June 22. FDR signs GI Bill (officially Servicemen's Readjustment Act); establishes veterans hospitals, provides vocational training, makes low-interest mortgages available, grants funds for continued education.

July. Bretton Woods Conference: world leaders establish International Monetary Fund, World Bank.

Aug. Dumbarton Oaks Conference: representatives of Britain, U.S., Soviet Union, China outline future peacekeeping organization; basic concept of UN Security Council.

Oct. Gen. MacArthur lands on Philippines; establishes practical U.S. control by July 1945.

Nov. Michigan native Thomas E. Dewey (now governor of New York) is Republican nominee for presidency; defeated by incumbent Franklin Delano Roosevelt, who will serve unprecedented 4th term.

Dec. 16. Battle of the Bulge; Allies pour into Germany after failure of last Nazi offensive.

Charles De Gaulle becomes president of France's provisional government (to 1946).

Olympics are canceled due to World War II.

Cultural Progress

United Negro College Fund founded.

Comedian Bob Hope tops bestseller lists with *I Never Left Home,* his account of entertaining the troops.

Journalist Ernie Pyle's *Brave Men,* third compilation of his columns covering World War II, widely read.

American composer Aaron Copland writes *Appalachian Spring.*

Scientific and Commercial Progress

U.S. Navy's Grace Murray Hopper writes first functional computer program, for Harvard-developed Mark I computer (first automatic calculator).

U.S. military accepts first jet fighter plane.

1945

Detroit and Michigan

Jan. 31. Hamtramck-born soldier Eddie Slovik is executed by firing squad in France: Court-martialed for desertion under fire, he was sentenced to death as a deterrent to other would-be World War II deserters. (Remains are returned to Michigan decades later.)

April 14. Detroit stops work at hour of President Franklin D. Roosevelt's funeral service.

May 8. Detroit celebrates V-E Day.

Red Wings lose Stanley Cup finals to Toronto Maple Leafs.

June. Michigan Senator Arthur H. Vandenberg (Republican) helps frame charter of United Nations.

July 13. Wilson Theater purchased as new home for Detroit Symphony Orchestra; renamed Music Hall.

Aug. 9. Kaiser-Frazer Corp. organized; by 1947 they will be 4th-largest automaker.

Aug. 14–15. Detroit celebrates Japanese surrender, end of World War II.

Automakers have produced 92% of vehicles, 87% of aircraft bombs, 85% of helmets, 50% of engines, 56% of tanks, and 47% of machine guns needed to fight World War II. After V-J Day, they resume car production.

Sept. 21. Henry Ford steps down as head of Ford Motor Co.; grandson Henry II takes helm.

Oct. Detroit Tigers win pennant and go on to claim World Series.

Nov. 15. Detroit holds armistice parade.

Surveys reveal 75% of Detroit's female workforce wants to remain on job at end of war. But with veterans returning to their jobs, most women return home.

College of Nursing added at Wayne University.

Parke, Davis and Co. introduces Promin, first effective chemotherapeutic agent for leprosy.

Harold "Prince Hal" Newhouser, who joined the Detroit Tigers in 1939, wins his second Most Valuable Player award; only pitcher to win consecutive MVP honors.

Future jazz great Betty Carter (born in Flint, educated in Detroit) begins singing in Detroit clubs with noted bebop musicians including Charlie "Bird" Parker.

World History

U.S. unemployment, 1.9%.

More than one-third of U.S. nonagricultural workers are union members; hospital insurance coverage, paid vacations, pensions among World War II era gains.

Jan. 20. President Franklin D. Roosevelt inaugurated; 4th term.

Jan. 26. Allied troops liberate Auschwitz.

Feb. Roosevelt, Churchill, Stalin hold Yalta Conference.

Feb. 13–14. Dresden bombing raid.

March. Allied troops capture Germany's industrial Ruhr Valley.

April 11. U.S. troops led by Gen. George Patton liberate Buchenwald.

April 12. President Roosevelt dies; succeeded by Vice President Harry S Truman, 33rd U.S. president.

April 25. Allied Army enters Berlin.

April 28. Benito Mussolini is killed after caught trying to escape to Switzerland.

April 30. Adolf Hitler commits suicide in Berlin.

May 7. Germany surrenders.

May 8. V-E Day declared by President Truman.

June 21. Japanese surrender Okinawa.

June 26. United Nations chartered (international conference began April); approved by required number of countries Oct. 24.

July 16. U.S. tests first A-bomb at Alamogordo, New Mexico.

Aug. 6 & 9. Allies drop A-bombs on Hiroshima and Nagasaki, Japan; 240,000 civilians are killed.

Aug. 14. Japan surrenders.

Sept. 2. Japan signs terms of surrender aboard U.S.S. *Missouri*; V-J Day proclaimed in U.S.

President Harry Truman advocates civil rights legislation, national health insurance.

Nov. 25. Trials at Nuremberg open: International Military Tribunal hears testimony in cases of Nazi leaders charged with conspiracy, war crimes, crimes against humanity. Proceedings (to Sept. 30, 1946) document Nazi atrocities. Of the 22 charged 19 are found guilty on 1 or more counts.

During Holocaust Nazis killed about 6 million Jewish men, women, and children—more than two-thirds of the Jews in Europe.

Anticolonialism gains steam around globe: 57 nations (including 6 super powers) now recognized; by end of century, world map has 182 nations.

Cultural Progress

Mary Chase's *Harvey* wins Pulitzer Prize for drama.

Ebony magazine first published.

A. B. "Happy" Chandler is named commissioner of baseball, succeeding Kenesaw Landis after his death.

Oct. Detroit Tigers defeat Chicago Cubs in World Series, 4 games to 3.

Scientific and Commercial Progress

Penicillin becomes commercially available as an antibiotic. British scientists Alexander Fleming, Howard Florey, Ernst Chain share Nobel Prize for medicine for discovery, development.

Ballpoint pen goes on sale.

1946

Detroit and Michigan

Jan. 1. Department of Street Railway fares raised from 6 cents to 10 cents; streetcar fares now equal bus fares.

Feb. 18. Archbishop Edward Mooney of Detroit is made Cardinal.

March 14. UAW strike settled when General Motors Corp. agrees to pay 18.5 cent hourly wage increase. (Strike called Nov. 21, 1945.)

March 27. Walter Reuther elected president of UAW.

April. Detroit telephone directory published in 2 volumes for first time.

May 6. Citywide brownout ordered because of coal shortage.

June 9. Detroit celebrates golden jubilee of automobile and sesquicentennial of first raising of U.S. flag in city.

School of Business Administration added at Wayne University.

Slade-Gragg Academy of Practical Arts opens; first African American vocational school in Detroit and first black-owned and operated business located on Woodward Ave.

Music Hall (formerly Wilson Theatre) becomes home to Detroit Symphony Orchestra, which moves from Masonic Auditorium.

Eighteen-year-old Gordie Howe begins rookie season with Red Wings.

Chevrolet is first automaker to advertise on network television.

Detroit becomes home to first automated car wash: Paul's Automatic Car Wash opens at 541 West Fort St.

Network of Detroit freeways in the works: Fisher, Lodge, and Chrysler freeways to radiate outward from downtown to suburbs; Ford freeway crosstown route.

World History

Labor strikes cripple U.S.: shortage of consumer goods, suspension of services result.

Jan. 10. First meeting of United Nations held in London.

April 1. Tidal wave hits Hilo, Hawaii, destroying waterfront; claims 150 lives.

March. Winston Churchill coins term *Iron Curtain.*

July. U.S. tests A-bomb on Bikini Atoll, South Pacific.

July 4. Philippines declared independent.

Nov. 23. French bomb Haiphong, Vietnam.

Soviets install communist governments in Romania and Bulgaria.

Americans John R. Mott (YMCA founder) and Emily Greene Balch (of Women's International League for Peace and Freedom) share Nobel Peace Prize.

Cultural Progress

Songwriter Irving Berlin has another banner year; composes music for stage (*Annie Get Your Gun*) and film (*Blue Skies*).

Summer. Bikini bathing suit debuts on Paris runways.

Oct. American playwright Eugene O'Neill's *The Ice Man Cometh* opens.

Nov. George Balanchine choreographs *Four Temperaments.*

Mildred "Babe" Didrikson Zaharias begins golf winning spree (to 1947): claims 17 tournaments in a row.

Scientific and Commercial Progress

Jan. Army Signal Corps reach moon with radar beam.

Feb. ENIAC begins operation; world's first general-purpose electronic digital computer.

U.S. tests first supersonic rocket.

Ford assembly line becomes automated.

Tupperware debuts.

1947

Detroit and Michigan

Kim Sigler, Republican, governor (to 1948).

Beulah Cain Brewer becomes first black principal in Detroit Public Schools.

Jan. 29. Webster Hall taken over by Wayne University as dormitory and student center.

March 4. Common Council approves City Plan Commission's riverfront development plan.

March 4. WWJ-TV begins broadcasting; among first television stations in U.S. Hires radio newscaster Fran Harris, making her first woman in Michigan to broadcast TV news. WXYZ (Channel 7) and WJBK (Channel 2) soon go on air, with stations competing for small audience, numbering only 6,400 homes by next year.

April 7. Henry Ford dies at age 83.

Ford Foundation becomes largest in world when it receives Ford Motor Co. nonvoting stock in Henry Ford's will.

May 29. Willow Run becomes commercial airport for passenger carriers.

July 9. City adopts smoke abatement code.

Nov. 4. Eugene Van Antwerp elected mayor of Detroit.

Tigers draw their largest crowd ever, 58,369 attend doubleheader with Yankees.

World History

Taft-Hartley Act prohibits certain labor strikes, establishes rules for union organizing, abolishes closed shops, allows government delay of strikes affecting nation's health and safety.

Truman Doctrine marks beginning of cold war.

Congress passes National Security Act; establishes Central Intelligence Agency (CIA).

June 5. Marshall Plan: U.S. Secretary of State George Marshall originates European Recovery Program; outlines plan for American aid to Europe.

Aug. 15. India achieves independence; Jawaharlal Nehru is first prime minister. Partition of Pakistan ignites violence.

Oct. 5. President Harry Truman makes first televised presidential address.

Nov. United Nations carves Israel out of Palestine region; divides rest of Palestine among neighboring Arab nations.

Studio executives assemble list of 300 alleged communist sympathizers in movie industry. "Hollywood Ten" refuse to testify before House Committee on Un-American Activities: Alvah Bessie, Herbert Biberman, Lester Cole, Edward Dmytryk, Ring Lardner Jr., John Howard Lawson, Albert Maltz, Samuel Ornitz, Adrian Scott, Dalton Trumbo draw short prison sentences, are blacklisted.

Doomsday clock first appears, on cover of *Bulletin of the Atomic Scientists*.

U.S. sends aid to aid government of Greece.

Dead Sea Scrolls discovered.

Hungary and Poland controlled by communists.

Diary of Anne Frank published in Europe; account of Jewish family's suffering during Nazi occupation of Netherlands.

Cultural Progress

Robert Lowell's *Lord Weary's Castle* wins Pulitzer Prize for poetry.

Tennessee Williams's *Streetcar Named Desire* opens on Broadway (wins Pulitzer Prize, 1948).

Charles Ives's Symphony No. 3 wins Pulitzer Prize for music.

"Divine One" Sarah Vaughan has her first hit recordings, "Tenderly" and "It's Magic."

New York artists Wilhelm de Koonig, Jackson Pollock paint abstract expressionist works.

April 19. Jackie Robinson breaks pro baseball's color barrier; begins playing with Brooklyn Dodgers.

National Basketball Association holds first championship: Philadelphia Warriors beat Chicago Stags, 4 games to 1.

Scientific and Commercial Progress

U.S. has 227,146 miles of railway.

U.S. continues testing pilotless rocket planes, reaching speeds of 1,500 mph.

Edward Land demonstrates new photographic process to produce positive print in camera 1 minute after exposure; continues development of "instant camera."

1948

Detroit and Michigan

Jan. Eugene Van Antwerp takes office as mayor of Detroit.

April 20. Assassination attempt on Walter Reuther in his home; labor leader suffers arm injuries.

May 12. UAW stages walkout at Chrysler over wages; strike ends 17 days later after automaker concedes to 13-cent-per-hour raise.

May 29. UAW contract with General Motors ties wages to cost-of-living index.

Red Wings, anchored by "Production Line" (Gordie Howe, Ted Lindsay, Sid Abel) make it to Stanley Cup finals but lose in a sweep to Toronto Maple Leafs.

June 15. First night game at Briggs Stadium: Tigers defeat Philadelphia Athletics 4–1.

Sept. Labor Day: President Harry Truman kicks off "Give 'em Hell" campaign in Cadillac Square rally.

Sept. 20. State Hall opens at Wayne University—first of new buildings in university's planned campus.

Oct. 6. Parking meters installed on Detroit streets.

Nov. G. Mennen "Soapy" Williams wins gubernatorial election, defeating Kim Sigler and ushering in new era of politics.

Rear-engine Tucker 48 introduced; though short-lived, due to legal woes of founder Preston Tucker, car features several safety and style innovations that become standard, including pop-out windshield and safety steering wheel.

Third and final addition made to downtown Detroit Hudson's store, which now covers entire city block.

Among worst trades in baseball history, Tigers send pitcher Billy Pierce to Chicago White Sox for catcher Aaron Robinson; Robinson fades after 2 seasons, while Pierce becomes Chicago staff mainstay for 13 seasons.

World History

Jan. 30. Indian nationalist, spiritual leader Mahatma Gandhi is assassinated by Hindu extremist.

Feb. 25. Communists rise to power in Czechoslovakia.

April. President Harry Truman approves Marshall Plan: U.S. to send more than $13 billion in aid in Europe.

May 14. Israel, independent Jewish state, established; David Ben-Gurion is head of provisional government.

June 24. After announcement of formation of West Germany, Soviet troops blockade West Berlin (to May 12, 1949); U.S., British, French begin airlift.

June 24. President Truman signs peacetime draft.

June 26. Berlin airlift begins.

July 26. Executive Order bars segregation in U.S. armed forces.

Nov. 4. U.S. presidential election: *Chicago Tribune* headline, put to press before results are tallied, reports "Dewey Defeats Truman." But President Truman wins; photo of him holding false newspaper headline widely publicized.

Supreme Court ruling in *McCollum* v. *Board of Education* bans religious instruction from schools.

Anne R. Davidow (Detroit) is first woman to argue before U.S. Supreme Court that sex discrimination violates women's constitutional rights (in case of *Goesaert* v. *Cleary*).

Communists take control of Czechoslovakia.

South African apartheid policy formalized: whites have supremacy over majority non-whites; distinguishes among various ethnic groups.

Cultural Progress

James Michener's *Tales of the South Pacific* wins Pulitzer Prize for fiction.

W. H. Auden's *The Age of Anxiety* wins Pulitzer Prize for poetry.

Photographer Gordon Parks begins working for *Life* magazine.

Walter Piston's Symphony No. 3 wins Pulitzer Prize for music.

New York City Ballet founded.

French fashion designer Christian Dior's "new look" reaches U.S.

Drive-in movie theaters have their heyday.

Supreme Court rules that movie studio control over production, distribution, and exhibition constitutes illegal monopoly; orders studios to divest their movie theaters.

June 20. *Ed Sullivan Show* (originally *Toast of the Town*) makes network debut; becomes Sunday night habit in millions of households.

Sept. 21. NBC-TV begins broadcasting *Texaco Star Theater,* featuring Milton Berle; Berle becomes so popular during program's 8-year run he earns sobriquets "Mr. Television" and "Uncle Miltie."

Nov. 29. ABC-TV broadcasts performance of Verdi's *Otello*; first opera televised from Metropolitan Opera House.

Winter Olympics held in St. Moritz, Switzerland.

Summer Olympics held in London.

Scientific and Commercial Progress

Bell Laboratories announces development of the transistor.

Alfred Kinsey publishes groundbreaking work, *Sexual Behavior in the Human Male.*

Superpowered telescope is dedicated at Mount Palomar Observatory (California).

March 20. First simulcast over television, AM, FM.

1949

Detroit and Michigan

Jan. 1. G. Mennen Williams, Democrat, inaugurated governor; goes on to serve 6 terms (to 1960).

Jan. 1. Fort Wayne (active since 1837) transferred from U.S. government to city of Detroit, which turns facility into military museum.

Jan. 13. Northwestern Health Center opens.

May 24. Another attack on the Reuther family: labor leader Victor Reuther (Walter's brother) is shot while sitting in his living room; loses vision in right eye. No one is convicted.

Toronto Maple Leafs sweep the Red Wings in Stanley Cup finals second year in a row.

July 19. Supreme Court Justice Frank Murphy dies in Detroit.

Sept. 11–Nov. 20. "For Modern Living" exhibit at Detroit Institute of Arts gains national attention.

Nov. 8. Albert E. Cobo elected mayor of Detroit.

Mary V. Beck is first woman elected to Detroit Common Council.

Detroit suffers serious municipal problems including financial losses of Department of Street Railway, lax welfare policies, housing shortage.

United Foundation is organized; consolidates fund-raising for nearly 200 agencies. Inaugural Torch Drive gets under way with public lighting of torch.

Detroit Symphony Orchestra disbands. (*See* Oct. 18, 1951.)

Bois Blanc officially renamed Bob-Lo; park comes under new ownership, transforming island to include rides, fun house, zoo, mini railroad.

World heavyweight champion Joe Louis, one of Detroit's favorite sons, retires from boxing after 12 years on top. He successfully defended title 25 times, 21 by knockouts.

Heirs of Gen. Russell A. Alger donate family home on Lake Shore Dr. in Grosse Pointe Farms to community for use as cultural center.

Delayed by postwar strikes and conversion to peacetime production, work finally begins in Warren on GM Tech Center.

Ford Motor Co. and UAW enter into contract for worker pensions wholly financed by company.

Chrysler introduces key ignitions.

Michigan-Wisconsin Pipeline completed for bringing natural gas from Texas to Detroit.

World History

Jan. 20. President Harry Truman inaugurated.

April 4. NATO military alliance formed: North Atlantic Treaty Organization signed by U.S., Britain, France, Italy, Belgium, Netherlands, Denmark, Luxembourg, Norway, Portugal, Iceland, Canada.

Sept. 23. Soviet test of A-bomb (Aug. 29) announced by President Truman; arms race begins.

Left-wing rebellion crushed in Greece.

Zionist leader Chaim Weizmann is elected Israel's first president. National boundaries redrawn.

Peasant revolt in China; Red Army enters Beijing, overthrowing Nationalists. Mao is named chairman of People's Republic of China.

Cultural Progress

George Orwell publishes futuristic novel *1984*.

Simone de Beauvoir publishes *The Second Sex,* attacking oppression of women in Western society.

Renowned playwright and University of Michigan alumnus Arthur Miller wins Pulitzer Prize for drama for *Death of a Salesman.*

Kiss Me Kate (music by Cole Porter) and *South Pacific* (Rodgers and Hammerstein) are Broadway draws.

After 5 years as leading box office movie star, Bing Crosby moves to second; surrenders top spot to Bob Hope.

Canasta is popular card game.

Scientific and Commercial Progress

Feb. 26–March 2. U.S. Air Force makes round-the-world nonstop flight: Captain James Gallagher, Lt. Arthur Neal, Captain James Morris pilot B-50 *Lucky Lady II* on 94-hour flight; plane is refueled 4 times in the air by B-29 tanker planes.

Cotton picking machine goes into mass production.

LP records debut.

Postwar prosperity: increased wages, improved benefits, advertising (radio and TV) combine to create new spirit of consumerism in U.S.

GM, Ford, Chrysler set new production records to keep up with demand. GM sets net profit record of $656 million.

1950

Detroit and Michigan

Michigan's population, 6,372,009 (corrected figure).

Detroit's population, 1,849,568; ranks 5th in size among U.S. cities.

Detroit metropolitan (tri-county) area population, 3,016,197.

Jan. Albert E. Cobo takes office as mayor of Detroit.

Detroit loses two leaders: John C. Lodge dies in Feb.; Edward J. Jeffries in April.

March 11. Ford Motor Company and Ford and Lincoln-Mercury dealers announce $2.5 million gift to city for Henry and Clara Ford Memorial Auditorium in new Civic Center.

Groundbreaking for Douglass (May 5) and Jeffries (July 19) housing projects.

May 6. UAW strike against Chrysler ends—having lasted 102 days—with company-paid pension plan but without union shop clause.

May 17. American Cancer Society's new detection center opens on John R St.

May 23. UAW and General Motors agree to 5-year contract including guaranteed annual wage increases, cost-of-living adjustments, modified union shop, $100-monthly pensions at age 65 after 25 years of service.

After two consecutive years of Stanley Cup finals losses, Detroit's hockey team finishes on top: Red Wings defeat New York Rangers to take the trophy. Ted Lindsay begins tradition of hoisting Cup over his head and skating around the rink.

June 11. Veteran's Memorial Building opens; first unit of new Civic Center. Marshall M. Fredericks carved 30-foot sculpture of eagle for northwest wall.

June. J. L. Hudson Co. announces plans for huge suburban shopping center (Northland).

July 13. Jerome H. Remick music shell dedicated on Belle Isle.

Edsel Ford Expressway opens to traffic.

Nov. Ruth Thompson (of Muskegon) is first Michigan woman elected to U.S. Congress (House of Representatives).

Charline Rainey White (Detroit) elected to Michigan House of Representatives; first African American woman elected to state legislature. Serves 11th District until 1959.

Nov. Michigan gubernatorial election settled by recount: G. Mennen Williams reelected. First Democratic governor to win consecutive second term.

Nash introduces compact car, the Rambler.

Grosse Pointe property values have soared, as have taxes and wages for domestic help. Mansions built by Detroit's early industrialists can no longer be maintained; many are sold and razed to make way for subdivision.

World History

U.S. population, 150,697,361.

U.S. unemployment, 5.3%.

Some 16% of U.S. children have mothers who work outside the home.

Jan. 20. U.S. public official Alger Hiss found guilty of perjury; case polarizes nation, with many believing Hiss was framed for political reasons.

Feb. Senator Joseph McCarthy claims to have list of 205 known communists in U.S. government.

June 25. Communist North Korea invades South Korea, beginning war.

June 29. U.S. sends troops to aid South Korea.

Sept. 22. American diplomat Ralph Bunche (born in Detroit) is awarded Nobel Peace Prize for 1948–49 work as UN mediator in Palestine; first African American Nobel Laureate.

Oct. 7. American forces invade North Korea.

Nov. 1. Two Puerto Rican nationalists make assassination attempt on President Harry Truman.

Nov. 26. China sends 200,000 troops to aid communist North Korea.

China invades Tibet.

Mother Teresa founds order of Missionaries of Charity in Calcutta; opens Pure Heart home for dying poor (1952), orphanage (1953).

TV broadcasts Kefauver hearings (to March 1951): U.S. Senator Estes Kefauver and Senate committee question alleged mobsters about organized crime.

Cultural Progress

William Faulkner wins Nobel Prize for literature; in acceptance speech states his theme is "the human heart in conflict with itself." (1949 award was delayed to this year.)

Guys and Dolls a Broadway hit.

Gian Carlo Menotti's *The Consul* wins Pulitzer Prize for music.

Approximately 9% of U.S. households have televisions.

June 11. Golfer Ben Hogan makes comeback following auto accident; wins U.S. Open.

Detroit Red Wings defeat New York Rangers 4 games to 3 to claim Stanley Cup.

Sept. 27. In comeback attempt Joe Louis defeated by heavyweight champ Ezzard Charles.

Scientific and Commercial Progress

Jan. 31. U.S. orders development of hydrogen (super) bomb.

Conquest of many diseases during first half of century has increased life expectancy; inspired interest in geriatrics, medicine of old age.

American Express card is introduced.

Beauty now a billion dollar industry.

U.S. automakers reach peak production: 7,950,000 cars produced this year.

FCC approves color television.

In annual reports, 19 American corporations cite sales over $1 billion; GM tops list at $7.53 billion.

1951

Detroit and Michigan

Detroit city government operations cost approximately $1 million per day.

Feb. 8. Fire in Lansing's State Office Building causes damage, especially to books in State Library.

Feb. 20. Sherwood Forest Branch Library opens in new building on West 7 Mile Rd., culminating several years of unprecedented branch library development.

April 1. Cornerstone placed for new International Institute building on Kirby near John R.

April 18. U.S. Senator Arthur H. Vandenberg dies. Succeeded in senate by Detroit newspaperman Blair Moody.

April 21. Department of Street Railway operators strike halts public transportation for 59 days. (Strike ends June 19; DSR's longest strike.)

June 23. St. Clair Metropolitan Beach opens; developed by Huron-Clinton Metropolitan Authority.

July 24. New Detroit Historical Museum opens on Woodward and Kirby.

July 28. Grand parade depicting history and development of Detroit and lighting of giant cake in Grand Circus Park are highlights of yearlong festivities celebrating Detroit's 250th birthday.

Oct. 18. First concert by revived Detroit Symphony Orchestra.

Mary Ball is first woman publicity director for Detroit.

Fund-raising campaign begins for convention and exhibits building in Civic Center and community arts building on Wayne University campus.

Kresge Library is completed at Wayne University.

Detroit Edison adds another powerhouse to Connors Creek Generating Station; twin stacks, which stand near Seven Sisters (1914), become known as Two Brothers.

Chrysler introduces power steering, on the Imperial.

World History

The 22nd Amendment to U.S. Constitution ratified; limits the presidential tenure to two terms of office.

April 11. President Harry Truman dismisses Gen. Douglas MacArthur for making statements advocating U.S. invasion of China.

Spring. United Nations begins moving into New York headquarters.

Cultural Progress

Carl Sandburg wins Pulitzer Prize for *Complete Poems*.

Mambo joins Latin dance craze; samba and rumba already popular.

I Love Lucy debuts on CBS; sets standard for sitcoms.

Search for Tomorrow debuts; first successful TV soap opera.

Michigan defeats California in the Rose Bowl.

Pro boxer and Detroit native Sugar Ray Robinson turns from welterweight to middleweight. Wins 5 world championships by 1960 and is later considered by many as the best fighter in history.

Scientific and Commercial Progress

Construction of Levittown, New York, begins; prototype of planned suburban development. Move from cities to suburbs aided by improved roads, low lending rates for GIs.

Dec. Electricity generated by atomic energy for first time.

U.S. Census Bureau uses UNIVAC computer.

1952

Detroit and Michigan

Oct. 3. On Lake St. Clair the retired steamer *Put-in-Bay* is deliberately burned to facilitate salvage of steel hull.

Cora Mae Brown (Detroit) is first black woman elected to Michigan senate.

Purdy Library is completed at Wayne University.

Rachel J. Rice Andersen founds international exchange program Youth for Understanding in Ann Arbor; headquarters later relocated to Washington, D.C.

Red Wings win Stanley Cup.

Detroit Lions win National Football League championship; team's second title. Team features Heisman Trophy winner and American football great Walter Doak.

Small ferry service (begun in 1882) to Belle Isle is discontinued.

Operation of Detroit Tank Arsenal is transferred to Chrysler Corp.

World History

More than 21,000 cases of paralytic polio are reported in U.S.

Nov. 1. U.S. explodes first hydrogen bomb.

Nov. 4. Dwight D. Eisenhower, Republican, elected president.

In 71 years of recordkeeping, Tuskegee Institute reports first year with no lynchings in U.S.

The International Planned Parenthood Federation is founded.

Puerto Rico adopts constitution; becomes U.S. commonwealth with autonomy in internal affairs.

Greece and Turkey join NATO.

Cultural Progress

Jan. 14. NBC's *Today* show debuts; network television's first and longest-running morning show.

Ralph Ellison publishes *Invisible Man.*

Herman Wouk's *The Caine Mutiny* wins Pulitzer Prize for fiction.

Musical *Singin' in the Rain* in movie theaters.

American musician and Detroit native Milton Jackson founds Modern Jazz Quartet (MJQ).

Winter Olympics held in Oslo, Norway.

Detroit Red Wings defeat Montreal Canadiens 4 games to 0 to win Stanley Cup.

National Football League championship won by Detroit Lions.

Summer Olympics held in Helsinki, Finland.

Scientific and Commercial Progress

British Airways initiates passenger service aboard jet airplanes, De Havilland Co.'s Comets.

In Memphis, Tennessee, first Holiday Inn opens; motel chain grows quickly to cater to American family motor travel.

1953

Detroit and Michigan

Hudson's downtown department store thriving: occupying 40 acres of space in its multi-story building on Woodward, store has 12,000 employees, makes as many as 100,000 sales per day. Its 5 restaurants serve 14,000 meals, including signature Maurice salad, each day.

June 16. Closed during World War II and extensively remodeled afterward, ultramodern Ford Rotunda reopens to public. Includes massive dome designed by R. Buckminster Fuller; first commercial application of his geodesic dome.

June 16. Ford Motor Co. celebrates 50th anniversary.

Detroit Lions win National Football League championship for second year in a row.

Tiger rookie outfielder Al Kaline gets his first major league hit, a single off Luis Aloma of White Sox.

Detroiter Irene M. Auberlin organizes World Medical Relief; provides medical supplies throughout globe for more than 40 years.

First section of John C. Lodge freeway opens.

Sheldon Shopping Center opens.

Chevrolet introduces Corvette, first true American sports car.

Chrysler Corp. purchases automotive plants and machinery of Briggs Manufacturing Co.

Multimillion dollar fire destroys General Motors Transmission plant in Livonia.

Mayoral elections mark the change in Detroit mayor's term from 2 to 4 years.

World History

Jan. 20. Dwight Eisenhower inaugurated; 34th U.S. president.

March 5. Joseph Stalin dies; struggle for power among top Soviet leaders.

May 29. New Zealander Sir Edmund Hillary ascends Mount Everest as part of British-led expedition; followed by fellow climber Tenzing Norgay, Nepalese Sherpa. First people known to reach summit of world's highest mountain.

June 2. Britain's Queen Elizabeth II crowned; succeeds her father, King George VI, who died Feb. 6.

July 27. Armistice ends Korean War.

June 19. Ethel and Julius Rosenberg are electrocuted as 10,000 protesters fill New York's Union Square. Death sentence of pair (guilty of espionage) disputed, viewed as epitome of cold war hysteria.

Earl Warren is appointed chief justice of Supreme Court (to 1969); guides court in several landmark civil rights and individual liberties decisions.

U.S. Department of Health, Education, and Welfare created.

Bureau of Internal Revenue dramatically reorganized to create Internal Revenue Service (IRS).

American physicist J. Robert Oppenheimer, former director of Los Alamos A-bomb laboratory, is suspended from U.S. Atomic Energy Commission, investigated for opposing U.S. development of hydrogen bomb.

Minute hand of doomsday clock positioned at 2 minutes before midnight after U.S. and Soviet Union each test hydrogen bombs.

Albert Schweitzer wins Nobel Peace Prize for humanitarian work (1952 award delayed a year).

Cultural Progress

Ernest Hemingway's *The Old Man and the Sea* wins Pulitzer Prize for fiction.

Hank Williams's "Your Cheatin' Heart" gains wide popularity for country music.

Irish playwright Samuel Beckett's tragicomedy *Waiting for Godot* acclaimed in Paris opening.

Make Room for Daddy premieres on CBS; stars Detroit's own Danny Thomas. Later renamed after its star, highly successful show runs to 1965.

National Football League championship again won by Detroit Lions.

Scientific and Commercial Progress

Jonas Salk announces formulation of polio vaccine.

Scientists James Watson and Francis Crick identify structure of chromosomes, develop model of DNA.

World's first color television broadcast.

1954

Detroit and Michigan

March 22. Northland Center, first large regional shopping center in nation, opens in Southfield. More than 50 stores cluster around J. L. Hudson's. Suburban location, which boasts parking for more than 10,000 cars, was made possible by metro Detroit's growth, new freeway system. Model adopted by shopping center planners across nation.

Automotive History Collection of Detroit Public Library is opened to public.

Red Wings win Stanley Cup.

Detroit's annual auto show moves to Michigan State Fair Grounds.

Ford introduces Thunderbird.

Nash-Kelvinator Corp. and Hudson Motor Car Co. merge into American Motors Corp.

Vernor's Ginger Ale moves operations from downtown (making way for Civic Center) to Woodward and Warren plant (on site of old convention center). Visitors can view bottles speeding along conveyor at rate of 350 per minute.

Construction begins on Mackinac Bridge.

World History

Nov. 29. Ellis Island is closed; immigration quotas have curtailed immigration eliminating need for the processing center. (Island designated national historic site, 1965; restored for visitors, 1980s).

Jan. 12. U.S. Secretary of State John Foster Dulles announces doctrine of "massive retaliation" against communist aggression.

April–June. Army-McCarthy hearings televised live; senator accuses Army of "coddling communists." Joseph McCarthy censured by U.S. Senate (Dec. 2).

May 7. In Indochina war, Vietnamese troops defeat French at Dien Bien Phu. North and South Vietnam established by international convention at Geneva. Ho Chi Minh takes control of communist North Vietnam.

Cultural Progress

May 17. *Brown* v. *Board of Education*: Supreme Court overturns separate-but-equal ruling of *Plessy* v. *Ferguson* (1896): High court rules school segregation violates 14th Amendment; orders desegregation of public schools "with all deliberate speed."

Ernest Hemingway wins Nobel Prize for literature for his novels and short stories.

Theodore Roethke, native of Saginaw, Michigan, wins Pulitzer Prize for poetry, for *The Waking*.

Joffrey Ballet founded in New York; modern repertory. Choreography by Robert Joffrey, Alvin Ailey, Twyla Tharp, others.

Elvis Presley releases first commercial recording, "That's All Right, Mama."

On the Waterfront in movie theaters.

Some 55.7% of U.S. households have televisions—5-fold increase in less than 5 years.

Sept. 27. *Tonight* premieres on NBC; first late-night desk-and-sofa show. Steve Allen hosts; followed by Jack Paar (1957), Johnny Carson (1962).

TV's golden age under way: Big Three networks capture more than 90% of viewing audience; live variety shows and drama anthology programs are mainstays, spur television sales.

Sports Illustrated first published.

Detroit Red Wings defeat Montreal Canadiens 4 games to 3 to win Stanley Cup.

Boston Red Sox great Ted Williams, returning from broken collarbone, turns in astonishing performance in Detroit doubleheader; goes 8 for 9, hits 2 home runs, drives in 9 runs.

Nov. 7. Supreme Court ruling orders desegregation of public golf courses, parks, swimming pools, playgrounds.

Scientific and Commercial Progress

Americans John Enders, Thomas Weller, Frederick Robbins win Nobel Prize for medicine for discovering simple method for growing polio virus in test tubes making widespread administration of vaccine viable.

Dec. 23. Harvard physicians perform world's first successful kidney transplant.

1955

Detroit and Michigan

Michigan is first state to require driver's education course before licenses can be issued to new drivers.

Charles C. Diggs Jr. (Detroit) is elected Michigan's first black member of U.S. House of Representatives; he takes office in 1955.

City-County Building (East Jefferson and Woodward) completed. Sculptor Marshall M. Fredericks's 25-foot bronze statue *Spirit of Detroit* placed in front of building on Woodward.

Wayne University's School of Medicine and Detroit hospitals plan Detroit Medical Center—to be built around Children's, Woman's, Grace, and Harper hospitals.

Mariner's Church is moved to southwest corner of East Jefferson and Randolph St.; square tower and rose window are added to 1849 edifice.

Old Firemen's Hall (Jefferson and Randolph) is torn down to make way for Civic Center.

Construction begins on 78-acre urban redevelopment project surrounding 19-acre Lafayette Park; internationally renowned architect Mies van der Rohe is principal designer and planner.

Detroit United Foundation drive surpasses $14,450,000; said to be world's largest.

Ford Auditorium, wedge-shaped structure of granite and marble, is completed on riverfront.

Red Wings win their second consecutive Stanley Cup; Detroit's hockey powerhouse has claimed 4 Cups in the last 6 seasons. (*See* Cultural Progress.)

Al Kaline—youngest American League batting champion ever, with .340 average—enjoys biggest single game of his career, collecting 6 RBIs and 4 straight hits, including 3 home runs against Kansas City.

Ford moves Lincoln manufacturing operations out of Detroit (to Wayne), selling West Warren buildings to Detroit Edison.

New copper mine is opened in White Pine, near Ontonagon, in Upper Peninsula.

Dual Motors Corp. of Detroit introduces limited production sports car called Firebomb.

World History

May. Warsaw Pact: Soviet allies meet in Poland; 8 Eastern bloc countries sign military agreement (in response to NATO).

Aug. Hurricane Diane hits New England.

West Germany joins NATO.

Dec. 1. Seamstress Rosa Parks refuses to yield her seat to a white passenger; local activists, led by Martin Luther King Jr., begin (Dec. 5) year-long Montgomery bus boycott, launching civil rights movement.

Ku Klux Klan reemerges during nation's struggle over civil rights.

Dec. 5. AFL and CIO reunite.

Cultural Progress

Wallace Stevens's *Collected Poems* wins Pulitzer Prize.

First rock and roll summer: Chuck Berry releases "Maybellene"; Bill Haley and the Comets' "Rock Around the Clock" is first international rock hit.

Marian Anderson becomes first African American to sing with the Metropolitan Opera.

Rebel Without a Cause, starring James Dean, in movie theaters (Dean dies in car crash Sept. 30; becomes lasting image of youthful rebelliousness).

For second year in a row, Detroit Red Wings defeat Montreal Canadiens 4 games to 3 to win Stanley Cup.

Scientific and Commercial Progress

April. Polio vaccine (tested at University of Michigan) pronounced safe and effective. Jonas Salk is awarded congressional gold medal, citation from President Dwight Eisenhower.

1956

Detroit and Michigan

April 3. Tornadoes ravage Michigan; 18 killed in Grand Rapids area.

April 7. Detroit's last streetcar makes final run.

Interstate Highway Act provides funding for construction of links from Detroit to Chicago (I-94), Lansing (I-96), and northern Michigan (I-75).

Wayne University becomes part of the system of universities supported by the State of Michigan; adopts name Wayne State University. Three-year transition begins July 1.

Mother Waddles founds Perpetual Mission in Detroit; privately funded social services agency provides comprehensive assistance programs to needy.

Detroit Symphony Orchestra moves from Music Hall to Ford Auditorium; gives first concert in new home.

Montreal Canadiens vindicated: after losing Stanley Cup to Detroit Red Wings two years in a row, the Canadiens turn things around to take the trophy, 4 games to 1.

Hammond Building (1890) is torn down to make way for new headquarters of National Bank of Detroit; original Union Trust Building, among city's first steel skeleton skyscrapers (1895) is also demolished for new project.

GM begins 2-year process of moving workers into Warren Tech Center; new facility consists of research, engineering, design, environmental, manufacturing, testing areas as well as headquarters for several GM divisions. Buildings cluster around 22-acre man-made lake.

Ford builds new headquarters in Dearborn.

Studebaker buys Packard Motor Car Co.

Ford Motor Co. stock has initial public offering; more than 10 million shares are offered at $64.50 per share.

Approximately 17,000 Detroiters displaced by new freeways: Chrysler (I-75) freeway divides African American neighborhood; John Lodge freeway bisects neighborhoods including Boston-Edison district.

Under court order, Briggs heirs sell Tiger stock for $5.5 million to syndicate of 11 radio and television men headed by John Fetzer, Fred Knorr (new president), Kenyon Brown.

World History

Feb. 14. Soviet Premier Nikita Khrushchev reveals, condemns Joseph Stalin's crimes; begins program of de-Stalinization.

March 1. Autherine Lucy, University of Alabama's first black student, is expelled after white students riot in protest.

March 25. European Common Market established by Treaty of Rome.

July 26. Suez Crisis: Israel, France, Great Britain attack Egypt over its takeover of Suez Canal. UN intervention brings cease-fire.

Oct. Soviet troops put down Hungarian rebellion. Government reforms under way in Poland.

Oct. 31. Egypt invaded by France, Britain, Israel.

Nov. 6. Dwight Eisenhower reelected president.

Interstate Highway Act signed into law. Work begins on U.S. highway system: 41,000 miles of modern freeways are planned to span country and connect major cities; federal government pays 90% of cost.

Cultural Progress

Elizabeth Bishop's *Poems: North & South—A Cold Spring* wins Pulitzer Prize.

Beat Generation writer Allen Ginsberg publishes "Howl."

Frank Sinatra releases *Songs for Swingin' Lovers*; "The Voice" hits his stride.

Elvis Presley appears on *Ed Sullivan Show*; "Heartbreak Hotel" tops charts; by 1969 Presley has seventeen number one records.

April 2. CBS introduces new soap operas *As the World Turns* and *The Edge of Night* on same day.

Winter Olympics held in Cortina, Italy.

Summer Olympics held in Melbourne, Australia.

Scientific and Commercial Progress

Polio vaccine is widely administered.

1957

Detroit and Michigan

Detroit Mayor Albert Cobo dies; succeeded by City Council President Louis Miriani, who is elected mayor Nov. 5.

Mary V. Beck becomes first woman president of City Council.

Nov. Mackinac Bridge opens to traffic; spans 18,615 feet connecting Michigan's Lower and Upper peninsulas. World's longest suspension bridge.

Father Solanus Casey dies; founded Detroit-based Capuchin Kitchen, which feeds hundreds of local families.

Alfred and Matilda Wilson donate 110-room Meadow Brook Hall, 1,400 acres to Michigan State University for establishment of new college (Oakland University).

Fort Wayne Pistons become Detroit franchise in National Basketball Association (NBA).

In giant 13-player deal, Tigers obtain second baseman Billy Martin, outfielders Gus Zernial and Lou Skizas, catcher Tim Thompson, and pitchers Tom Morgan and Mickey McDermott from Kansas City.

Detroit Lions bring home their 4th National Football League championship.

Annual auto show held at Detroit Artillery Armory.

Eastland Mall opens; patterned after Northland and anchored by J. L. Hudson's.

Ford introduces Edsel model; quickly rejected by public.

Ford stops production of 2-seater Thunderbird to make way for 4-passenger model.

World History

Jan. 20. President Dwight Eisenhower inaugurated; 2nd term.

Feb. 14. Southern Christian Leadership Conference (SCLC) founded; Martin Luther King Jr., president.

Sept. 25. Army troops dispatched to Little Rock, Arkansas, to protect African American students.

Aug. 29. Voting Rights Bill passed.

Oct. 4. Soviet Union launches *Sputnik,* first artificial satellite; begins space race with West.

Nov. 3. Soviet Union launches *Sputnik 2,* carrying first living creature into space. Two-year-old female dog Laika dies of oxygen starvation 7 days into journey.

Dec. 6. AFL-CIO expels Teamster Union on evidence of corruption. Labor leader Jimmy Hoffa rises to presidency of Teamsters.

Vietnam War (to 1975): Vietcong, communist-led guerillas, begin campaign to overthrow South Vietnamese government. North Vietnam launches full-scale invasion of South.

Cultural Progress

Beat Generation writer Jack Kerouac publishes highly influential novel *On the Road.*

West Side Story is a Broadway sensation. Composed by Leonard Bernstein; choreographed by Jerome Robbins.

Buddy Holly records "Peggy Sue."

Oct. *Leave It to Beaver* premieres on CBS; moves to ABC next year and runs to 1963.

National Football League championship won by Detroit Lions.

Scientific and Commercial Progress

Anthropologist Mary Leakey discovers skull of humanlike creature at Tanzania's Olduvai Gorge; "Nutcracker Man" (later called *Australopithecus boisei*) lived some 1.75 million years ago. First of many significant Leakey family finds at Olduvai.

1958

Detroit and Michigan

Mayor Louis Miriani announces plans of city government to economize in face of recession.

Leon M. Wallace is named director-secretary of Loyalty Investigation Committee, first African American to be part of city commission.

Wayne State University's MacGregor Memorial Conference Center completed. Highly praised facility designed by noted American architect and longtime Detroit resident Minoru Yamasaki (formerly of architectural firm Smith, Hinchman and Grylls).

School Art Guild of Society of Arts and Crafts moves to new quarters on East Kirby Ave.

Nearly 2 million Detroit-area homes have televisions.

First International Freedom Festival is held along Detroit River.

Tigers obtain infielder Ozzie Virgil and first baseman Gail Harris from San Francisco Giants for a third baseman and cash; Virgil is first African American to play for Detroit.

Ford Motor Co. produces 50 millionth vehicle.

World History

Jan. 31. U.S. launches first satellite, *Explorer 1*.

Charles De Gaulle again president of France (to 1969); now as head of newly formed Fifth Republic.

Communist Party Secretary Nikita Khrushchev officially takes power as Soviet premier; begins period of detente with West.

Great Leap Forward in China triggers widespread famine; 20 million die.

Cultural Progress

James Agee's *A Death in the Family* wins Pulitzer Prize for fiction.

Vladimir Nabokov's novel *Lolita* causes sensation.

Bestseller *Anatomy of a Murder* is set in Upper Peninsula; written by Robert Traver (pseudonym of Michigan State Supreme Court justice John Voelker).

Samuel Barber's *Vanessa* wins Pulitzer Prize for music.

Alvin Ailey Dance Company founded.

Scientific and Commercial Progress

Jack Kilby of Texas Instruments develops integrated circuit (computer chip).

1959

Detroit and Michigan

Michigan has record high year for field crop production.

Detroit Police Department patrol car crews are integrated.

Wayne State University completes 3-year transition to state control.

Deteriorated area of Corktown, west of downtown, is cleared to make way for West Side Industrial Project.

Plans for 23-acre downtown redevelopment project announced.

Rosa Parks, known as mother of civil rights movement, moves with her husband to Detroit.

Former autoworker Berry Gordy Jr. buys house on Detroit's west side and puts up sign reading "Hitsville USA"; soon cuts first record for company to be known as Motown.

Detroit News and *Detroit Times* both raise weekly price from 7 to 8 cents.

Detroit TV stations draw young audiences with dance shows: "Saturday Dance Party," "Swinging Time," and "Dance Party" feature local teens and latest recordings.

Tiger Al Kaline gets his 1,000th career hit, a single, against Chicago White Sox.

Kern's closes; Crowley's and Hudson's remain as Detroit's downtown department stores.

National Bank of Detroit completes 14-story headquarters on entire block in heart of downtown.

Chevrolet introduces Corvair to compete with small imports.

Pontiac Motor Division of General Motors produces 7 millionth car.

Ford Motor Co. establishes Ford Motor Credit Co.

Ford discontinues the Edsel; failure cost company estimated $350 million.

Little Caesars Pizza Treat opens (May 8) in Garden City; first franchise opens 2 years later in Warren, launching international pizza chain whose owner, Mike Ilitch, becomes important force in Detroit.

World History

Jan. 1. Revolutionary leader Fidel Castro leads rebels into Havana, Cuba; Batista's dictatorship ends.

Jan. 3. Alaska admitted to Union.

Aug. 21. Hawaii admitted to Union; 50th state.

Sept. Soviet Premier Nikita Khrushchev visits U.S., meets with President Dwight Eisenhower.

Nov. 2. Quiz show scandal: in subcommittee hearing, Charles Van Doren, winning contestant on TV's popular *Twenty One,* admits show was fixed.

Payola scandal: payoffs of radio disk jockeys revealed.

Nov. 7. Taft-Hartley Act provides basis of Supreme Court ruling to break 116-day steel strike in Pennsylvania.

Anti-China uprising in Tibet suppressed; Dalai Lama, priests flee to India.

Cultural Progress

Lorraine Hansberry's *A Raisin in the Sun* opens; first play by a black woman to be produced on Broadway.

Jazz great Miles Davis records *Kind of Blue* in New York City.

Saxophonist John Coltrane releases *Giant Steps.*

Some Like It Hot in movie theaters.

Police drama *The Untouchables* debuts; highly popular show draws criticism from Italian American groups for portrayal of stereotypes; others attack show's violence.

Scientific and Commercial Progress

COBOL (Common Business Oriented Language) introduced; highly successful computer programming language for business.

St. Lawrence Seaway opens to traffic.

American Airlines introduces first U.S. jet airplane passenger service; Boeing Co.'s 707s transport passengers between New York and Los Angeles.

Barbie doll debuts.

Pantyhose introduced.

1960

Detroit and Michigan

Michigan's population, 7,824,018 (corrected figure).

Detroit's population, 1,670,144; ranks 5th in size among U.S. cities.

Census figures show Detroit has large community of Mexican Americans who have migrated to city in postwar era.

Mayor Louis Miriani vetoes 1% income tax bill.

Michigan 4% state sales tax amendment adopted.

Preliminary amendment for calling state constitutional convention adopted.

Houghton-Hancock Bridge in the Upper Peninsula completed.

Cobo Hall and Convention Center, named for former mayor, is completed as part of Detroit Civic Center along riverfront. Cobo becomes home to Detroit's annual National Auto Show.

National Auto Show, for first time held in Detroit at new 10-acre Cobo Hall, draws 1,403,872 guests.

Myra Wolfgang becomes officer of Hotel, Motel, and Bartenders International; first woman to hold office in major union.

Dec. Detroit Police Department is placed on 6-day workweek.

Detroit News acquires rival *Detroit Times*.

Cass Tech student Diana Ross becomes first black bus girl in downtown Hudson's basement cafeteria.

Work begins on Detroit Medical Center; to cover 250-acre site.

Ford Rotunda in Dearborn a national tourist attraction; ranks behind Niagara Falls, Great Smoky Mountains National Park, Smithsonian Institution, and Lincoln Memorial as destination. Showcases history of roads, motor cars, auto industry.

Chrysler discontinues De Soto car line, begun 1928.

Tom Monaghan opens Domino's pizza outlet in Ypsilanti; builds it into nationwide pizza delivery chain.

World History

World population passes 3 billion.

U.S. population, 179,323,175.

U.S. unemployment, 5.5%.

Feb. 1. Black students stage sit-in at Greensboro, North Carolina, lunch counter; initiates wave of protests in South.

April 15–17. Student Nonviolent Coordinating Committee (SNCC) founded; leader in civil rights movement.

May 1. Soviets shoot down American U2 spy plane.

May 22. Earthquake, measuring 9.5 on Richter scale, shakes Chile. Quake spawns tsunamis that reach Hawaii, Japan, and the Philippines.

Sept. 26. Presidential debate televised for first time.

Nov. 8. John F. Kennedy, Democrat, elected president.

Dec. *Boynton v. Virginia*: Supreme Court ruling declares public facilities are for use of all citizens, regardless of color.

Cultural Progress

Some 35.3% of B.A. degrees in U.S. are awarded to women (according to U.S. Department of Education and National Center for Educational Statistics).

Paperback books popular: 300 million sold this year.

296

Andy Warhol paints Campbell's soup can; beginning of pop art.

Elliott Carter's String Quartet No. 2 wins Pulitzer Prize for music.

Detroit's Motown Records scores its first million-selling record: "Shop Around."

African American soprano Leontyne Price performs title role in *Aida* at La Scala in Milan, Italy.

Saxophonist Ornette Coleman reshapes jazz with recording *Free Jazz*.

Chubby Checker's "Twist" a rock and roll hit.

Alfred Hitchcock's *Psycho* in movie theaters; music by Bernard Herrmann.

Some 87.1% of U.S. households have televisions; up from just 9% a decade ago.

Winter Olympics held in Squaw Valley, California.

Summer Olympics held in Rome.

First Daytona 500 is held; Lee Petty wins.

Scientific and Commercial Progress

Laser technology first demonstrated.

U.S. auto ownership dramatically up since 1940: from 27.5 million to 61.5 million registered vehicles. Out of every 4 Americans, 3 own a car.

FDA approves birth control pill.

Aug. 12. First communications satellite is launched.

1961

Detroit and Michigan

Old City Hall demolished; site renamed John F. Kennedy Plaza in 1964.

John B. Swainson, Democrat, governor (to 1962).

Jerome P. Cavanagh elected mayor of Detroit.

Michigan voters authorize constitutional convention to revise state constitution (1908).

Motown hits number-one spot on charts: "Please, Mr. Postman" by Marvelettes.

After 5 years of domination by Montreal Canadiens, Stanley Cup contest is between two American teams—Chicago and Detroit. Blackhawks take the trophy, defeating Red Wings 4 games to 2.

Briggs Stadium is renamed Tiger Stadium.

John Fetzer becomes sole owner of Detroit Tigers, purchasing remaining interests of Fred Knorr estate.

Tiger great Ty Cobb dies of cancer in Georgia.

Chevrolet produces its 44 millionth vehicle.

Detroit's 25-story J. L. Hudson's is world's tallest department store; its 2 million square feet include 5 basements, 51 passenger elevators, 17 freight elevators, 51 display windows, 706 fitting rooms.

Fisher Theater is renovated.

World History

Jan. 20. John F. Kennedy inaugurated; 35th U.S. president.

The 23rd Amendment to U.S. Constitution ratified; grants residents of Washington, D.C., the right to vote in presidential elections.

U.S. begins boycott of trade with Castro-controlled Cuba.

March 1. Peace Corps authorized.

April 12. Cosmonaut Yuri A. Gagarin is first person in space; makes 1 hour 48 minute orbit aboard Soviet Union's *Vostok 1*.

April 17. Bay of Pigs: U.S. backs unsuccessful invasion of Cuba.

May 5. Astronaut Alan Shepard is first American in space; pilots suborbital craft *Freedom 7* to altitude of 116.5 miles.

May. Freedom Rides test desegregation of public facilities, transportation.

May 20. Freedom Riders mobbed, beaten in Montgomery, Alabama.

Nov. 25. President Kennedy announces U.S. will land a man on the moon by end of decade.

Dec. U.S. steps up involvement in Vietnam: 3,000 to be sent as "advisers" in conflict.

Russians build Berlin Wall.

FCC Chairman Newton Minow proclaims television a "vast wasteland."

South Africa withdraws from British Commonwealth over apartheid policy.

Cultural Progress

Harper Lee's *To Kill a Mockingbird* wins Pulitzer Prize for fiction.

George Shirley, graduate of Detroit Public Schools and Wayne State University, becomes first black male singer to perform with the Metropolitan Opera under a long-term (11 years) contract.

Singer-songwriter Bob Dylan begins performing in Greenwich Village; gains approval of critics, influences other musicians.

Breakfast at Tiffany's, starring Audrey Hepburn and Detroiter George Peppard, is in theaters; becomes film classic.

The Dick Van Dyke Show debuts on CBS.

1962

Detroit and Michigan

Jan. Jerome Cavanagh takes office as mayor of Detroit.

City income tax of 1%, sponsored by Jerome Cavanagh, established.

Nov. 9. Ford Rotunda is destroyed by fire.

International Bridge, connecting Upper Peninsula and Ontario, is completed at Sault Ste. Marie.

Arthur Coar founds Friends of African and African American Art, new auxiliary group at DIA.

Minnesota Twins slugger Harmon Killebrew is first player to hit home run over left field roof at Tiger Stadium.

Red Wing Gordie Howe earns his 1000th NHL point on an assist and his 500th NHL goal.

Downtown Hudson's still attracting customers, marking two $1 million days this year.

Famous high-wire daredevils the Great Wallendas perform in Detroit; suffer terrible accident when their pyramid falls, killing two family members and leaving another paralyzed.

World History

Feb. 20. Astronaut John Glenn becomes first American to orbit earth; circles 3 times aboard spacecraft *Friendship 7*.

May 17. U.S. troops are sent to Laos, Cambodia.

Sept. 30. University of Mississippi admits black student, James Meredith; white students riot in protest.

Oct. 10. Thalidomide tragedy: thousands of women given drug during pregnancy give birth to deformed babies in Europe; banned by FDA in U.S.

Oct. 11. Pope John XXIII convokes 2nd Vatican Council

Oct. 22–28. Cuban Missile Crisis: major confrontation brings U.S. and U.S.S.R. close to war over presence of Soviet nuclear-armed missiles in Cuba.

Cesar Chavez organizes California grape pickers into National Farm Workers Association. (Becomes United Farm Workers Organizing Committee, 1966; United Farm Workers of America, 1973.)

Rachel Carson publishes *Silent Spring*; bestseller launches environmental movement.

Black South African leader Nelson Mandela is imprisoned for political activities.

American Linus Pauling wins Nobel Peace Prize for efforts to ban nuclear weapons and testing.

Cultural Progress

John Steinbeck wins Nobel Prize for his novels, especially *The Winter of Our Discontent*.

The Beatles release "Love Me Do."

Beach Boys' "Surfin' U.S.A." a hit; launches surf craze.

Lawrence of Arabia in movie theaters.

Scientific and Commercial Progress

Sept. ABC begins color telecasts; 68% of NBC's prime time programming is color; CBS still broadcasting in black and white.

1963

Detroit and Michigan

George W. Romney, Republican, governor (to 1969).

April 1. Michigan voters approve new state constitution by narrow margin of about 7,000 votes. Among changes is governor's term in office, which increases from 2 to 4 years.

Martin Luther King Jr. marches with others in Detroit to protest racial injustices; gives preview of "I Have a Dream" speech 2 months before March on Washington.

Aug. 28. Michigan composer and choral director Eva Jessye conducts official choir for March on Washington led by Martin Luther King Jr.

Detroit Police Commissioner George Clifton Edwards Jr. appointed to U.S. Appeals Court.

Detroit Medical Center launches nation's first anticancer drug research program.

Wings added to Detroit Public Library's main facility on Woodward Ave.

Detroit Red Wings lose Stanley Cup finals to Toronto Maple Leafs, 4 games to 1.

Tigers extend team errorless streak to 12 games, all-time Major League record.

The Twenty-eight-story Detroit Bank and Trust Co. building goes up on West Fort in Financial District.

The 32-story Michigan Consolidated Gas Co. (later American Natural Resources) Building is completed on West Jefferson, fronting Civic Center.

Chrysler freeway opens.

Founder's great-nephew, J. L. Hudson Jr., becomes head of department store chain.

World History

Civil rights demonstration in Birmingham, Alabama: peaceful protesters subdued by police with dogs, fire hoses. Media coverage helps win public support for nonviolent movement, reform.

June 10. Congress passes law guaranteeing women equal pay.

June 12. Civil rights leader Medgar Evers shot and killed outside Jackson, Mississippi, home.

Betty Friedan publishes *The Feminine Mystique*; challenges status quo, heralds new age of feminism.

June 16. Cosmonaut Valentina Tereshkova is first woman in space; circles earth for 3 days aboard Soviet Union's *Vostok 6*.

June 17. Supreme Court ruling in *Schempp* v. *Abington Township* bars prayer and Bible reading in public schools.

Aug. 5. The Supreme Court decision in *Gideon* v. *Wainwright* ensures all felony defendants in U.S. receive legal representation.

Aug. 5. U.S., United Kingdom, and Soviet Union sign nuclear test ban treaty.

Aug. 28. March on Washington: 250,000 gather to urge passage of civil rights bill; Martin Luther King delivers "I Have a Dream" speech.

Sept. 15. Bomb explodes in Sixteenth Street Baptist Church, Birmingham, Alabama, as 200 people worship inside—4 African American girls are killed. Bombing provokes race rioting, claiming 2 more young lives.

Nov. 22. President John F. Kennedy assassinated while riding in Dallas motorcade; Lee Harvey Oswald arrested for his murder. Vice President Lyndon B. Johnson sworn in; 36th U.S. president.

Nov. 24. While under police arrest, presumed assassin Lee Harvey Oswald is shot and killed by Jack Ruby.

Nov. 25. John F. Kennedy's funeral held in Washington, D.C.; burial at Arlington National Cemetery.

Cultural Progress

William Carlos Williams's *Pictures from Brueghel* wins Pulitzer Prize for poetry.

James Baldwin publishes *The Fire Next Time*.

Motown's "Little" Stevie Wonder (a Michigan native, just 13 years of age) scores first hit record with pop single "Fingertips, Part 2."

The Beatles' "Please, Please Me" tops charts.

The Freewheelin' Bob Dylan gives voice to protest movement with songs "Blowin' in the Wind," "A Hard Rain's A-Gonna Fall."

At age 43, Dame Margot Fonteyn forms dance partnership with Rudolf Nureyev.

Evening television news broadcasts begin to threaten existence of evening paper.

1964

Detroit and Michigan

Michigan's new constitution goes into effect.

NAACP urges Michigan Civil Rights Commission to study alleged police brutality against African Americans.

Dec. Downtown Hudson's puts up 9-story Christmas tree of lights on side of building.

Supremes chart 3 hits: "Where Did Our Love Go?," "Baby Love," "Come See about Me." Motown Sound sweeps nation.

Meadow Brook Music Festival (at Oakland University) is created as summer home for DSO.

Detroit Red Wings again lose Stanley Cup finals to Toronto Maple Leafs, 4 games to 3.

Tigers draw their smallest crowd for night game: 2,173 watch home team play L.A. Angels.

Stroh Brewery Co. buys rival Goebel.

Ford introduces Mustang, immediate bestseller; Chrysler responds with Barracuda.

Julie Candler (Birmingham) begins writing "Woman at the Wheel" column for *Woman's Day* magazine; first monthly automotive column for women to appear in national magazine.

World History

Jan. In State of the Union address, President Lyndon Johnson proclaims war on poverty.

Jan. 23. The 24th Amendment to U.S. Constitution ratified; outlaws poll tax in federal elections and primaries.

March 9. Supreme Court ruling in *New York Times* v. *Sullivan* narrows libel law for public figures.

March 28. Great Alaskan earthquake: measuring 9.2 on Richter scale, quake generates 220-foot tidal wave.

May. Palestinian Liberation Organization (PLO) founded to establish Palestinian homeland; headed by Yasir Arafat.

July 2. President Lyndon Johnson signs Civil Rights Act, which passes Congress after long Senate debate: bans discrimination on basis of color, race, national origin, religion, or sex; establishes Equal Employment Opportunity Commission.

July 18. Race rioting in Harlem sparks disturbances in 6 major U.S. cities (to Aug. 30).

Aug. 7. Congress passes Tonkin Gulf resolution: authorizes U.S. military action in Southeast Asia as a response to alleged attack of American destroyers; President Johnson (and later President Richard Nixon) uses resolution to engage nation in Vietnam War.

Aug. At Democratic national convention, Mississippi Freedom delegates are denied seats.

Economic Opportunity Act signed into law; allocates $1 billion to fight poverty.

Sept. 27. Warren Commission report concludes Lee Harvey Oswald acted alone in assassinating President John F. Kennedy.

Oct. 14. American clergyman and civil rights leader Martin Luther King Jr. is awarded Nobel Peace Prize.

Soviet Premier Nikita Khrushchev ousted; Leonid Brezhnev, Communist Party head, gains power.

Nov. 3. Lyndon Baines Johnson elected president in his own right; defeats Republican Barry Goldwater.

Teamster Jimmy Hoffa secures master trucking agreement.

Free speech movement launched at Berkeley, California; begins decade of student protests around the nation.

Pope Paul VI makes pilgrimage to Holy Land; first pope to leave Italy in many years; meets with Ecumenical Patriarch Athenagoras I in Jerusalem. Rift between Eastern Orthodox churches and Roman Catholic Church healed.

Indian Prime Minister Jawaharlal Nehru dies.

Cultural Progress

Beatlemania sweeps U.S.: Fab Four are met by 10,000 screaming fans at New York's Kennedy Airport (Feb. 7); appear on *The Ed Sullivan Show* (Feb. 9); secure top 5 spots on U.S. singles charts (April); release rock movie *A Hard Day's Night.*

Sidney Poitier wins Academy Award for best actor (for 1963's *Lilies of the Field*); first black to win Oscar for starring role.

Dr. Strangelove in movie theaters.

Soap opera hits prime time: *Peyton Place* a success for ABC.

Feb. 25. Cassius Clay (Muhammad Ali) wins world heavyweight championship with knockout of Sonny Liston.

Winter Olympics held in Innsbruck, Austria.

Summer Olympics held in Tokyo.

Scientific and Commercial Progress

Bell Laboratories scientists discover cosmic radiation; supports big bang theory of cosmology.

Jan. 11. U.S. Surgeon General issues warning that smoking causes cancer.

1965

Detroit and Michigan

City of Detroit, along with Shreveport, Louisiana, wins first American Institute of Architects urban redevelopment award.

Mayor Jerome Cavanagh reelected.

Civil rights worker Viola Liuzzo (from Detroit) is murdered in Alabama.

Astronaut James A. McDivitt is Michigan's first man in space. (*See also* Scientific and Commercial Progress.)

Woman's Hospital in Detroit is renamed in honor of Eleonore Hutzel, health and social reform leader.

The 23-story First Federal Building completed on Woodward at Michigan (former site of Majestic Building), overlooking Kennedy Plaza.

Pontchartrain Hotel opens in new building at Civic Center; first major hotel built in Detroit since 1927.

Westland Mall opens; unlike Northland and Eastland, shopping center is enclosed.

Detroit physician Charles Wright establishes International Afro-American Museum. West Grand Blvd. facility houses dozens of exhibits.

Motown's Diana Ross and Supremes continue to top charts with 3 new hits, "Stop! In the of Love," "Back in My Arms Again," and "I Hear a Symphony."

Al Kaline gets his 1,000th career RBI in game against Kansas City.

Dodge introduces Charger.

Pontiac's GTO "muscle car" an instant hit.

U.S. motor vehicle industry grants $10 million to University of Michigan to establish highway research institute.

Ford Motor Co.'s stamping plant opens in Woodhaven.

General Motors dedicates new training center in Detroit.

Heinz Prechter launches American Sunroof, making preproduction installations of sunroofs viable.

World History

Fourth wave of U.S. immigration begins (to end of century).

Jan. 2. SCLC launches voter registration drive in Selma, Alabama. Becomes national protest movement.

Jan. 20. President Lyndon Johnson inaugurated.

Feb. U.S. bombs North Vietnam.

Feb. 21. Black Muslim leader Malcolm X is assassinated in Harlem.

March 6. Civil rights marchers near Selma, Alabama, attacked by state troopers.

March 8. U.S. combat troops arrive in Vietnam; by July, 125,000 American soldiers land.

Voting Rights Act outlaws poll tax, other suppression of minority votes.

Antiwar movement begins with demonstration protesting U.S. military involvement in Southeast Asia.

Aug. 11–16. Police brutality protest turns to violent race riots in Watts neighborhood of Los Angeles; 34 dead, 3,500 arrested, $225 million in property damages.

Sept. 8. Hurricane Betsy sweeps over Florida, moves into Mississippi, Louisiana.

Oct. 3. Congress passes Immigration Reform Act; national quotas abolished.

Oct. Communists massacred in Indonesia.

May 11. Supreme Court ruling in *Griswold* v. *Connecticut* articulates constitutional "right to privacy."

Great Society (to 1967): President Lyndon Johnson advocates legislation expanding social and welfare programs, establishing Medicare and Medicaid, reforming immigration laws.

U.S. Department of Housing and Urban Development created.

New York City's East Village and San Francisco's Haight-Ashbury are havens for hippie movement's flower children.

Cultural Progress

National Endowment for the Arts, National Endowment for the Humanities founded.

African American collage artist Romare Bearden has first exhibition at major museum, Washington, D.C.'s Corcoran Gallery.

Motown's Smokey Robinson and the Miracles have a hit with "The Tracks of My Tears." Written by Robinson, who pens many hits for the Detroit label, and who singer/songwriter Bob Dylan calls "America's greatest living poet."

Bob Dylan releases *Highway 61 Revisited*.

Rolling Stones' "(I Can't Get No) Satisfaction" a hit.

Rock band Grateful Dead founded by Jerry Garcia.

Miniskirt first appears in London.

I Spy makes network debut; features Robert Culp and Bill Cosby. First American TV series to star a black actor.

Scientific and Commercial Progress

June 4. Edward Higgins White II is first U.S. astronaut to leave craft while in outer space: goes on 21-minute "spacewalk" as part of 4-day flight with fellow astronaut James A. McDivitt.

BASIC computer programming language developed.

Consumer advocate Ralph Nader publishes *Unsafe at Any Speed*.

1966

Detroit and Michigan

Jan. Mayor Jerome Cavanagh sworn in; 2nd term.

Michigan State University football team loses Rose Bowl to UCLA, 17-10.

Sept. Grand Opening of Detroit's planned artist community along Plum St.: Gov. Romney, Senator Griffin, and Mayor Cavanagh attend event.

Nov. Voters go to polls to elect Michigan's governor and lieutenant governor, who now run for office as a team. Republican George Romney reelected with running mate, William Milliken.

State begins experiments to adapt salmon to Great Lakes.

Construction completed on Terminal 2 (North Terminal) at Detroit Metropolitan Airport. Six airlines relocate from Willow Run, bringing number of scheduled operators to thirteen.

Detroit Red Wings lose Stanley Cup finals to Montreal Canadiens, 4 games to 2.

Ailing Tigers manager Charlie Dressen dies of a heart attack at age 67; Mayo Smith is named new Tiger manager.

World History

Robert C. Weaver is appointed secretary of housing and urban development; nation's first black cabinet member.

National Traffic and Motor Vehicle Safety Act sets motor vehicle safety standards.

June 13. Supreme Court ruling in *Miranda* case sets police standard for reading of rights upon arrest.

June. National Organization for Women (NOW) founded.

July 1–9. Student Non-Violent Coordinating Committee (SNCC) and Congress of Racial Equality (CORE) endorse Black Power, stressing black community development, self-reliance, and armed self-defense; SCLC and NAACP stay course of pursuing integration.

Oct. Black Panther party founded by Huey P. Newton, Bobby Seale.

Dec. 26. African Americans in California begin marking Kwanza, weeklong festival celebrating 7 principles of black culture: unity, self-determination, working together, sharing, purpose, creativity, faith.

U.S. Department of Transportation created.

Mao Tse-tung launches Great Cultural Revolution in China.

Indira Gandhi is elected Indian prime minister.

Cultural Progress

Katherine Anne Porter's *Collected Stories* wins Pulitzer Prize for fiction.

Beach Boys release influential concept album *Pet Sounds*.

The Beatles release *Revolver*.

That Girl makes network debut.

1967

Detroit and Michigan

May. Drive to recall Mayor Jerome Cavanagh is shown to have strong racial overtones; African American leaders rally to mayor's side.

June 15. Patrolmen begin sick-out to back Police Officer Association demands for pay increase.

July 23. In predawn hours, Detroit police raid illegal after-hours establishment in predominately black neighborhood; crowd gathers but police refrain from acting to disperse it. Violence breaks out; black civic leaders who attempt to calm rioters are pelted with stones. Begins 8 days of race riots that claim 43 lives, send thousands to hospital for treatment; $45 million in property damages. National Guard and U.S. Army troops are called in to restore order. Gov. Romney declares state of emergency (lifted Aug. 6).

New Detroit founded as nation's first urban coalition; aims to improve education, employment, housing, and economic development in city.

First phase completed of urban renewal project Elmwood Park (east of Lafayette Park).

African Americans boycott Detroit public schools to protest racism in education system.

Mayor-appointed study group issues report calling for major overhaul of government poverty programs and agencies; urges creation of 2 superagencies, one to deal with human problems and other to handle physical renewal.

Michigan adopts state income tax; funds to go toward education, mental health programs, welfare.

Dec. 9. City government presents massive rebuilding program for 12th St., scene of July rioting.

Marion Isabel Barnhart is first woman professor at Wayne State University Medical School.

Detroit Tigers fall short of pennant by one-half game as they lose second game of double-header at home.

World History

Jan. 27. NASA disaster: Flash fire inside *Apollo 1* capsule kills astronauts Virgil "Gus" Grissom, Edward White, Roger Chaffee.

The 25th Amendment to U.S. Constitution ratified; clarifies vice presidential and presidential succession.

Carl B. Stokes elected mayor of Cleveland, Ohio, making him the first African American mayor of a major American city.

April 21. Colonels' Coup in Greece ousts civilian government.

April 30. Heavyweight champion Muhammad Ali refuses draft; boxing commission strips him of title.

Black Power movement gains momentum; many civil rights activists turn backs on pursuit of integration.

May 1–Oct. 1. Long Hot Summer: race riots or disturbances erupt in more than 100 U.S. cities.

June. Six-Day War: Israel responds to Egyptian provocation; Israeli troops occupy West Bank, Gaza Strip, Golan Heights, Sinai Peninsula.

Aug. 30. Thurgood Marshall is first black justice on U.S. Supreme Court.

Oct. 21. Vietnam protesters march on Pentagon.

Dec. 31. Yippie movement launched with founding of Youth International Party (YIP).

Revolutionary leader Che Guevara killed in Bolivia during attempted coup.

Cultural Progress

Bernard Malamud's *The Fixer* wins Pulitzer Prize for fiction.

Anne Sexton's *Live or Die* wins Pulitzer Prize for poetry.

305

Edward Albee's *A Delicate Balance* wins Pulitzer Prize for drama.

Diary of Anne Frank published in U.S.

The Beatles release *Sgt. Pepper's Lonely Hearts Club Band.*

Aretha Franklin's Atlantic Records debut *I Never Loved a Man (The Way I Loved You)* electrifies audiences; earns Detroit musician nickname "Queen of Soul."

New York's new Metropolitan Opera House opens; features murals by Marc Chagall.

The Graduate in movie theaters.

End of an era: last newsreels are screened.

Corporation for Public Broadcasting established by Public Broadcasting Act. PBS soon vies with Big Three networks for viewers.

Jan. First Super Bowl played: Green Bay Packers (NFL) defeat Kansas City Chiefs (AFL), 35–10.

NHL launches expansion effort to double number of teams, now just 6, including Detroit Red Wings.

Scientific and Commercial Progress

Dec. 3. World's first heart transplant performed in Cape Town, South Africa; first U.S. heart transplant performed Dec. 7 by New York surgeon.

Big Three TV networks broadcast entirely in color.

Computerworld begins publication.

First microwave oven produced.

1968

Detroit and Michigan

Michigan State Senator Coleman Young is first black member of Democratic National Committee.

Nov. Michigan voters approve bond issues expanding recreational areas, reducing water pollution.

Michigan Women's Commission established by state legislature.

Detroit police receive pay raise from $8,335 to $10,000 per year, highest in nation; firemen receive similar increase.

April 5. State of emergency declared in Detroit after scattered violence breaks out: looter is killed by police, 2 African Americans are shot by unknown persons. Calm restored within few days.

Detroit Free Press receives Pulitzer Prize for its reporting of 1967 riots.

Detroit Tigers win American League pennant, their first since 1945.

Oct. After falling behind 3 games to 1 in World Series, Tigers storm back to defeat St. Louis Cardinals and claim the baseball championship.

Dec. 30. Detroit Common Council approves Federal Model Cities program.

World History

Jan. Tet offensive jolts American public, deepens antiwar sentiment: Vietcong and North Vietnamese forces launch all-out attack, seizing provincial capitals and raiding American embassy compound. American journalist sizes it up as "the more we kill, the better they get." Secretary of Defense Clark Clifford reports to President Lyndon Johnson war cannot be won.

March. President Johnson announces he will not run for reelection; ends political career.

April 4. Martin Luther King Jr. is assassinated in Memphis, Tennessee; sparks rioting across country.

May. Students and workers stage protest in Paris against U.S. involvement in Vietnam, for a better educational system, and for working-class rights.

June. Robert F. Kennedy is assassinated in California while campaigning for presidency; Arab nationalist Sirhan Sirhan, reportedly angered by RFK's support of Israel, is arrested.

June. Nuclear Nonproliferation Treaty signed.

At Summer Olympics in Mexico City, 2 American track medalists, Tommie Smith and John Carlos, raise gloved, clenched fists in support of Black Power.

Aug. 20. Soviet troops invade Czechoslovakia; assert authority.

Aug. 26–29. Vietnam protesters and police clash during Democratic national convention; Chicago 7 charged with inciting riot (found not guilty, Feb. 1970).

Nov. 5. Richard M. Nixon, Republican, elected president.

Student strike begins at San Francisco State University; other student protests occur, including at Columbia University, in Paris, Mexico City, Tokyo.

Women's liberation movement gains momentum: Feminists protest Miss America pageant in Atlantic City; picketers dump bras, girdles, false eyelashes, copies of *Playboy*, other symbols of oppression into "freedom trash can."

Violence between Catholics and Protestants intensifies in Northern Ireland; emergence of republican Catholic civil rights movement there.

Paul Ehrlich's *The Population Bomb* asserts population growth will outpace earth's natural resources; Zero Population Growth organization founded.

Fair Housing Act bars racial discrimination in U.S. sales and rentals.

Cultural Progress

William Styron's *The Confessions of Nat Turner* wins Pulitzer Prize for fiction.

Dance Theater of Harlem established; first world-renowned African American ballet company is founded by Arthur Mitchell of NYC Ballet.

Motown Records signs The Jackson 5. Tops charts with "ABC," "I'll Be There."

Stanley Kubrick's *2001: A Space Odyssey* in movie theaters.

Sept. 24. CBS debuts *60 Minutes*. Pioneers "newsmagazine" concept; becomes television institution.

Winter Olympics held in Grenoble, France.

Summer Olympics held in Mexico City.

Oct. Detroit Tigers defeat St. Louis Cardinals to win World Series.

Scientific and Commercial Progress

Federal government issues its first antipollution standards for automobiles.

1969

Detroit and Michigan

Jan. 22. Gov. Romney resigns post to become U.S. secretary of housing and urban development. Succeeded by Lt. Gov. William G. Milliken, Republican, governor (to 1982).

Feb. 7. Unarmed civilian patrol of African American youths wearing semi-military clothing begins patrolling high crime areas; part of effort to address problems in Detroit's African American community.

March 30. One unarmed patrolman is killed and another injured when they approach group of armed African American men outside west side New Bethel Baptist Church where black nationalist group Republic of New Africa meet. Police arrest 135 men inside church; all but 10 are later freed by Judge George W. Crockett Jr.

Jerome Cavanagh to retire at end of term; Roman S. Gribbs elected Detroit mayor.

First Michigan chapter of National Organization for Women is founded. Patricia Hill Burnett of Detroit, organizer.

Plum St., Detroit's planned art district (launched 1966) fails: of some 40 establishments once operating, fewer than 10 remain.

Tiger pitcher Denny McLain posts his 8th season shutout, tying Hal Newhouser's club record.

Detroit-based Hudson's is bought by Minnesota-based Dayton Corp. to form Dayton-Hudson.

Somerset Mall opens in Troy; new center for Detroit area's upscale shopping.

World History

Jan. 20. Richard Nixon inaugurated; 37th U.S. president.

Shirley Chisholm, New York, is first black woman to serve in U.S. House of Representatives.

May. Student protest at People's Park, Berkeley, California.

President Richard Nixon begins withdrawing American troops from Vietnam; U.S. bombs Cambodia.

June. Stonewall riot in Greenwich Village: police raid gay bar provoking violent reaction. Launches gay rights movement.

July 20. Astronaut Neil Armstrong is first person to walk on moon: steps out of *Apollo 11* lunar module *Eagle* followed by Buzz Aldrin, utters famous words, "That's one small step for man, one giant leap for mankind."

Aug. Charles Manson leads Helter-Skelter slayings in Los Angeles.

Aug. Rioting in Northern Ireland; British troops dispatched.

Aug. 17. Hurricane Camille strikes Mississippi and Alabama with 190-mile-per-hour winds; later reaches Virginia.

Nov. 15. Vietnam Moratorium Day: 250,000 antiwar protesters participate in rallies.

Nov. 20. American Indian movement leaders seize Alcatraz, San Francisco Bay.

Georges Pompidou, president of France (to 1974).

Stephen Biko founds South African Student's Organization; part of Black Consciousness Movement and leader in fight against apartheid.

Golda Meir becomes prime minister of Israel.

Cultural Progress

Supreme Court rules U.S. schools must end segregation immediately.

Feb. End of an era: *Saturday Evening Post* magazine ceases publication.

N. Scott Momaday is first Native American writer to win Pulitzer Prize for fiction (for *House Made of Dawn*).

The National Football League (NFL) and the American Football League (AFL) merge into the National Football Conference (NFC).

Woodstock: New York music and art festival draws 300,000.

Easy Rider and *Butch Cassidy & the Sundance Kid* in movie theaters.

Sesame Street debuts on PBS; first production of Children's Television Workshop (CTW). Quickly gains wide audience; sets new standard for children's programming.

The Brady Bunch makes ABC debut; popular TV program later a cult favorite.

Scientific and Commercial Progress

Government-developed ARPAnet allows computers to exchange large quantities of information; origin of Internet.

1970

Detroit and Michigan

Roman Gribbs takes office as mayor of Detroit.

Michigan's population, 8,881,826.

Detroit's population, 1,511,482; ranks 5th in size among U.S. cities.

March 7. Urban Institute and Detroit Police Department announce experiment in decentralized police patrolling: 1 sergeant commands 21 patrolmen who work in high crime areas.

June 28. New requirements for Detroit police officers announced: must complete one year of college before taking promotion examinations.

Frank B. Murphy Hall of Justice is constructed on St. Antoine, near county jail.

The 29-story McNamara Federal Building completed on West Michigan, consolidating offices of 5,000 government employees in downtown area.

Police Commissioner Patrick V. Murphy is appointed New York City police commissioner; John F. Nichols is named Detroit's new commissioner Oct. 17.

May 9. UAW leader Walter Reuther and wife, May, die in plane crash.

Olga Madar is first woman named international vice president of United Auto Workers (UAW) in Detroit.

Clara Stanton Jones becomes director of Detroit Public Library; first African American in nation to direct major public library.

Robert Tannahill bequeaths impressionist and post impressionist paintings to DIA.

Restoration of Orchestra Hall begins; crusade to save 1919 building led by DSO musicians, friends.

Detroit Dance Co. is founded by Carole Morisseau.

Ethnic Festivals begin on Detroit riverfront.

After final game of season, Tiger manager Mayo Smith is fired; Billy Martin is named manager.

Warner Lambert acquires Detroit pharmaceutical company Parke-Davis.

Chrysler expands and reorganizes Highland Park headquarters.

Business leaders found Detroit Renaissance, Inc.

Southland Mall opens in Taylor.

Hudson's begins scaling back operations in downtown store, now 1 of 15.

World History

U.S. population, 203,235,298.

U.S. unemployment, 4.9%.

Women account for 38% of U.S. labor force outside the home; account for 98% of secretaries.

My Lai massacre (March 1968) comes to light: frustrated American soldiers rounded up and repeatedly shot 200 unarmed Vietnamese civilians, mostly women and children. Cover-up lasting 21 months kept atrocity under wraps.

April 13. "OK, Houston, we've had a problem": oxygen tank explosion on moon-bound *Apollo 13* damages heat shield; world watches, waits while NASA engineers work to save astronauts Jim Lovell, Jack Swigert, Fred Haise. Results in "successful failure": astronauts splash down safely in Pacific April 17.

April. U.S. invades Cambodia.

National student strikes protest U.S. involvement in Vietnam: National Guard guns down 4 antiwar protesters at Kent State University, Ohio (May 4); officers kill 2 students at Jackson State University, Mississippi (May 14).

Aug. 26. Women march in support of Equal Rights Amendment.

Black September massacre: Palestinians killed in Jordan.

Cyclone strikes East Pakistan (Bangladesh); estimated fatalities, 500,000.

Rock and roll legends Jimi Hendrix and Janis Joplin die of drug overdoses.

Dec. Congress passes Clean Air Act.

Congress establishes Amtrak. Formally called the National Railroad Passenger Corp., Amtrak is a federally supported corporation that will operate nearly all intercity passenger trains in U.S. Assumes control of passenger service from the nation's private rail companies the next year.

Environmental Protection Agency (EPA) and Occupational Safety and Health Administration (OSHA) founded.

Labor leader Cesar Chavez, United Farm Workers spearhead California grape boycott. Raises public awareness of (Mexican) migrant workers' condition.

Cultural Progress

Journalist and Detroit native Helen Thomas becomes UPI's chief correspondent to White House; first woman to hold such position on permanent basis for national news agency.

Maya Angelou's *I Know Why the Caged Bird Sings* is released.

African American poet Robert Hayden (who grew up in Detroit and now teaches at University of Michigan) publishes poetry collection *Words in the Mourning Time.*

April 10. End of an era: The Beatles announce breakup.

The Mary Tyler Moore Show debuts on CBS; enjoys 7-year run. Hailed as model sitcom.

Leisure suit is fashionable.

Scientific and Commercial Progress

Floppy disk introduced to store computer data.

April 22. First Earth Day.

1971

Detroit and Michigan

Jan. 27. *Detroit Free Press* announces price increase from 10 to 15 cents.

Sept. 3. Kresge Co. (K-Mart Corp.) announces it will donate its headquarters to Detroit Institute of Technology; the retail giant plans move to suburbs (*See* 1972).

Sept. 27. District Court Judge Stephen J. Roth rules Detroit Public Schools were deliberately segregated over long period.

Oct. 4. Federal Court orders Michigan Education Board to propose integration plan for metropolitan area including Detroit and some suburbs.

Detroit Police Department creates STRESS (Stop the Robberies Enjoy Safe Streets), special unit to control escalating street crime; after black youths are killed by STRESS officers, public rally is held to call for unit's suspension. (*See* 1972, 1974.)

Detroit Mayor Roman Gribbs calls for statewide campaign to ban handguns; reaction to city's rising murder rate.

Henry Ford II, head of Detroit Renaissance Inc., announces plan for $500 million complex of office buildings, retail space in downtown. Renaissance Center will be privately financed.

Motown releases influential soul record *What's Going On* by Marvin Gaye.

Detroit hosts Major League Baseball's annual All-Star Game.

Orchestra Hall, spared from wrecking ball last year in great effort staged by DSO musicians and friends, is added to National Register of Historic Places.

On nearly 12 acres of urban renewal land, Blue Cross/Blue Shield of Michigan completes its new office center, just west of Chrysler freeway.

Children's Hospital moves into new location in Medical Center.

World History

The 26th Amendment to U.S. Constitution ratified; lowers voting age to 18.

Memorial Day becomes official U.S. holiday; last Monday in May set aside to honor nation's war dead.

April 20. Supreme Court ruling upholds practice of busing to desegregate schools.

Sept. 9–13. Attica prison uprising: 1,500 troopers storm penitentiary; 43 dead.

Pentagon Papers are leaked to *New York Times*; documents detail U.S. policy in Vietnam War.

Vietnam veterans march in Washington in protest against U.S. involvement in Southeast Asian conflict.

Reverend Jesse Jackson founds People United to Save Humanity (PUSH; later People United to Serve Humanity).

Cultural Progress

W. S. Merwin's *The Carrier of Ladders* wins Pulitzer Prize for poetry.

Best-selling fiction focuses on auto industry: Arthur Hailey's *Wheels,* Harold Robbins's *The Betsy.*

Pilobolus Dance Theater founded; experimental repertory.

The French Connection in movie theaters.

Scientific and Commercial Progress

Two new galaxies discovered adjacent to Milky Way.

First manned vehicle on moon is Lunar Roving Vehicle built by General Motors.

Texas Instruments introduces first pocket calculator.

Intel introduces first microprocessing chip.

Cigarette advertising banned from television.

1972

Detroit and Michigan

March 9. Wayne County Sheriff's deputy is killed and 3 wounded (all victims are black) by gunfire during Detroit police raid of apartment where off-duty deputies were playing cards. Black policemen are accused of shooting first; acquitted (Aug. 11). "Gun-happy" STRESS unit involved in case.

Michigan establishes state lottery; money is earmarked for schools.

Mary Stallings Coleman (Battle Creek) is first woman elected to Michigan Supreme Court.

Erma Henderson is first African American woman elected to Detroit City Council.

Detroit Tigers win American League Eastern Division championship.

Oct. 12. Oakland Athletics defeat Tigers to win American League pennant.

Motown Records founder Berry Gordy Jr. moves label from Detroit to Hollywood.

K-Mart Corp. (formerly Kresge) moves headquarters from Detroit to Troy.

Jeffries freeway opens.

World History

Jan. Violence in Derry, Northern Ireland, claims 13 Irish Catholics.

Feb. 20–27. President Richard Nixon visits People's Republic of China.

Father's Day becomes official U.S. holiday; to be celebrated 3rd Sunday in June.

March 22. Senate approves Equal Rights Amendment; grants that "equality of rights under the law shall not be denied or abridged by the United States or any state on account of sex." Sent to states for ratification.

May. Nixon visits Moscow, signs Strategic Arms Limitation Treaty.

June 29. Supreme Court ruling declares death penalty unconstitutional.

July. Break-in at Democratic national headquarters, Watergate.

At Summer Olympics in Munich, 11 Israeli athletes are killed by Arab terrorist group Black September.

Hurricane Agnes batters northeastern U.S.

Oct. *Washington Post* reveals Watergate scandal.

Nov. 7. Richard Nixon reelected president.

Dec. Hanoi and Haiphong, Vietnam, bombed.

Senate ratifies Strategic Arms Limitation Treaty (SALT I) with Soviet Union.

Eisenstadt v. *Baird* ruling interprets 1965's *Griswold* v. *Connecticut* decision as protecting right of unmarried people to use birth control.

Cultural Progress

Education Amendments Act passed by Congress; includes Title Nine, prohibiting federally funded schools, colleges from discriminating on basis of sex. Applies to admissions, athletics, curriculum.

Wallace Stegner's *Angle of Repose* wins Pulitzer Prize for fiction.

July. *Ms.* Magazine founded.

New York's World Trade Center completed; world's tallest building. Designed by Detroit architect Minoru Yamasaki.

Berry Gordy Jr. encourages Michael Jackson to go solo.

The Godfather in movie theaters.

Time Warner's HBO begins beaming signal to customers on subscription basis; becomes driving force in development of cable TV.

Winter Olympics held in Sapporo, Japan.

Summer Olympics held in Munich, West Germany.

Scientific and Commercial Progress

Improved Polaroid instant camera introduced: takes color pictures that develop outside camera within seconds.

1973

Detroit and Michigan

Jan. 16. Federal Appeals Court agrees to rehear full arguments on school desegregation plan for Detroit schools and 52 suburban districts. (*See* June 12.)

May 14. Detroit school custodial and service officials strike; a third of city's 10,500 teachers refuse to cross picket lines May 15.

June 12. Federal Appeals Court in Cincinnati rules that to achieve racial balance in schools, black Detroit schoolchildren be bused to suburban schools; suburban students bused to Detroit schools.

Detroit teachers strike the day before scheduled opening of classes.

Oct. 15. Detroit teachers approve new contract.

Nov. 6. State Senator Coleman A. Young, Democrat, is elected first African American mayor of Detroit, narrowly defeating Detroit Police Chief John F. Nichols. Young secured more than 90% of city's black voters, about 10% of white voters.

Voters approve new city charter for Detroit.

College of Lifelong Learning added at Wayne State University.

First women's studies association in nation is founded at Michigan State University

First lawsuit to challenge Little League Baseball's no-girls policy is filed in Detroit on behalf of Carolyn King. Courts throw case out, but it leads to similar lawsuits culminating in organization's ban on sex discrimination.

World History

Jan. 20. President Richard Nixon inaugurated; 2nd term.

Jan. 22. *Roe* v. *Wade:* Supreme Court ruling in class-action lawsuit establishes woman's right to terminate a pregnancy; overturns state laws restricting access to first trimester abortions.

Feb. 28. Oglala Sioux lead American Indian movement protest at Wounded Knee, South Dakota; demand U.S. recognize treaties.

March 29. Last American troops withdrawn from Vietnam.

May 17. Watergate hearings begin.

May 29. Thomas Bradley is elected first black mayor of Los Angeles. Mayoral races in Atlanta (Oct. 16, Maynard Jackson elected) and Detroit (Nov. 6, Mayor Coleman Young elected) also won by black candidates.

June 21. Supreme Court ruling leaves definition of pornography to be decided by community standards.

Sept. 11. Gen. Augusto Pinochet leads coup in Chile; democratically-elected leader, Salvador Allende is murdered.

Oct. 6. Yom Kippur War begins: Egypt, Syria, Iraq attack Israel on holy day. Heavy losses for both sides; ends in cease-fire (1974).

Oct. 10. Vice President Spiro Agnew forced to resign for income tax evasion. Michigan Representative Gerald Ford is named vice president.

Oct. 17. OPEC embargo causes fuel prices to soar; triggers inflation, recession, unemployment.

Representative Martha Griffiths (Michigan) reintroduces Equal Rights Amendment in Congress, 15 years after amendment was first introduced; Griffiths guides passage through House.

Barbara Jordan (Texas) is elected to U.S. House of Representatives; first African American woman from southern state to serve in Congress.

Spanish leader Francisco Franco steps down; to be succeeded by Juan Carlos (becomes king on death of Franco, 1975).

Cultural Progress

Eudora Welty's *The Optimist's Daughter* wins Pulitzer Prize for fiction.

Pablo Picasso dies but impact of prolific artist endures. Created some 35,000 works during his lifetime.

Bob Marley and the Wailers' *Burnin'* puts reggae on international music map.

American Graffiti in movie theaters.

Sheila Young of Detroit is first American woman to win World Cycling championship.

Sept. 20. Billie Jean King defeats Bobby Riggs in highly publicized tennis match.

1974

Detroit and Michigan

Coleman Young takes office as mayor of Detroit.

Controversial STRESS anticrime unit disbanded. (*See* 1971, 1972.)

Michigan legislature passes Criminal Sexual Conduct Act, labeling rape as violent crime and ensuring victim's privacy; law becomes model for other states.

Recession hits auto industry: GM lays off 38,000 workers indefinitely; another 48,000 put on short-term leave.

Coalition of Labor Union Women (CLUW) founded, with "first lady of labor" Olga Madar (Detroit) first president.

Ann Arbor's Belita Cowan organizes National Women's Health Network, only consumer organization in country devoted to women's health.

After 22-year Major League career, Tiger legend Al Kaline announces retirement from baseball.

Twelve-year-old Laura Cross wins Detroit Soap Box Derby; dedicates achievement to "womanhood."

Detroit Free Press parent company Knight merges with Ridder newspapers.

Dec. 1–2. Detroit socked with more than 19 inches of snow; second-greatest single snowfall on record. Storm claims 27 lives.

World History

Jan. U.S. oil prices have jumped 350% over 1 year ago, causing energy crisis.

Congress passes legislation dropping national speed limit to 55 mph to reduce gasoline consumption.

Auto industry in recession; American Motors Co. is only U.S. car producer with increased sales—90% of AMC cars are compacts.

July. Judiciary Committee of House of Representatives prepares articles of impeachment against President Richard Nixon.

Aug. 8. Nixon resigns; succeeded by Vice President Gerald Ford, 38th U.S. president.

Sept. 8. President Ford pardons Richard Nixon for Watergate break-in, cover-up.

Sept. 12. South Boston busing protest turns into riot.

Valery Giscard d'Estaing is president of France (to 1981).

India tests nuclear bomb.

Palestinian Liberation Organization (PLO) is recognized by United Nations and Arab countries as governing body of Palestinian people.

Cultural Progress

Equal Educational Opportunity Act makes bilingual instruction available to Hispanic students in U.S. public schools.

Chicago's Sears Tower completed; world's tallest building.

Disco music moves from clubs to radio airwaves.

April 8. Baseball great Hank Aaron hits 715th home run; breaks Babe Ruth's long-standing (1928) record.

1975

Detroit and Michigan

Detroit's (est.) population, 1,335,000; 28% decrease over 25 years ago. African Americans comprise 54% of city's population.

Detroit tricounty area (est.) population, 4,163,300.

City of Detroit police officials make an agreement with Detroit Police Officers Association to prevent layoffs.

Aug. 14–18. Estimated 700 sanitation truck drivers strike.

Nov. 4. Judge Robert DeMascio rules city school system must begin integration by Jan. 26, 1976.

Nov. 10. Ore carrier *Edmund Fitzgerald* is foundered during Lake Superior storm; all 29 crewmen perish.

Center for Creative Studies is completed near Wayne State University to house art and music schools for Society of Arts and Crafts and Detroit Community Music School.

Detroit Free Press raises Sunday edition price from 35 to 50 cents.

WXYZ-TV's Jeanne Sullivan Findlater is nation's first woman program director of network-owned TV station.

Pontiac Silverdome, 10-acre indoor arena with inflated roof, completed; Detroit Lions move into their new home.

World History

U.S. unemployment, 8.5%.

Jan. 10–11. Blizzard hits upper Midwest; 90 mile-per-hour winds, wind chills as low as 80 degrees (F) below zero. Claims 80 lives; farmers lose 55,000 head of livestock.

April. Cambodia falls to communist Khmer Rouge; revolutionary leader Pol Pot institutes reign of terror—killing fields.

April 30. North Vietnam takes Saigon; all of Vietnam now under communist control.

July. Teamster Jimmy Hoffa disappears; assumed dead.

Sept. Two assassination attempts on President Gerald Ford.

Cultural Progress

Journalist and Detroit native Helen Thomas, of UPI, becomes president of White House Correspondents Association.

Michael Shaara's *The Killer Angels* wins Pulitzer Prize for fiction.

One Flew Over the Cuckoo's Nest and *Jaws* in movie theaters.

Oct. 11. *Saturday Night Live* premieres on NBC; features Detroit native Gilda Radner as one of Not Ready for Prime Time Players. Radner creates memorable characters, contributing to show's popular and critical success.

Sony introduces Betamax, first videocassette recorders (VCRs).

Tennis great Arthur Ashe is first black man to win Wimbledon singles championship; first to be ranked number one internationally.

Scientific and Commercial Progress

American car registration passes 100 million mark.

Bill Gates and Paul Allen found Microsoft.

1976

Detroit and Michigan

Michigan passes nation's largest container deposit law for returnable bottles and cans, leading the nation in waste reduction and recycling efforts.

Jan. 26. Court-ordered busing of students begins peaceably; attendance off by 1/3 but is near normal next day.

Mayor Coleman A. Young announces plans to eliminate 4 city departments, along with permanent and temporary layoffs.

City government begins 3-day sale of unneeded items, accumulated over last 60 years.

June 12. Mayor Young, acting to enforce long-standing city statute requiring city employees reside within city, suspends several employees without pay; majority are white firemen and policemen.

Massive sick-out to protest layoffs; Police Chief Philip Tannian warns officers to return or face dismissal.

Summer. Following downtown rock concert, rampaging youth gangs create night of terror, attacking concertgoers; city recalls 450 laid-off police officers.

Sept. 28. Mayor Coleman Young names William L. Hart as city's first African American police chief.

Oct. Mayor Young forms Economic Growth Council to reorganize city government operations and tax structure.

Cassandra Smith-Grey becomes Detroit assessor; first black woman in nation to hold that municipal job.

Michigan Indian Tuition Waiver Law is passed.

Facilities of Harper and Grace hospitals (recently merged) are completed in Medical Center.

Sheila Young (Detroit) is triple-medal winner at Winter Olympics; picks up gold, silver, bronze medals in speed skating at Games held in Innsbruck, Austria.

Tiger rookie pitcher Mark "The Bird" Fidrych wins his first big-league start against Cleveland Indians. Catcher Bill Freehan draws his release after brilliant 15-year career.

Fairlane Town Center opens in Dearborn.

American Motors moves headquarters from Detroit to Southfield.

World History

World population reaches 4 billion.

June. South Africa's Soweto uprising.

July 2. Supreme Court reinstates death penalty.

July 4. Americans celebrate U.S. Bicentennial.

July 28. Earthquake rocks Tangshan, China, killing 250,000 (some estimates as high as 750,000) and destroying 89% of homes and 78% of area's industrial buildings.

Sept. 16. Hyde Amendment passed by Congress; bans federal funding of abortions.

Texas Representative Barbara Jordan is first black keynote speaker at a Democratic national convention.

Nov. 2. James E. (Jimmy) Carter, Democrat, elected president.

Congress forges Conrail out of 6 failed U.S. railroads.

Cultural Progress

Congress officially names February Black History Month.

Saul Bellow's *Humboldt's Gift* wins Pulitzer Prize for fiction; American novelist also awarded Nobel Prize for literature this year.

Rocky in movie theaters.

Winter Olympics held in Innsbruck, Austria.

Summer Olympics held in Montreal.

Scientific and Commercial Progress

Two U.S. Viking spacecraft touch down on Mars.

1977

Detroit and Michigan

Detroit hires 700 new policemen.

Detroit School Board approves layoff of 692 teachers.

Mayor Coleman Young reelected; to serve 2nd term in office.

Mayor Young loses fight to keep Michigan State Police on Detroit freeways; State Police restored to Detroit freeways under Governor James Blanchard in the 1980s.

Detroit Public Library Director Clara Stanton Jones is first black person elected president of American Library Association (ALA).

Detroit Science Center opens.

Construction begins on $15 million, 3-year modernization project at Tiger Stadium; includes renovation of clubhouses; new press box; luxury boxes; electronic scoreboard.

Renaissance Center opens; 5 cylindrical towers are home to offices, hotel rooms, shops, theaters, restaurants. Two additional towers are planned. Developed and promoted by

Henry Ford II as renewal of Detroit, critics charge that design isolates complex from rest of downtown. Its central tower rising 73 floors, RenCen claims title of Detroit's tallest building. It is among largest renewal projects undertaken in U.S.

World History

Jan. 20. Jimmy Carter inaugurated; 39th U.S. president.

Seabrook, New Hampshire, protest: 2,000 demonstrators call for end of nuclear power.

U.S. Department of Energy created.

Sept. 7. U.S. and Panama sign treaty returning control of canal to Panama in 2000.

Aug. Black South African student leader Stephen Biko is arrested; killed by his jailers.

Britain's Queen Elizabeth celebrates silver jubilee.

Egyptian President Anwar Sadat visits Israel to discuss peace.

Communist leader Deng Xiaopang again rises to power in China.

Cultural Progress

Jan. 27–Feb. 3. ABC-TV broadcasts 8-part *Roots* television series, based on novel by Alex Haley; tops ratings.

Punk rock is born.

Annie Hall and *Star Wars* in movie theaters.

Saturday Night Fever (movie and soundtrack) bring disco to height of popularity.

A. J. Foyt wins Indianapolis 500 for 4th time—a new record.

Scientific and Commercial Progress

Macintosh begins selling Apple II personal computers; first mass-market PC.

1978

Detroit and Michigan

Jan. Mayor Coleman Young sworn in; 2nd term.

Jan. 26–27. Detroit gets 19 inches of snow; third-greatest single snowfall on record.

Shake-up in Ford's senior management: Lee Iacocca, president, is dismissed.

Chrysler hires Lee Iacocca to lead company's turnaround.

Detroit Zoo celebrates 50th anniversary of Royal Oak facility.

Fall. Detroit agrees to lease land between John R and Brush to International Afro-American Museum, which has outgrown original quarters on West Grand Blvd.

Headlee Amendment to state constitution approved by voters; prohibits property tax increases without voter approval.

Chemical spill in Detroit River kills more than 100 ducks, other wildlife.

Monument to Polish patriot Tadeusz Kosciuszko unveiled at Michigan Ave. and Bagley.

Detroit's Stroh Brewery Co. now distributes beer to 17 states; acquires F&M Schaefer Brewing Co.

World History

Aug. 2–8. New York's toxic Love Canal declared unsafe; federal emergency assistance approved for cleanup, relocation of residents. Years of chemical dumping have caused high rates of cancer, miscarriages, birth defects, other illnesses.

Supreme Court decision in Bakke case rules against admissions quotas but fails to provide clear direction to universities on how to achieve desired racial mix.

California's Proposition 13 cuts property taxes; slashes funding for public education.

July 25. Louise Brown is born in Bristol, England; world's first test-tube baby.

Oct. John Paul II is elected pope; first non-Italian pope since 1523, first Polish pope.

Palestinian guerillas in Lebanon launch air raid on Israel; Israeli troops dispatched to south Lebanon. UN intervenes.

President Jimmy Carter holds meetings at Camp David (Maryland) with Israel's Menachem Begin and Egypt's Anwar Sadat. (Begin and Sadat awarded Nobel Peace Prize for efforts.)

Cultural Progress

TV's *Dallas* debuts; nighttime soap becomes smash hit. 1979–80 season ends with "who shot J.R.?" cliffhanger.

1979

Detroit and Michigan

Former Mayor Jerome Cavanagh dies.

Second recession seriously hurts Detroit's automakers; Chrysler particularly hard hit.

Mayor Coleman Young unveils $224.7 million downtown development plan.

Detroit Receiving Hospital and Health Care Institute open in Medical Center.

The 20,000-seat Joe Louis Arena is completed in Civic Center. Pistons and Red Wings move from Cobo Arena to new venue.

Riverfront Philip A. Hart Plaza completed near intersection of Jefferson and Woodward; includes open-air amphitheater; space for festivals; ice skating rink; Isamu Noguchi's Dodge Fountain.

WXYZ-TV's Jeanne Findlater becomes vice president and general manager of network affiliate.

Detroit businesswoman Marilyn French Hubbard founds National Association of Black Women Entrepreneurs.

Hudson's turns over operation of annual Thanksgiving Parade to Detroit Renaissance.

Michigan State University Spartans win NCAA basketball championship.

Sparky Anderson assumes control of Tigers from interim manager Dick Tracewski.

World History

Feb. Revolution in Iran.

March 26. Camp David Accords signed in Washington: Egypt to regain lands lost to Israel in 1967 war.

U.S. President Jimmy Carter and Soviet Premier Leonid Brezhnev sign SALT II, strategic arms limitations treaty.

March 28–April 1. Near meltdown at nuclear power plant at Three Mile Island, outside Middletown, Pennsylvania; radiation leaks, fear of explosion prompt evacuation of area. Eventually contained.

U.S. Department of Health, Education, and Welfare reorganized to spin off Department of Education; original agency renamed Department of Health and Human Services.

Nicaraguan revolution: Sandinista movement overthrows despotic leader Anastasio Somoza.

Margaret Thatcher is elected first woman prime minister of Great Britain.

Pro-democracy movement begins in Beijing, China.

Nov. 4. Iranian revolutionaries seize U.S. embassy in Teheran; hold 52 Americans hostage (to 1981).

Dec. Soviet troops invade Afghanistan to suppress anticommunist movement.

Mother Teresa awarded Nobel Peace Prize for tireless humanitarian work in India.

Cultural Progress

The Stories of John Cheever wins Pulitzer Prize for fiction.

Rap music has first hit with Sugarhill Gang's "Rapper's Delight."

Scientific and Commercial Progress

Herbert Charles Brown (taught at Wayne State University, 1943–47) and George Wittig win Nobel Prize for chemistry for pioneering work with inorganic and organic boron compounds.

Smallpox wiped out; vaccine credited with eradication of disease.

Electronic mail in use; modems connect computers via telephone lines.

Sony Walkman, personal stereo, debuts.

1980

Detroit and Michigan

Michigan's population, 9,262,078.

Detroit's population, 1,203,339; ranks 6th in size among U.S. cities.

Recession felt hard at home: Michigan's unemployment rate highest in nation.

Chrysler Corp. reorganizes; secures loan guarantee from U.S. government, warding off bankruptcy.

To make way for General Motors Poletown plant, demolition of Dodge Main and Hupp plants (in Milwaukee Junction Industrial District) begins.

Chrysler Corp. introduces K car.

Detroit hosts 32nd Republican National Convention at new Joe Louis Arena.

Detroit-Montreaux Jazz Festival begins on riverfront.

Tigers retire Al Kaline's number 6; first Tiger player to be so honored.

World History

U.S. population, 226,545,805.

U.S. unemployment, 7.1%.

Congress passes Comprehensive Environmental Response, Compensation, and Liability Act, establishing multibillion dollar Superfund to clean up nation's worst toxic sites.

April 24. Failed U.S. rescue attempt of Americans held hostage in Iran.

May 17. Race rioting in Miami; 15 dead.

May 18. Washington's Mount St. Helens erupts.

320

U.S. and 62 other noncommunist countries (including Japan and Federal Republic of Germany) boycott USSR-hosted Olympic Games to protest Soviet invasion of Afghanistan (1979).

July. Supreme Court upholds minority quotas in government contracts.

Aug. Solidarity movement begins: Lech Walesa leads federation of 50 labor unions in protest of Poland's communist government.

Aug. 11. ABSCAM trials open in New York: FBI sting operation results in prosecution of corrupt government officials.

Sept. Iran-Iraq War (to 1988).

Nov. 4. Ronald Reagan, Republican, elected president. Landslide victory.

Nov. 20. China's Gang of Four are tried for counterrevolutionary acts, including sedition, conspiracy to overthrow government, plotting to assassinate Mao.

Nov. 21. Fire at MGM Grand, Las Vegas, kills 85, injures 600. Prompts revision of local fire codes across nation.

Dec. 8. John Lennon is shot dead in New York City.

Dec. 10. Prime lending rate hits 20%.

Japanese auto production outpaces U.S.

Cultural Progress

Norman Mailer's *The Executioner's Song* wins Pulitzer Prize for fiction.

PBS airs Carl Sagan's 13-part *Cosmos*.

Ted Turner's Cable News Network (CNN) begins broadcasting news 24 hours a day.

TV series *Magnum P.I.* debuts; starring Detroit native Tom Selleck, hit show remains on air to 1988.

Winter Olympics held in Lake Placid, New York.

Summer Olympics held in Moscow.

1981

Detroit and Michigan

Mayor Coleman Young reelected; to serve 3rd term in office.

Mayor Young urges Detroit voters to approve tax increase.

Detroit City Council approves $1.6 billion budget.

Detroit schools prepare to expand busing for further racial integration.

Detroit Public Library adds Arabic-language collection to respond to city's changing demographics.

City begins razing homes in I-94/I-75 area for General Motors' $750 million Poletown plant.

Stroh Brewery ranks 7th in nation in beer sales.

World History

Jan. 20. Ronald Reagan inaugurated; 40th U.S. president.

Jan. 20. Hostages held at U.S. embassy in Iran are released.

Feb. President Reagan defends U.S. intervention in El Salvador.

Reagan administration pursues program of supply-side economics.

March 30. Assassination attempt on President Reagan.

May. Assassination attempt on Pope John Paul II.

June. François Mitterrand is elected president of France, representing national move toward left.

July 29. Britain's Prince Charles marries Lady Diana Spencer in grand ceremony watched around the world.

Sept. 21. Sandra Day O'Connor is first woman appointed to Supreme Court.

Oct. President Ronald Reagan proposes increase in defense spending; cuts in social programs.

Oct. Egyptian President Anwar Sadat assassinated in Cairo.

New York Times reports on identification of AIDS (called GRID, Gay Related Immune Deficiency).

Cultural Progress

Music Television (MTV) is launched.

Scientific and Commercial Progress

Aug. IBM begins manufacturing PCs to compete with upstart Apple.

Pac-Man video game debuts.

1982

Detroit and Michigan

Jan. Mayor Coleman Young sworn in; 3rd term.

Ongoing state financial crisis prompts cuts in funding for education, mental health services, welfare, other programs.

Detroit's Neighborhood Services Department established; Michigan's largest community action agency.

Nov. James Blanchard, Democrat, elected governor; running mate Martha Griffiths is Michigan's first woman elected lieutenant governor.

Betty Lackey is first woman president of Detroit chapter of NAACP.

DSO premiers *Cityscapes,* concerto for jazz quartet and orchestra composed by Wayne State faculty member Dr. James Hartway; work is nominated for Pulitzer Prize.

Detroit entrepreneur Mike Ilitch (founder of Little Caesars) buys Detroit Red Wings, signaling turnaround for once-glorious team (now derided by followers as "Dead Things").

Detroit hosts first Grand Prix international racing event in streets of downtown.

Super Bowl XVI is played at Pontiac Silverdome.

Public relations professional Beverly Beltaire is first woman to chair Greater Detroit Chamber of Commerce.

Hudson's holds last Downtown Detroit Days shopping fest.

Stroh Brewery Co. buys Schlitz Brewing Co. to become 3rd-largest brewery in nation.

Chrysler reintroduces the convertible.

New Center One office/retail complex completed in Detroit's New Center.

Magnum Oil affirmative action deal with city of Detroit criticized.

World History

U.S. unemployment, 9.7%.

Jan. Judge orders breakup of communication giant AT&T.

May. Falkland war heats up.

June 30. Equal Rights Amendment fails when only 35 of the required 38 states ratify it before 10-year deadline. Interpretation of ERA's language prevented adoption.

Oct. Tylenol tampering scare; 7 die.

Estimated 1 million protesters attend rally in New York's Central Park for nuclear freeze, disarmament.

Leonid Brezhnev dies; succeeded by Yuri Andropov as Soviet premier.

Spain joins NATO.

Cultural Progress

John Updike's *Rabbit Is Rich* wins Pulitzer Prize for fiction.

Sylvia Plath's *Collected Poems* wins Pulitzer Prize.

Roger Sessions's Concerto for Orchestra wins Pulitzer Prize for music.

Sept. 15. *USA Today* debuts on newsstands.

E.T. The Extra-Terrestrial in movie theaters.

1983

Detroit and Michigan

James Blanchard, Democrat, governor (to 1990).

Jan. Hudson's closes landmark Detroit store, ending 72 years at Woodward and Gratiot site and 102 years downtown.

Improved auto sales boost state's economy, easing financial crisis.

Chrysler, under leadership of Lee Iacocca, rebounds and repays sizeable loan 7 years early.

International Salt closes Detroit mine.

Agnes Mary Mansour, head of state Department of Social Services, resigns from religious order in dispute with Vatican over state-funded abortions.

Mayor Coleman Young orders audit of Detroit Institute of Arts spending.

Esther Gordy Edwards founds Motown Museum.

Red Wings draft 18-year-old Steve Yzerman as no. 1 pick; rookie is scoring machine, posting new records in his first season.

Commuter rail service that began as Detroit & Pontiac Railroad ends; last of Metro area's light rail lines.

Ground is broken for Detroit People Mover.

World History

Some 35.3 million Americans live below poverty line; highest rate in 19 years.

March. Star Wars strategic defense initiative (SDI) unveiled by Reagan administration.

April 12. Chicago gets its first black mayor when Harold Washington is elected.

June 18. Astronaut Sally Ride is first American woman in space; she and 4 other crew members make 6-day flight aboard *Challenger*.

June 22. Louisiana legislature repeals last racial classification law in U.S.

Sept. 1. Soviets shoot down Korean Airlines flight 007, which had entered Soviet air space; 269 civilians dead.

Oct. 23. U.S. Marine servicemen are killed in Beirut, Lebanon, when truck bomb explodes; U.S. withdraws forces.

Oct. 25. U.S. troops invade Grenada.

Nov. Stock market hits new high.

Cultural Progress

National Commission on Excellence in Education issues "A Nation at Risk" report.

Alice Walker's *The Color Purple* wins Pulitzer Prize for fiction.

Ellen Taafe Zwilich is first woman to receive Pulitzer Prize for music.

Michael Jackson's *Thriller* tops charts; sells 21 million copies.

Feb. 28. Estimated 125 million watch final episode of *MASH*.

1984

Detroit and Michigan

Michigan's unemployment rate drops to 7.2%.

General Motors Hamtramck (Poletown) Assembly Plant opens; first major new auto plant built in Detroit since 1928, when Plymouth Motor Corp.'s Lynch Rd. Assembly Plant went up.

Settlement of class action lawsuit against *Detroit News* results in improved working conditions for newspaper's women reporters, other women on editorial staff.

Domino's Pizza founder Tom Monaghan buys Detroit Tigers.

For second time in major league baseball history, a team is in first place from first day of season to last: Detroit Tigers win American League pennant.

Oct. Detroit Tiger victory in World Series (*See* Cultural Progress) inspires fans to go wild: cars are set on fire, other property damaged in riotous celebration. Photos of aftermath are published in media around the world.

World History

Soviets boycott Summer Olympic Games.

April 1. Motown great Marvin Gaye is killed in domestic dispute.

July 18. Gunman in California kills 21 inside McDonald's restaurant.

Geraldine Ferraro (Democrat) is first woman vice-presidential nominee of major U.S. political party.

Nov. 6. Ronald Reagan reelected president.

Dec. 3. Poisonous gas leak at Union Carbide pesticide plant in Bhopal, India, kills 3,000 (unofficial tolls as high as 10,000); affects thousands more.

Dec. 22. New York subway vigilante Bernhard Goetz shoots 4 youths.

Reverend Jesse Jackson founds Rainbow Coalition to gain political power for blacks and other people of color.

New York is first state to require drivers, front seat passengers, and children under 10 to wear seatbelts.

U.S. media coin term *Yuppies* (acronym for young urban professionals) to describe new force in nation's economy and society.

Indian Prime Minister Indira Gandhi is assassinated by her Sikh security guards.

Nonviolent antiapartheid movement gains strength under leadership of Anglican bishop Desmond Tutu, who wins Nobel Peace Prize for efforts.

Cultural Progress

David Mamet's *Glengarry Glen Ross* wins Pulitzer Prize for drama.

Rocker Bruce Springsteen's *Born in the U.S.A.* a bestseller.

Madonna releases highly successful *Like a Virgin* record. Bay City, Michigan-born singer uses business savvy to become international superstar by end of decade.

The Cosby Show a monster hit; launches NBC Thursday night powerhouse. First TV show featuring all-black cast to gain widespread appeal.

Winter Olympics hosted in Sarajevo, Yugoslavia.

Summer Olympics hosted in Los Angeles.

Oct. Detroit Tigers defeat San Diego Padres in World Series, 4 games to 1.

Michael Jordan plays first season of pro basketball; playing for the Chicago Bulls, Jordan leads NBA in points, is named Rookie of the Year.

Scientific and Commercial Progress

Kathryn Sullivan is first U.S. woman astronaut to walk in space.

Apple Computer introduces the Macintosh; first PC with graphical user interface (GUI).

1985

Detroit and Michigan

College of Urban, Labor, and Metropolitan Affairs added at WSU.

May 21. Ground is broken for new facility for International Afro-American Museum; name is changed to Museum of African American History.

Detroit Public Library offers free tax assistance program.

Detroit holds crime control rally.

Detroit Tigers win divisional flag but lose pennant to Kansas City Royals.

Oct. 30. Press assembles from around world to cover Detroit's annual Devil's Night arson fires.

Mayor Coleman Young reelected; to serve 4th term in office.

Entertainment center Trapper's Alley opens on Monroe in Detroit in renovated 1800s buildings erected by German-American businessman Traugott Schmidt to house his furrier/tannery business.

Millender Center opens on East Jefferson; hotel, retail, apartment space is connected to Ren Cen and City-County Building via above-the-street walkways.

Detroit's first heart transplant surgery is performed at Henry Ford Hospital.

GM announces formation of Saturn Corp.

World History

Jan. 20. President Ronald Reagan inaugurated; 2nd term.

Congress passes Superfund Amendments and Reauthorization Act; includes community-right-to-know provision (citizens may know what chemicals are produced, stored, buried in neighborhoods).

March. Mikhail Gorbachev becomes Soviet leader; soon announces programs of *glasnost* (openness) and *perestroika* (restructuring).

Aug. 12. Japan Air Lines Boeing 747 crashes into a mountain on a domestic flight; 520 dead.

Sept. 19. Mexico City rocked by earthquake.

Achille Lauro incident in Mediterranean: hostage drama ends when U.S. fighters prevent terrorists' escape.

Soviet Premier Gorbachev and U.S. President Reagan have first meeting.

Nov. 13. Colombia's Nevada del Ruiz volcano erupts; claims 23,000 lives.

Cultural Progress

Stephen Sondheim and James Lapine win Pulitzer Prize for drama for *Sunday in the Park with George.*

July 13. Live Aid rock concert held in London for famine relief in Africa.

Scientific and Commercial Progress

Americans Michael S. Brown, Joseph L. Goldstein win Nobel Prize for medicine for explaining role of high cholesterol in heart disease.

American business becoming characterized by mega-mergers and subsequent downsizing.

1986

Detroit and Michigan

Jan. Mayor Coleman Young sworn in; 4th term.

Detroit releases data showing city owns some 8% of land parcels in city.

Harbortown, 48-acre residential/commercial project on East Jefferson Ave., is developed.

College of Fine, Performing, and Communication Arts added at WSU.

Sculpture unveiled at intersection of Woodward and Jefferson; monument honors Joe Louis, Detroit native and heavyweight boxing champion of world. Bronze arm and clenched fist, by artist Robert Graham, hangs from open pyramid of bronze beams. Popularly known as Big Fist, it is among most controversial pieces of civic art in nation.

Chrysler begins $1.2-billion project to update and rebuild its Jefferson Assembly plant.

Construction begins on Chrysler Tech Center in Auburn Hills.

Northwest Airlines and Republic Airlines merge, creating larger hub at Detroit Metropolitan Airport.

June. More than 500,000 fans jam riverfront to watch Gold Cup races in Detroit River.

Red Wings hire new coach, Jacques Demers; Steve Yzerman (21 years old) is named captain.

World History

U.S. unemployment, 7.0%.

Jan. 16. Bronze bust of Martin Luther King Jr. placed at nation's Capitol; first day commemorating slain civil rights leader marked Jan. 20.

Jan. 28. U.S. space shuttle *Challenger* bursts into flames shortly after takeoff, claiming lives of all 7 crew members: teacher Christa McAuliffe; commander Francis Scobee; pilot Michael Smith; specialists Ellison Onizuka, Ronald McNair, Judith Resnick, Gregory Jarvis. Investigators learn O-ring seals on shuttle's solid rocket boosters failed; government commission recommends complete redesign, other safety reforms. Manned space program suspended.

Feb. 25. Ferdinand Marcos's dictatorship of Philippines ends; Corazon Aquino claims presidency.

May 14. Soviet leader Mikhail Gorbachev appears on national television to make official announcement of April 26 disaster at Chernobyl Nuclear Power Plant, near Kiev, Ukraine.

Explosions killed 2 workers immediately and some 30 others soon after, sent radioactive gasses into atmosphere. Long-term death toll could surpass 6,500, officials say.

Nov. Iran-Contra affair revealed: high-level officials in President Ronald Reagan's administration involved in 1985 arms-for-hostages trade, diversion of funds to Nicaraguan rebels.

American Elie Wiesel awarded Nobel Peace Prize for efforts to help oppressed and victims of racial discrimination.

Cultural Progress

U.S. names first national poet laureate: Robert Penn Warren's works include Pulitzer Prize–winning *All the King's Men* (1946).

Platoon in movie theaters.

Oprah Winfrey Show goes into syndication; gains national audience.

Scientific and Commercial Progress

Soviets launch space station *Mir.*

1987

Detroit and Michigan

Michigan celebrates 150 years of statehood.

Detroit People Mover opens; 3 miles of elevated tracks carry passengers in monorail cars in a downtown loop.

Summer. Northwest Airlines jet departing from Detroit Metropolitan Airport crashes on takeoff, killing 161.

Restoration of Detroit's Wayne County Courthouse (built 1902), on Randolph, is completed; renamed Wayne County Building.

Museum of African American History opens in Detroit's Cultural Center. At 28,000 square feet, the museum houses permanent exhibit on African American heritage—from African continent, through Middle Passage, to freedom.

Michigan Women's Historical Center and Hall of Fame opens in Lansing.

Detroit's Aretha Franklin, known internationally as Queen of Soul, is first woman inducted into Rock and Roll Hall of Fame.

Center for Creative Studies graduate and high school teacher Tyree Guyton begins work on Heidelberg Project: at abandoned houses in 3600 block of Heidelberg St. (between Gratiot and Mount Elliott), Guyton creates works of art out of found objects—old tires, furniture, road signs, pipes, other cast-off items. Project ignites firestorm of controversy.

Detroit Pistons win Central Division title.

Detroit Red Wings win Norris Division championship but lose to Edmonton Oilers in semifinals.

Parent companies of *Detroit News* (Gannett) and *Free Press* (Knight-Ridder) agree to Joint Operating Agreement (JOA).

Ten-year-old Renaissance Center is remodeled to address design problems that hinder access and use.

Detroit Renaissance Inc. finances Strategic Planning Task Force to make plans for Detroit's future.

World History

Iran-Contra investigation: covert actions revealed in nationally televised hearings.

U.S. trade gap hits all-time high: $17.6 billion.

Oct. 19. U.S. stock market crash.

Dec. 8. Palestinian *intifada:* uprising in Gaza Strip, West Bank against Israeli occupation.

Cultural Progress

Peter Taylor's *A Summons to Memphis* wins Pulitzer Prize for fiction.

Rita Dove's *Thomas and Beulah* wins Pulitzer Prize for poetry.

August Wilson's *Fences* wins Pulitzer Prize for drama.

Singer Anita Baker (who, while growing up, sang in church choirs in Detroit) wins two Grammy Awards for her album *Rapture* (1986).

Exhibit of Robert Mapplethorpe photos stirs discussion over public funding of arts in U.S.

1988

Detroit and Michigan

Speed limit is raised to 65 mph on all federally designated highways in Michigan.

Controversy develops over Detroit newspapers' Joint Operating Agreement.

Second Annual Festival of Arts takes place in Detroit.

Detroit Red Wings win Norris Division championship.

Detroit Pistons make it to NBA championship play: after winning Eastern Conference by defeating the venerable Boston Celtics, Pistons are defeated by Los Angeles Lakers, who take 4 games to Pistons' 3 to claim the championship. Nevertheless, Pistons are on the upswing.

Berry Gordy Jr. sells Motown to MCA.

Fox Theatre, one of few remaining movie palaces in nation, is restored by Detroit businessman Mike Ilitch.

Elwood Bar and Grill, Art Deco diner (built 1937), is restored as part of revitalization of Detroit Theater District.

Borman, Inc. sells Farmer Jack supermarket chain to Atlantic & Pacific Tea Co. (A&P).

Michigan Central Depot, built in 1913, is closed with no plans for renovation.

World History

July 3. U.S. warship *Vincennes* in Persian Gulf mistakes Iran Air A300 Airbus for attack plane; shoots it down, killing 290 civilians.

Sept. 29. NASA sends first shuttle into space since 1986 *Challenger* disaster.

Nov. 8. George Bush, Republican, elected president.

Nov. 15. PLO declares Palestinian state.

Dec. 21. Pan Am 747 explodes over Lockerbie, Scotland, killing all 259 on board, 11 on ground. Investigators conclude explosion caused by terrorist bomb.

Lauro Cavasos becomes first Hispanic U.S. secretary of education.

Terrorists kill 9 tourists aboard Aegean Sea cruise ship.

Benazir Bhutto of Pakistan is first woman to lead a Muslim nation.

Cultural Progress

Toni Morrison's *Beloved* wins Pulitzer Prize for fiction.

Winter Olympics held in Calgary, Alberta.

Summer Olympics held in Seoul, South Korea.

Scientific and Commercial Progress

Influential physicist Stephen Hawking publishes *A Brief History of Time: From the Big Bang to Black Holes*; bestseller.

1989

Detroit and Michigan

Jan. University of Michigan Wolverines football team wins Rose Bowl.

Detroit School Board reform results in stabilized school finances.

Problem of abandoned housing in Detroit neighborhoods gains attention.

U.S. Attorney General approves Gannett and Knight-Ridder's Joint Operating Agreement for *Detroit News* and *Free Press*: advertising, business, production, circulation departments merge under newly formed company, Detroit Newspaper Agency.

Mayor Coleman Young reelected; to serve 5th term in office.

Auto show renamed Detroit International Auto Show.

Four-year, $225 million expansion of Cobo Center completed; among nation's largest exhibit spaces.

Sept. 15. Detroit Symphony Orchestra returns to original home—a renovated Orchestra Hall, following 19-year absence.

Deborah Borda is named executive director of Detroit Symphony Orchestra; first woman executive director of major American symphony.

University of Michigan Wolverines win NCAA basketball championship.

Detroit Pistons turn things around: finishing the season with 63 wins, Pistons go on to defeat last year's NBA champions, L.A. Lakers, 4 games to 0. Led by Ishiah Thomas, the "Bad Boys" powerhouse is Bill Laimbeer, Mark Aguirre, Vinnie Johnson, Dennis Rodman, Rick Mahorn, James Edwards, and John Salley.

Red Wings draft Niklas Lidstrom, Sergei Fedorov, Vladimir Konstantinov; Dino Ciccarelli and Paul Coffey are added to offense—paving way for future.

Detroit City Airport is expanded.

World History

Jan. 7. Japanese Emperor Hirohito dies; ruled 62 years.

Jan. 20. George H. W. Bush inaugurated; 41st U.S. president.

March. Exxon *Valdez* oil spill in Alaska; largest in U.S. history.

March 15. In England, 95 soccer fans crushed to death, 2,000 more injured in arena melee.

April. Student democracy demonstrations in Beijing's Tiananmen Square suppressed by military police.

Aug. President Bush signs bill approving $166 billion to bail out failed savings and loans.

Aug. 10. Colin Powell is appointed chairman of Joint Chiefs of Staff; first African American to hold the job.

Sept. Hurricane Hugo strikes Virgin Islands, Puerto Rico, Carolinas.

Oct. Earthquake rocks San Francisco area.

Nov. Berlin Wall is opened to West; symbol of fall of Communism in Eastern Europe. Wall totally dismantled by 1990.

Dec. 16–30. Popular revolution in Romania. Tyrannical communist leader Nicolae Ceausescu and wife Elena killed by firing squad after 1-hour "trial."

Dec. 20. U.S. invades Panama; General Manuel Noriega surrenders to American troops.

Ronald Brown named chairman of National Democratic Committee; first African American to hold position.

Antonia Novello becomes first Hispanic U.S. surgeon general; Manuel Lujan Jr. becomes first Hispanic U.S. secretary of the interior.

African American Thomas Bradley is reelected mayor of Los Angeles; will serve unprecedented 4th term.

White South African leader F. W. de Klerk is elected president.

Dalai Lama is awarded Nobel Peace Prize for leading nonviolent struggle to free Tibet from China.

Salman Rushdie's *Satanic Verses* banned by the Ayatollah. Death sentence on author forces Rushdie into hiding.

Cultural Progress

Anne Tyler's *Breathing Lessons* wins Pulitzer Prize for fiction.

Wendy Wasserstein's *The Heidi Chronicles* wins Pulitzer Prize for drama.

Jazz vocalist Betty Carter (who got her start in Detroit's nightclubs) scores a Grammy Award for her album *Look What I Got* (1988).

Detroit Pistons win their first NBA championship.

Scientific and Commercial Progress

Voyager II spacecraft returns report on Neptune.

Americans J. Michael Bishop and Harold E. Varmus win Nobel Prize for medicine for research on cancer-causing genes.

1990

Detroit and Michigan

Michigan's population, 9,328,784; 8th-largest state.

Detroit's population, 1,027,974; ranks 7th in size among U.S. cities.

Detroit metropolitan area's population, 3,698,000; 5th-largest in U.S.

Jan. Mayor Coleman Young sworn in; 5th term.

Fermi II nuclear plant in Monroe temporarily closed.

Neal Shine is named publisher of Detroit *Free Press*.

Neeme Järvi is named music director of Detroit Symphony Orchestra.

Preservation Wayne and DIA Founders Society promote plan for East Ferry Arts and Heritage District.

Dayton-Hudson Corp., parent company of Hudson's, buys Marshall Field's of Chicago to become dominant department store chain in Midwest.

Automakers introduce air bags as standard feature in some new model cars.

World famous Lawrence Scripps Wilkinson toy collection opens at Detroit Historical Museum.

Detroit Pistons repeat: NBA champions stay on top, defeating Portland Trail Blazers, 4 games to 1 for the title.

Madden Building, first major office complex built downtown in nearly a decade, is completed at 150 West Jefferson Ave.

World History

U.S. population, 249,632,692.

U.S. unemployment, 5.6%.

Ellis Island reopens to public as immigration museum.

May 29. Boris Yeltsin elected president of Russia.

July 26. Congress passes Americans with Disabilities Act.

Aug. 2. Iraq invades Kuwait.

Oct. 3. Germany is reunited.

Nov. 21. Junk-bond dealer Michael Milken sentenced to 10 years for insider trading.

Conservative party leader, John Major, becomes British prime minister (to 1997), succeeding Margaret Thatcher.

Black South African leader Nelson Mandela released after 28 years in prison.

Elections in Poland; voters pick Solidarity leader and Nobel laureate (1983) Lech Walesa as president. Poland's Communist Party dissolves.

Mikhail Gorbachev awarded Nobel Peace Prize for efforts to reduce tensions between communist and noncommunist nations.

Cultural Progress

Oscar Hijuelos (*The Mambo Kings Play Songs of Love*) is first Hispanic to win Pulitzer Prize for fiction.

Goodfellas in movie theaters.

More than 98% of U.S. households have televisions.

Cable gains more viewers this decade; Big Three (NBC, ABC, CBS) reach only about 60% of TV audience.

Detroit Pistons win 2nd consecutive NBA championship.

Scientific and Commercial Progress

Americans Joseph E. Murray, E. Donnall Thomas win Nobel Prize for medicine for work in transplanting human organs and bone marrow.

Dow Jones Industrial Average hits 3,000.

Microsoft releases Version 3.0 of Windows; graphical user interface (GUI) for PCs.

U.S. launches Hubble telescope.

1991

Detroit and Michigan

John Engler, Republican, governor (through 2002).

Residential projects worth $1.5 to $2 billion are scheduled to begin in Detroit.

Oct. Chairman Lee Iacocca dedicates Chrysler Corp.'s new headquarters in Auburn Hills; automaker moves out of Highland Park offices.

Chrysler Corp. builds Jefferson North Assembly plant.

Demolition of Tyree Guyton's controversial Heidelberg project begins on Detroit's east side.

Out of original 367 homes in Indian Village, 349 are still in existence.

One Detroit Center, 50-story, $200 million office tower, opens.

World History

Jan.17. Iraq fails to withdraw from neighboring Kuwait despite warnings; U.S.-led coalition bombs Iraq, beginning Gulf War (to Feb. 28).

March 3. African American Rodney King is beaten by Los Angeles police; incident caught on videotape.

May. Cyclone packing 145-mile-per-hour winds, 20-foot waves sweeps over Bangladesh coastal plain; death toll estimated in the hundreds of thousands.

Aug. KGB coup attempt thwarted in Russia.

Sept. 3. Fire in Hamlet, North Carolina, chicken-processing plant claims lives of 35 workers; emergency exits locked.

Oct. Law professor Anita Hill charges Supreme Court nominee Clarence Thomas with sexual harassment.

Carol Moseley Braun (Illinois) is first black woman elected to U.S. Senate.

U.S., Soviet Union sign Strategic Arms Reduction Treaty (START). Scientists reposition minute hand of doomsday clock to 17 minutes before midnight; farthest the minute hand has ever been from striking the hour.

Nov. 7. Basketball star Magic Johnson announces he is HIV positive.

Dec. Soviet Union falls apart. Warsaw Pact ends.

Dec. Shiite Muslims release hostage Terry Anderson (AP correspondent), ending 7-year ordeal.

South African government repeals apartheid laws; system of segregation officially abolished.

Cultural Progress

Neil Simon's *Lost in Yonkers* wins Pulitzer Prize for drama.

Michigan's Tim Allen stars in new prime-time family sitcom *Home Improvement*; set in suburban Detroit, program includes many regional references.

Scientific and Commercial Progress

World Wide Web (invented 1990) becomes part of the Internet; ups usage.

E-mail widely used.

1992

Detroit and Michigan

Scenic River Act passed; state legislation protects areas along 14 Michigan rivers from development.

Nov 5. Fatal beating of black motorist Malice Green by 2 white Detroit police officers again thrusts city into national spotlight on issue of race, police brutality.

College of Science added at WSU, bringing Wayne State's total number of schools to 14.

DSO performance broadcast live to 25 million radio listeners in Western and Eastern Europe.

Detroit Grand Prix moves to Belle Isle.

Detroit Boat Club on Belle Isle files for Chapter 11 bankruptcy.

Detroit Institute of Arts manages financial crisis.

Detroit Red Wings win Norris Division championship.

Pizza Kings transfer ownership of Tigers: Mike Ilitch buys Detroit ball club from Tom Monaghan.

Michigan experiences cloudiest year since 1938.

World History

U.S. national debt exceeds $3 trillion.

U.S. unemployment, 7.5%.

The 27th Amendment to U.S. Constitution ratified; prevents Congress from passing immediate salary increases for itself.

Jan. 6. FDA halts further use of silicon breast implants; Dow Corning faces charges of insufficient testing.

March. Bosnia-Herzegovina declares independence from Yugoslavia; move is opposed by Bosnian Serbs and civil war breaks out. Fighting with Croats centers around capital city, Sarajevo. Evidence surfaces that Serbs, led by Radovan Karadzic, engage in ethnic cleansing.

April 29. Verdict in Rodney King case causes rioting in Los Angeles.

April. Operation Rescue activists block abortion clinics.

May 1. Navy Tailhook scandal revealed.

June 28. Earthquake jolts Los Angeles.

Aug. 24. Hurricane Andrew slams south Florida. Most damaging hurricane in U.S. history, it leaves some 250,000 homeless.

Oct. Multimillionaire H. Ross Perot announces independent run for presidency; analysts predict he'll split Republican vote.

Nov. 3. William Jefferson (Bill) Clinton, Democrat, elected president.

Dec. U.S. troops land in Somalia as part of international peacekeeping force. Launches series of United Nations or U.S.–led interventions for humanitarian causes during decade.

Dec. 24. President George Bush pardons Iran-Contra conspirators.

U.S. closes Philippines naval base.

Voters Assistance Act makes bilingual voting information available to U.S. Hispanic voters.

Maastricht Treaty signed by 12 European countries for greater economic cooperation.

Rigoberta Menchu awarded Nobel Peace Prize for work to gain recognition of rights of Guatemala's Indians.

Cultural Progress

Port Huron–born African American writer Terry McMillan's *Waiting to Exhale* tops the bestseller lists; novel is later adapted to the big screen (1995).

Nirvana's *Nevermind* tops Billboard album chart; highly successful, influential recording ushers in grunge movement.

The Unforgiven in movie theaters.

May 22. End of an era: popular late-night host Johnny Carson leaves *The Tonight Show.*

Winter Olympics held in Albertville, France.

Summer Olympics held in Barcelona, Spain. American Jackie Joyner-Kersee is first woman to repeat as heptathlon champion.

Scientific and Commercial Progress

First joint U.S.-Japan space shuttle mission.

June. Earth Summit held to address global warming, species preservation, other environmental issues.

1993

Detroit and Michigan

Detroit Police officers Larry Nevers and Walter Budzyn are convicted of second degree murder in 1992 death of motorist Malice Green.

Schools in Kalkaska, Michigan, close 2 months early because of financial problems.

In nationally publicized case, court rules that adopted daughter of the De Boers family of Ann Arbor must be returned to her biological parents in Iowa.

Former State Supreme Court Judge Dennis Archer elected mayor of Detroit; to succeed Coleman Young, who retires after 5 terms in office.

Under direction of new coach Scotty Bowman and with Chris Osgood in net, Detroit Red Wings win Norris Division championship.

World History

Jan. 20. Bill Clinton inaugurated; 42nd U.S. President.

Feb. 26. Bomb explodes at World Trade Center, killing 6 people, injuring hundreds more.

March. Great Blizzard strikes U.S. eastern seaboard.

April 19. Branch Davidian compound burns outside Waco, Texas.

May 25. UN sets up war crimes tribunal to try former Yugoslavian leaders.

Spring–Summer. Great Flood: heavy rainfall causes Mississippi, Missouri rivers to overflow banks. Some 85,000 are displaced from their homes, 50 die, property and crop losses tally $15 billion.

Sept. 13. Oslo Accord signed by Israel and PLO, which officially recognize each other. Agreement provides interim framework of Palestinian autonomy in West Bank and Gaza Strip.

Dec. 8. President Clinton signs North American Free Trade Agreement (NAFTA).

Jocelyn Elders is first black U.S. surgeon general. Henry Cisneros is first Hispanic U.S. secretary of housing and urban development; Federico Peña is first Hispanic U.S. secretary of transportation (named secretary of energy, 1997).

President Clinton orders bombing of Iraqi intelligence center; in retaliation for assassination plot on former President George Bush.

Nelson Mandela and F. W. de Klerk win Nobel Peace Prize for efforts to end South African apartheid.

Cultural Progress

Jan. 20. Maya Angelou reads her poem "On the Pulse of the Morning" at U.S. presidential inauguration.

Toni Morrison is awarded Nobel Prize for literature; first African American woman Nobel laureate.

Holocaust Memorial Museum opens in Washington, D.C.

Fox becomes first new national TV network since 1950s.

Scientific and Commercial Progress

Most U.S. offices equipped with voicemail systems.

U.S. experiences slow economic growth; harbinger of unprecedented prosperity.

1994

Detroit and Michigan

Jan. Dennis Archer takes office as mayor amidst hopes he can forge coalition between Detroit and suburbs and state officials.

Jan. Detroit hosts National Figure Skating competition; reigning champ Nancy Kerrigan prepares to defend title but is attacked, injured. Rival skater Tonya Harding revealed to be behind assault.

Michigan sharply reduces use of property taxes in financing public schools.

City loses battle for 1990 census recount.

Detroit receives Federal Empowerment Zone grant.

Detroit Press Club closes.

DSO radio broadcast is heard by 4.5 million listeners in Europe and countries of former Soviet Union.

Astronaut, physician, and WSU alumnus Jerry Linenger flies a Discovery mission.

Detroit Red Wings win Central Division championship.

Detroit hosts World Cup soccer: games played at Pontiac Silverdome are first soccer championship games played indoors.

World History

Blacks vote in South Africa for first time: African National Congress (ANC) wins control of parliament; Nelson Mandela elected president.

Jan. Zapatistas rebel in Chiapas, Mexico.

Feb. Serbian siege of Sarajevo ends.

April–June. Rwanda in crisis: Hutu rebels kill 800,000 Tutsis in genocide.

Nov. Midterm elections benefit Republican party; GOP wins Congress. Speaker of the House Newt Gingrich issues Contract with America.

Dec. 11. Russian troops invade breakaway province Chechnya.

PLO leader Yasir Arafat, Israeli leaders Yitzhak Rabin and Shimon Peres receive Nobel Peace Prize for efforts to bring peace to Middle East.

Cultural Progress

Pulp Fiction in movie theaters.

Chicago Hope debuts on CBS; among hospital drama's stars is Michigan's Christine Lahti.

Winter Olympics held in Lillehammer, Norway.

Scientific and Commercial Progress

Tunnel opens beneath English Channel, connecting England and France; known as the Chunnel.

1995

Detroit and Michigan

Workers at *Free Press* and *Detroit News* strike.

Oct. 30. Decline in Devil's Night arson fires in Detroit; community activism is credited.

Michigan mourns losses of Temptation singer Melvin Franklin, radio announcer J.P. McCarthy, photographer Tony Spina, former Gov. George Romney.

Pope John Paul II declares Detroit's Father Solanus Casey (who died in 1957) "venerable"; second-to-last step before sainthood is bestowed.

Tiger Stadium Fan Club protests organization's move to build new facility. (*See* 1996.)

Tiger greats Sparky Anderson, Lou Whitaker, Alan Trammel take final bows at Michigan and Trumbull.

Detroit Red Wings in Stanley Cup play for first time in nearly 20 years: after winning Central Division and Western Conference titles, they suffer crushing defeat, losing finals to New Jersey Devils in 4-game shutout. Season still had its glory: Steve Yzerman scored his 500th career goal, Paul Coffey garnered his 1,000th career assist, and Red Wings broke all-time single-season record with 62 victories.

Troy-based K-Mart Corp. cuts 900 jobs in cost-cutting campaign.

World History

Jan. 17. Earthquake rocks Japan.

April 19. Truck bomb explodes outside Alfred P. Murrah Federal Building, Oklahoma City. Most destructive act of terrorism in U.S. history claims 168 lives (including 19 children), injures 500 more. Timothy McVeigh and Terry Nichols are indicted Aug. 10, on 11 charges each.

May. Ebola virus strikes Zaire.

Oct. 1. World Trade Center bombing case: federal jury finds 10 Muslim extremists guilty of conspiring to carry out terrorist campaign to force U.S. to abandon support of Israel and Egypt.

Oct. 3. Former football player O. J. Simpson is acquitted in the 1994 murders of Nicole Brown Simpson and Ronald Goldman.

Hurricane Opal hits Florida's panhandle.

Nov. 4. Israeli Prime Minister Yitzhak Rabin is assassinated by extremist.

Dec. Dayton Accord ends civil war in Bosnia; arranges power-sharing among factions.

Jacques Chirac (conservative party) elected president of France; announces nation will resume participation in NATO's military wing.

Cultural Progress

Morton Gould's *Stringmusic* wins Pulitzer Prize for music.

Michigan's Tim Allen voices animated Buzz Lightyear in Disney box office hit *Toy Story.*

Get Shorty a box office hit; based on novel by Michigan's Elmore "Dutch" Leonard.

Scientific and Commercial Progress

Americans Mario Molina, F. Sherwood Rowland, and Dutch Paul Crutzen win Nobel Prize for chemistry for work leading to discovery of "hole" in earth's ozone layer.

1996

Detroit and Michigan

April. Renovated Detroit Opera House opens; gala includes performance by Luciano Pavarotti.

Voters approve casino gambling in Detroit.

Focus Hope founder Father William Cunningham announces he has cancer.

Jack Kevorkian's assisted-suicide trial begins in Pontiac; he is acquitted. (*See* 1999.)

Veteran's Administration facility, affiliated with Wayne State's School of Medicine, opens in Detroit Medical Center.

DSO announces $80 million development project for Orchestra Place, adjacent to Orchestra Hall.

Bob-Lo Island's heyday past, steamers *Columbia* and *Ste. Claire* are auctioned.

Detroit Mayor Dennis Archer, Mike Ilitch, William Clay Ford Jr. announce plans for new Lions and Tigers stadium in downtown Detroit.

Former Piston great Isiah Thomas' number is retired at the Palace.

Detroit Red Wings acquire Brendan Shanahan, win Central Division title 1996–97 season.

World History

Jan. Palestinians in Gaza Strip and Palestinian-controlled areas of West Bank set up self-rule; Yasir Arafat is elected president.

March 13. Gunman kills 16 kindergartners in Dublane, Scotland.

April. Unabomber suspect Theodore Kaczynski arrested.

May 29. Israel elects Benjamin Netanyahu, defeating incumbent Shimon Peres.

June 25. Truck bomb explodes outside U.S. military installation in Saudi Arabia; 19 dead, hundreds injured.

July. Bombing at Olympic Park in Atlanta, Georgia, casts shadow over Summer Games.

Aug. President Bill Clinton signs bill limiting how long people can receive welfare benefits, shifting welfare administration from federal government to states.

Oct. 12. Hispanic March for Justice on Washington, D.C.

Nov. 5. Bill Clinton reelected president.

South Africa's Truth and Reconciliation Commission begins investigations of political crimes committed under apartheid.

Cultural Progress

Twin Petronas Towers completed in Kuala Lumpur, Malaysia; measure 1,483 feet to claim title as world's tallest.

Fargo in movie theaters.

Michigan's Christine Lahti wins Academy Award for directing short live-action film *Lieberman in Love*.

April 24. NBA announces Board of Governors' approval of Women's National Basketball Association (WNBA).

Scientific and Commercial Progress

U.S. AIDS deaths decline for first time since disease was recorded.

Media industry consolidation under way: record distributors, entertainment companies, publishers involved in mergers and acquisitions.

March. Soviet space station *Mir* and U.S. space shuttle *Atlantis* dock.

1997

Detroit and Michigan

Michigan unemployment rate hits low 3.9%, almost a full point lower than national rate.

Jan. 12. WSU alumnus Jerry Linenger (Medical School, 1981) becomes third American astronaut to board Russian space station *Mir* (until May 1997).

Jan. 26. Public and private interests initiate plan to transform Detroit riverfront.

April. WSU's oldest building, Old Main, reopens following $42 million renovation.

April 12. Third generation of Museum of African American History (now Charles H. Wright Museum of African American History), 120,000-square-foot facility, opens its doors at corner of East Warren and Brush.

May. Total number of living WSU alumni is more than 198,000.

Former Detroit mayor Coleman Young and Focus Hope founder Father William Cunningham die.

June. Red Wings win first Stanley Cup since 1955; Detroit savors victory; regales team in Woodward Ave. parade and Hart Plaza rally, attended by hundreds of thousands of fans.

July 2. Severe storms move through Michigan, spawning tornadoes. Northwest Detroit, Hamtramck, Detroit's Focus Hope campus, and Grosse Pointe are hard hit. Hundreds of metropolitan Detroit residents homeless as residences are reduced to rubble; 337,000 homes without power; more than 100 people injured; death toll, 16.

Summer. Red Wing Vladimir Konstantinov and team masseur Sergei Mnatsakanov are severely injured in limousine accident.

Nov. Mayor Dennis Archer reelected.

Detroit Recorders Court merges with Wayne County Circuit Court.

City of Detroit hands over Detroit Institute of Arts to privatization.

Restored Gem Theater is moved to make way for new stadia.

World History

Women account for 46.2% of U.S. labor force outside the home.

Jan. 20. Bill Clinton inaugurated; 2nd term.

Feb. 4. O. J. Simpson found liable in wrongful deaths of his ex-wife and her friend; ordered to pay damages to families.

March. Mass suicide of Heaven's Gate cult members in California.

Cigarette manufacturer Liggett admits its product is addictive.

June. Timothy McVeigh found guilty of murder and conspiracy in 1995 bombing of Oklahoma City's federal building; jury sentences him to death. Co-conspirator Terry Nichols found guilty (in separate trial) of conspiracy, involuntary manslaughter; sentenced to life in prison.

July. Economic recession begins in Asia.

July 4. NASA lands Pathfinder on Mars; deploys 2-foot-long robotic rover Sojourner to collect 2.3 billion pieces of data about planet, 8.5 million temperature and pressure measurements; takes 16,500 pictures.

Aug. 31. Britain's Princess Diana dies in car crash in Paris.

Sept. 5. Mother Teresa dies; hailed by world leaders as "apostle of peace and love," "unique example of genuine holiness."

Tony Blair becomes British prime minister in landslide victory of Labour Party.

Cultural Progress

Some 55.4% of B.A. degrees in U.S. are awarded to women (according to U.S. Department of Education and National Center for Educational Statistics).

Frank McCourt's *Angela's Ashes: A Memoir* wins Pulitzer Prize for autobiography.

Wynton Marsalis's *Blood on the Fields* wins Pulitzer Prize for music.

After 4 straight games, Red Wings beat Philadelphia Flyers to end the 42-year Stanley Cup drought for Detroit. (*See* Detroit and Michigan.)

Oct. 30. Eight cities (Charlotte, Cleveland, Houston, Los Angeles, New York, Phoenix, Sacramento, Salt Lake) are selected to be homes to Women's National Basketball Association charter teams.

Scientific and Commercial Progress

Feb. Scientists clone sheep in Scotland.

Dec. Kyoto Treaty on global warming signed; limits emissions for 34 industrialized nations.

1998

Detroit and Michigan

Metropolitan Detroit (est.) population, 4.8 million.

Michigan has about 118,000 miles of roads.

Jan. Mayor Dennis Archer sworn in; 2nd term.

Jan. University of Michigan Wolverines football team wins Rose Bowl.

Federal agents indict 17 suspected metro Detroit Mafia members.

Daimler-Benz merges with Chrysler Corp. to form DaimlerChrysler Corp.

Auto workers go on strike against General Motors in Flint, causing 54-day shutdown.

Ann Arbor's Michigan Stadium undergoes renovation, adds 5,000 seats; sets NCAA single-game attendance record as 111,012 fans watch Wolverines defeat rival Michigan State, 29–17, in the Big Ten Conference opener for both squads, Sept. 26.

Oct. 24. J. L. Hudson Building in downtown is imploded at cost of $7.1 million; Detroit People Mover tracks are damaged in process forcing several-month closure.

Jennifer Granholm becomes first woman elected Attorney General of Michigan.

Grosse Pointe teen and 3 friends are charged with having sex with minors; 4 boys plead guilty to lesser charges. Scandal shakes community.

Total fall enrollment at WSU is 31,203; 92% are from Michigan; 85% from tri-county area.

First phase of Orchestra Place project completed; DSO moves its offices to new facility.

Detroit Red Wings repeat: win second straight Stanley Cup. Team dedicates season to injured team members Vladimir Konstantinov and Sergei Mnatsakanov.

Detroit gets WNBA franchise: the Shock bring women's pro basketball to the Palace.

Construction begins on new Tiger Stadium in Theater District.

Detroit plans new urban park in historic Campus Martius, area currently occupied by Soldiers and Sailors Monument, on Woodward at juncture of Michigan, West Fort, Cadillac Square, and Monroe.

Corktown condominium development begins.

World History

World population, 5.9 billion. Most populous cities are Tokyo, Mexico City, São Paulo.

U.S. population, 269 million.

U.S. unemployment, 4.6%.

Average weekly earnings (U.S.), $435; average workweek, 37.9 hours.

U.S. postal rate for first-class mail, 33 cents.

U.S. has 2 million farms; 3% of American workers are employed in agriculture.

Average U.S. life expectancy, 76; median age, 35.

Infant mortality per 1,000 live births (U.S.), 6.3.

Spring. U.S. Census Bureau report cites 9.6% of U.S. residents are foreign-born; highest percentage since 1930s (11.6% were foreign-born). Latin Americans account for roughly half of new arrivals; one-fourth are Asian; one-fifth are European.

Out of 103 million American households, 43% report at least 1 adult works at home; roughly half of those are "spillover" workers, employees completing office work at home.

Some 68% of U.S. children have mothers who work outside the home.

Jan. President Bill Clinton denies affair with White House intern; House of Representatives impeaches president.

April 10. Good Friday peace accord signed by Catholic and Protestant leaders in Northern Ireland; agree to form multiparty administration by Oct. General elections (May 22) support initiative.

May. India and Pakistan test nuclear weapons. Scientists forward minute hand of doomsday clock to 9 minutes before midnight.

U.S. Undersecretary of State Stuart Eizenstat issues report detailing wrongdoings of Switzerland, other self-proclaimed neutral countries during World War II.

Aug. 15. Violence renewed in Northern Ireland: car bomb explodes in Omagh, killing 28 people, injuring 220 others. Dissident group Real IRA claims responsibility.

Oct. Wye River Memorandum: Israeli prime minister Benjamin Netanyahu and Palestinian leader Yasir Arafat sign land-for-peace settlement.

Oct. Yugoslav President Slobodan Milosevic agrees to NATO demand that Serbian-led army end its crackdown of separatist force Kosovo Liberation Army. Nevertheless violence against ethnic Albanians in Kosovo province continues.

Dec. U.S. House of Representatives brings charges of impeachment against President Clinton, saying he has perjured himself and obstructed justice.

Cultural Progress

Best-selling book in U.S., *Cold Mountain,* historical novel by American Charles Frazier.

Popular NBC sitcom *Seinfeld* signs off after 9-season run.

Michigan's Christine Lahti wins Emmy Award (best actress in drama) for CBS's *Chicago Hope.*

A Simple Plan is in theaters; directed by Michigan native Sam Raimi.

Detroit Red Wings win Stanley Cup for second year in a row.

St. Louis Cardinal Mark McGwire hits 70 home runs this season; new record (rivaled by Chicago Cubs player Sammy Sosa, who had 66 home runs).

Winter Games held in Nagano, Japan.

Scientific and Commercial Progress

Internet usage surpasses 50 million individual users.

1999

Detroit and Michigan

- Michigan unemployment rate is among lowest in nation: strong economic rebound over past decade is due in part to strength of Big Three automakers, but growth of non-auto sector also robust.

Jan. 1. William Clay Ford Jr. becomes chairman of the board of Ford Motor Co.

Jan. 1. Detroit hit with worst snowstorm in 25 years: snarls Detroit Metropolitan Airport where hundreds of flights are delayed or canceled; leaves numerous Detroit residents without power; city streets remain unplowed for several days causing schools to close.

Feb. 1. Explosion and fire at Ford Rouge River plant kills 6 workers; injures 34 others.

March. "Dr. Death" Jack Kevorkian is convicted of second-degree murder in injection death of Thomas Youk, who suffered from Lou Gehrig's disease. Kevorkian later sentenced to 10–25 years in prison.

April. Ground is broken for new Detroit High School for Fine and Performing Arts (behind Orchestra Hall). Orchestra Hall expansion slated to begin next year.

After 14-year career, Piston Joe Dumars moves off the court and into team's front office; Dumars was 2-time NBA champion, 6-time All-Star, 4-time member of NBA's All-Defensive First Team, and finished career as Detroit's franchise leader in points (16,401) and games (1,018).

Pistons have retired: number 2 (Chuck Daly); number 4 (Joe Dumars); number 11 (Isiah Thomas); number 15 (Vinnie Johnson); number 16 (Bob Lanier); number 21 (Dave Bing); number 40 (Bill Laimbeer).

Detroit Red Wings are Central Division champions (1998–99 season).

Sept. 27. Farewell to the Corner: sellout crowd turns out to say good-bye to Tiger Stadium. Detroit's ball club to begin next season at new stadium, Comerica Park, in heart of downtown.

Dec. Rosa Parks is awarded Congressional Medal of Honor by Vice President Al Gore during a tribute held at Orchestra Hall, Detroit.

Since Music Director Neeme Järvi joined DSO in 1990, orchestra has recorded more than 30 compact discs (released on Chandos and DSO labels).

Businessman Peter Karmanos and Mayor Dennis Archer announce plan for suburban Detroit's Compuware Corp. to build 14-story office complex at Woodward and Monroe, downtown. Hailed as part of overall redevelopment plan that will again make Campus Martius city's center.

The 149-year-old Stroh Brewery Co. announces sale of its brands to Pabst Brewing Co. and Miller Brewing Co.

World History

World population reaches 6 billion.

World braces for Y2K and the threat of millennium bug.

Jan. Senate prepares to hear impeachment charges against President Bill Clinton.

Feb. 1. President Clinton announces budget surplus.

Feb. 12. Senate acquits President Bill Clinton of charges against him.

March 12. Poland, Czech Republic, Hungary join NATO.

March. U.S. and NATO forces bomb Yugoslavia to force resolution to Kosovar province crisis. Serbian President Slobodan Milosevic accepts NATO peace plan (June).

April 20. Columbine, Colorado, high school shooting; tragedy rocks nation.

May 17. Israel elects moderate leader Ehud Barak; many view his election as referendum on Middle East peace process.

July 7. President Clinton is first sitting chief executive since President Franklin D. Roosevelt to visit Indian country, touring South Dakota's Pine Ridge Reservation to visit with Oglala Sioux nation.

July 16. John F. Kennedy Jr., wife Carolyn Bessette Kennedy, sister-in-law Lauren Bessette die when plane piloted by young Kennedy crashes off Martha's Vineyard en route to a family wedding.

Sept. 21. Australian troops land in East Timor on peacekeeping operation.

Nov. 29–Dec. 4. Seattle meeting of World Trade Organization (WTO) protested by unions, political activists as statement against continued globalization of industry.

Dec. 31. Russian President Boris Yeltsin resigns; turns over power to Prime Minister Vladimir Putin until presidential elections in March 2000.

Second gilded age under way in U.S.: Unprecedented economic prosperity is fueled by rapid growth of technology sector and booming stock market.

Cultural Progress

Detroit journalist Mitch Albom's *Tuesdays with Morrie* climbs bestseller lists; HBO movie in the works.

Tom Brokaw's *The Greatest Generation* renews interest in Americans who survived Great Depression, fought World War II.

Pulitzer Prize winners: *The Hours*, Michael Cunningham; *Gotham* by Edwin G. Burrows, Mike Wallace; *Lindbergh*, A. Scott Berg; and *Blizzard of One Poems*, Mark Strand.

American Beauty, The Matrix, Star Wars Episode I, The Talented Mr. Ripley, Cider House Rules, The Green Mile, The Hurricane in movie theaters. Sam Raimi's *For the Love of the Game* tells story of aging Detroit Tigers pitcher.

Tool man Tim Allen says so-long to prime time: ABC's *Home Improvement* ends 8-year run with series finale that draws more than 35 million viewers.

Scientific and Commercial Progress

May 3. Dow Jones Industrial Average soars to all-time high of 11,000.

Judge finds Microsoft is a monopoly.

2000

Detroit and Michigan

Jan. 1. The University of Michigan defeats Alabama in the Orange Bowl.

April 11. The Detroit Tigers play their first game at the new Comerica Park, beating the Seattle Mariners 5–2. Hamtramck native Maggie Dewald, age 11, throws out the ceremonial first pitch.

Van Gogh exhibit at the Detroit Institute of Arts draws huge crowds.

Nov. Sparky Anderson, former manager of the Detroit Tigers, and Turkey Stearnes of the Detroit Stars (Negro League) are inducted into the Baseball Hall of Fame.

Dec. 21. Opera tenor Luciano Pavarotti sings at the Detroit Opera House.

World History

April 14. Earth Day marks the 30th anniversary of the environmental event.

April 22. U.S. Federal Marshals, in a pre-dawn raid, remove 6-yr. old Elian Gonzalez from the home of his Miami relatives, and take him to Washington D.C. where he is reunited with his father. Elian and his father return to Cuba.

May 4. Love Bug virus, originating in the Philippines, spreads rapidly through computers world-wide destroying files when it is opened in e-mail. Security experts estimate that the bug infected more than half of U.S. large businesses and "tens of millions" of computers worldwide.

July 11. Mideast peace summit takes place at Camp David. Palestinian leader Yasir Arafat, Israeli Prime Minister Ehud Barak, and U.S. President Bill Clinton attempt to secure peace in the Middle East.

Aug. 9. Firestone tire recall. Repeated tire failures on Ford Explorers have caused innumerable accidents and resulted in at least 148 deaths according to the National Highway Traffic Safety Administration.

Aug. 13. Russian nuclear submarine Kursk becomes trapped and crippled in the Barents Sea. Several countries send aid to rescue the crew, but arrive too late. All 118 sailors aboard the sub die.

Oct. 12. U.S.S. *Cole* attacked by suicide bombers in Aden, Yemen, while in the harbor for refueling. Seven sailors are killed and 39 injured. No one claims responsibility and an investigation is ongoing.

Nov. 7. U.S. presidential election held with Democrat Al Gore and Republican George W. Bush. Gore wins popular vote, but the outcome of the election is not determined until Dec.12 when Florida's electoral votes fall to George Bush after a U.S. Supreme Court decision.

The 2000 U.S. Census puts U.S. population at 281,421,906.

Kim Dae-jung, president of South Korea, wins the Nobel Peace Prize for his efforts to establish relations with communist North Korea.

Cultural Progress

July 8. *Harry Potter and the Goblet of Fire* is released worldwide; fourth book in J. K. Rowling's series sells over 3.8 million copies on first printing.

Gao Xingjian, a self-exiled Chinese political refugee and writer living in France, wins the Nobel Prize for literature. His writing is banned in China.

Scientific and Commercial Progress

June 26. Researchers announce they have completed a draft of the master blueprint of the human genome; promises to revolutionize medicine in coming decades.

July 12. Russia launches critical International Space Station (ISS) module *Zvezda* containing flight controls, sewage system, and crew sleeping quarters; makes further development of ISS possible.

Appendix A

French Commanders of Detroit

1701	Antoine de la Mothe Cadillac
1704 (fall)–1706 (Jan.)	Alphonse de Tonty (temporary)
1706 (Jan.–Aug.)	Sieur de Bourgmont (temporary)
1706–11 (summer)	Antoine de la Mothe Cadillac
1711–12 (June)	Joseph Guyon du Buisson
1712 (June)–1714	Francois Daupin, Sieur de la Forest
1714 (Nov.)–1717	Lt. Jacques Charles Sabrevois
1717	Louis de la Poste, Sieur de Louvigny
1717 (July)–1720	Henri de Tonty
1720	Charles Joseph, Sieur De Noyelle
1720–27 (Nov.)	Alphonse de Tonty
1727 (Dec.)–1728	M. le Chevalier Lepernouche
1728	Jean Baptiste Deschaillons de St. Ours
1728	Charles Joseph, Sieur Noyelle
1728–34 (June)	M. de Boishebert
1734	Hughes Jacques Péan, Sieur de Livandière
1734–38	Jacques Charles Sabrevois
1738–41	Charles Joseph, Sieur de Noyelle
1741 (July)–1742	Pierre Poyen de Noyan
1742–43	Pierre de Celeron, de Blainville
1743–47	Joseph Lemoyne, Sieur de Longueil
1749	Jacques Charles Sabrevois
1751 (Feb.)–1754 (March)	Pierre de Celeron, Sieur de Blainville
1754–58 (May)	Jacques d'Anon, Sieur Muy
1758–60	François Picoté, Sieur de Bellestr

Appendix B

English Commanders of Detroit

Appendix C

Mayors of Detroit

1824–25 ....John R. Williams
1826 ....Henry J. Hunt
1827–28 ....John Biddle
1829 ....Jonathan Kearsley
1830 ....John R. Williams
1831 ....Marshall Chapin
1832 ....Levi Cook
1833 ....Marshall Chapin
1834 ....Charles C. Trowbridge
1834 ....Andrew Mack
1835–36 ....Levi Cook
1837 ....Henry Howard
1838 ....Augustus S. Porter
1838 ....Asher Bates
1839 ....De Garno Jones
1840–41 ....Zina Pitcher
1842 ....Douglass Houghton
1843 ....Zina Pitcher
1844–47 ....John R. Williams
1847 ....James A. Van Dyke
1848 ....Frederick Buhl
1849 ....John Ladue
1850 ....Charles Howard
1851 ....Zachariah Chandler
1852–53 ....John H. Harmon
1854 ....Oliver M. Hyde
1855 ....Henry Ledyard
1856–57 ....Oliver M. Hyde
1858–59 ....John Patton
1860–61 ....Christian H. Buhl
1862–63 ....William C. Duncan
1864–65 ....K. C. Barker
1866–67 ....Merrill I. Mills
1868–72 ....William W. Wheaton
1872–76 ....Hugh Moffat
1876–77 ....Alexander Lewis
1878–79 ....George C. Langdon
1880–84 ....William G. Thompson
1884–86 ....S. B. Grummond
1886–88 ....M. H. Chamberlain

1888–90 ....John Pridgeon Jr.

1890–97 **(March 22)** ....Hazen S. Pingree

1897**(March 22–April 5)** ....William Richert

1897 **(April 5)–1904** ....William C. Maybury

1905–6...George P. Codd

1907–8...William B. Thompson

1909–10 ....Philip Breitmeyer

1911–12 ....William B. Thompson

1913–18 ....Oscar B. Marx

1919–22 ....James Couzens

1922 **(Dec. 5)–1923 (April 9)** .....John C. Lodge

1923 **(April 9)–1924 (June 10)** ...Frank E. Doremus

1924 **(June 10–Aug. 2)**................Joseph A. Martin

1924 **(Aug. 2–Nov. 21)**................John C. Lodge

1924 **(Nov. 21)–1928** ....John W. Smith

1928 **(Jan. 10)–1930** ....John C. Lodge

1930 **(Jan. 14)–1930 (Sept. 22)**..Charles Bowles

1930 **(Sept. 23)–1933 (May 10)**.Frank Murphy

1933 **(May)–1938 (Jan. 4)** ....Frank Couzens

1938–40 **(Jan. 1)**...........................Richard Reading

1940–48 ....Edward J. Jeffries

1948–50 ....Eugene I. Van Antwerp

1950–57 ....Albert E. Cobo

1957 **(Nov. 5)–1962** ....Louis C. Miriani

1962–69 ....Jerome P. Cavanagh

1970–73 ....Roman S. Gribbs

1974–93 ....Coleman A. Young

1994–...Dennis W. Archer

Sources

Print

Angelo, Frank. Yesterday's Detroit. Miami: E. A. Seemann, 1974.

Axelrod, Alan, and Charles Phillips Holbrook. What Everyone Should Know about American History: Two Hundred Events that Shaped the Nation. Holbrook, Mass.: Bob Adams, 1998.

Bald, Frederick Clever. Michigan in Four Centuries. New York: Harper & Row, 1954.

Burton Historical Collection, specialized extensive clippings files, Detroit Public Library, Detroit.

Cantor, George. Historic Landmarks of Black America. Detroit: Gale Research, 1991.

Carney Smith, Jessie, ed., with Casper L. Jordan and Robert L. Johns. Black Firsts: Two Thousand Years of Extraordinary Achievement. Detroit: Visible Ink, 1994.

CNN and Newseum's 100 Top Stories of the Century, 1999.

Destination Detroit Spring 2000

The Detroit News: "Michiganians of the Century." January 5, 2000.

The Detroit News: Special Section, "The American Journey." January 1, 2000.

The Detroit News: Special Section, "Michigan at the Millennium." Various dates in 1998 and 1999.

Dunbar, Willis F., and George S. May. Michigan: A History of the Wolverine State. 2d ed. Grand Rapids: W. B. Eerdmans Pub. Co., 1970.

Farmer, Silas. History of Detroit and Wayne County and Early Michigan: A Chronological Cyclopedia of the Past and Present. 1890. Reprint, Detroit: Gale Research, 1969.

Ferguson, Rebecca. The Handy History Answer Book. Detroit: Visible Ink Press, 1999.

Ferry, W. Hawkins. Buildings of Detroit. Detroit: Wayne State University Press, 1968.

Grun, Bernard. Timetables of History: A Horizontal Linkage of People and Events, Based on Werner Stein's Kulturfahrplan. 3d ed. New York: Simon and Schuster, 1991.

Harley, Rachel Brett, and Betty MacDowell. Michigan Women: Firsts and Founders. Lansing: Michigan Women's Studies Association, 1995.

Hartford, Courant: "To Sort Out Music of the 20th Century, Here's Where to Start." Reprinted in the Ann Arbor News, January 3, 2000.

The Nation January 10–17, 2000

Zilboorg, Caroline, ed. Women's Firsts. Detroit: Gale Research, 1997.

Electronic

Discovering U.S. History. CD-ROM. Detroit: Gale, 1996.

Discovering World History. CD-ROM. Detroit: Gale, 1996.

Web sites

CNN (cnn.com)

Detroit Free Press (freep.com)

Detroit Institute of Arts (dia.org)

Detroit Lions (nfl.com/lions)

Detroit News (detnews.com)

Detroit Pistons (nba.com/pistons)
Detroit Public Library (detroit.lib.mi.us)
Detroit Red Wings (detroitredwings.com)
Detroit Shock (wnba.com/shock)
Detroit Tigers (detroittigers.com)
Encyclopedia Britannica (www.eb.com)
University of Michigan (umich.edu)
Wayne State University (wayne.edu)

Index

American Hotel, Detroit, 114
American Indians: grand council of 1761, Detroit, 40; concede to treaties in Northwest Territory, 96; rights of inheritance, 163; civil rights movement, 308, 313
American Institute of Architects, 172, 302
The American Journal of Science, 100
American Library Association, 156
American Marconi Company, 185
American Medical Association, 126, 154
American Mercury, 18
American Motors Corp., 289, 315, 317
American Museum, New York, 121
American Museum of National History, New York City, 149
American Philosophical Society, 21, 31
American Railway Express Co., 238
American Railway Union, 175, 176
American Red Cross, 162
American Republican party, 123
American Revolution, 49
American Society for the Prevention of Cruelty to Animals, 146
American Sunroof, 303
Americans with Disabilities Act, 331
American Telephone and Telegraph Co., 166, 323
American Tobacco Co., 172, 227
American Woman Suffrage Association, 149, 171
America (schooner), 131
America's Cup, 131
AME Zion Church, Detroit, 191
Amherstburg, 188
Amistad. 118
Amnesty Act, 152
Ampère, Andre, 102
Ams, Frederick, 126
Amtrak, 310
Amundsen, Roald, 217, 227
Anatomy, 18
Anatomy of the Human Body, Descriptive and Surgical (Gray's Anatomy), 137
Ancram, William, 56, 346
Andersen, Rachel J. Rice, 287
Anderson, Cora Reynolds, 249
Anderson, Hans Christian, 114
Anderson, Julia, 128
Anderson, Marian, 268, 291
Anderson, Sparky, 319, 336, 342
Anderson, Terry, 332
Andre, John, 54
Andropov, Yuri, 323
Anel, Dominique, 15
Anesthesia, 122, 125, 133
Angelou, Maya: I Know Why the Caged Bird Sings, 310; "On the Pulse of the Morning," 334
Anglo-Irish Treaty, 243
Animated motion pictures, 226, 254
Ann Arbor, 104
Anne, Queen of England, 8, 10, 12, 13, 14, 15
Annie Hall, 318
Ann McKim (Baltimore Clipper), 111
Anson, George, 29, 31
Antarctic Circle, 47
Antheil, George: Ballet mécanique, 252
Anthony, Susan B., 133, 149, 152
Anthracite coal, 62, 100
Anthrax, 156, 164
Anti-apartheid movement, 324

Antibiotics, 275
Anti-colonialism, 278
Anti-draft riots, 142
Antietam, Battle of, 141
Anti-Saloon League of America, 178
Anti-Semitism, 158, 177
Antiseptics, 125, 144
Anti-slavery movement. See Abolitionism
Antitoxic immunity, 172
Anti-war movement, 303, 305, 310
Antoinette, Marie, 46, 49, 64
Antonopoulos, Demetrios, 177
Apache Indians, 167
Apartheid, 281, 298, 308, 337
An Appeal to the Colored People of the World, 108
Appert, Nicolas-François, 66, 93
Apple Computer, 325
Aquino, Corazon, 326
Arafat, Yasir, 301, 335, 337, 340, 343
Arapahoe Indians, 144
Archer, Dennis W., 334, 335, 337, 338, 339, 341, 348
Argand, Aimé, 57
Arithmometer Co., 216
Arizona: organized as territory, 142; admitted to Union, 228
Arkansas, admitted to Union, 115
Arkwright, Richard, 46
Armenian genocide, 233
Armistice Day, 237, 240, 246
Armour, Philip, 148
Armour & Co., 148
Arms Race, 283
Armstrong, Louis, 250, 254
Armstrong, Neil, 308
Army Signal Corps, 279
Arnat, Thomas, 179
Arnold, Benedict, 54
Arnold, Lucy M., 149
ARPAnet, 309
Arsenals, federal, 65
Arsenic and Old Lace, 272
Art Deco, 242
Arthur, Chester, 162
Arthur, Clara B., 217, 222, 228
Articles of Confederation, 51, 54
Artillery shell, 89
Arts and crafts movement, 231
Ascot Races, 13
Ashe, Arthur, 316
Ashmum Institute, 135
Ashraf, Afghani Shah of Persia, 20, 23
Asia: drought, 158; economic recession, 338
Askin, John, 87
Ask Me Another, 252
Aspdin, Joseph, 105
Assembly line, 230, 231, 254, 279
Associated Press, 127
Association for the Study of Negro Life and History, 233, 251
As the World Turns, 292
Astor, John Jacob, 94
Astoria, 94
Astronomy, 22, 27, 28, 34, 68
Atlantic Charter, 272
Atlantic Monthly, 136
Atlantis, 338
Atlas, Charles, 245
Atomic bomb, 269, 273
Atomic energy, 286

Royal Palace, Madrid, 28
Royal Society of Art, London, 40
Royal Society of London, 15
Royal Society of Medicine, France, 52
Royal William (steamship), 112
Rozier, Jean-François Pilâtre de, 56
Rubaiyat of Omar Khayam, 138
Rubber processing, 103
Ruby, Jack, 300
Rugby football, 104
Rules of Golf, 37
Rumba, 286
Rumble seat, 223
Rumsey, James, 59
Rural Electrification Act, 265
Rural Free Delivery (RFD), 179
Rush-Bagot pact, 99
Rushdie, Salman: Satanic Verses, 330
Russel, George B., 132, 156
Russel, George H., 156
Russel, Walter S., 156
Russell House, Detroit, 79
Russell House Hotel, Detroit, 104, 161
Russel Wheel and Foundry Co., 156
Russia: occupies Poland, 12; war with Turkey,
    13, 21, 26; expulsion of Jesuits, 17; pogroms,
    31; occupation of Berlin, 40; Cossack upris-
    ing, 48; annexes the Crimea, 56; Napoleon
    marches into, 95; frontier treaty with U.S.,
    104; declares war on Turkish Ottoman
    Empire, 107; emancipation of serfs, 136,
    140; wages war with Turkey, 157; Jews perse-
    cuted in, 162; famine, 173
Russian Academy of Sciences, 20
Russian Cossacks, 47
Russian Revolution, 220
Russo-Japanese War, 219, 220
Russo-Turkish War, 45, 108
Russo-Turkish War, Second, 59
Rutgers University, 44
Ruth, Babe, 250, 253, 262
Rutherford, Daniel, 47
Rutherford, Ernest, 182
Rwanda, 335

S. S. South American, 270
Saarinen, Eero, 257
Saarinen, Eliel, 247, 251, 257, 259
Sabrevois, Jacques Charles, 14, 25, 33, 345
Sacajawea, 89
Sacco, Nicola, 243
Sadat, Anwar, 318, 319, 322
Safety razor, 178
Sagan, Carl, 321
Saginaw Indians, 100
Saginaw river valley, 7
Saimi, Sam, 340
St. Aloysius Roman Catholic Church, Detroit,
    153
St. Clair, Arthur, 67
St. Clair Metropolitan Beach, 286
St. Clair Township, Wayne County, 67
St. Florian Church, Detroit, 222, 253
St. Genevieve, 26
St. John's German Evangelical Church, 111
St. Joseph, fort at, 7, 40, 43
St. Lawrence Seaway, 295
St. Louis, Missouri, 43
St. Louis Post-Dispatch, 158
St. Louis World's Fair, 219
St. Mary's Catholic Church, Detroit, 120, 122

St. Mary's River, 69
St. Ours, Jean Baptiste Deschaillons de, 22, 345
St. Peter Claver Mission, Detroit, 227
St. Petersburg, Russia, 8
St. Petersburg Academy of Science, 21
St. Vincent, British West Indies, 53
St. Vincent's Catholic Female Orphan Asylum,
    130
St. Vincent's Hospital, Detroit, 124
Ste. Anne's Church, Detroit: 1701, 2; founding
    of, 7; church records first inscribed Parish of
    Ste. Anne's, 19; new church erected, 20; in
    1730, 23; Father Daniel, pastor of, 26;
    Father Morinie, pastor of, 27; Father
    Bocquet, pastor of, 36; rebuilt, 37; in 1796,
    67; Father Gabriel Richard, pastor of, 88;
    cornerstone laid for new, 99; new, 1828, 107;
    torn down, 166; new (1887), 167
Ste. Claire (steamer), 226
Saints Peter and Paul Church, Detroit, 127
Salic law, 118
Salk, Jonas, 288, 291
Salley, John, 329
Salman Rushdie: Satanic Verses, 330
Salmon, 304
SALT II, 319
Salt Lake City, 126
Salt mining industry, 139
Salvation Army, 145
Samba, 286
San Antonio, Texas, 17
Sandanista movement, 320
Sandburg, Carl: Chicago Poems, 235; Complete
    Poems, 286
Sand Creek Massacre, 144
Sanders, Fred, 155
Sandusky Bay, 27
Sanford, Amanda, 149
San Francisco earthquake, 221, 329
San Francisco Examiner, 161
Sanger, Margaret, 234
San Juan Hill, Battle of, 181
Santa Anna, Antonio Lopez de, 112, 115
Santa Fe Trail, 103, 129
Santo Domingo, Haiti, 62, 65, 87, 88
Sarajevo, Serbian siege, 335
Sargent, John Singer: The Three Graces (The
    Wyndham Sisters), 184
Sargent, Winthrop, 67
Sargent Township, Wayne County, 67
Sarnoff, David, 251
Saturday Evening Post, 103, 242, 308
Saturday Night Fever, 318
Saturday Night Live, 316
Saudi Arabia, U.S. military installation bombing,
    337
Sauerbrun, Baron Karl von Drais de, 99
Sault (Soo) Canal, 134, 178, 240
Sault Ste. Marie, Treaty of, 101
Savannah, Georgia, 25
Savannah (sailing ship), 101
Sax, Adolphe, 125
Saxon Motor Plan, Detroit, 235
Saxophone, 125
Scarab Club, Detroit, 234, 255
Scarlet fever, 26, 27
Scenic River Act, 332
Schempp v. Abington Township, 300
Schiaparelli, Giovanni, 157
Schiller, Johann: William Tell, 89
Schlegel, August von, 68

386

388

Titles in the Great Lakes Books Series

Michigan Lumbertowns: Lumbermen and Laborers in Saginaw, Bay City, and Muskegon, 1870–1905, by Jeremy W. Kilar, 1990

Detroit Kids Catalog: The Hometown Tourist, by Ellyce Field, 1990

Waiting for the News, by Leo Litwak, 1990 (reprint)

Detroit Perspectives, edited by Wilma Wood Henrickson, 1991

Life on the Great Lakes: A Wheelsman's Story, by Fred W. Dutton, edited by William Donohue Ellis, 1991

Copper Country Journal: The Diary of Schoolmaster Henry Hobart, 1863–1864, by Henry Hobart, edited by Philip P. Mason, 1991

John Jacob Astor: Business and Finance in the Early Republic, by John Denis Haeger, 1991

Survival and Regeneration: Detroit's American Indian Community, by Edmund J. Danziger, Jr., 1991

Steamboats and Sailors of the Great Lakes, by Mark L. Thompson, 1991

Cobb Would Have Caught It: The Golden Age of Baseball in Detroit, by Richard Bak, 1991

Michigan in Literature, by Clarence Andrews, 1992

Under the Influence of Water: Poems, Essays, and Stories, by Michael Delp, 1992

The Country Kitchen, by Della T. Lutes, 1992 (reprint)

The Making of a Mining District: Keweenaw Native Copper 1500–1870, by David J. Krause, 1992

Kids Catalog of Michigan Adventures, by Ellyce Field, 1993

Henry's Lieutenants, by Ford R. Bryan, 1993

Historic Highway Bridges of Michigan, by Charles K. Hyde, 1993

Lake Erie and Lake St. Clair Handbook, by Stanley J. Bolsenga and Charles E. Herndendorf, 1993

Queen of the Lakes, by Mark Thompson, 1994

Iron Fleet: The Great Lakes in World War II, by George J. Joachim, 1994

Turkey Stearnes and the Detroit Stars: The Negro Leagues in Detroit, 1919–1933, by Richard Bak, 1994

Pontiac and the Indian Uprising, by Howard H. Peckham, 1994 (reprint)

Charting the Inland Seas: A History of the U.S. Lake Survey, by Arthur M. Woodford, 1994 (reprint)

Ojibwa Narratives of Charles and Charlotte Kawbawgam and Jacques LePique, 1893–1895. Recorded with Notes by Homer H. Kidder, edited by Arthur P. Bourgeois, 1994, co-published with the Marquette County Historical Society

Strangers and Sojourners: A History of Michigan's Keweenaw Peninsula, by Arthur W. Thurner, 1994

Win Some, Lose Some: G. Mennen Williams and the New Democrats, by Helen Washburn Berthelot, 1995

Sarkis, by Gordon and Elizabeth Orear, 1995

The Northern Lights: Lighthouses of the Upper Great Lakes, by Charles K. Hyde, 1995 (reprint)

Kids Catalog of Michigan Adventures, second edition, by Ellyce Field, 1995

Rumrunning and the Roaring Twenties: Prohibition on the Michigan-Ontario Waterway, by Philip P. Mason, 1995

In the Wilderness with the Red Indians, by E. R. Baierlein, translated by Anita Z. Boldt, edited by Harold W. Moll, 1996

Elmwood Endures: History of a Detroit Cemetery, by Michael Franck, 1996

Master of Precision: Henry M. Leland, by Mrs. Wilfred C. Leland with Minnie Dubbs Millbrook, 1996 (reprint)

Haul-Out: New and Selected Poems, by Stephen Tudor, 1996

Kids Catalog of Michigan Adventures, third edition, by Ellyce Field, 1997

Beyond the Model T: The Other Ventures of Henry Ford, revised edition, by Ford R. Bryan, 1997

Young Henry Ford: A Picture History of the First Forty Years, by Sidney Olson, 1997 (reprint)

The Coast of Nowhere: Meditations on Rivers, Lakes and Streams, by Michael Delp, 1997

From Saginaw Valley to Tin Pan Alley: Saginaw's Contribution to American Popular Music, 1890–1955, by R. Grant Smith, 1998

The Long Winter Ends, by Newton G. Thomas, 1998 (reprint)

Bridging the River of Hatred: The Pioneering Efforts of Detroit Police Commissioner George Edwards, by Mary M. Stolberg, 1998

Toast of the Town: The Life and Times of Sunnie Wilson, by Sunnie Wilson with John Cohassey, 1998

These Men Have Seen Hard Service: The First Michigan Sharpshooters in the Civil War, by Raymond J. Herek, 1998

A Place for Summer: One Hundred Years at Michigan and Trumbull, by Richard Bak, 1998

Early Midwestern Travel Narratives: An Annotated Bibliography, 1634–1850, by Robert R. Hubach, 1998 (reprint)

All-American Anarchist: Joseph A. Labadie and the Labor Movement, by Carlotta R. Anderson, 1998

Michigan in the Novel, 1816–1996: An Annotated Bibliography, by Robert Beasecker, 1998

"Time by Moments Steals Away": The 1848 Journal of Ruth Douglass, by Robert L. Root, Jr., 1998

The Detroit Tigers: A Pictorial Celebration of the Greatest Players and Moments in Tigers' History, updated edition, by William M. Anderson, 1999

Father Abraham's Children: Michigan Episodes in the Civil War, by Frank B. Woodford, 1999 (reprint)

Letter from Washington, 1863–1865, by Lois Bryan Adams, edited and with an introduction by Evelyn Leasher, 1999

Wonderful Power: The Story of Ancient Copper Working in the Lake Superior Basin, by Susan R. Martin, 1999

A Sailor's Logbook: A Season aboard Great Lakes Freighters, by Mark L. Thompson, 1999

Huron: The Seasons of a Great Lake, by Napier Shelton, 1999

Tin Stackers: The History of the Pittsburgh Steamship Company, by Al Miller, 1999

Art in Detroit Public Places, revised edition, text by Dennis Nawrocki, photographs by David Clements, 1999

Brewed in Detroit: Breweries and Beers Since 1830, by Peter H. Blum, 1999

Detroit Kids Catalog: A Family Guide for the 21st Century, by Ellyce Field, 2000

"Expanding the Frontiers of Civil Rights": Michigan, 1948–1968, by Sidney Fine, 2000

Graveyard of the Lakes, by Mark L. Thompson, 2000

Enterprising Images: The Goodridge Brothers, African American Photographers, 1847–1922, by John Vincent Jezierski, 2000

New Poems from the Third Coast: Contemporary Michigan Poetry, edited by Michael Delp, Conrad Hilberry, and Josie Kearns, 2000

Arab Detroit: From Margin to Mainstream, edited by Nabeel Abraham and Andrew Shryock, 2000

The Sandstone Architecture of the Lake Superior Region, by Kathryn Bishop Eckert, 2000

Looking Beyond Race: The Life of Otis Milton Smith, by Otis Milton Smith and Mary M. Stolberg, 2000

Mail by the Pail, by Colin Bergel, illustrated by Mark Koenig, 2000

Great Lakes Journey: A New Look at America's Freshwater Coast, by William Ashworth, 2000

A Life in the Balance: The Memoirs of Stanley J. Winkelman, by Stanley J. Winkelman, 2000

Schooner Passage: Sailing Ships and the Lake Michigan Frontier, by Theodore J. Karamanski, 2000

The Outdoor Museum: The Magic of Michigan's Marshall M. Fredericks, by Marcy Heller Fisher, illustrated by Christine Collins Woomer, 2000

Detroit in Its World Setting: A Three Hundred Year Chronology, 1701–2001, edited by David Lee Poremba, 2001